THE ACADEMIC PROFESSION

THE ACADEMIC PROFESSION

National, Disciplinary, and Institutional Settings

Edited by
BURTON R. CLARK

UNIVERSITY OF CALIFORNIA PRESS
Berkeley   Los Angeles   London

University of California Press
Berkeley and Los Angeles, California

University of California Press, Ltd.
London, England

Library of Congress Cataloging in Publication Data

The Academic profession.

Based on papers presented at an international conference held at the Villa Serbelloni, Bellagio, Italy, in 1984, and sponsored by the Rockefeller Foundation.
Includes bibliographies and index.
1. College teachers—Congresses.   2. Universities and colleges—Faculty—Congresses.   I. Clark, Burton R.   II. Rockefeller Foundation.
LB2331.7.A23   1987   378'.12   86-30916
ISBN 0-520-05940-9 (alk. paper)

Printed in the United States of America

1 2 3 4 5 6 7 8 9

Contents

Acknowledgments

This volume required the efforts of ten experts from the United Kingdom, the Federal Republic of Germany, France, Belgium, and the United States who prepared eight basic papers for an international conference and then revised them for publication. Their task was not easy, especially since the academic profession has received little serious analysis in most countries, including the major ones in Europe; it is to this group that I, as editor, am first indebted. Critical discussion of these papers took place among twenty-six scholars during a four-day seminar at the Villa Serbelloni, Bellagio, Italy, in midsummer 1984, a meeting that also drew scholars from Sweden, the Netherlands, and Italy as well as from the countries named above. The combined expertise of the group ranged widely, reaching as far as Japan and Latin America. To this larger group the authors of the papers and I are indebted for their prepared critiques and stimulating discussion that helped to highlight basic points and to draw out critical cross-national differences.

Three foundations assisted our collective effort. The Rockefeller Foundation was our host during the week in Bellagio: we are indebted to the foundation and especially to the director and immediate staff of the Villa Serbelloni for hospitality that aided thought and reflection. The Exxon Education Foundation and the Carnegie Foundation for the Advancement of Teaching provided grants that supported the travel, administrative, and editing expenses of the meeting, including the preparation of this volume. We are grateful for their essential support.

The larger effort of which this volume is a part was initiated in 1983 mainly as an intensive field study of the academic profession in the United States, a three-year endeavor carried out at UCLA and supported by the Carnegie Foundation for the Advancement of Teaching. The results of this domestic study are reported in a separate volume, *The Academic Life: Small Worlds, Different Worlds* (1987). The 1984 international meeting was conceived as a cross-national effort that would inform the American study while it also linked scholars working in comparative higher education; the outcome was to be a basic volume for a wide audience. This broader effort has served effectively on both counts, contributing to the perspective I adopted in the domestic study, while offering a set of cross-national, analytical views not previously available. On both grounds I am deeply indebted to my international colleagues.

In organizing the topics for this collective effort, I was joined by Sydney Ann Halpern, Gary Rhoades, and Kenneth P. Ruscio, postdoctoral research scholars during 1983 and 1984 in the Comparative Higher Education Research Group at UCLA. Adele Halitsky Clark helped to administer the conference, to edit the papers, and to prepare the final manuscript. It is a pleasure to thank all the above for their contribution.

Burton R. Clark

Santa Monica, California
June, 1985

Contributors

Tony Becher is professor of education at the University of Sussex, England. He served for some years on the editorial staff of Cambridge University Press while teaching at Cambridge, and later was director of the Nuffield Higher Educational Group, which studied innovations in undergraduate teaching. His principal publications include: (with Jack Embling and Maurice Kogan) *Systems of Higher Education: United Kingdom,* 1978; (with S. MacLure) *The Politics of Curriculum Change,* 1978; and *Accountability in Education,* 1979; (with Maurice Kogan) *Process and Structure in Higher Education,* 1980; and "The Cultural View," in *Perspectives on Higher Education,* edited by Burton R. Clark, 1984.

Burton R. Clark is Allan M. Cartter professor of higher education and sociology and chairman of the Comparative Higher Education Research Group, University of California, Los Angeles. He taught previously at Stanford and Harvard Universities, the University of California, Berkeley, and Yale University in departments of sociology and schools of education; from 1974 to 1980, he was chairman of the Yale Higher Education Research Group. His publications include: *The Open Door College,* 1960; *The Distinctive College,* 1970; *Academic Power in Italy,* 1977; *The Higher Education System,* 1983; (editor) *Perspectives on Higher Education,* 1984; and (editor) *The School and the University,* 1985.

Erhard Friedberg is associate director, Centre de Sociologie des Organisations and senior researcher at the Centre National de la Recherche Scientifique (CNRS), both in Paris. Born in Vienna, he has been living in France since 1960. He teaches regularly at the Paris Institute of Political Science and has conducted research in public administration in both France and Germany. From 1974 to 1977 he was a research fellow at the Science Center in West Berlin. He is now directing a major comparative study in the organizational dynamics of French and German universities. His publications include: (with Michael Crozier) *Actors and Systems*, 1979; and (with Philippe Urfalino) *Le Jeu du Catalogue*, 1984.

Sydney Ann Halpern is assistant professor of sociology at the University of Illinois, Chicago. Before and after taking her Ph.D. in sociology from the University of California, Berkeley, she held research positions at the University of California School of Medicine, San Francisco, as well as on the Berkeley campus. During 1983–1984 she was a postdoctoral research scholar at the UCLA Comparative Higher Education Research Group, where she worked on a study of the American academic profession. Her publications include: *The Emergent Profession: A Social History of American Pediatrics* (University of California Press, forthcoming) and (with Neil J. Smelser) "The Historical Triangulation of Family, Economy and Education," in *Turning Points: Historical and Sociological Essays on the Family*, 1978.

Walter P. Metzger is professor of history at Columbia University, where he has taught since 1950. He was the author of *Academic Freedom in the Age of the University*, part two of *Development of Academic Freedom in the United States* (with Richard Hofstadter), 1955. During 1956–1957 he was a fellow at the Center for Advanced Study in the Behavioral Sciences, Palo Alto. He has served as consultant and board member of many organizations, notably the American Association of University Professors, where he has been a member of Committee A on Academic Freedom and Tenure since 1957. He has edited a forty-volume series for Arno Press (1977) on the academic profession. He has written extensively about the history of academic freedom and tenure, the delocalization of academic institutions, and institutional neutrality. Currently he is completing a major historical study of the American academic profession.

Wolfgang J. Mommsen is professor of modern history at Düsseldorf University, a position he again assumed after having served between 1977 and 1985 as director of the German Historical Institute in London. He has held many visiting professorships, including ones at Cornell, Oxford, and Johns Hopkins universities, and he was a visiting member of the Institute of Advanced Study in Princeton in 1968. His major publications include: *Das Zeitalter des Imperialismus*, 1968; *Max Weber und die Deutsche Politik*, 1974 (English edition, *Max Weber and German Politics*); *The Age of Bureaucracy*, 1974; and *Imperialismustheorien*, 1977 (English edition, *Theories of Imperialism*).

Christine Musselin, a research fellow at the Centre de Sociologie des

Organisations in Paris, did her undergraduate work at the Ecole Supérieur de Commerce de Paris and completed course work leading to a Master's degree in sociology at the Paris Institute of Political Science. She was awarded a fellowship by the Franco-German Exchange Program in 1984–1985 and spent that year doing research in Germany. Currently she is preparing a doctoral dissertation on French and German universities.

Guy Neave is professor of comparative education, University of London. After completing his Ph.D. in French political history at University College, London, in 1967, he taught modern European history for several years before he changed careers to become a researcher in the sociology of education. Between 1976 and 1985, he served as director of research for the Institute of Education and Social Policy of the European Cultural Foundation, Paris and Brussels. He has consulted widely on problems of education in Europe. His publications include: *How They Fared*, 1975; *Patterns of Equality*, 1976; *The EEC and Education*, 1984; and "France" in *The School and the University*, edited by Burton R. Clark.

Harold J. Perkin is professor of history, Northwestern University. Before coming to the United States in 1985, he was for many years professor of social history and director of the Centre of Social History, University of Lancaster, England. A graduate of Jesus College, Cambridge, he has also served at Manchester, Princeton, and Rice universities, has been president of the British Association of University Teachers (A.U.T.) in 1970–1971, and editor of the series *Studies in Social History* for Routledge and Kegan Paul since 1957. He is currently writing the second volume of his study of English social history, a sequel to *The Origins of Modern English Society, 1780–1880*. Other publications include: *Key Profession: The History of the A.U.T.*, 1969; and *New Universities in the United Kingdom*, 1970.

Gary Rhoades is assistant professor of higher education, University of Arizona. After completing his doctorate in sociology at UCLA in 1981, he served for five years as a postdoctoral research scholar in the UCLA Comparative Higher Education Research Group. His work in progress includes a manuscript on conflicting values and interests in higher education, tentatively entitled *The Profession and the Laity*, and a comparative study of the influence of higher on secondary education. His early publications include: "Conflicting Interests in Higher Education" (*American Journal of Education*, May 1983); and "Conditioned Demand and Professional Response" (*Higher Education*, April 1984). Forthcoming is "Higher Education in a Consumer Society," to be published in *The Journal of Higher Education*.

Kenneth P. Ruscio is assistant professor of political science at Worces-

ter Polytechnic Institute, Worcester, Massachusetts, a position he assumed after having been for two years (1983–1985) a postdoctoral
scholar at the UCLA Comparative Higher Education Research Group.
He holds the MPA and the Ph.D. from the Department of Public
Administration, Maxwell School, Syracuse University. He has served
as a doctoral research fellow in the U.S. General Accounting Office
and as visiting assistant professor in the Department of Political Science, University of Kansas. His publications include: "Prometheus
Entangled: Academic Science in the Administrative State" (*Public Administrative Review,* July/August 1984); "The Changing Context of Academic Science" (*Policy Studies Review,* November 1984); and "From
Juridical Democracy to Judicial Bureaucracy: Constitutionalism in the
Administrative State" (*American Review of Public Administration,* Spring
1985).

Introduction

The academic profession is an oddity among professions. For some eight centuries in the West, it has trained the members of such other leading professions as medicine and law. In recent times it has accommodated a host of would-be professions that have come to it for training and legitimation. Other advanced occupations thereby take up residence within it, imparting their habits and interests and shaping, if not controlling, the professional schools and faculties that represent them within universities. This embrace alone insures a unique confederation, a profession composed of medicine and law and architecture and engineering, incorporating such immense traditional fields as schoolteaching and such emerging specialties as computer science. And the medley of occupational fields is only the beginning of a vast reach. The profession is also rooted in a large number of disciplines that are based primarily in the academic system itself, stretching from archeology to zoology in the alphabet of academic interests and passing through all the many specialties of the natural and social sciences, the humanities, and even some of the arts. With the higher education system serving as the principal home for knowledge, the occupation of those who carry out the primary tasks of professional education, general education, and research cannot have other than an unparalleled variety. In its modern nature it is many disciplines as well as many professions.

This characteristic internal variety has been greatly extended by the remarkable expansion of higher education in the last half of the twentieth century. In many developed and modernizing societies, the profession had doubled, tripled, quadrupled—at times it has increased tenfold—its membership in the short span of a decade or two. Its student base steadily shifts from elite to mass. Its coverage of expanding and proliferating fields tends everywhere to become wider and deeper. Fueled by a knowledge explosion in a learning society, this confederative profession stretches more than any other. As the production and distribution of knowledge evolve, so does the profession reap.

For many reasons, then, the academic profession ought to arouse our curiosity and elicit serious study. It trains the members of an increasing number of leading fields outside the academy; its ideas speak to economy and politics, to social order and culture; and its leading scientists produce knowledge and technique in such world-transforming fields as atomic energy, biotechnology, and computerization. In so many ways, and more than before, it touches the lives of the general public. Yet, in the face of such importance, how much do we know about the development of this profession in other than simple numerical terms? What does it mean for a profession to be a loosely coupled array of disciplines and professional fields, each having a history, a sense of nationhood, and a momentum that makes it a going concern in its own right? Observers have long noted that academicians study everything but themselves, a remarkable failing in an estate composed of scholars and researchers devoted to the task of assisting others to understand the natural and social phenomena that make a difference in shaping the modern world. Of this we can be sure: the academic profession makes a difference. We can hardly know too much about it. In the mid-1980s we still know so little.

The academic profession is shaped by many social settings. Prominent among them is national context: the profession takes a different shape, even radically so, in France than in the United States, in Mexico or Brazil than in the United Kingdom or Sweden. If we wish to search for basic differences (and similarities) in the profession, to study their causes and unearth their consequences, it is wise to search first among nations. Discipline or field of study is a second primary setting: the profession takes a different shape in physics than in political science, in biology than in classics, in engineering than in education. Thus we must pursue the disciplines and search for similarities and differences across them. Increasingly, institutions are a third structuring context: in France the academic occupation is different in the *grandes écoles* than in the universities; in the United States it is radically different in community colleges than in research-based universities. What has generally been thought of as a university profession has become a more complicated postsecondary occupation in which professors and teachers are dispersed in various nonuniversity settings as well as in different types of universities.

To ignore such primary types of settings is to fall back on misleading general statements about "academic man": that a universal type extends across nations; that the profession is essentially the same across disciplines within an institution; that academics have a similar culture across radically different types of institutional constraints. We move from stereotype to reality as we look at variation by context. Large areas of similarity may still exist, but they ought to be found, not assumed. They ought to be induced from empirical observation, not deduced from traditional images and statements of personal preference.

This volume is an international effort to explore the variety and uniformity of the profession, its differentiation and integration as shaped by these three contexts of nation, discipline, and institution. The chapters were prepared initially for a seminar held during midsummer 1984 at the Bellagio Conference Center, Italy, where each paper was critically reviewed by over twenty-five experts drawn from six countries. The papers were subsequently revised, several extensively, and edited for this volume. We have divided our collective effort into two parts: the first is devoted to four national contexts—the United Kingdom, The Federal Republic of Germany, France, and the United States—the major centers of learning in the Western world; the second is organized around disciplinary and institutional components, with special attention to the enormous variety in American higher education. To introduce the chapters that follow, I will highlight the approach taken by each author and note one or two central findings or recurring themes that connect one discussion to another.

In earlier work Harold Perkin has written extensively about the historical development of higher education in the United Kingdom, arguing cogently that the academic field has become the key profession. His opening chapter in this volume reviews the rise of the profession in Britain, spells out "the rules of the professional game," and then concentrates on the vulnerabilities of the profession in present-day Britain. A mere quarter of a century ago (1960), the academic profession in Britain was arguably the most stable and self-confident one in the world, with unusual autonomy rooted in the age-old traditions and exceptional status of Oxford and Cambridge, high standards of teaching and research, a relationship of trust between academic and government officials, and oligarchical control provided by the leading academics who served on the University Grants Committee and research-granting national bodies. But structural changes and governmental actions already underway by the mid-1960s brought hard times by the late 1970s and early 1980s, greatly weakening the confidence of the profession and rendering it considerably more vulnerable. The British flow of change and the sources of vulnerability evidenced there can be studied profitably by other countries. The profession seems unrepresentative of society, even isolated from it. Financial support is heavily dependent on a single source, the national government, and there is provided mainly by one funding bureau. That solitary source has imposed sharp cuts from above, forcing a rise of managerialism. Arbitrarily, institutions have been told to close up or to amalgamate, or to define certain proportions of their academic staff as redundant. Job opportunity and mobility has been lowered to the point of promoting a brain drain to other countries, notably to the United States but also to those on the European continent. The British academic profession is undergoing painful adjustments. The dons are living in "a cold climate."

After delineating the heritage of nineteenth-century higher education in Germany and the impact of the fascist period, Wolfgang Mommsen concentrates on changes that have occurred during the last two decades, portraying the 1960s as a great divide in German higher education. For the professoriat in the Federal Republic of Germany, there has been a considerable shift in power. With expansion, the junior faculty has become much larger and has sought greater influence locally, regionally, and nationally. Government interference has risen sharply in the form of court decisions applied across the nation as well as through political dictates and bureaucratic standardization. Expanding nonuniversity sectors have become more influential, pressing hard for a parity of esteem with universities. Reforms have been enforced from the outside; nasty struggles have occurred over student access. Mommsen notes that the responses of the old professoriat through these troubled decades have been confused and ineffectual. High among the lasting effects of the recent changes has been a lessening of competition among institutions, with a concomitant decline in mobility within the profession. Here, as in Britain, we see a profession in transition, one permanently altered from the traditional form that was so highly praised and imitated in the nineteenth century, one that still preoccupied the German professoriat as late as the 1945 to 1960 postwar years of reconstruction. The German case makes the point, perhaps more sharply than anywhere else, that an elite academic profession will never be elite throughout its ranks again, once its support system has shifted in numbers and in functions from elite to mass.

In chapter 3, Erhard Friedberg and Christine Musselin specify the historical evolution that has cast French higher education in the form of three highly autonomous institutional sectors. They then proceed to demonstrate how these "institutional foundations" have critically shaped the structure of the academic profession. The grandes-école sector has had a favored status for a century and a half, with extremely selective recruitment of staff and students. But internally it is surprisingly varied, anarchic, and competitive. A highly influential research sector, based in academies and laboratories, hires full-time researchers and provides them with separate careers. This sector is strongly organized and mainly administered by scientists. The university sector is largest in numbers of faculty and students, but it may be the least important of the three: clearly, it is least in favor and most in trouble. Its historical roots lie in the examination of secondary school students, a framework initially little given to research and graduate study. It falls under a strong state bureaucracy, with government ministers almost compelled by the logic of their situation to come forth with top-down commands and reforms, against which professors as well as students stand in opposition. At the same time the professors are individually well protected by their position in the civil service. Overall, there is much bureaucratization and politicization, with the faculty turning, layer by layer, to the countervailing power of unionization. Friedberg and Musselin portray the profession in France as highly atomized and as having severe problems of blockage and low motivation in the large university sector. Among the four countries in this volume, France is the clear case of an academic profession making its way almost entirely within a national state system, with fascinating effects.

Walter Metzger, in the last of the nation chapters, covers in rich detail the long growth of American higher education to its present-day colossal size and wide coverage of subjects. The American academic profession was destined to become large, diffuse, and open. During the last decades of the nineteenth century, the system and the profession became unusually responsive, affiliating new programs, dividing old subjects, and giving dignity to occupational studies that elsewhere would be kept out. The curriculum became eclectic rather than pure; it was driven by restless institutional competition and aggrandizement rather than controlled by national oligarchs and state bureaucrats. By the turn of the century the profession had become a peculiarly heterogeneous work force. It increasingly included individuals who did not fit the image of Mr. Chips, or the great scientist, who were soon to draw the ire of such diverse purists as

Thorstein Veblen, Abraham Flexner, and Robert Hutchins. This internal diversity increased greatly in the twentieth century as the clientele of American higher education became virtually anyone who wished to enter. Hence the profession's problems of integration have become immense, its size and diversity affecting its mentality. A basic split in orientation was reflected in a growing division in the American Association of University Professors (AAUP) during the 1970s, between those who have clung to the older collegial posture, that authority ought to be softly shared with administrators, and those who believe in the more adversarial posture of collective bargaining between workers and management.

Chapter 5, by Guy Neave and Gary Rhoades, initiates the second part of this collective effort. In this section the organizing principle shifts from national settings to organizational and disciplinary contexts. Centered on the situation of academics as teachers and researchers in Western European countries, their analysis spans the gap between the national-system papers and the later chapters on disciplines and institutional sectors. They highlight the critical differences in public and scholarly definitions of academia between continental Europe and Anglo-American settings, that is, between an academic estate and an academic profession. In France, as emphasized by Friedberg and Musselin, there is no overtone of profession—that is left for such "learned professions" as medicine and law. Rather an individual belongs to one of the *grands corps de l'état*, or more precisely to *les corps universitaires*, a legal term for the university sector of employment. Beyond the tighter state-based definition there is only *le milieu universitaire et scientifique*, a phrase that broadly conveys an academic environment that embraces intellectuals. And so it is, for example, in Germany, Sweden, and Holland, where such defining conceptions as *Korporationen der Professoren* (the professorial corporation), *Högskollerar* (comprehensive university teacher), and *Wetenschappelijk Lid* (member of the scientific body) do not suggest "profession" but instead portray an estate closely related to, or intimately a part of, the state. The independence inherent in the concept of profession in English does not seem to apply. This fundamental distinction emerged (in a most confusing fashion) during the critical review of the country papers at the 1984 Bellagio conference and is greatly clarified in chapter 5 by the juxtaposing of "profession" and "estate."

The Neave-Rhoades analysis of the impact of organizational forms also highlights another fault line in the differentiation of academics— that between junior and senior faculty. This division by rank has not developed in a major way in Britain and the United States, where collegial norms or gradations of rank or both have suppressed it. But in recent decades, in Western European systems this division has been impressively strengthened, the roots of the conflict lying in the traditional chair-and-faculty structure and the reactions to it following expansion.

In Tony Becher's presentation we enter into a rich form of analysis that draws on the history and sociology of science as well as on the direct study of academic institutions. The individual disciplines and the professional areas of study are clearly the primary units of membership and identification within the academic profession, and sharply so in the leading institutions. How they fragment the profession—or integrate it—become critical but perplexing questions. Becher offers four categories upon which to focus our thinking about the disciplines: how recruits are attracted and initiated; the nature of social interaction within a field; the type and degree of specialization within it; and the modes of change in internal structures and external boundaries of fields and in the career lines that cause individuals to move between specialties, to shift from research to administration, or to remain in the same specialty to benefit from long experience and accumulated wisdom. His discussion on how we think about the academic profession as simultaneously "the one and the many" has helped set the general framework of the volume and informs my concluding comments in the final chapter.

Chapters 7 and 8, based on new research undertaken in a 1983–1986 UCLA study of the academic profession, concentrate on some primary divisions in the American professoriat. Among disciplinary differences none is more basic than the divide between professional schools and liberal arts departments. Sydney Halpern's analysis centers on the nature of academic thought and practice in American professional schools, preeminently in medicine where elaborate specialization around professional practice is most advanced. Since the professional school must combine practical and academic missions, the contrast with letters and science departments is striking. The dual professional and scholarly commitments of the professional school produce structural ambiguity: there must be a "clinical" as well as a scholarly faculty, hence a dual appointment system, with possibly a nontenure track and members who have little or no interest in tenure. During one period the professional school may move toward the central norms of the university—research production and all the other customary responsibilities and obligations—to strengthen its position within the university itself. It "goes academic." But then in a subsequent period its inherent duality will pull and push it toward practice, then to obey the norms of the outside practicing profession, orienting itself, in the case of medicine, to patient care. The stretch increases: roles are differentiated to serve in opposite directions; faculty members are as much outside the academy as inside; the complexities of the outside profession are brought inside, for example, the practices of the health industry penetrate the medical schools. With the majority of American university academics now located in professional schools, Halpern's analysis of what we might call "the professional-school difference" becomes central to our understanding of the changing nature of academic work, thought, and authority.

Kenneth Ruscio explores the layering of the profession in the United States by institutional sector. No other society has such a range of types of postsecondary institutions, a differentiation that produces an extreme division of labor among academics. About one-third of the work force is in community colleges, where faculty teach largely first-year students and nonmatriculated adults. Their duties then resemble those of teachers in the secondary school more than those of instructors in the graduate school. Another one-third are in four- and five-year colleges, public and private, where again the context deflects university norms. From intensive interviews with academics in a wide range of institutions, Ruscio details the imposing differences in work, authority, and belief which divide the American profession institutionally into "the many." The differing on-the-job mandates are striking. Yet he also notes the powerful counterforce of common socialization to scientific, scholarly, and university-rooted norms whch occurs during graduate training. The strain between the one and the many may be in part a strain between prejob socialization that unites and on-the-job imperatives that divide.

In the concluding chapter I seek to weave together the ideas presented in the earlier essays and to establish a framework for future thought and inquiry. I begin with the observations found in the earlier essays on how academics and their work are conditioned by national settings, are differentiated by institutional sectors, and are affected by the increasingly powerful thrust of the disciplines. These three contexts interact with and shape one another, as in certain European countries where both state bureaucracy and academic oligarchy have restrained disciplinary development to the point of measurably slowing scientific advance. The analysis then deals with the question of academic authority, highlighting the guildlike forms intrinsic to the profession which provide the foundation for larger forms of collegial-professional authority. Simultaneously, these forms serve to provide some integration and to form a self-government resistant to political and bureaucratic controls, even when the estate is situated within the state. I then turn to the structural and normative dimensions that appear to integrate academics into a larger whole; here I suggest that there are some intangible bonds of identity and morality, alluded to in some of the earlier chapters, which we understand poorly because they are so remote to objective inquiry and so couched in cliché and cant. Finally, I turn briefly to the relationship of this profession with the rest of society to emphasize three points. The critical relation is the degree of closeness to government; the services of the profession now vary enormously in kind and must be approached institutional sector by institutional sector, discipline by discipline; and beyond the immediate services to government, individuals, and groups there lie long-term fiduciary responsibilities to knowledge and culture and to future generations. There are grains of truth among the elaborate claims of altruism that this profession as much as any other manages to mount.

The final chapter, indeed the entire volume, reflects a bias toward organizational explanation: we study the structural foundations of any social system in order to understand the primary forms that set incentives that in turn shape motivations that steer behavior. The motivations and behaviors of academics are considerably determined by the incentives that reside in different forms of academic organization—from those that support advanced training at the beginning of careers to those that provide for retirement. Those forms are best pursued initially by searching for similarities and differences across national, disciplinary, and institutional contexts.

PART I
NATIONAL SETTINGS

1

The Academic Profession in the United Kingdom

Harold J. Perkin

In the expansive days of the Robbins era in Britain, with new universities springing into existence and student numbers surging on all sides, I wrote a book on the twentieth-century development of university teaching in the United Kingdom, which I chose to call *Key Profession*. I argued that, in an increasingly professional society, university teaching was the key profession because academics had become the educators and selectors of the other professions. In a world increasingly dominated by the professional expert, on whose competence, reliability, and integrity society had come to depend for not merely the functioning of our complex industrial, or postindustrial, service-oriented society, but for the very survival of civilization and the human race itself (here I am thinking of the destruction that might be wreaked by a few incompetent, unreliable, or dishonest experts), the organized application of trained intelligence, of which the universities were the embodiment and the gatekeepers, was the key both to economic survival and to cultural progress.

That was in the warm, sunny optimistic days of the 1960s, lightly shadowed perhaps by the challenge to academic complacency represented by student unrest and the demand, undoubtedly justified, for the customers to have some say in the nature of the gate to which their mentors held the key. According to A. H. Halsey and Martin Trow, who were writing their much larger analysis, *The British Academics*,[1] at precisely the same time, about two-thirds of the British

university teachers, despite apprehensions about maintaining standards, welcomed the Robbins expansion, and about half their sample
would have liked to see an even higher proportion of the age group
in British higher education by the 1980s.[2]

Those warm, sunny, springlike days have gone; British academics
now live in a cold climate, with the searing winds of change, of
economic depression and public expenditure cuts blowing down the
corridors of power from the Department of Education and Science
and the Treasury. Robbins's blissful dawn has been succeeded by the
Thatcher government's *Attack on Higher Education* chronicled by Maurice and David Kogan, and lamented on all sides as part of a larger
Crisis of the University (Peter Scott's title) and of higher education in
general.

In this much colder climate, unforeseen in the torrid 1960s or even
in the chilly 1970s, the academic profession seems to have lost its
leading role as the key profession and is losing out both in status and
in material rewards. The buyers' market in academic jobs has been
replaced by a fear of redundancy, and the profession is declining in
size and influence. Yet in a cold climate one does not give up working
and taking exercise, unless one is a hibernating snake or tortoise; one
does it all the more deliberately and carefully, and with a shrewder
eye to survival into warmer climes. Far from wringing our hands and
lamenting our plight, we academics should ask ourselves what went
wrong, why we slid overnight from being the custodians of the future
to being the pariahs of the present—in short, why we are losing out
in the game of life—and attempt to regain our position in the league
table of the professions by learning how to play the game to win.
This means coolly analyzing what the game is about, and how it is
played by more successful professionals.

I want to do four things in this paper: (1) to trace briefly the history
of the academic profession in Britain and to show how its fragmented
and hierarchical structure evolved to create the present amorphous
team in the game of life. This will mean looking at the changing social
function of the universities and colleges in successive societies; (2) to
set out the nature of the game and the context in which it is played.
This will mean introducing a more operational and dynamic theory
of the professions and how they interact with society than that usually
found in the literature; (3) to explain why and how the academic
profession in Britain came to lose its winning streak. This will mean
examining both the resources of skill and persuasion it brought to the
game and the ill winds that have blown against it in the last decade;
(4) to demonstrate that, despite the current pessimism, the game is

by no means lost, and that hard times can be turned to good account if present adversities are accepted as a challenge to reform the profession and to create a better system of higher education and a more responsive society. Happily, recent signs indicate that the profession is at last coming together to field a united team in the game of life.

THE RISE OF THE KEY PROFESSION

The present academic profession in Britain is the product of a long historical development; it is impossible to understand its amorphous shape and many divisions without a brief look at its history. Until the 1820s there were only two universities in England and Wales: Oxford and Cambridge, founded in the thirteenth century; and four Scottish ones: St. Andrews, Aberdeen, Glasgow, and Edinburgh, founded in the fifteenth and sixteenth centuries. Until the Reformation they were mainly clerical institutions concerned with educating clergy for the two national churches, though they also had postgraduate facilities of law and medicine. After the Reformation the English and Scottish universities went separate ways. Oxford and Cambridge, in Hugh Kearney's words, "underwent a change of social function. They were transformed from being institutions geared to training for a particular profession into institutions which acted as instruments of social control." They began to cater to the governing elite of landowners who ruled the country, mainly on an amateur basis, as justices of the peace and the like, for the next three and one-half centuries:

Some time between 1530 and 1570 laymen from the landed gentry began to go up to Oxford and Cambridge in large numbers. The universities ceased to be the educational organs of the Church. They began to cater in part at least for the educational needs of the lay ruling elite.[3]

For about a hundred years the two English universities thrived as educators of the sons of the landed class and of the intending clergy. Student numbers expanded, and the tutors, the college fellows, became in effect prosperous servants of the ruling class and often benefited from their pupils' patronage in the shape of rich livings of the church. Soon after the English Civil War in the mid-seventeenth century, however, the numbers began to decline, and did not recover their old level again until the mid-Victorian age.[4] The reasons for the decline are obscure, but they have to do with the counterattractions of the continental grand tour as a finishing school for young gentlemen and also with the decay of lecturing and serious academic work

on the part of overendowed and self-indulgent university dons. Eighteenth-century college fellows were notorious for eating and drinking
and neglecting their duties. Most of them were comparatively young
men who were simply waiting in comfort for a college living in the
church and the chance to marry, since only the few who became
professors or masters of colleges escaped the celibacy rule.

Nevertheless, the few who did take their duties seriously could
claim to be engaged in higher education. In Scotland, a much poorer
country with a very scattered population, the undergraduate faculties
of the four universities became, in effect, the main secondary schools
of Scotland, catering to the same early teenage group that attended
the so-called public schools (they were the endowed grammar, especially boarding, schools) in England. The different educational level
is confirmed by the tradition that the wealthier Scottish graduates
pass on to Oxford or Cambridge to take a second undergraduate
degree. The Scottish universities, however, did provide for a poorer
class of boys and a larger swathe of society than the English and
enabled the "lad o' pairts," with talents and little or no money, to
rise from peasant or artisan stock and become a minister of the kirk,
a lawyer, or a physician. Thus Scotland came to export to England,
and to the growing empire, a stream of poor but able men of letters,
professional men, and such "feelosophers" as James Mill and Thomas
Carlyle, the like of which were rare among English graduates.

The Scottish universities never experienced the twilight of teaching
and scholarship of eighteenth-century Oxbridge, however. Because
of their poverty they were forced to abandon the expensive tutorial
system that required each tutor to teach the whole syllabus to a handful of students. Instead, they adopted the much cheaper system of
using professors expert in a single subject as lecturers to large classes,
a system urged by Andrew Melville in the sixteenth century, which
became general by the eighteenth. This economizing device, paradoxically, encouraged a small number of professors to specialize in
one subject and to become advanced thinkers and researchers in mathematics, astronomy, natural philosophy (physics), moral philosophy
(social science), law, humanity (classics), and a host of other subjects.[5]
The result was the renascence of learning known as the Scottish Enlightenment, when professors like Colin Maclaurin, Newton's precocious pupil, pioneered advanced mathematics, Joseph Black inau-
gurated experimental chemistry and encouraged James Watt's
experiments with steam power, David Hume developed his skeptical,
iconoclastic philosophy, William Roberts his multidisciplinary history, and Adam Ferguson, Adam Smith, and John Millar the origins

of modern social science and economics and, long before Marx, the economic interpretation of history.[6]

These two competing traditions of the academic profession, the Oxbridge tradition of the college tutor devoted to his well-to-do pupils and as much concerned with developing their characters as their minds and the Scottish tradition of the research-oriented professor, remote from his numerous and often poor students, concerned with stimulating their intellect, have struggled for supremacy in British higher education ever since. The Oxbridge tutorial tradition was an elitist one, designed to rear future rulers and key professional men; the Scottish professorial one represented "the democratic intellect" and was meritocratic in encouraging talent wherever it could be found. When the Industrial Revolution of the late eighteenth century, which itself owed very little to either kind of university, began to stimulate the demand for higher education from a rapidly expanding industrial and commercial middle class, it was the Scottish tradition they wanted, because it was more specialized and tailored to their needs for expertise, because it was much cheaper than the Oxbridge alternative, and because it was home-based in the great commercial cities where the middle class lived in large concentrations.[7]

Thus it is not surprising that when London University, the first new university in England since the Middle Ages, was founded in 1826, significantly by graduates of Edinburgh University like Henry Brougham and Thomas Campbell and their Dissenting and agnostic friends, it should have adopted the Scottish professorial system as the basis of its teaching and organization. That its Anglican rival, King's College London, should have adopted the same system is more surprising, but this shows that its manifest advantages for a middle-class clientele living at home outweighed the English upper-class preference for the more expensive tutorial system.[8] The Anglican cathedral chapter's University of Durham adopted the same mode in 1834, as did the many new civic university colleges that followed the example of Owens College, Manchester (1951) in Leeds Liverpool, Birmingham, Sheffield, and Bristol, in a steady stream down to the First World War.[9]

Meanwhile, even Oxford and Cambridge were forced, partly by external pressure of critics like James Heywood and the Benthamite *Westminster Review*, partly because of the internal agitation of reforming dons like Thomas Arnold, Mark Pattison, and Henry Sidgwick, to accept reform, much of it imposed by Parliament and the Royal Commissions of the 1850s and 1870s. The revolution of the dons, in Sheldon Rothblatt's phrase, in effect professionalized university teaching in the ancient English universities, got rid of the Anglican monopoly, introduced modern teaching of modern subjects, including laboratory sciences, strengthened the university and the professoriat against the colleges and the tutorial fellows, and transformed the celibate Anglican don into the professional academic "of any religion or none." Even so, the Oxbridge professor remained an honorific but remote and nearly powerless figure (except with the few graduate students or where he controlled an important laboratory), and the college fellows continued to dominate the education of the undergraduates.[10] The revolution in short was a conservative one; it accepted just enough of the alternative tradition to keep Oxford and Cambridge in front in social prestige and intellectual eminence.

The revolution within the universities belatedly reflected the revolution in society at large. The Industrial Revolution had created a larger-scale, more complex society based on great cities and requiring a wider range of expert services. The old universities had been ill-equipped to provide these and a host of new institutions, Dissenting academies, mechanics' institutes, medical schools, and private-venture colleges had grown up to meet the demand for skilled technicians, managers, accountants, doctors, local public officials, and the like. The older universities were slow to meet these demands, but their reform coincided with the introduction of entry by examination to the civil service between 1854 and 1870 and also to the Indian civil service and the Empire generally. Oxford and Cambridge seized on these opportunities for employment and came to exercise a near-monopoly of the new administrative grade of the civil service. They also refurbished their medical and law schools, established science and engineering faculties, and in the 1890s developed appointment boards to find jobs for their graduates in industry and commerce.[11] The Scottish universities and the major English civics, though less prominent in the public service occupations, developed closer links with local industries through such eminent professors as Sir Henry Roscoe and Sir William Perkin of Manchester in chemicals and dyestuffs, Sir Richard Redmayne and Lord Cadman of Birmingham in mining, Sir Charles Wheatstone and J. F. Daniell of King's College London in electricity, Lewis Gordon and Lord Kelvin of Glasgow in Atlantic cables, and McQuorn Rankin of Glasgow and Alfred Ewing of Dundee in shipbuilding. Oxford and Cambridge were not without such links—C. F. Jenkin of Oxford helped with aircraft engineering in the First World War, and Sir James Dewar of Cambridge invented the vacuum flask and was coinventor of cordite—but their science gravitated to the "pure" kind whose ultimate value to future industry, like Clerk Maxwell's work on electromagnetic radiation or J. J. Thompson's on X rays, might be immense, but whose immediate applications were not so clear. The older universities acquired their reputation for keeping aloof from contemporary money-making industry and commerce which they have retained ever since.[12]

The demands of industry and the new society could not entirely be met, especially at middle management, technician, and skilled worker levels, by either kind of university, new or old, and the Victorian age burgeoned with colleges below the university level. By 1851 there were no less than twenty-nine such general colleges and nearly sixty medical colleges. Several of them became or merged with the new university colleges, such as Owens College, Manchester or Mason College, Birmingham, but others remained to provide subdegree training for skilled craftsmen, technicians, law clerks, and lesser professions of all kinds, often on a part-time basis, like the Manchester Mechanics' Institute that became the Manchester Technical College (later the University of Manchester Institute of Science and Technology) or the Regent Street Polytechnic in London.[13] Many of these were eventually carried up on the escalator of "academic drift" to become full universities, but most remained technical colleges and became ancestors of the public sector of higher education, catering to a great variety of nondegree students taking courses for the City and Guilds examinations and later for the present elaborate system of technical qualifications, mainly the Ordinary and Higher National certificates and diplomas. It was always possible, from 1858 on, for some of their students to take external degrees from the University of London, and most of the university colleges served their university apprenticeship by this means before the Council for National Academic Awards largely took over that function in the 1960s. But for the most part the technical colleges together with the art and design schools and the normal schools (teacher training colleges) of the Victorian age provided a layer of "higher and further education" below the university level, which was of great importance to the lower middle and skilled working classes and was to evolve into the state sector (strictly, the local authority and denominational sector) of the modern binary system.[14]

In this haphazard and completely unplanned way, the multilayered hierarchy of the British higher education system and its fragmented academic profession came into existence. It is important to note that the size of and balance between the various institutions and sectors changed continually. In 1900 when only 1.2 percent of nineteen-year-olds in Britain were in full-time education, there were only about

20,000 full-time students in universities, 5,000 in teacher training, and none in further education, which had an unknown but fairly small number of part-time students. By 1938, when 2.7 percent of the age group entered higher education, there were 50,000 full-time students in universities, 13,000 in teacher training, and 6,000 in further education. By 1963, when the Robbins Committee on Higher Education reported, 8.5 percent of the age group was involved, and the numbers were 118,000, 55,000, and 43,000, plus 54,000 part-time students in advanced courses in further education.[15] Today (1984) when the age participation rate is 13.2 percent, there are 259,000 home full-time students at universities, 256,000 in the public sector, plus 45,000 overseas students divided between the two. There are also 300,000 part-time advanced students, 192,000 of the latter in the public sector, 75,000 at the Open University, and 66,000 at the universities.[16] It can readily be seen that on top of the enormous growth in student numbers, from 1 percent to 13 percent of the age group (still far short of most other advanced countries), the balance has shifted from an overwhelming preponderance in the university sector to an approximate fifty-fifty division of full-timers between university and nonuniversity sectors, and in the public sector, to a preponderance of advanced part-timers.

Since the academic staff has, until the last four years, increased almost pari passu with student numbers, the balance of the academic profession has shifted in the same direction. Staff-student ratios are somewhat more generous in the universities (though not so generous as appears at first sight, the university ratios being weighted with the staff-intensive schools of medicine, veterinary science, and agriculture), since polytechnic and further-education staff are not required to do research, though many do; but the public-sector lecturers, providing for some 470,000 full-time and part-time advanced students as against the universities' 325,000 (excluding the Open University), not to mention the large number of nonadvanced part-time students, already far outnumber the university professors and lecturers. As against the 44,100 university teachers at the peak in 1980, there were 77,600 public-sector lecturers in 1979, 31,800 of them graduates.[17]

Within the university sector, too, the balance among different kinds of universities has profoundly changed. In 1900 about half of the 2,000 university teachers taught in Oxford and Cambridge. By 1963 only one in twelve (8.6 percent) of the then 20,000 taught in those universities, and today the proportion of the now 43,000 is even less (7.5 percent). Yet that small minority, as A. H. Halsey has pointed out, "have retained their commanding position."[18] They attract the best students: 74 percent of their entrants in the 1970s had A-level scores of 13 points (A B B) or better out of a maximum of 15, as against 59 percent for other universities. They publish, on average, more books and articles than other academics. One or the other ancient university is voted as the best place for study and research in most, though not quite all, of the leading subjects (the London School of Economics leads them in the social sciences and Imperial College London in engineering). And on the test of envy ("Which university would you rather be at?") they consistently attract more preferences than any other.[19]

The reasons for their high status, reputation, and attractiveness are fairly obvious: they have the largest endowments, the finest accommodation, cuisine, and wine cellars, the best libraries, laboratories, and other facilities, and—a factor that cannot be too strongly emphasized—the gravitational pull of first-class academics and students for each other. Indeed, this pull has become stronger since the Second World War, as the increasingly generous student-grant system has encouraged the most able applicants from every social class to gravitate there (there is still, however, a powerful bias toward entrants from the fee-paying schools) and as the same trend has affected the meritocratic selection of the dons. Indeed, a self-perpetuating momentum is at work; good people attract good people, and good people recommend those they think are good for honors and promotion. Halsey and Trow point out that Oxford and Cambridge have more than their share of fellows of the Royal Society and the British Academy,[20] but since they run the Royal Society and the British Academy this is not altogether surprising.

Oxford and Cambridge are the British equivalent of the French *grandes écoles*, of the American Ivy League, of the great To-Dai (Tokyo University) and Kyoto University in Japan, of the Russian academies of science, and so forth. They are at the head of the academic hierarchy of prestige, achievement, and reputation known to every academic, professional, and businessman in Britain. The pecking order descends from them via London University, the great civic universities (Manchester, Birmingham, Leeds, Liverpool, Sheffield, and Bristol) and the major Scottish universities (Aberdeen, Glasgow, and Edinburgh), and the minor civics (e.g., Leicester, Hull, Reading, Cardiff, and Swansea) and smaller Scottish (St. Andrews, Dundee) to the ex–colleges of advanced technology (CATs) promoted to university status in the 1960s (e.g., Aston, Bradford, Salford). By and large, status has normally gone with age. The one exception to this is the new universities of the 1960s (Sussex, Kent, Warwick, Lancaster, etc.), the so-

called green-field campuses that were founded as autonomous de-
gree-granting institutions from the beginning and so were able to
experiment with new subjects, new curricula, new methods of teaching and examining, and so on—what Asa Briggs had called "the new
map of learning." Some of these were able to leapfrog the minor civics
and the ex-CATs in prestige and attractiveness, but not the University
of London and the major civics, still less Oxford and Cambridge. With
that minor exception, the rule that old is beautiful continues to apply,
as indeed it does in many other countries.

Further down, the polytechnics and other colleges take their place
in the pecking order not from their founding date but from when
they first began to teach substantially to degree standard. For the
most part this meant from the time they were designated as polytechnics in the 1960s. They too have their pecking order, with Oxford
Polytechnic and Central London Polytechnic at the top and the more
remote from the southeastern academic heartland further down. Although the polytechnics were meant to be different from universities
and to concentrate on applied and vocational subjects, in practice
they have less science and technology and more social science, including management and business studies, than the universities. In
the eyes of students they have become a lesser alternative to a university course. A recent study shows that the best polytechnic has
an average A-level score for its entrants of 6.5 (between C D D and
C D E) out of 15 points compared with 8.5 for the worst university
(between C C C and C C D); what matters is not whether the scores
are meaningful but where the students with the better scores prefer
to go.[21] Similarly with the academics: according to Halsey's 1976 survey, more appointees with first-class honors gravitate to universities
(43 percent of the staff) than to the polytechnics (19 percent), far more
of the university staff publish regularly, and though 47 percent of the
polytechnic lecturers would take a university post at a lower salary,
over half the university teachers would not take a polytechnic post
even at a higher salary.[22]

The history of higher education in Britain, as in many other countries, has left a legacy of hierarchy and fragmentation. Does it matter?
Perhaps not, insofar as meritocracy has increasingly, though not completely, replaced social background as the main principle of selection
and appointment. But given the key role of universities as educators
and selectors of all the major professions in a postindustrial society,
and given the well-known preference of the civil service, the higher
professions, and the major business corporations for graduates from
Oxford and Cambridge—an arts graduate from one of them is con-

sistently preferred by management recruiters to a scientist or engineer from elsewhere—the pecking order does have a profound effect on the character of leadership in British business and public administration, and, some would say, on the success of the British economy. Sir Alastair Pilkington, former chairman of Pilkington Glass and inventor of the world-renowned float process of glass manufacture, in his recent presidential address to the British Association for the Advancement of Science, joined the long-standing chorus of criticism of our universities for not producing enough graduates interested in industry, and of industry and the civil service for employing arts graduates in preference to applied scientists and engineers.[23] Mr. Kenneth Durham, chairman of Unilever, told an international higher education conference at York that

as a group, educationists do not understand the process by which wealth is created and a few of them are actively opposed to the idea of profit and free enterprise. The education system seems inimical to industry, and their grasp of the role or even the meaning of innovation is entirely feeble.[24]

And a recent study of employers' views of graduate job applicants by a team of researchers at Brunel University led by Dr. Chris Boyes found that those recruiting potential managers preferred Oxbridge graduates with good degrees in traditional subjects to those from other universities with more relevant and work-related training, and those with any kind of degree from a university to the most technically qualified graduate from a polytechnic. One personnel manager said:

I still believe the Oxbridge qualification carries clout and I would like my son to be exposed to what, after all, are top academics. . . . But I must confess to an appalling lack of knowledge of the other universities and polytechnics.[25]

The traditional anti-industrial spirit of the English (not so much the Scottish) universities has been chronicled by Sheldon Rothblatt and Martin Wiener, who have traced it to the domination of the educational ethos by Oxbridge and the public boarding schools.[26] Its ultimate springs, I believe, lie deep in English society, as young people imbibe these attitudes long before they arrive at the university, and their preference for the arts and social sciences over natural science and technology can be measured by the A-level grades demanded for university entrance to the former compared to the latter. To the extent that Oxford and Cambridge share that anti-industrial spirit and help to transmit it to the rest of the university system, they must bear some of the responsibility for what is a uniquely English prejudice.

In France, Germany, America, Russia, and Japan, as indeed in every other advanced industrial country, engineering schools are at or near the head of the academic hierarchy and can reject all but the best qualified applicants. In Britain they are at the bottom, and the best qualified students go into the humanities and pure sciences. Far from this being an aberration on their part, the students are making a rational, maximizing decision: they know that they will have a higher status at the university and a better chance of a highly paid job with prospects afterward than if they choose a "more useful" subject. They have consciously and intelligently equipped themselves for the game of life as it is played in Britain, not as it is played by different rules in countries better geared to life and work in the new postindustrial society. Yet by contrast the key profession itself, the academic profession that trains and selects these students for their future roles, has not discovered how best to equip itself for its own future role and, for reasons we shall see, has in recent years begun to lose out in the professional game of life.

THE PROFESSIONAL GAME OF LIFE

The academic profession may be the key profession, but it is nonetheless only one profession among many and must learn how to play by the rules of the professional game. It is admittedly a very peculiar profession in that most university and other higher education teachers have a double allegiance, primarily to the discipline in which they were trained and only secondarily to the institution that employs them.[27] Most academics look first to their discipline for their reputation and psychic rewards (these of course have a determinate cash value), and to their national and international standing with their peers in the same area of study, on which appointment, promotion, and translation to chairs depend. This is why research and publication are so vital, not only because they are more subject than teaching to peer review but because they can influence far more people, including students at other institutions. Publication, it is too often forgotten, is a vital form of teaching, as reading is a vital part of learning, and although the immediate connection between research and good teaching may be exaggerated, nonpublishers do not necessarily make better teachers. On the contrary, those who cannot explain themselves in print often cannot explain themselves in class. For better or worse, teaching, the weaker link, binds them to their local colleagues; research and publication, far stronger links, bind them to the national and international world outside the walls.

To the extent, however, that the discipline outweighs the institution in their allegiance, it represents a centrifugal force that fragments and weakens the unity of the profession and reduces its effectiveness in the game of life. It is true that many employed professionals—accountants, lawyers, economists, and engineers who work for the government or a private corporation, for example—have the same double allegiance and may, and with the professional and scientific branches of the civil service, pay for it in lower salaries and status than the mainline managers or administrators, but in no other profession does every member look outward for his or her primary loyalty. The strength of this loyalty varies among disciplines: inordinately strong among medical and legal academics, less strong among linguists and historians. In Britain, with its early specialization and commitment for most academics to a single honors subject from their admission to the first degree, fragmentation of the profession has gone so far that many colleagues cannot speak one another's language, a significant fact to which we shall return.

Such an idiosyncratic occupation is exceptionally difficult to fit into the traditional concept of the professions presented by sociologists and historians. Most such theory has been completely static, and is based on a crude division of all occupations into prestigious "liberal" or "learned" professions and nonprestigious nonprofessions, sometimes with a twilight zone of quasi or semiprofessions in between. Sociologists have vied with each other in delineating the three, six, or fourteen traits that distinguish the professional sheep from the unprofessional goats.[28] The six traits most commonly cited are: (1) a skill based on theoretical knowledge; (2) intellectual education and training; (3) the assessment and certification of competence; (4) the exclusion of the unqualified; (5) a code of conduct; and (6) fiduciary service in the affairs of others. Some or all of these features might in a small number of cases be reinforced by legislation and state registration, but this has been by no means universal to the recognized professions—indeed, the oldest of them, the clergy and the bar, have never sought legislative recognition, while the state-employed professions, the civil service and the officer corps, have not needed it.

Some sociologists have adopted a less static approach by treating the traits as steps on the path to professional status, up which each aspiring occupation would climb as far as it could, before finding its own level in the hierarchy.[29] Such movement was always one way, and the rise of one occupation, however successful, did not displace any other. The long upward climb still led, generally for the few, to the summit where the "true" professions looked down on the hyphenated professions below. The fact that in addition to the many prestigious, often university-educated, professions now sitting on the crowded top of the pyramid, there are hundreds of others sweating up the sides, throws doubt in a society increasingly composed of professional and would-be professional groups on the whole model of traits and steps, especially as it applies to those seemingly endless professions that have come to be increasingly trained by, and therefore represented in, the academic profession.

What is needed therefore is a more dynamic or operational theory of the professions and professionalization, one that allows occupations to sink as well as rise on the professional escalator, and is in perpetual motion to accommodate the changing fortunes of each and every professional occupation, however grand and seemingly invulnerable or however lowly and aspiring. Such an approach is part of the wider theory of the game of life. According to this theory, society consists of an endlessly shifting market for people, people with particular skills and abilities who bargain and jostle for the rewards— social, psychic, and political as well as material and economic—which they can persuade the rest to pay them. This is of course a much wider and more sophisticated market than the ecomomic labor market, which is only one small aspect of it. The short-term bargains over pay and perquisites are real and important enough, but they pale into insignificance beside the long-term bargains over status and power that affect the more persistent standing of each occupation and therefore its capacity to make repeatedly advantageous short-term economic bargains over the generations.

The operation of the market for people is like a gigantic game of Monopoly. In it the players do not start from scratch but with very different stakes; and the play never ends. Those who sit on prestigious properties (Chancery Lane or Harley Street? Whitehall or the City?) can charge high fees for the use of their facilities; but they can, if they are unlucky or careless, lose them to luckier or more skillful players coming from behind. The properties are, of course, "human capital," but not just the human capital of Gary Becker or Pierre Bourdieu, which is principally the product of past educational investment, paid for by the family or by the state.[30] Over and above this, it is, like so much material capital, in large part the product of capital gains, much of it artificially induced by persuasive advertising and restrictive practices. Some players, like opera singers, fashionable painters, pop stars, leading lawyers, or inventors of computer games or Rubik cubes, can play as individuals, and bid for "jackpot" rewards in terms of fame as well as fortune, but most players for practical reasons prefer to play as teams and share the benefits. Professional organization is a species of collective bargaining, not necessarily with a real or putative client or employer, but with all the other players in the game. Instead of playing against one another and perhaps reducing their winnings by internal competition, members of the same occupation choose to rise or fall together by joining forces and pooling their competitive resources.

The resources a typical profession brings to the game consist of its expertise, based on its specialized education and training; its provision of an esoteric and preferably fiduciary service, one that is beyond the immediate judgment of the laity, who must therefore take it on trust; and above all, the trust of the clients themselves, be they individuals, corporate employers, or the state. This trust, in turn, is based on the profession's collective capacity to persuade, to raise its market reputation, to establish its charisma. The one resource that can mobilize all the rest, which lies more within the profession's power to control, is organization. By skillfully choosing their team, by restricting it to the right-sized group of players, large enough to be an effective power block but small enough not to spread the gains too thinly, and by excluding just those competitors who are threats rather than allies, they can maximize their chances of establishing a winning team position. Thus those "devices of closure" remarked by shrewder sociologists like Anthony Giddens and Frank Parkin[31]—control of admission by prior qualification and examination, exclusion of "quacks" and "charlatans" by state registration, and the like—are not so much an altruistic concern for high standards or a cynical bid for monopoly (though they may be those, too) as an integral part of the professional game. By a curious paradox, professional organization in the market for people is an attempt to rig the free market in labor to prevent competition by the excluded from pulling down the profession's rewards to the free market level.[32] One can see why the advocates of the free market readily set their faces against professional monopoly and restrictive practices, as for example in Britain the solicitors' monopoly of conveyancing or the universities' pre-1964 monopoly of degrees.[33] Professionalism is an attempt to control and limit the free market in the interests of professional rewards, which is not to say that it cannot also benefit the client in the shape of higher standards or a guaranteed service.

The best way of persuading the client, the employer, and society (through the state) that a particular professional service is vital and worth protecting from free competition by statutory or other privileges is to provide an undoubtedly vital and trustworthy service. Ultimately, no professional organization can create a permanent quasi monopoly without inspiring the belief that what it has to offer is worth paying for, and the best way to inspire that belief is by believing in it oneself. The priesthood that becomes so "honest to God" that God no longer exists in a form the faithful can accept soon loses its believers and most of its income. The physician who will not heal himself or at least take his own medicine will soon find his surgery empty. Only in the never-never land that some purist academics and philosophic clergymen inhabit can the game be played so quixotically. In the real world of hardheaded professionalism, the professionals really believe in the wares they cry up.

On the whole, however, if British academics have lost out, it is not by *not* believing in their wares. If anything, they have believed in them so much they did not think they needed to cry them up at all. "Effortless superiority," inherited from an older world where Oxbridge and the public schools serviced an effortlessly superior imperial dream, has been their stock in trade. Martin Wiener, following Sheldon Rothblatt, has attributed the decline of the industrial spirit in Britain to the survival of aristocratic values in English higher education.[34] This seems to me to mistake the influence of the aristocracy, which always had and still has an enterprising eye for the fast buck, and to underrate that of the dons themselves, who for too long have looked down on the industrial money-grabbing on which their private endowments and public funding have rested. Yet the problem is more complicated than this. It is not true that the British universities have neglected science and technology; they in fact provide proportionately more places in those subjects than in most other countries. Britain has a larger ratio of Nobel prize–winners to population in the sciences than any other country except Sweden, and Oxford and Cambridge have the largest share of them as well as of Fellows of the Royal Society.[35] Even the charge that there is too much pure science and not enough applied science is belied by the close relations many universities have developed with industry, not only in science and technology, but in business management, operations research, information technology, and many other "high tech" developments. University business and science parks are currently all the rage, and there is scarely a university without a scheme involving local industry. And yet the universities are constantly criticized for not showing more concern for problems of production and economic growth and for turning out graduates who prefer jobs in government, teaching, the social services, leisure industries, and the media, and who spurn productive industry. To some extent the criticism is based on a misunderstanding of postindustrial society and its economy, increasingly based on services rather than on material production, but the academic profession has certainly failed to put over to the public either the realities of the new productive system or the nature of their key role within it. It may not be the fault of the dons that British students prefer nonvocational courses and that British graduates turn their backs on industry—they have learned those attitudes long before they reach the university—but British academics have done little either to change those attitudes or to justify them to society at large. They have thus failed a basic test in the game of life.

CHARACTERISTICS OF THE BRITISH ACADEMIC PROFESSION

The British academic profession has at least six important features that, though defensible in themselves and not fundamentally different from those of other nations, become in their British variants potential handicaps in the game of life. It is split between different sectors and kinds of institutions and is not organized to play as a unified team. It is not divided vertically into equal sectors, whatever the theory of the binary system, but hierarchically into layers of different prestige and importance, according to a rigid pecking order. It is fragmented yet another way by specialization and departmentalism, and often the specialists can no longer talk to each other. It is unrepresentative of the population as a whole, and particularly neglects talent among the working class, women of all classes, and immigrants of different race and color from the majority. Its salary structures discourage mobility between institutions. And finally the principle of tenure, one of the best safeguards a profession might have, also entails costs in discouraging effort and innovation. All these features it shares in some degree with academic professions elsewhere. Disunity, hierarchy, o-verspecialization, and unequal opportunities for the underprivileged by class, sex, or race are common enough in most societies, and more or less equal salary scales and early tenure leading to immobility and lack of motivation are not unknown elsewhere.

Yet there is a sense in which these characteristics are intensified in Britain by the peculiarities of British society and the rigidities of its higher education system. The division between the two sectors, the universities and the polytechnics, is not a difference of function but of status, living and working conditions, and resources, and has become enshrined in the government policy of the binary system that seeks to perpetuate that division. The hierarchy is not based purely on academic merit as in France, America, Russia, and Japan, but on a class-ridden school system that gives competitive advantages at the higher level to those who can pay for private education at the secondary level. Specialization between arts and science and among individual subjects begins at a much earlier age in Britain than elsewhere, so that the lack of a common intellectual background and language is more deeply ingrained. Unequal opportunities for workers' children, women, and colored immigrants are defended on principles of "fairness" which preempt any discussion of "positive discrimination." The centralized salary structure (or structures—there are really two, for the universities and the public sector, both equally determined by the government) is unique in its rigidity below the professorial level, while at all levels it discourages mobility among institutions except on nonmaterial grounds of reputation and status. Finally, university tenure is awarded earlier than in any other country, after three or four years, and usually before a lecturer can produce any real evidence of scholarly achievement. In all these ways the British academic profession raises problems common to other systems to a higher level of difficulty. These six features would in normal times be harmless enough, if in some cases regrettable. But the 1980s are not normal times, and what in the past have been merely characteristics worthy of note have now become potential handicaps in the game of life.

The first potential handicap is that the British academic profession is far from a united or even readily identifiable team. Indeed, it has not yet decided where it begins and where it ends. There are still many academics who think it should be confined to a handful of "real" universities and that "more means worse" applies to teachers as much as to students.[36] At the other end of the scale are those who belive in "multiversities," huge comprehensive institutions that would unite all academics under the same administrative umbrella, if not under the same roof. The profession stretches all the way from Oxbridge to the smallest college of further education where a Council for National Academic Awards or a London external degree can be taken. As we have seen, more academics teach in the public sector than in the universities. In 1980 there were 35,100 full-time university teachers and 9,000 researchers (including those financed by research councils and other bodies as well as by the universities themselves). In 1979 there were 77,571 teachers in the public-sector colleges, 16,699 of them in the polytechnics. Only 41 percent of the total were graduates; the rest were mainly certificated teachers.[37]

Some university academics would argue that because the government insists that the polytechnic and other further education teachers are not required to do research the latter cannot be academics in the fullest sense, advancing as well as transmitting knowledge. According to a survey conducted by A. H. Halsey in 1976 only 60 percent of polytechnic lecturers claimed to be engaged in scholarly or research work meant for publication, as compared with 93 percent of university teachers. One-third of the university teachers had published at least one book and seven out of eight at least one article, compared with one in eight and one in two of the polytechnic lecturers. Half the polytechnic lecturers had published *something*, however, while a not inconsiderable number in the universities, 23 percent, had not published an article or book in the last two years, compared with 68 percent in the polytechnics.[38] And if scholarship—keeping abreast of one's subject—is to count as the more realistic test of academic status, then all teachers on both sides of the binary divide are required to pretend to it, however specious in some cases the pretense.

Whether or not it would pay the British academic profession to aim at a narrower or a more inclusive definition is a moot question. To take an analogy from the history of the medical profession, the university-educated physicians in the eighteenth and early nineteenth centuries did well for generations by excluding the apprentice-trained surgeons and apothecaries but were eventually forced to make common cause with them to obtain the protective monopoly of the 1858 Medical Registration Act. Yet the three together conspired, from the 1840s, to exclude the chemists and druggists under the 1858 Act, along with a long tail of unqualified and ancillary practitioners, and have held that line to their considerable profit to this day.[39]

As in medicine, discrimination between consultants and general practitioners within the profession is nearly as important as the exclusion of outsiders, and the second potential handicap of the British academic profession is its tendency to hierarchy, which is multidimensional. Over and above the career-oriented hierarchy of professor, reader, senior lecturer, and lecturer, and its equivalent in the public sector, a hierarchy that is plausibly defensible in terms of merit, age, and experience, there is the more debatable hierarchy based on institution of origin and of current allegiance. This is not just a matter of distinguishing between university sheep and further-education goats. As we have seen, every institution in the land has its historically determined place in the academic pecking order, which rubs off on the lowliest and most undeserving of its graduates and current members. One of the most revealing sections of Halsey and Trow's 1971 study was that on mobility preferences, which clearly showed where most academics' hearts lay. Of those who wished to move from their current university, nearly half would have preferred to go to Oxford or Cambridge, a quarter to London or a major redbrick university, one in eight to a new English university, and less than one in six to all the rest. A full third, significantly, would have preferred a college fellowship at Cambridge to a professorship at Sussex or Leeds or a readership at London. This was confirmed by Halsey's 1976 survey, which showed an increase in those preferring the Cambridge post from 33 to 35 percent. It is significant, however, that this closely matches the one-third of the profession who were educated at Oxford or Cambridge—a straight example of alumni loyalty, perhaps.[40] Although certainly not based on economic preference, as salaries, grade for grade, were the same in all universities with the partial exception of Oxford and Cambridge, this pecking order was not irrational. As Halsey and Trow pointed out, it was to some extent self-reinforcing: the best academics, as measured by first-class degrees, Ph.D.'s, Nobel prizes, F.R.S.'s and F.B.A.'s, tended to gravitate to the more attractive universities in terms of libraries, laboratories, and not least, life-style and access to men of power in government, industry, the professions, and the media.[41] In the hard times of the 1980s, when all universities are suffering from expenditure cuts, placing in the hierarchy matters: in the 1981 cutback, 8 percent on average, Cambridge and Oxford suffered very small cuts of 3.7 and 5.1 percent; Aston and Salford, massive cuts of 18 and 27.5 percent.[42] The hierarchy, as in so many other countries, is no doubt justified by academic merit, but the pecking order fragments the profession and encourages complacency in the face of the adversity of others. While some universities were at their wits' end at how to cope with losses of up to one-third of their staff, the vice-chancellor of Oxford was praising the University Grants Committee (UGC), the body applying the selective cuts, saying that we must "do everything possible to support its authority." Such insensitivity to the problems of professional colleagues undermines the team's capacity to play a united game.

In the polytechnics there is a further turn of the screw. In addition to the hierarchy of institutions with the polytechnics at the top and lesser colleges lower down the scale of esteem, there is over and above the teaching grades from lecturer to head of department a tall superstructure of administrative grades from permanent dean through various assistant and deputy directors to the director, a system admittedly not unlike the average American university. Unlike British universities, where the administrators are "civil servants" parallel in pay and status to the academics, and the professors and lecturers bear much of the administrative load, the polytechnic administrators are paid more than the teaching staff, do very little teaching, and often administer smaller faculties and departments than are found in the universities. The structure enables the polytechnic directors and lecturers to claim that their highest teaching staff are fewer in number and are paid less than full professors in universities, while studiously ignoring the overpaid administrators. It is a situation in which junior academics carry very heavy teaching loads and have very little influence on institutional policy, and it explains why few university teachers contemplate migrating to the public sector. Yet in the cost-cutting of the 1980s it has been the public-sector lecturers, not the bureaucrats, who have borne the burden of redundancy.

A third potential handicap, stronger in Britain than elsewhere, springs from specialization and departmentalism. Universities and colleges everywhere are somewhat arbitrary clusters of departments and faculties, most of which look for their identity, raison d'être, and objectives to similar subunits elsewhere. The subunits were not always so tightly cocooned. From the Middle Ages down to the nineteenth-century revolution of the dons, all students and teachers went through the same learning experience, the same grounding in a literal common language, and acquired in the medieval arts or Aristotelian philosophy the same tools and instruments of thought. While no one would wish to revive "a little Latin and less Greek" for everyone, a thorough grounding in English composition and mathematics would be a welcome novelty in most students and, since every academic was a student once, most faculty, too. The specialized disciplines, through an excess of professionalism, have come to pride themselves on their inaccessability to the uninitiated and often adopt their own "device of closure" in the form of jargon, acronyms, and mind-set which frustrates communication across disciplinary boundaries. This would matter less if they had all begun from a common starting place, so that learning the new language was akin to learning Romanche or Catalan for a Latinist.

In England (much less in Scotland), where specialization begins earlier than anywhere else (effectively at sixteen, and as between arts and sciences often at fourteen), the barriers to communication within the same institution are of longer and sturdier growth than in the United States or Europe, where general education continues to age eighteen or beyond. British academics have an even better excuse than others for misunderstanding each other. To paraphrase what Bernard Shaw said of the English in general, one English academic can scarcely open his mouth without being despised by another one. The mutual misunderstanding is more than verbal. It penetrates to the very fabric of what constitutes academic work. A physical scientist will assume a linguist to be playing with words, while the latter will consider the former to be playing with things, both equally "useless" occupations. A social scientist will imagine a historian to be merely "fact-grubbing," collecting and collating facts, perhaps for his benefit, while the latter imagines the former to be dreaming up theories without evidence, making bricks without straw, building castles in the air. Even scientists in adjacent fields may express disrespect for one another: "Atomic physics is physics; chemistry is applied atomic physics." Such mutual misunderstanding and disdain lead them to undervalue one another's professional worth; this, in turn, encourages outsiders to do the same. A fragmented and mutually critical profession does not make for a united team.

In social composition, by contrast, the profession has the wrong kind of unity, too middle-class, too masculine, and too racially uniform. This makes for a fourth potential handicap, the unrepresentativeness of academics in terms of social class, sex, and ethnic origin. In this they perhaps do not differ markedly from other leading professions, notably law, medicine, and the civil service, but in terms of the greater need of the universities for public sympathy and support, it is for them a more dangerous handicap. Halsey's 1976 survey shows that there has been very little change in the social origins of university teachers since Halsey and Trow's 1964 survey, my own in 1968, and Williams, Blackstone, and Metcalf's for 1969: only 25 percent of university teachers and 35.4 percent of polytechnic lecturers came from the manual working class (including lower-grade technicians and manual supervisors), compared with 49.2 percent and 40.7 percent from the professional, administrative, and managerial classes (the rest, 25.7 percent and 23.9 percent, came from the families of routine nonmanual employees, small proprietors, and self-employed artisans).[43] Williams, Blackstone, and Metcalf argue that the academic profession is a surer route for the upwardly mobile working-class boy (much more rarely girl) than professions more reliant on ascribed characteristics rather than merit.[44] Nevertheless, the social recruitment of academics is far removed, as one would expect, from the census distribution of occupations. In 1951 (when most fathers of these samples were heads of households) only 3.3 percent of the population were in the higher and 18.8 percent in the lesser professional and managerial class, 12.3 percent were in the routine nonmanual and 65.5 percent were in the manual working class. The disparity is wider in the ancient universities: in Halsey and Trow's 1964 sample, the professional and managerial middle class supplied 72 percent of the academics at Oxford and Cambridge, 68 percent at the London colleges, and 53 to 59 percent at all the rest. Thus the profession is preponderantly middle class in origin, tempered with a minority of upwardly mobile recruits from the nonmanual and manual working class, and is not in close rapport with the majority of the society that sustains it.

Women, that other majority of the population, are disproportionately underrepresented in the British academic profession. Women in higher education diminish in number the higher one goes. In 1983 they constituted 57 percent of students in nonadvanced further education, 46 percent of advanced courses in the public sector, 40.5 percent of university undergraduates, and 36.7 percent of postgraduates.[45] In polytechnics they were only 14.5 percent of all lecturers. In universities they averaged 14 percent of all faculty, 6.5 percent of readers and senior lecturers, and 2.3 percent of professors (99 out of 4,258). By discipline there were 30 women out of 779 full professors in business and social studies, 29 out of 760 in the arts and language studies, 25 out of 940 in the medical faculties, 8 out of 1,042 in the natural sciences, 6 out of 122 in education, only 1 out of 452 in engineering and technology, and none at all out of 60 in architecture and related subjects and out of 96 in agriculture, forestry, and veterinary science.[46] The reasons for this scarcity of women academics given to Williams, Blackstone, and Metcalf by women in their 1970 sample—lack of career orientation, social pressure to marry and have children, role conflict and domestic commitments, consequent lack of sustained ambition and therefore of administrative experience, research, and publication—point to deep-seated causes in the wider society but are still inadequate to account for it. It is interesting that the small minority of married women academics with children had published books and articles at the same rate as the men and far more than the single and the childless married women. This suggests that a new breed of women academics committed to both family and career is beginning to emerge, but they have not yet had time to overcome the masculine bias of the profession.[47]

The growing ethnic minorities also have, one feels (there are no surveys whatsoever), much less than their share of university students (most of the many ethnic students in universities and polytechnics being in fact foreigners on temporary visas) and a negligible share of the academic profession. Perhaps it is too early for second-generation immigrants to make much impact, and it will be interesting to see if, as in British small business and American academe, the Asians, who are already as well qualified as their white neighbors, take more advantage of what opportunities there are than those, mainly West Indians, of African origin.[48] To the extent that British universities and colleges have made little provision for nonwhite citizens, we can expect that there will be insignificant opportunity for them in the profession, the members of which can only be drawn from the student body. Once again we see that British higher education, out of complacency rather than ill will, is neglecting its links with and responsibilities to the wider society.

Paradoxically, another potential handicap is the nationally unified salary structure, different from both the free professorial market of American academia and from the state-administered academic bureaucracy of most European countries. In British universities nonprofessorial salary scales are everywhere the same; at the professorial level each university receives from the University Grants Committee the same average amount per full professor, which it then distributes as it thinks fit. Academically controlled Oxford and Cambridge pay the same salary to each professor; major civic universities with stronger lay (mostly business) control tend to pay high salaries to scientists and engineers and low ones to arts and social science professors; some, mostly minor civics, operate scales based on age and experience up to the average professorial salary; only a few make a conscious effort to relate salaries to scholarly reputation, though others are forced to do so by the market for scarce subjects or eminent individuals. This curious system, unlike most others in the Western world (Sweden and the Netherlands excepted), has a deleterious effect on professional mobility. Between the first appointment as a junior lecturer and the translation to a professorial chair (not always in a different university), there is very little staff movement among British universities. Even at the professorial level the occasional move to a prestigious chair at Oxbridge or London is often at some sacrifice to the individual, since the increase in salary is rarely worth the physical upheaval or the higher cost of housing. The result is that most British academics are trapped in their institutional framework like flies in a web, and that, since the founding of the new universities of the 1960s, there has been little opportunity for the almost automatic shake-up for both individuals and institutions that comes from migration. There are now many academics who have spent all their careers in one, at most two, institutions. In that situation it takes great character not to succumb to institutional stagnation and individual *melancholia academica*—not the best mental condition in which to play the game of life.

The final potential handicap is the one the profession values most. Tenure is the invaluable safeguard of academic liberty, without which, it is argued, there would be no freedom to teach or research, and above all, to "speak truth to power." Freedom to criticize is especially important in an increasingly centralized society with few alternative centers of criticism. Such freedom is vital, and the universities would be foolish to relinquish any part of the safeguard without putting something equally powerful in its place. Every benefit has its cost, however, and the price of tenure is to intensify the stagnation induced by the rigid salary and career structure. As the author of the case which the Association of University Teachers successfully presented to the Prices and Incomes Board in 1968 to reduce probation for new entrants by abolishing the old assistant lecturer grade, I now have to admit that three or four years is too short a period in which to decide an academic's fitness to hold a job for life. Not all the dead wood is at the bottom of the tree, however. The highest cost of tenure often appears higher up among those who, if they had ever been sapient green wood, have now withered on the branch; they not only frustrate promotion of livelier shoots from below but by their weight divert growth in fruitless directions. Tenure, in any case, is not so secure in, it is claimed, one-third or more of British universities as most academics think and is nonexistent in the public sector; and tenure based on academic freedom is not perhaps the best defense of job security.[49] Meanwhile, it *is* a problem, and the public belief that university teachers are protected from the rigors of economic depression and unemployment in a way denied to other occupations, however justified, once again weakens the position of the academic profession in the game of life.

All six leading characteristics of the British academic profession in the game of life—its uncertain extent and identity, its divisive pecking order, its premature specialization, its unrepresentativeness and failure to relate to a majority of society, its structural immobility, and its nursing of its own deadwood—are potential handicaps that could be a drag on its success even in a warm, hospitable climate. In the cold climate of the 1980s, they invite frostbite.

DONS IN A COLD CLIMATE

In the professional game of life no team is likely to be popular with all the rest. Though they may respect them and admire their skill, doctors do not love lawyers, professional managers do not love trade union leaders, and civil servants and professional politicians do not love academics. On the contrary, academics are envied and feared by most other professions, above all by those in government, for their "leisure" or command of unstructured time, which enables them to apply their not inconsiderable talents to the criticism of society and of public policy. True, private corporations and government departments make use of the talents of some academics as consultants and researchers, but these by definition are exceptional and generally handpicked for their "freedom from academic bias," like the "poverty lobby" who advise Labour governments on welfare policy or the monetarist economists who provide the Conservative government with its economic policy.

Even at the best of times, therefore, a cool skeptical breeze, healthy and invigorating perhaps, blows from business and government in the face of critical academics. At the height of the Robbins expansion civil servants at the Department of Education and Science (DES) and the Treasury, annoyed at both parties' too ready acceptance of the report, set out to frustrate it. One ploy, foisted on Anthony Crosland, Labour Secretary of State for Education and Science in 1965, was the "binary policy" under which the two sectors were kept separate, no more new universities were to be created, and institutions in the public sector, especially the new polytechnics, were no longer to be allowed to climb the ladder to university autonomy (Burgess and Pratt's "academic drift").[50] Two other tactics were the transfer of the University Grants Committee's accountability from the Treasury to the DES in 1964 and the auditing of university books from 1968 by the comptroller and auditor-general, two more steps toward state control. These changes had the paradoxical effect of making the "private sector" of higher education more vulnerable to direct pressure from the central government than the "public sector," which was protected by a more powerful buffer than the University Grants Committee, the politically influential Local Education Authorities (LEAs) that owned the polytechnics and further-education colleges.

At what stage the normal skepticism of the professional bureaucrats and politicians toward the "excessive" demands of the universities changed from a cool breeze to a "blue northerly" it is difficult to say. No doubt the weather would have turned colder anyway, since the massive expansion of public spending on higher education could not be sustained indefinitely, and the world recession provoked by the oil crisis of October 1973 hit the weak British economy much harder than most. Recurrent exchequer grants to the universities (not counting capital grants and student fees and maintenance) rose from £228 million in 1970 to £979 million in 1980; while that to further education (over one-third of it, to advanced education) and teacher training outside the universities rose from £409 million to £1,305 million over the same time period.[51] To this we should add public expenditure on university fees, mostly paid by the state through the LEAs, which rose from about £20 million to £337 million between the same dates, and also expenditure on maintenance grants to students in both sectors—a far more generous allotment than elsewhere, as Britain spends more than twice the percentage of the gross domestic product as most Organization for Economic Cooperation and Development (OECD) countries on student support and welfare,[52] which rose from £125 million to £630 million.[53] All these figures must of course be deflated to take account of the massive inflation of the 1970s. Retail prices rose 3.69 times between 1971 and 1981, reducing the increase in government grants to universities from 379.4 percent to only 16.4 percent in real terms, compared with a 30.3 percent increase in student numbers (partly compensated for by an increase in student fees).[54] The difference represented a 10 percent decline in the "unit of resource" (cost per student). The rising cost of the open-ended "Robbins-plus" expansion began to alarm governments of both parties.

The first Wilson government in the late 1960s tried to get the universities to economize so as to accommodate more students at the same cost. In 1969 the universities rejected the famous "13 points" of Shirley Williams, Minister of State for Higher Education, on the grounds that the economics could threaten academic standards. The government therefore turned to the polytechnics, which became the overspill for frustrated university applicants. Compared with an increase in full-time university students from 235,000 in 1970 to 308,000 in 1981, full-time advanced students in polytechnics and other public-sector colleges increased only from 221,000 to 236,000, but if we allow for the rundown in teacher education colleges, predominantly for women, the comparable percentage growths for male students were 14 percent in the universities and 29 percent in the public sector.[55] (For women students there was a welcome 74 percent increase in the universities compared with a decrease of 4 percent in the public sector, entirely due to the decrease in teacher training.)[56] This trend was in line with DES policy of upgrading the public sector on the grounds that it was more responsive to the needs of society for more applied scientists and technologists, though in practice it was mainly due to the student demand for more places in the humanities and social sciences than the universities could provide.

Another sign of changing climate was the change in policy toward overseas students. The 1970s saw a near-doubling of such students in universities, from 18,300 to 33,500, and a trebling in public-sector higher education, from 6,200 to 19,800.[57] The policy of raising fees to overseas students began almost by accident in the late 1970s when an attempt by the Labour Government to raise university fees generally—representing very little saving on the home undergraduate majority whose fees were automatically paid through the local education authorities—was successfully, if temporarily, resisted by the universities and ended by falling only on foreign students. Complaints by the European Economic Community countries, where most universities did not charge fees, later restricted it to non-Common Market students. Whether or not the differential fee was worth the cost in lost goodwill and the future loss of influence and perhaps orders for books, machinery, and other exports, as the Foreign Office feared, the cost-conscious Conservative government in 1980 determined to charge foreign students "full cost fees." There was an immediate 11 percent fall in the intake of overseas students (later reduced to 7 percent). Despite the outcry from the universities and foreign governments, the government refused to give ground, except to award aid through the Foreign Office to select students from favored, mainly Commonwealth countries.

The final sign of the coming freeze was the handling of the student numbers crisis. In the 1970s, after years of expansion ahead of the Robbins forecasts, planned student numbers were revised downward. The DES estimate for 1981 was cut back by the 1972 white paper, *Education: A Framework for Expansion,* from 850,000 to 750,000 full-time advanced students, half in the universities and half in further education. This was still considerably more than 463,000 students of 1972; but during the 1970s the estimate was gradually reduced to the actual figure of 556,000 of 1981, close to the original Robbins forecast of 560,000. Since the Robbins principle of providing places for all qualified applicants who wished to take them was still operative, the chief factors in the decline, not of numbers but of expectations, were the size of the eighteen-year-old age group and the age participation rate, which in turn depended on the qualified participation rate, the percentage of school-leavers qualified for degree courses (by two General Certificate of Education—GCE—A-levels or three Scottish Higher Certificate passes) who entered higher education. By 1978, the trough of the birth rate, it had become obvious that the 34 percent fall in births since 1964 would lead, after a "hump" of eighteen-year-olds in the early 1980s due to the birthrate bulge of the mid-1960s, to a steep fall in the student age group down to a trough in the mid-1990s. The DES therefore issued a "brown paper" (discussion document), *Higher Education into the 1990s* (February 1978) which offered five alternative models for coping less with the ultimate decline than with the more immediate problem of the hump. The models in turn envisaged: (1) expanding and contracting the higher education system and its manpower in line with student numbers, which may lead to a demoralizing wave of redundancies; (2) freezing the system at the 1981 level of about 560,000 students, which would mean abandoning the Robbins principle of providing a place for every qualified student who wanted one; (3) economizing by renting short-term accommodation, hiring temporary staff, and stretching the staff-student ratio nearer to the 1:10 envisaged by the 1972 white paper, all of which would be difficult and probably not save enough to be worthwhile; (4) "tunneling through the hump" by shortening courses, switching some students to part-time courses, or deferring entry for others so as to spread the load into later and easier years, which would require up to 70 percent of all applicants being switched or deferred at the peak of the "hump"; (5) seizing the opportunity of permanently expanding the system so as to cater to more children from the manual working class, more mature students, more women, and more entrants from the ethnic minorities, which would be expensive and require a major change of policy.

Not surprisingly, the whole academic profession (except the tiny "more means worse" brigade) plumped for model 5, which for the first time offered a chance of expanding the system beyond its traditional role of providing for an elite of eighteen-year-olds drawn mainly from the middle classes. The new Conservative government elected in 1979 had other ideas, however: the reduction of taxation and public expenditure before all else. Maurice and David Kogan have given a blow-by-blow account of *The Attack on Higher Education* by the Conservative government of 1979–1983 in their timely polemic.[58] As they see it, the attack was not a premeditated change in educational policy designed to provide a higher education system better suited to the country's purse and needs, but a makeshift attempt to make education bear its full share of the general cuts in public spending. Only as an afterthought did ministers, especially Sir Keith Joseph, produce ex post facto arguments to justify the policy, urging the concentration of resources on science and technology, particularly information technology, and away from the "softer" social sciences, minority subjects like Russian and Eastern bloc studies, and "luxuries" like archaeology and drama. Even the attack on tenure was a belated response to the cost and practical difficulties of making one in six university teachers redundant. Marked in the Kogans' view by inconsistency, bias, and lack of foresight, government policy was an attempt to save £120 million a year on higher education, a paltry sum, they said, compared with the £400 million per annum spent on the Falklands policy. The unforeseen consequences of the policy led to subsequent retractions: the Foreign Office provided £46 million to aid selected overseas students; overseas student fees were reduced from "full average cost" to a level near marginal cost; nearly 700 "new blood" posts were provided for teaching and research (230 a year in science and technology and 30 a year in the arts for three years); special funds were granted for information technology (70 new teaching posts, 45 research fellows, and 5,000 additional students); and the public sector was expanded (unintentionally) to provide for the 18,000 to 23,000 home students and about 5,000 overseas students lost to the universities.

The extent of the cuts can be measured by the reduction in government annual grants to universities: an average decline of 13 percent in real terms between 1979–1980 and 1983–1984. One cut alone, that of 8.1 percent imposed in July 1981, ranged from 2.1 percent in Bath and 3.7 percent in Cambridge to 19.1 percent in Bradford and 27.5 percent in Salford.[59] This was followed in September 1983 by the announcement of "a progressive reduction of the order of, say, 5 percent to 10 percent overall by the end of the decade and a further 5 percent in the five years beyond that."[60] One in six university teachers was to be dismissed either by means of early retirement or by redundancy, voluntary or compulsory; meanwhile, student numbers were not to decline below the 1979 level until the early 1990s so that teaching "productivity" was to be increased. After an unexpected overflow of students into the polytechnics, similar cuts were imposed on the public sector: 6.5 percent between 1980–1981 and 1981–1982, and 10 percent the following year. This meant a similar loss of one in six lecturers to teach a student body still growing to meet the overspill from the universities.[61] When the Committee of Vice-Chancellors and Principals and the Association of University Teachers (AUT) protested that it would cost more in the short run to make academics redundant than to retain them, they were told that the government was determined to force redundancies whatever the cost.[62]

In his letter rejecting the plea from the vice-chancellors of the five worst-hit universities that staff losses would cripple and unbalance their teaching programs, Sir Keith Joseph put the blame on the universities themselves for becoming too dependent on the state:

It always seemed to me anomalous that universities that have allowed themselves to become dependent for the great bulk of their income upon the voting of funds by Parliament should have denied themselves the capacity to respond feasibly to changes in the level of that support.[63]

He then went on to repudiate tenure:

Academic tenure exists to protect freedom of thought and of expression—in teaching and research. These are vital freedoms. But their cause is not served by the abuse of academic tenure to protect not freedom but individual jobs irrespective of the consequences to the universities, other members of staff and the students.

How the universities could protect academic freedom without protecting individual jobs he did not venture to say.

This letter, with its lack of sympathy for academics who have spent most of their careers specializing in disciplines that are unsalable outside the universities and polytechnics, is typical of the level to which the respect of professional politicians and civil servants for the academic profession has sunk. Some of this is due to the suspicion of the right wing of party politics that universities are full of left-wing dissidents who constantly indoctrinate their students with disaffected views, a suspicion "confirmed" by the past behavior of some student unions and a handful of vociferous faculty. It is of course true that academics are politically peculiar in that they are predominantly to the left of the middle class to which they belong and nearer to the position of the working class, in that in 1964 and 1970 only 35 percent and 33 percent of them supported the Conservative Party as compared with 77 percent and 79 percent of the professional middle class generally, and 33 percent of the working class on both occasions. On the other hand, this by no means meant they belonged en masse to the hard left. At both dates only 5 percent belonged to the "far left," while 48 percent and 40 percent belonged to the "moderate" left, and a further 28 percent and 27 percent claimed to belong to the center (including, presumably, the 14 percent and 20 percent who supported the Liberals).[64] This is a far cry from the image put about by some politicians and the press, and could, as in the United States, be due to academics' stance as objective critics of government policy.

More to the point, however, is that academics apparently have singularly little effect on the political views of their students, which seem to have been largely formed before they arrive at the university or the polytechnic. Students, like most other voters in Britain, tend to follow the political allegiance of their parents, which in their case means predominantly middle class and therefore Conservative.[65] Ironically, both the economic and educational policies of the Thatcher government are derived from right-wing academics, such as Dr. Friedrich von Hayek, Professor James Ball of the London Business School, Lord Beloff, until lately vice-chancellor of the newly chartered University of Buckingham, and the authors of the *Black Papers*. The political disunity of the profession helps to account for its weakness in the face of government criticism and pressure. This has led to its isolation not only from the government but also from the opposition parties and in great measure from the political process itself, from which alone in contemporary Britain it can hope to obtain the resources necessary for its survival and prosperity.

THE ISOLATION OF THE INTELLECTUALS

The British academic profession has, in comparison with other countries, fallen between two stools. It is, on the university side, neither an arm of the state bureaucracy as in most European countries, wholly supported by the government and protected in the Western democracies by a well-understood Humboldtian tradition of *Lehrfreiheit* and *Lernfreiheit;* nor is it, as in the United States private sector, a truly independent profession, selling its services of teaching and research on the open market to all students willing to be taught, all corporations and government agencies willing to contract for research and all donors willing to buy goodwill and prestige. It has become a poor relation among the professions, a compound of dependent pauperism and faded gentility, dependent on an unsympathetic state and no longer enjoying the support of the church or the great cities.

This lack of sympathy and respect for the academic profession is not confined to the Conservative Party. The Labour Party and its educational advisers believe that *all* universities are elitist and predominantly middle class and that the polytechnics are the true "people's universities," the "comprehensives" of the tertiary-education sector, and the main hope of what Harold Wilson once called the "white hot technological revolution." This ignores the reality that the public sector, with some 6 percent of the age group in full-time advanced courses as against the universities' 7 percent, is nearly as elitist as the universities, and that with their humanities and social science courses, the polytechnics have become almost as middle class as and less technological than the universities. Labour's greatest education minister, Anthony Crosland, former Oxford don and author of the binary policy, was no friend of the universities. His reply to an AUT question about why he favored the local authority colleges was, "How many votes have the university teachers?"[66] More recently, in *Labour's*

Programme 1982 the section on "Education after Eighteen" almost ignores the universities. "University" appears only three times, twice after "Open" and once before "Grants Committee." As for the Social Democratic Party Liberal Alliance, Dr. David Owen's insensitive speech to the AUT national lobby of Parliament in November 1981 showed that he was more concerned with the problem of tenure and early retirement to meet the fall in the age group than with expanding educational opportunities; he condemned the universities' "attitudinal rigidities which have resisted sensible economies and rational readjustments over many years."[67]

How did the British academic profession come to be in such low repute with professional politicians and bureaucrats and, unkindest cut of all, with the academics who advise them? How did they come to face the icy blast with such threadbare protection? There is some truth in the view that they oversold their wares in the expansionist 1960s and are now paying the price by falling back to their true value. As Adam Smith put it:

The usual reward of the eminent teacher bears no proportion to that of the lawyer or physician; because the trade of the one is crowded with indigent people who have been brought up to it at the public expense; whereas those of the other two are encumbered with very few who have not been educated at their own.[68]

In the 1960s the universities educated too many graduates and recruited too many of the best ones as academics for their own long-term good. In a falling labor market, a glut lowered both the demand and the price of intellectual labor.

Yet there must be more to it than that. The universities produced large numbers of other professionals too, including lawyers and physicians, and now just as much at the public expense; yet their stock has not fallen. In the game of life, lawyers and medical doctors are grand masters, and know that the key to success is to control the market, not to let the market control you. Throughout the Robbins expansion the doctors, through the General Medical Council, have kept a tight hold on admissions to medical schools while the lawyers, through the Inns of Court and the Law Society, have refused to accept a university law degree as a sufficient qualification to practice. They do not always win: the doctors are becoming vulnerable, as in the United States, to malpractice suits that reduce income by increasing insurance premiums, and the solicitors are about to lose their monopoly of property conveyancing. But unlike academics, they do not readily give up control of the supply of professional labor.

Academics are, like the teaching profession generally, in a dilemma over control of the market. In the short run it pays them to cry up education and expand it as much as possible, but in the not so very long run the market becomes overstocked. However, the Civil Service has also expanded despite government efforts to cut it, and it is, if anything, even more unpopular with ministers and the public than the university teachers, since it can annoy many more people. Yet, whereas between 1979 and 1983 the university lecturer maximum salary rose by 21 percent (compared with 41 percent for retail prices and 55 percent for average earnings), the Civil Service principal grade maximum went up by 42 percent—as rapidly as prices, but still short of average earnings, a measure of their greater but still limited strength.[69] The latter's success, presumably, rests on their greater cohesion as well as their more immediate opportunity to make their discontent felt.

The academic profession lacks cohesion and is organizationally divided into three bodies: the Association of University Teachers, the National Association of Teachers in Further Education, and the relatively new Association of Polytechnic Lecturers. Yet they have all three made great efforts in the last decade to organize and unify their own sector. The AUT, the most gentlemanly of professions, which in the 1960s repeatedly refused to register as a trade union and eschewed the very notion of a strike, not only registered as a trade union in 1972 but joined the Trade Union Congress in 1976; it has contemplated, and in some cases actually called, token one-day stoppages of the universities.[70] It may be argued, however, that a really powerful profession or trade union does not need to withdraw labor, and that to call a strike, even a token one, is a sign not only of weakness but of proletarianization, that is, the loss of independent control of one's labor power. Certainly the increased organization and apparent consensus among university teachers and polytechnic lecturers on the need for a more confrontational style is a response to adversity rather than a mark of strength.

But the weakness of the British academic profession lies deeper than any of these causes. It lies in the long-standing attitudes of British society to intellectuals and to the value of education. Unlike most other industrial countries, Britain's early success in economic growth and modernization owed almost nothing to the universities or even to formal technical education. As Sheldon Rothblatt and W. J. Reader have shown, the universities long drew their skirts away from industry and commerce and concentrated instead on educating young men, often sons of the business class, for the church and the professions, government, and the empire.[71] Even today, as we have seen, applied science and engineering have lower status and less attraction for students in British higher education than in any other advanced country. Indeed, the very urgency with which politicians of all parties press for the expansion of technology and business studies is evidence of the lack of a spontaneous industrial spirit. Industry and business have responded to this ambivalently. On the one hand, they ask for more graduate recruits in science and technology. On the other, they habitually recruit "the best man for the job" (only occasionally the best woman) in terms of personality and managerial potential, who, because of the low status and attraction of technology, often turns out to have an arts or social science degree. There are still strong negative feelings among university graduates toward industry, and industry reacts, understandably if perhaps unfairly, by blaming the universities, even though the problem begins long before university entrance, in the wider society. British society, not just the universities that merely reflect it, is basically anti-industrial.

This is not to absolve the academic profession from all blame. They have obviously not done enough to counteract a prejudice that, if it is one of the main causes of Britain's relative economic decline and incipient deindustrialization, may kill the goose that laid the golden eggs for the universities. As the chairman of Unilever says: "Industry provides the resource by which the rest is met. You have to ask yourselves whether a no-growth society would be a more humane, a more tolerant, even a more comfortable society."[72] To put the problem in perspective, however, there is no imaginable reform of the higher education system, either to make it leaner and fitter or to widen access to American or Japanese levels, however desirable, which could of itself cure Britain's economic problems or loosen the structural rigidities of British society. The key profession may educate a widening range of other professions, but it has so far proved incapable of doing the one thing needful, which is to change basic social attitudes toward education as a tool for growth and progress, both of the individual and of society as a whole.

HOW TO WIN FRIENDS AND INFLUENCE PEOPLE

What could bring about such a change? How could the academic profession play its part in bringing it about and at the same time improve its position in the game of life? As a historian of the social causes and effects of industrialization, economic progress, modernization—call it what you will—I have been struck by the perception that education, especially higher education, has played a key role in the process in practically every successful country except Britain. The French *grandes écoles*, the German universities and *Technischehochschulen*, the American land-grant colleges, the Russian academies and research institutions, and the Japanese westernized universities all played a crucial role in the later stages of their industrial revolutions; they were founded and supported by the states to that end. Only the British, who took for granted the provision of skills—professional, managerial, and manual—as a sort of providence from God, could afford, for a limited time, to leave higher and technical education to the self-taught man and the private philanthropist. The result has been a quasi-private university system geared, down to the Second World War, to the production of a professional establishment and an imperial elite, propped up by a socially and materially inferior public technical-education system mainly for part-time students. The divisive pecking order of British higher and further education is based on the underlying hierarchy and class division of British society.

By contrast the American university system, which is also hierarchical but presents its inequality as a meritocratic challenge to the able to compete for its rewards chiefly in the form of top jobs in the outside world rather than in the universities themselves, is based on a deep respect for education and the willingness of its alumni to prove that respect with generous donations, and of the public to vote taxes for its own state universities. Where else in the world will you find people driving cars with the name of their alma mater in gold letters on the back windows, even though it may only be the local state college? That respect for education has been burned deep in the American character (as it is in the French, German, Russian, and Japanese characters) from the beginning of the modern era, but it is still not left to chance. The universities and colleges work at it, devoting large sums and whole administrative departments to public relations, glossy publications and appeals to their alumni, continuous contacts with philanthropic foundations, and persistent lobbying of city, state, and federal governments. The result is that, within a framework of law and taxation favorable to institutional support, the universities thrive and provide higher education for nearly half the age group. The academic profession, though it is not as well rewarded as many other professions, is respected and rewarded according to its merits: academic mobility is such that the poor boy from Cincinnati or Memphis can end up at Harvard or Berkeley, all the more so because the rich kids among those they teach will prefer to end up on Wall Street or Madison Avenue.

There is of course no way in which the British academic profession could move directly to an American situation, even if that were desirable and they were willing to pay the not inconsiderable price in competitiveness and insecurity. But they could learn from the Americans how better to play the game of life. They could put far more effort into improving their relations with the public, with legislators, and with their own graduates. If Sir Keith Joseph wants academics to raise more resources from the private sector, they could seize the opportunity to lobby for a change in the tax laws to make giving more attractive to individual and corporate taxpayers. They could be more flexible about tenure and separate the question of academic freedom from that of job security by negotiating cast-iron safeguards for the first (statutory due procedure, as now provided by most charters) together with a permanent redundancy compensation scheme at least as generous as that for company directors and top civil servants. They could be more flexible about entrance requirements and ask, not for departmental guarantees that the schools have done half their job for them before the students arrive, but for a general assurance that they have the basic literacy and numerical skills to tackle any course of higher education. On this basis they could abandon, at least in the first year, the single honors approach that forces students to guess in complete ignorance whether they are suited to a particular subject, and give them instead a chance to discover their forte among a choice of related disciplines. They could shift their focus from providing for a narrow elite at high costs, with overgenerous staff-student ratios and full maintenance grants, to accommodating larger sections of the population who could, like so many American students, help to support themselves by working their way through college. Instead of boasting about their low failure rate, they could devise a system by which students could get credit for each year of higher education accomplished (and held in store for future extension) instead of labeling everyone who drops out a failure. Above all they could show that they themselves care for education, in the true sense of enabling students to prepare themselves for life, not just for one highly specific job; students must be able to tackle the tasks and problems of a future that may be unlike anything the academics themselves can imagine. Finally, they could learn to judge themselves (as the best already do) not by where they took their degree or by where they now practice their craft, but by their current skill and achievements in their calling of teaching and research. In such ways the key profession could better learn to play the game of life.

POSTSCRIPT

In the fall of 1984, some signs have appeared that the British academic profession has begun to organize itself to win friends and influence people more effectively. The most hopeful one is that the University Grants Committee on behalf of the universities and the comparatively new National Advisory Body representing the public sector of higher and further education have come together to present (in September 1984) a joint statement on a policy for higher education for the rest of the century.[73] This is the first time these bodies, especially the UGC, have given their advice to the government of the day in public—a measure of their new awareness of the need to get public support for their views on the urgency of the crisis facing the universities and polytechnics in their present weakened state.

The joint statement reaffirms and updates the four objectives essential to higher education set by the Robbins Committee in the expansionist sixties: instruction in skills; promotion of the general powers of the mind; the advancement of learning; and the transmission of a common culture and common standards of citizenship. Instruction in skills and promotion of the powers of the mind remain the main teaching purposes of higher education, both for the needs of the economy and for the personal and career needs of the individual. But in the rapidly changing economy of today, specific knowledge quickly becomes outdated and the need is for flexible and transferable intellectual skills and for their frequent updating by continuing education. Continuing education is also needed for its contribution to personal development and social progress, and is now so important that it ought to be elevated to a new fifth objective to add to the Robbins four.

Central to the Robbins report was equality of opportunity and the axiom that courses of higher education ought to be available for all who are qualified by ability and attainment to pursue them and who wish to do so. This axiom was too narrowly based on the idea of qualification by means of a fallible examination system and should now be redefined to read "courses of higher education should be available for all those who are able to benefit from them and who wish to do so." The beneficiaries should include not only students from different social classes, especially those previously underrepresented, but also from different ethnic groups and from mature students and women of all classes.

Robbins's third objective, the advancement of learning, is still at the heart of the educational process. Through research activity higher education makes a major contribution to the continued health of the nation's industry and commerce; to curtail it would impoverish the nation materially and culturally.

Finally, the transmission of a common culture and common standards of citizenship might sound somewhat old-fashioned in the 1980s, but common values are still needed to give society cohesion and stability. These include the need to protect the free expression and testing of ideas and the examination of cases and arguments on their merits. It is in this context that equal access for all groups in society, all classes, both sexes, all ages and all ethnic groups, becomes important. The principle is also concerned with the relationship between each institution and its locality, so that the university or polytechnic ought to contribute both to the cultural and to the economic life of its community.

Among the remedies for the current malaise, the two bodies suggest not merely an expansion of the resources devoted to higher education and an increase instead of a decrease in student numbers in the 1990s but also broader curricula in the schools and modular courses and credit transfer in the universities and polytechnics to discourage too early and too much specialization. The UGC goes so far as to say: "In particular we believe that school learners today can be regarded as having a balanced education only if they have followed courses in both arts and sciences throughout their secondary schooling." In British terms this in itself would be a revolution that may transform the pattern of student choice and the flexibility of manpower planning and produce graduates far more appropriate to a postindustrial society.

The UGC is also tackling the difficult and unpopular reform of tenure; it is suggesting that it ought to be possible to get rid of faculty for idleness and incompetence as well as for financial exigency (redundancy), though it is seeking some ways of guaranteeing academic freedom while implementing these policies, a controversial and difficult aim.[74] These and similar recommendations would go a long way toward meeting some of the necessary reforms I have put forward.

The joint statement of the UGC and the NAB is a sustained argument for the primacy of higher education in the reproduction of society and in support of the intellectual, cultural, and economic progress of the nation. As such, it is an implicit claim for the academic profession as the key profession in British society. It is also the first attempt by an official body representing the whole academic profession since the Robbins Committee to "speak truth to power" about the need for a strong and effective higher education system and the dangers for the nation of running down support for it. For the first time in twenty years the academic profession (except for the inevitable handful of politically motivated *clercs de trahison*) is united as a team to play the game of life. Whether they will succeed in increasing the resources needed to strengthen and expand the profession and to make the service it provides accessible to all those who need and could benefit from it remains to be seen. But at last the British academic profession has become aware that it is involved in the game of life, that to play it requires a united team spirit as well as the skills, however brilliant, of individual players.

NOTES

1. See Halsey and Trow, *British Academics*, pp. 243–247; Williams, Blackstone, and Metcalf, *Academic Labour Market*, chap. 3, "Attitudes to Expansion."

2. For the following history of the profession, see Perkin, *Key Profession*, chap. 1, and (for developments in the early 1970s) Perkin, "Professionalization of University Teaching"; Armytage, *Civic Universities*; Kearney, *Scholars and Gentlemen*; Stone, ed., *University in Society*.

3. Kearney, *Scholars and Gentlemen*, pp. 23, 33.

4. Stone, ed., *University in Society*, chap. 1.

5. Scotland, *History of Scottish Education*, vol. 1, chap. 11.

6. Rendell, *Origins of the Scottish Enlightenment, 1707–76*; Davie, *Democratic Intellect*; Anderson, *Education and Opportunity in Victorian Scotland*.

7. See Perkin, *Key Profession*, pp. 14–24.

8. Harte and North, *World of University College London*; Huelin, *King's College London*.

9. Armytage, *Civic Universities*, chaps. 9, 10.

10. Rothblatt, *Revolution of the Dons*; Ward, *Victorian Oxford*; Engel, "From Clergyman to Don."

11. Sanderson, *Universities and British Industry*, chap. 2.

12. Ibid., pp. 39, 42, 160–162.

13. Armytage, *Civic Universities*, p. 174, and chap. 10.

14. Argles, *South Kensington to Robbins*, passim.

15. Lord Robbins, *Higher Education (Robbins Report)*, pp. 13–16.

16. *DES Report on Education*, no. 100, July 1984.

17. *Hansard*, vol. 54, 16 Feb. 1984, answer by Mr. Peter Brooke of DES; DES, *Statistics of Education, 1979*, vol. 3, *Further Education*, p. 3.

18. Halsey, "Decline of Donnish Dominion?" pp. 217–218, and n. 17.

19. Ibid., pp. 218–225.

20. Halsey and Trow, *British Academics*, pp. 217–218.

21. *The Guardian*, 12 Sept. 1984.

22. Halsey, "Teachers in Universities and Polytechnics," pp. 6, 13 (unpublished paper kindly supplied by the author).

23. *The Guardian*, 3 Sept. 1984.

24. *Times Higher Education Supplement*, 14 Sept. 1984, p. 7.

25. *The Guardian*, 3 Sept. 1984.

26. Rothblatt, *Revolution of the Dons;* Wiener, *English Culture and the Decline of the Industrial Spirit.*

27. See Clark, *Higher Education System*, pp. 28–34; and Becher, "Cultural View."

28. See, among others, Greenwood, "Attributes of Profession"; Merton, "Some Thoughts on Professionalization in American Society," and Millerson, *Qualifying Professions*, pp. 4–6 and 9–13. For a critique of the traits approach see Johnson, *Professions and Power*, pp. 23–32.

29. See, among others, Moore, *Professions*, pp. 5–16; Vollmer and Mills, eds., *Professionalization*, pp. 2, 34; and on a slightly different, functional approach, Parsons, "Professions."

30. See, for example, Becker, *Human Capital;* Bourdieu, *Reproduction in Education, Society and Culture;* Gouldner, *Future of the Intellectuals;* and Giddens, *Class Structure of the Advanced Societies*, p. 107. For a different concept of specifically professional capital see Perkin, *Professionalism, Property and Engish Society Since 1880.*

31. Giddens, *Class Structure*, pp. 164–170; and Parkin, *Class Inequality and Political Order*, pp. 29, 49–60.

32. Larson, *Rise of Professionalism*, pp. 51–52.

33. See Monopolies Commission, *Professional Services.*

34. Cf. Wiener, *English Culture and the Decline of the Industrial Spirit*, pp. 12–24; he acknowledges his debt to Rothblatt, *Revolution of the Dons*, on pp. 23–24.

35. Halsey and Trow, *British Academics*, pp. 217–218; Arimoto, "Beikoku no Daigaku Kyojushijo no Tokoshitsu."

36. See Cox and Dyson, *Black Papers*. See also Williams, Blackstone, and Metcalf, *Academic Labour Market*, chap. 5, "Were More Dons Worse Dons?"

37. Hansard, vol. 54, 16 Feb. 1984, answer by Mr. Peter Brooke of DES; DES, *Statistics of Education, 1979*, vol. 3., *Further Education*, p. 3.

38. Halsey, "Teachers in Universities and Polytechnics," tables 12 and 13 (unpublished article kindly supplied by the author). Williams, Blackstone, and Metcalf, *Academic Labour Market*, p. 387, found that 59 percent of their 1970 interview sample (57 percent of men and 77 percent of women academics) had not published a book; and 23 percent of men and 44 percent of women had not published an article in the previous two years.

39. Parry and Parry, *Rise of the Medical Profession*, chap. 6.

40. Halsey and Trow, *British Academics*, pp. 228–235; Halsey, "Decline of Donnish Dominion?" p. 221.

41. At Oxford and Cambridge most fellows and lecturers are on a scale that embraces both lecturer and senior lecturer and are paid somewhat more than elsewhere, including extra payments for tutorial and pastoral work, examining, colleges offices, and so on, and such perquisites as free meals

and free or subsidized housing. See Halsey and Trow, *British Academics,* pp. 180, 206–207, 214–215; Williams, Blackstone, and Metcalf, *Academic Labour Market,* chap. 8, "Mobility."

42. University Grants Committee, Sir Edward Parkes, Chairman, letter to Vice-Chancellors and Principals, Circular No. 10/81, 1 July 1981.

43. Halsey, "Teachers in Universities and Polytechnics," table 30; Halsey and Trow, *British Academics,* p. 216; Perkin, *Key Profession,* p. 262; Williams, Blackstone, and Metcalf, *Academic Labour Market,* pp. 28–32.

44. Williams, Blackstone, and Metcalf, *Academic Labour Market.*

45. *Social Trends, 1984,* pp. 49–50.

46. University Grants Committee, *University Statistics, 1981–82,* vol. 1, *Students and Staff,* p. 46; DES, *Statistics of Education, 1979, 3, Further Education,* p. 3.

47. Williams, Blackstone, and Metcalf, *Academic Labour Market,* chap. 19, "Women Academics."

48. According to Smith, *Racial Disadvantage in Britain,* pp. 338–339, only 2 percent of West Indian men in Britain in 1974 had completed their education at 20 or more years of age as compared with 18 percent of Asians and 5 percent of white men, and less than 1 percent of West Indian men had a degree as compared with 4 percent of Asians and 4 percent of white men. (The Asian men had mostly Asian degrees—M.A., M.Sc., or better.)

49. DES, Sir Keith Joseph's letter to Lord Flowers, Chairman of the Committee of Vice-Chancellors and Principals, 8 May 1984, proposing that Statutory Commissioners limit tenure for new entrants to university teaching by compulsory revision of university statutes.

50. Boyle and Crosland, *Politics of Education,* pp. 193–195; Pratt and Burgess, *Polytechnics,* pp. 23–30.

51. UGC, *University Statistics, 1981–82,* vol. 2, *Finance,* p. 5; *Social Trends, 1984,* p. 55.

52. *O.E.C.D. Observer,* March 1984: the U.K. spends 0.8 percent of GDP on student support and welfare compared with 0.1 percent to 0.4 percent by all other OECD countries.

53. *Social Trends, 1984,* p. 55.

54. Ibid., p. 82.

55. Ibid., p. 50.

56. Ibid.

57. Ibid.

58. Kogan and Kogan, *Attack on Higher Education.*

59. UGC, Sir Edward Parkes, Chairman, letter to Vice-Chancellors and Principals of Universities, July 1981.

60. DES, Sir Keith Joseph's letter to Sir Edward Parkes, Chairman of UGC, 11 September 1982, on "Development of a Strategy for Higher Education."

61. Kogan and Kogan, *Attack on Higher Education,* p. 129.

62. DES, Sir Keith Joseph's letter to Dr. A. Kelly, Vice Chancellor of University of Surrey, May 1982.

63. Ibid.

64. Halsey and Trow, *British Academics*, chap. 15, "Politics," esp. pp. 403–406; Williams, Blackstone, and Metcalf, *Academic Labour Market*, chap. 20, "Political Attitudes," esp. pp. 405, 408. In 1974, 25.1 percent of university teachers and 24.7 percent of polytechnic lecturers voted Conservative. Halsey, "Teachers in Universities and Polytechnics," table 28. For American comparisons see Lipset, "Academia and Politics in America," and Lipset and Dobson, "The Intellectual as Critic and Rebel."

65. See Butler and Stokes, *Political Change in Britain*.

66. Perkin, *Key Profession*, p. 222.

67. Social Democratic Party, Speech of the Rt. Hon. David Owen, M.P. to the AUT National Lobby of Parliament, 18 November 1981.

68. Smith, *Wealth of Nations* (1905 ed.), 1:138.

69. AUT, *Salary Review, 1984*.

70. For example, on the day of AUT National Lobby of Parliament, 18 November 1981.

71. Rothblatt, *Revolution of the Dons*, pp. 86–93; Reader, *Professional Men*, app. 2, "Public Schoolboys' Occupations, 1807–1911"; Sanderson, *Universities and British Industry*, pp. 48–60, which, however, shows an increase of Oxbridge graduates entering business occupations from the establishment of the Oxford Appointments Committee in 1892 and the Cambridge Appointments Association in 1899, predecessors of the present appointments boards.

72. *Times Higher Education Supplement*, 14 Sept. 1984, p. 7.

73. Printed in full in *Times Higher Education Supplement*, 14 Sept. 1984.

74. Ibid. 21 Sept. 1984.

BIBLIOGRAPHY

Anderson, R. D. *Education and Opportunity in Victorian Scotland*. Oxford: Clarendon Press, 1983.

Argles, Michael. *South Kensington To Robbins: An Account of English Technical and Scientific Education Since 1851*. London: Longmans, 1964.

Arimoto, Akira. "Beikoku no Daigaku Kyojushijo no Tokushitsu" ("The Academic Market Place in the U.S."). In *Daigaku Ronshu* 6. Research Institute for Higher Education, Hiroshima University, 1978.

Armytage, W. H. G. *Civic Universities*. London: Arno, 1977.

Association of Commonwealth Universities. *Universities Facing the Challenge of the Eighties*. London, 1982.

Association of University Teachers. *The Real Demand for Student Places*. London, December 1983.

———. *The Future of Universities*. London, April 1984.

———. *Salary Review for Non-Clinical Academic and Related Staff, 1984*. London, 1984.

Becher, Tony. "The Cultural View." In *Perspectives on Higher Education: Eight Disciplinary and Comparative Views*, ed. Burton R. Clark. Berkeley, Los Angeles, London: University of California Press, 1984.

Becker, Gary S. *Human Capital.* New York: Columbia University Press, 1964.

Berrill, Kenneth, et al. *Excellence in Diversity: Towards a New Strategy of Higher Education.* Guildford, England: Society for Research into Higher Education, 1969.

Bligh, Donald, ed. *Accountability or Freedom for Teachers?* Guildford, England: Society for Research into Higher Education, 1982.

Bourdieu, Pierre. *Reproduction in Education, Society and Culture.* Beverly Hills, Calif.: Sage, 1977.

Boyle, E., and Anthony Crosland. *The Politics of Education.* Harmondsworth, Middlesex, England: Penguin Books, 1971.

Burgess, Tyrrell, and John Pratt. *Technical Education in the United Kingdom.* Paris: Organization for Economic Cooperation and Development, 1971.

Butler, David, and Donald Stokes. *Political Change in Britain.* London: Macmillan, 1969.

Clark, Burton R. *The Higher Education System: Academic Organization in Cross-National Perspectives.* Berkeley, Los Angeles, London: University of California Press, 1983.

Clark, Burton R., ed. *Perspectives on Higher Education: Eight Disciplinary and Comparative Views.* Berkeley, Los Angeles, London: University of California Press, 1984.

Committee of Vice-Chancellors and Principals. *Press Information.* London, 1981, 1984.

Cook, T. G., ed. *Education and Professions.* London: Methuen, 1973.

Cox, C. B., and A. E. Dyson, eds. *The Black Papers.* London: Critical Quarterly Society, 1968, 1969; Dent, 1975; Temple Smith, 1977.

Davie, G. E. *The Democratic Intellect: Scotland and Her Universities in the 19th Century.* Edinburgh: Edinburgh University Press, 1964.

Department of Education and Science. *Higher Education Into the 1990s: A Discussion Document.* London, February 1978.

————. *Statistics of Education, 1979.* Vol. 3, *Further Education.* London [1980].

————. Letter to Dr. A. Kelly written by Sir Keith Joseph. London, May 1982.

————. Letter to Sir Edward Parks written by Sir Keith Joseph on "Development of a Strategy for Higher Education." London, 11 September 1982.

————. Letter to Lord Flowers written by Sir Keith Joseph. London, 8 May 1984.

————. *D.E.S. Report on Education.* No. 100. London, July 1984.

————. *Press Notices.* London, 1982, 1984.

Engel, Arthur. "From Clergyman to Don: The Rise of the Academic Profession in 19th-Century Oxford." Ph.D. diss., Princeton University, 1975.

Fulton, Oliver. *Access to Higher Education.* Guildford, England: Society for Research into Higher Education, 1981.

Giddens, Anthony. *The Class Structure of the Advanced Societies.* London: Hutchinson, 1973.

Gouldner, Alvin. *The Future of the Intellectuals and the Rise of the New Class.* London: Macmillan, 1979.

Greenwood, Ernest. "Attributes of a Profession," *Social Work* 2 (1957): 45–55.

Halsey, A. H. "Teachers in Universities and Polytechnics." Unpublished paper.

—————. "The Decline of Donnish Dominion?" *Oxford Review of Education* 8, no. 3 (1982): 215–229.

Halsey, A. H., and Martin Trow. *The British Academics.* London: Faber and Faber, 1971.

Harte, Negley, and John North. *The World of University College London, 1828–1978.* London: University College London, 1978.

Huelin, Gordon. *King's College London, 1828–1978.* London: King's College London, 1978.

Johnson, T. J. *Professions and Power.* London: Macmillan, 1972.

Kearney, Hugh. *Scholars and Gentlemen: Universities and Society in Pre-Industrial Britain.* London: Faber, 1970.

Kogan, Maurice, with David Kogan. *The Attack on Higher Education.* London: Kogan Page, 1983.

Larson, Magali S. *The Rise of Professionalism.* Berkeley, Los Angeles, London: University of California Press, 1977.

Lindley, Robert, ed. *Higher Education and the Labour Market.* Guildford, England: Society for Research into Higher Education, 1981.

Lipset, Seymour M. "Academia and Politics in America." In *Imagination and Precision in the Social Sciences,* ed. T. V. Nossiter. London: Faber and Faber, 1972.

Lipset, Seymour M., and R. B. Dobson. "The Intellectual as Critic and Rebel: With Special Reference to the United States and the Soviet Union." *Daedalus* 101 (Summer 1972): 137–198.

Merton, Robert K. "Some Thoughts on Professionalization in American Society." In *Brown University Papers,* no. 37. Providence, R.I.: June 1960.

Millerson, Geoffrey. *The Qualifying Professions.* London: Routledge and Kegan Paul, 1964.

Monopolies Commission. *Professional Services: A Report on the General Effect on the Public Interest of Certain Restrictive Practices.* London: HMSO, Cmnd. 4463-1, 1970.

Moodie, Graeme C., and Rowland Eustace. *Power and Authority in British Universities.* London: Allen and Unwin, 1974.

Moore, W. E. *The Professions: Roles and Rules.* New York: Russell Sage, 1970.

Morris, Alfred, and John Sizer, eds. *Resource and Higher Education.* Guildford, England: Society for Research into Higher Education, 1983.

Oldham, Geoffrey, ed. *The Future of Research.* Guildford, England: Society for Research into Higher Education, 1982.

Organisation for Economic Cooperation and Development (OECD). *O.E.C.D. Observer* (March 1984).

Parkin, Frank. *Class Inequality and Political Order.* London and Dublin: MacGibbon and Kee, 1971.

Parry, Noel, and Jose Parry. *The Rise of the Medical Profession.* London: Croom Helm, 1976.

Parsons, Talcott. "Professions." In *International Encyclopaedia of the Social Sciences,* Vol. 12. London: Macmillan, 1968.

Perkin, Harold. *Key Profession: The History of the Association of University Teachers.* London: Routledge and Kegan Paul, 1969.

———. *The Professionalization of University Teaching.* In *Education and the Professions,* ed. T. G. Cook. London: Methuen, 1973.

———. *Professionalism, Property and English Society Since 1880.* (Stenton Lecture, 1980). Reading, England: University of Reading, 1981.

Pratt, John, and Tyrrell Burgess. *Polytechnics: A Report.* London: 1974.

Reader, W. J. *Professional Men: The Rise of the Professional Classes in Nineteenth-Century England.* London: Weidenfeld and Nicolson, 1966.

Rendell, Jane L., ed. *The Origins of the Scottish Enlightenment, 1707–76.* London: Macmillan, 1978.

Robbins, Lord. *Higher Education: Report of the Committee.* London: HMSO, Cmnd. 2154, 1963.

Robinson, Eric. *The New Polytechnics.* Harmondsworth, Middlesex, England: Penguin Books, 1968.

Robinson, Ken, ed. *The Arts and Higher Education.* Guildford, England: Society for Research into Higher Education, 1983.

Rothblatt, Sheldon. *The Revolution of the Dons: Cambridge and Society in Victorian England.* London: Faber, 1968. Reprint. Cambridge: Cambridge University Press, 1981.

Sanderson, Michael. *The Universities and British Industry 1850–1970.* London: Routledge and Kegan Paul, 1972.

Scotland, James. *The History of Scottish Education.* 2 vols. London: London University Press, 1969.

Scott, Peter. *The Crisis of the University.* London: Croom Helm, 1984.

Shattock, Michael, ed. *The Structure and Governance of Higher Education.* Guildford, England: Society for Research into Higher Education, 1983.

Shils, Edward. "Great Britain and the United States: Legislators, Bureaucrats and the Universities." In *Universities, Politicians and Bureaucrats,* ed. Hans Daalder and Edward Shils. Cambridge: Cambridge University Press, 1982.

Smith, Adam. *The Wealth of Nations.* 1776. Reprint. London: Bell, 1905.

Smith, D. J. *Racial Disadvantage in Britain.* Harmondsworth, Middlesex, England: Penguin Books, 1977.

Social Trends, 1984. London: HMSO, 1984.

Stone, Lawrence, ed. *The University in Society.* 2 vols. Oxford: Oxford University Press, and Princeton: Princeton University Press, 1974.

Swinnerton-Dyer, Sir Peter. "Prospects for Higher Education." *London Review of Books.* London: (19 November–2 December 1981): 9–10.

University Grants Committee. *University Statistics, 1981–82.* Vol. 1, *Students and Staff.* London: [1983].

——. *University Statistics, 1981–82.* Vol. 2, *Finance.* London: [1983].

——. *University Statistics.* Sir Edward Parkes, Chairman, Letter to Vice-Chancellors and Principals of Universities. Circular No. 10/81. 1 July 1981. London: 1980–1984.

Vollmer, H. M., and D. L. Mills, eds. *Professionalization.* Englewood Cliffs, N.J.: Prentice-Hall, 1966.

Wagner, Leslie, ed. *Agenda for Institutional Change in Higher Education.* Guildford, England: Society for Research into Higher Education, 1982.

Ward, W. R. *Victorian Oxford.* London: Cass, 1965.

Wiener, Martin. *English Culture and the Decline of the Industrial Spirit, 1950–1980.* Cambridge: Cambridge University Press, 1980.

Williams, Gareth, and Tessa Blackstone. *Response to Adversity: Higher Education in a Harsh Climate.* Guildford, England: Society for Research into Higher Education, 1983.

Williams, Gareth, Tessa Blackstone, and David Metcalfe. *The Academic Labour Market: Economic and Social Aspects of a Profession.* Amsterdam, London, and New York: Elsevier, 1974.

2
The Academic Profession in the Federal Republic of Germany

Wolfgang J. Mommsen

THE HERITAGE OF THE NINETEENTH CENTURY

The German university system began with the founding of the University of Berlin in 1808; it was a deliberate venture by the state of Prussia to mobilize the intellectual resources of the country at a moment of political humiliation and defeat. The system, which developed largely according to the principles formulated by Wilhelm von Humboldt, emphasized from the start that academic instruction and research ought to be institutionalized together, rather than remain separate as they had been during the seventeenth and eighteenth centuries. From the beginning, pioneers of the new university encouraged students to view academic research as an end in itself; they awarded the highest educational value to it, and they strongly advocated the primacy of original investigation. Vocational training was considered less important, and as conceptualized by Humboldt, philosophy and the humanities were designated core disciplines, a prominence that endured.[1]

The potential conflict between scholarly research and education (*Bildung*) and academic training for vocational purposes was not recognized for many years, but the seeds of discord were present from the start. The Prussian university system was obliged to fulfill substantial social functions: its mandate was to produce civil servants for the state—professionals and teachers (some of whom were to pass on to future generations the notion that higher learning was intrinsically valuable). The higher civil service, which ran the affairs of government, consisted mostly of university graduates, thus closely linking university and government. Nonetheless, universities gradually managed to extricate themselves from the role of merely training higher civil servants and professionals, and in time they established an important degree of independence from direct government interference. The state continued to set terms for examinations that permitted entry into government service or into positions within the professions, thereby determining the framework within which the universities were obliged to operate. But even with those conditions, they enjoyed considerable freedom, particularly in matters of research. Until the latter part of the nineteenth century, the undisputed close interrelationship between academic research and academic instruction sanctioned the notion that only those who had established themselves as scholars ought to have the right to teach. Vocational training was clearly marginal.

From the 1880s, in certain fields, the idealistic tradition that emphasized personality growth through research, not training, did not prevent an increasing professionalization of the university system. Almost imperceptibly, the humanities lost their hegemonial position. Because the knowledge base in the sciences and medicine exploded spectacularly in the last decade of the nineteenth and the first decades of the twentieth centuries, the government was often compelled to impose those disciplines on universities reluctant to develop more practical aspects of academic teaching and research—institutions often disinclined to consider expansionist measures that might disturb the corporate system, which granted substantial power to the professoriat.[2] The new *Technische Hochschulen*, geared more to the application of science than to pure research, faced a long, bitter struggle before they were recognized by universities as equals. The emphasis on Bildung and on the close relationship between research and instruction that favored competence in research rather than vocational qualification did not prevent the German university system from moving in leaps and bounds toward professionalization in the late nineteenth and early twentieth centuries.

In the earlier stages the boundaries between the disciplines tended to be narrow; professors could move easily from one major field to another. Academic degrees, like the Master of Arts in English universities today, led to careers in the most diverse fields. By the end of the nineteenth century, though, a narrowly defined professional-career system had emerged for students and professors alike. Only a very few academics could still manage to switch from an academic position in constitutional law to one in national economy (then economics) and eventually take a chair in sociology, as Max Weber had done.

The training of students also became more professionalized. In contrast to the Anglo-Saxon system, German students tended to be (and still are) older when they entered the university after passing the Abitur, which concluded their secondary school education. (The last two years at secondary school are often considered comparable to the first two years of American and English colleges or universities.) They were required to enroll in a specific field from the start, such as medicine, law, or economics; only in the humanities was some choice still possible. Employment requirements, usually defined in the state-examination regulations, frequently determined this choice. In spite of its origins in idealistic philosophy and rhetoric, which emphasized that universities were directed toward a search for the truth regardless of practical application, German universities by the end of the nineteenth century had become institutions of specialized professional training. They provided vocational training for the higher civil service, the professions, teaching, and increasingly for managers, engineers, and scientists, who helped develop the modern industrial system.

Fritz K. Ringer, among others, blamed academics during that period for an idealistic rhetoric that masked an antimodernist, antiliberal, and antidemocratic position, and which in some ways opposed the development of modern mass society.[3] Similarly, Konrad Jarausch has argued recently that the periodic contractions in the academic system during the later nineteenth and early twentieth centuries gave support to illiberal tendencies within the German academic profession.[4] There is no doubt some truth in these arguments, but they overestimate the antimodernist features of the system. The universities reflected the views of the upper middle classes, not those of the conservative elites. Given the conditions at that time, the academic community was a moderately progressive, not a reactionary, force, even after the revolution of 1848–1849. Further, it is misleading to assign to the later nineteenth-century German professoriat a distinctive role in politics. Throughout Europe, by the 1880s trends pointed to a decline in liberalism and to the reemergence of conservative social thought. This conservatism also characterized the academic profession. The political and social mentality of German academics probably never differed very strongly from that of the German upper middle classes, and by and large they appear to have shared their political views. Aristocratic traditions played a secondary role. Socially the German academic profession was closely intertwined with the upper middle classes, particularly with the higher civil service and with the professions that formed the mainstay of the classic liberal bourgeoisie. These relationships continued to be close in the later nineteenth century even though numbers of students and academic positions increased considerably.

If by 1900 substantial growth in the university system was beginning to undermine traditional teaching methods using small groups, especially in the sciences, the larger numbers of staff and students generally did not lead to major upheavals in university operations or to any significant changes in the social composition of the academic community. Kaelble has shown that the German academic profession was largely self-perpetuating until the 1960s. Socially it renewed itself by self-recruitment from its own ranks.[5] There was a high degree of social interchangeability between the upper middle classes—many had a university education—and the academic profession. The system was also open enough to provide an opportunity for individuals from a lower class to rise to social distinction (a feat usually almost impossible), although this process often took several generations.

Almost from the start, German academics were relatively independent of the federal states. The faculty enjoyed considerable prestige and could rely on public support in controversial cases. By the middle of the nineteenth century, the principle of state disengagement from university matters was generally accepted, even though there were many exceptions. Universities were largely autonomous in all academic matters; they were allowed to recruit younger scholars in accordance with their own standards and to appoint full professors at their own discretion, the government's legal final say notwithstanding. Universities then were self-governing islands within a semiauthoritarian state, if only because they readily adapted themselves to the predominant trends of the time.

The authorities did interfere, however, in a substantial number of cases; with hindsight we may view some of the outcomes as successful. Several German scholars of renown who helped to establish German academic prestige in the late nineteenth century would not have obtained professorships at prominent Prussian universities if the faculties had had their way. In contrast, academics, especially from the social sciences, strongly influenced government legislation and decision making. In the semiconstitutional system of imperial Germany, parliamentary votes were often less important than administrative decisions based on allegedly objective expertise; this was often provided, directly or indirectly, by prestigious academics, who also enjoyed academic freedom within clearly recognizable margins defined by the interests of the established monarchical system. In 1908 Max Weber pointed out with considerable bitterness in "The Alleged Academic Freedom of the Universities" (*Frankfurter Zeitung*) that " 'freedom of scholarship' exists in Germany only within the limits of political and ecclesiastical acceptability."[6] Social Democrats had absolutely no chance of entering an academic career, and other outsiders, notably Jews, found it very difficult indeed to be admitted to professorial status.

The comparatively high social standing of German academics received further support by the end of the nineteenth century. Prussia and other federal states deliberately favored the academically trained as a potential reservoir for high government office because the traditional aristocratic elite was no longer capable of supplying sufficient suitable candidates. In the military officer corps academic distinction also functioned to some degree as a substitute for aristocratic origins, and over time it became increasingly so.[7] This general climate contributed to the willingness of the managerial class to prefer graduates from universities or other institutions of higher learning; they thereby opened the floodgates to the professionalization of industrial management, which at the time was unparalleled in other countries.

Given such recognition, the German professoriat ("mandarins" in Ringer's word) should not be singled out as having antimodernist tendencies. Perhaps some philosophy and law and sciences faculties exhibit these traits—we know little about the attitudes of individual scholars in these fields—but generally, the German academic profession was a comparatively open elite, especially if compared with peers in France and Britain at that time. Self-recruitment prevailed in principle until the 1960s, but as noted previously the system was sufficiently flexible to allow gifted individuals to make headway within it and to climb socially and academically to high positions from rather low origins, though it often took two or three generations to achieve this. Besides, it was often social climbers, not scholars from traditional backgrounds, who acclaimed the new nationalism that was commonplace in German society before 1914.[8] Though the German academic profession was largely antiaristocratic in orientation and social composition, its members nonetheless were found in the conservative camp. To some degree, however, they initiated reform and modernization in welfare policies.[9]

Arguably, the substantial amount of research achieved in the German academic system in the last decades before 1914 was possible because the profession held a unique social status; it enjoyed an unusual degree of autonomy not experienced in other sectors of German society. The emerging nineteenth-century academic system organized both teaching and research around individual professorial chairs which, in theory at least, were to be given only to scholars of great distinction, who qualified for the job not only by a special examination, the Habilitation, but who had been teaching as *Privatdozenten* for some time without pay. It was clearly a hierarchical system; those scholars who held key chairs were to organize teaching and research according to their academic expertise, without much interference from university bodies or government. As a rule professorial chairs were endowed with special research units. Depending on the requirements of the particular discipline, these might have been institutes, seminars, laboratories, or even hospitals. Such institutional bodies employed many junior scholars and nonacademic staff. Traditionally, academic subjects were taught by arrangements of students and professors in small groups pursuing specific research projects, with students having a share, however small, in conducting the research. As numbers increased, however, these research units gradually evolved into academic "production units" that developed their own momentum. The classic rule was—in the Max Planck–Gesellschaft it still is—"one man, one institute." Only in a few disciplines, namely, the humanities, were research units run jointly by two or more professorial chairholders. By the early twentieth century, however, this transition was already taking place. By the 1960s and 1970s these research units mushroomed, sometimes beyond recognition, their substantial size making it often impossible for a single professor or director to govern and still teach and do research. But even today every German academic still aspires to command a research institute or at least a research unit.

Though ideal and reality began to diverge early, much of the success of the German university system, at least in its earlier stages, rested on these comparatively small and highly autonomous self-contained units of academic production. On this institutional basis it proved possible to organize teaching and research so that students could participate, in principle, as junior partners in the community of teachers and students. Admittedly, teaching and research were partly controlled by corporate bodies, particularly the faculties, who were to collectively organize research and teaching in such fields as humanities, law, or medicine, which comprised a large, steadily rising number of disciplines. Only recently has further differentiation of faculties taken place: today they have been supplanted by far more narrowly defined *Fachbereiche*. Faculties formed the core of the German university; they, not the senate or the rector who represented the interests of the university as a whole, were the wielders of power. Faculties were clubs of equals in which the deans, elected for one or at most two years, acted as a *primus inter pares*. Their authority was derived from these bodies alone. Faculties had control over all appointments and promotions and some control over the allocation of financial resources. They operated within the context of a strong academic ethos, which in some ways was a substitute for their limited formal power. Curricular organization and examination standards were largely left to the principal chairholders in individual disciplines.

This corporate structure was adopted by the more practical types of institutions, especially the technical universities, the *Handelshoch-schulen*, and other tertiary-level institutions that developed during the later nineteenth century. But teacher-training colleges, polytechnics, and other vocational schools were not part of the academic system; the wall separating academic education from mere vocational training was until recently upheld with great diligence and rhetoric. Even so, they gradually assumed the same organizational principles. This system of small, highly autonomous units of academic organization survived in principle into the 1930s and perhaps even into the 1950s, with some slight revisions. Both the strengths and the weaknesses of the German university system as it developed in the twentieth century were embodied in it. Though theoretically open, it nonetheless gave predominant influence to a fairly small body of professorial chairholders.

NATIONAL SOCIALISM AND THE GERMAN ACADEMIC SYSTEM

Surely the bulk of the German academic profession must be counted among the critics—even enemies—of the Weimar system, even though few professors openly declared their allegiance to parties or movements directly challenging that order. Only a minority were actual members or sympathizers of the National Socialist Party. Of the others, very few dared to actively resist its policies once Hitler had come to power; most publicly applauded that dictatorship. Undoubtedly, the universities shared greatly in the responsibility for the breakdown of the democratic system in the 1930s. German academic thinking in political matters in the interwar period was mostly reactionary. The universities were largely bulwarks of traditionalist thought; they idealized the age of Bismarck and William II even though the new democratic government went to considerable lengths to support the academic system in much the same way as had been done before. The irrational and distinctly anti-Western modes of thought that prevailed in those years were backed by a majority of academics; such scholars as Ernst Troeltsch and Alfred Kantorowicz, who argued in favor of a reorientation toward the West, always had a difficult time. Given this mental outlook, the German academic profession proved totally unable to resist the rising tide of National Socialism.[10]

But students, not professors, first entered the National Socialist camp; aggressive student demonstrations that appeared suddenly in most German universities against those professors considered to be sympathetic to left-wing causes were a new and frightening experience for many academics. They were bewildered and seemed unable to do much against the trends of the time. Some academics readily joined the party or the SA (Sturmabteilung) to further their careers, and such eminent scholars as Martin Heidegger and Carl Schmidt joined forces with National Socialism at a very early stage. Others offered almost no resistance to the elimination of Jews from university positions, a practice implemented from the start and first seen in the civil service law in 1934. Eventually the profession grudgingly suffered the National Socialist policies that eliminated traditional university autonomy and that attempted to govern the universities according to National Socialist ideas. But it cannot be said that the National Socialist attempt to bring the universities into line succeeded. Although the National Socialists succeeded in putting their men into key positions and although they introduced the leadership principle as opposed to academic self-government, they did not succeed in imparting to the universities a new National Socialist spirit.[11] Academics reacted to the attempts of the National Socialists to impose their political ideology on the universities by retreating to their traditional nonpolitical professional attitudes. The attempts by Walter Frank to create a new National Socialist history got nowhere.[12] Neither did the rather grotesque attempt to create a German physics succeed.[13] Nor did institutional changes, namely, the introduction of the leadership principle and the suppression of self-government, lead to the desired results.

The role of the German academic community in the 1930s and 1940s was clearly not reputable. When the National Socialist system eventually collapsed in 1945, with all Germany and many universities in ruins, the profession had to start anew, taking into account a much diminished morality. The spectrum of political views within the academic community had been greatly distorted by the policies of National Socialism, though this was not always fully realized at the time. Those scholars who represented the political left had either emigrated or died; the liberal center had been morally and politically compromised by its general collaboration with the National Socialist regime, if often only for opportunistic reasons. Only the conservatives had a relatively clean record; for the most part they had kept aloof from politics of any kind. Further, the German university system had lost many first-rate minds in diverse fields: those in physics, mathematics, art history, and social sciences were among the most prominent. Only a few emigrants to the West, such as Hans Rothfels or Ernest Fraenkel, who strongly influenced history and the social sciences, eventually did return to West Germany to help rebuild the university system.

The National Socialists had brutally suppressed the principle of academic freedom; they considered it an intolerable relic of bourgeois and liberal eras. To restore the principle of autonomy to the academic community in 1945 was considered vital. The neoliberal philosophy of the day, which hailed individual initiative rather than state action, also advocated the restoration of a university system governed by the academic profession. The Occupation authorities did make some effort to prevent the employment of professors who had been directly associated with National Socialist policies, but with limited lasting effect: the German academic profession escaped relatively unscathed. Only a small minority actually lost their jobs in 1945. Many who did were later reinstated, though occasionally in less important positions. But no major changes in the system were made; it was restored to much of its former structure of the 1920s.

RECONSTRUCTION 1945–1960

Reconstruction after 1945 exhibited a direct return to Weimar conditions. Traditional university self-government was restored in full, and the privileged position of the professoriat within the system was maintained almost unimpaired. The grand old men—Gerhard Ritter, Hans Rothfels, and Friedrich Meinecke from the humanities, for example—dominated German university life in the 1940s and 1950s. Since few emigrés returned, the balance of political views was tilted, albeit only slightly, in favor of the conservative and traditionalist elements within the profession; virtually no Socialists or Marxists were visible. This biased political outlook of the academic community was strengthened by the intellectual climate that emerged with the development of the Cold War.

German academics in charge after 1945 were slow to take up the idea of democratization. They readily accepted parliamentary democracy on the political level but otherwise dissociated themselves from any direct involvement in politics. Only a minority of scholars argued that the universities had an obligation to help spread democratic ideas among the young and for contributing actively to the restoration of democratic order. Instead, the bulk retired into professionalism and became relatively detached from day-to-day politics.

Slowly, a movement for reform within the universities came about; it was guided by the belief that mere professional instruction was not sufficient, that students ought to be given some moral and intellectual guidance to enable them to find their way in a free society. Thus the *studium generale* was introduced. These university courses for students of all disciplines were usually devoted to general themes from philosophy and the social sciences, with some attention given to current political and moral problems. Experiments were also undertaken to establish special colleges in which small groups of students were to live together with academic tutors. These colleges were intended to help students find a new orientation by living in small communities of their own, rather than by pursuing their studies in relative isolation, as had been the rule in German universities for many years. But these ventures lagged. With the exception of such outstanding figures as Alexander Mitscherlich, Eugen Kogon, or Ernst Fraenkel, older professors were largely reluctant to tackle current problems. Nor were the pragmatic, newer-generation academics morally willing to lead the student body; they were disillusioned, and they were uncertain about their values. Students were not very enthusiastic about studium generale programs. They were not keen to attend classes not apparently directly useful to their professional careers.

Clearly the university system in the form in which it had been reestablished after 1945 no longer sufficed. Being relatively secluded from society at large caused regret in many circles, where the argument was made for a more democratic and a more egalitarian institution. The cause was pleaded by academics who sympathized with groups of the political left such as the Oberaudorfer Kreis, and by others who repeatedly asked if the traditional combination of academic research and teaching was meeting the requirements of the day. Nor, it was argued, did universities sufficiently prepare students for their later professional roles. Universities were still primarily concerned with research, even though only a very small percentage of students would enter academic careers.[14] Groups, especially outside the universities, demanded that teaching and research be separated to make the system more effective. Such proposals met with little positive response either within or outside the university.

In the very influential *Einsamkeit und Freiheit*, published in 1963, Helmut Schelsky conceded that the old formula of research and instruction no longer covered all the functions scholars actually perform in a modern university. After listing the duties of a chairholding professor—research and research management, specialized instruction, participation in academic self-government, education, professional expertise—he nonetheless pleaded for maintaining the unity of research and teaching, albeit in a modified form.[15] In principle almost no one was prepared to embark on a fundamental reconstruction of the academic system, but many believed that more attention ought to be given to proper professional training instead of to research. The initiative for founding a new university, launched in 1963 by the Wissenschaftliche Gesellschaft für ein Neue Deutsche Universität, was based on similar premises.[16] It suggested a renewed German university system, founded on the "integrated results of unbiased empirical research" and to a lesser degree on philosophical doctrines. This was somewhat in line with the pragmatic philosophy of logical positivism then enjoying its heyday. But these initiatives got nowhere, partly because alternative models were confused, partly because university-system resistance to these types of major changes proved too resolute. Much the same was true of the demand to eliminate the existing barriers between universities and technical universities and between such institutions of higher learning as teacher training colleges and other vocational training institutions. An argument, primarily political, was made for the abandonment of the two-tier system on the grounds that greater equality within the system of higher education would then be achieved. But the universities successfully resisted such attempts at demoting their elevated status for some time.

REFORM 1964–1978

The dramatic economic recovery and the rapidly changing political climate of the Federal Republic gradually altered the framework within which the university system operated. The concentration on economic reconstruction after World War II now gave way to the demand for more social equality and a higher quality of life for everyone. Government was expected to create preconditions for continuous economic growth and to provide social security and a heightened degree of egalitarianism for the individual within a social-market economic system associated with Ludwig Erhard's policies of the late 1940s and early 1950s. The social-market economy had been hailed as the key to economic recovery, although its benefits were extended more to the propertied classes than to the workers. Education was now discovered as a possible corrective to the market forces that had not at all brought about greater equality. Suddenly the higher education system was confronted with far-reaching demands that could not be met within the existing framework, and a rising new demand for higher education developed among growing sections of the population. In 1964 Robert Picht published *Die Deutsche Bildungskatastrophe*, which prominently voiced these new tendencies.[17] Picht pleaded for a huge, speedy expansion of exisiting facilities for all sectors of education, including the university.

By now many more young people wanted a university education. Picht argued that a modern industrial society, like West Germany, would require a far higher proportion of professionals and experts trained in universities and other institutions of higher learning than had been envisaged in the past. He warned that economic growth in the Federal Republic would eventually come to a halt due to a lack of experts in many fields. The existing system of higher education was far too small and unsuitable to cope with the projected student increase. Picht pleaded for a sweeping expansion of the educational system, and he demanded an educational policy that would identify and tap potential students. At about the same time, Ralf Dahrendorf and others argued that the state had a moral duty to provide higher education for all those who demanded it. Dahrendorf stipulated a *Bürgerrecht auf Bildung*, an individual's constitutional right to attend higher education institutions if formal academic enrollment requirements could be met.[18] But he was merely reiterating what had already been accepted as a fundamental principle of German constitutional law, namely, the citizen's right to free access to higher educational institutions. His ideas were based on the then-current liberal philosophy that argued it was both a necessity and a moral duty to provide facilities for higher education in all regions of the country. To rely on the comparatively small number of existing universities and other institutions of higher learning dispersed unevenly throughout Germany was unacceptable. New universities were planned to eliminate inequality of opportunity for young people living in more remote areas. This development of a comparatively tight network of institutions of higher education extending throughout the Federal Republic was considered to be a primary goal; in so doing, hitherto undetected educational reserves might be tapped from a wider social spectrum.

This issue of increasing facilities for higher education was alarming. Was it a legitimate one in the political system of the Federal Republic of Germany? Few people disputed that complete equality was unattainable in a modern advanced industrial society, but most advocated equality of opportunity, the notion that all individuals ought to have a chance to achieve a respectable position in society by means of a proper education. Equality of opportunity was considered a substitute for orthodox egalitarian ideas, socialist or otherwise, and this idea corresponded to the dynamic entrepreneurial spirit that pervaded public opinion in the Federal Republic. The educational system—particularly the academic system—was seen as an instrument for providing a higher degree of social justice and a closer approach to equality in an advanced industrial society.

These political demands and postulates coincided with a dramatic increase of young people wanting to attend universities or other higher education institutions. Wilhelm Hennis pointed out that "West Germany was not exempt from the 'educational explosion' that took place in the industrialized countries after the Second World War."[19] To some extent this process may have been encouraged by the proponents of more social equality via a fair and open system of education. But it also reflected the rising standard of living, especially for the middle classes. A new stratum of the population began to send their children to secondary schools, and nearly all of them went on to a university or other institution of higher education. After leaving secondary school, only a handful found employment that did not require academic qualifications. More than ever before, secondary schools became merely preparatory for entry into the university, although initially this had not been envisaged by education authorities. The figures are dramatic. Within two decades the numbers of students entering universities increased about fivefold; sooner or later such expansion was bound to break the traditional mold of the system. During the winter term of 1950–1951, only 112,000 students enrolled at universities and technical universities; by 1960–1961 the figures had risen to 217,000, and by 1970–1971 to 350,000; in 1977 they reached 605,000. These figures do not include students who attended teacher training colleges, schools of art, or schools for vocational training.[20] In 1981–1982 the figure had risen to 822,363 excluding 77,880 students enrolled in the newly founded comprehensive universities.[21] These latter figures are not totally comparable because they include students who formerly would have attended teacher training colleges, polytechnics, and the like. But even so, they show dramatically that the German university system was torn asunder by the sheer rise in tides of students seeking a university education. Admittedly the figures are somewhat inflated because students took course work over considerably longer periods of time; it could be argued that the inability to provide proper instruction might have magnified the problems of swelling hordes of students, though perhaps more on paper than in actual fact. Universities that had 2,500 to 3,000 students throughout most of the nineteenth and early twentieth centuries suddenly had to cope with 10,000, and such universities as Munich, Munster, and Cologne reported enrollments of about 40,000 students. Needless to say, the facilities for accommodating these students in research laboratories, seminars, and libraries and for teaching them according to traditional patterns were becoming increasingly inadequate.

In the early 1960s the dramatically rising demand for higher education was seen universally as a positive development. Only a small minority of academics warned that unlimited expansion might severely damage the system, and they did so with occasionally authoritarian and elitist arguments that were not actually in tune with the democratic age.[22] As early as 1962, the new government advisory body, the Wissenschaftsrat, in a lengthy memorandum, suggested several urgent measures to meet the swelling press for higher education: it advised existing universities to expand as quickly as possible, and it proposed that comprehensive universities be created by adding new faculties to existing technical universities and professional schools. Accordingly, in 1964 the medical school at Düsseldorf was upgraded to a university, and the former Handelshochschule Mannheim was given university status. Many technical universities, such as Karlsruhe, Aachen, Braunschweig, Hannover, and the Technical University of Berlin, were also expanded by the addition of humanities faculties. But even though (with some encouragement and even financial aid from the federal government) the *Länder* governments embarked on a long-term program of expanding existing universities and establishing new ones, these measures were too little and too late to alleviate the dramatic student overpopulation of the next decade.

Little change was envisaged in the internal arrangements of the academic system. The predominant position of the professoriat was maintained in much the same way, although both the rising demands of instructing ever larger numbers of students and the increased requirements of more sophisticated institutional facilities for advanced research indicated that the existing system had reached its limits. If student numbers were continually to increase, most universities would find it difficult to remain both centers of advanced research and institutions of higher learning without substantial loss to either. The creation of new elitist reform universities might have been an answer to this dilemma; they were mandated to concentrate more on research than on teaching and if possible to accept only restricted numbers of highly qualified students. Thus the reform universities of Konstanz and Bielefeld came into being. But within a few years these lofty plans had largely evaporated.

The enormous student growth, compounded by these structural deficiencies, was bound to expose the profession to heavy strain. Professors had been accustomed to working with students in small, informal groups in a highly decentralized manner, but this no longer held; in some larger fields the ratio between staff and students deteriorated beyond all reasonable levels. Classically scholars and students were considered to be a community, jointly pursuing research projects; unrestricted communication between professors and students was assumed. For the most part this was no longer possible. Student numbers dictated more authoritarian forms of classroom teaching, and the gap between research and teaching, already a major problem, became ever wider.

The universities and educational authorities responded to the new situation caused by burgeoning numbers of students by disproportionately expanding the *Mittelbau,* the junior staff, which now took over expanding teaching as well as administrative duties. The alteration in the composition of the staff soon reached epic proportions. According to the figures provided by the Wissenschaftsrat in 1970, in 1960, 74.7 percent of all academic positions were held by junior staff. By 1966 this figure had risen to 82.1 percent, and it continued to rise even further.[23] Clearly the percentage of professors was much reduced. Although these figures do not provide precise information (chairholders and associate professors were not always listed separately), they established the trend toward quantitative growth of the "lower orders" within the academic profession, which in the long run was bound to undermine the near-monopolistic position of the professoriat. These statistics mask the total numbers in the shift toward the Mittelbau because the increases took place mainly in those disciplines that attracted large numbers of students, whereas the ratios remained much the same as before in the less popular disciplines.

A substantial change in the qualitative structure of the academic staff also took place. If before, most *Assistenten* (junior positions) had been considered academic apprentices, entitled to teaching introductory courses only, they now assumed a susbtantial teaching load. The old hierarchy that denied the Mittelbau any reasonable share in running the universities was gradually undermined: the monopolistic position of the *Ordinarien*, professors who usually directed the specialized research units, no longer appeared justified when a much larger share of teaching and research was actually being done by associate professors, Privatdozenten, and research assistants. The dramatic student explosion undercut the legitimacy of the traditional hierarchies. Not unnaturally, research assistants, who were required to assume an important share of the teaching of introductory courses and who also were obliged to demonstrate research techniques, grouped together to demand a thoroughgoing reform of the academic system.

At the same time institutions were changing; this further eroded the foundations of the older system. The small research institutes, laboratories, and other similar units, usually directed by full professors or sometimes by three or four professors jointly with a few assistants, now grew in size to meet the new demands. But they could no longer be managed by informal means alone. They ceased to be mere tools to be controlled and used by one distinguished scholar for both research and instruction. Instead they acquired a momentum of their own, particularly as they employed additional academic and nonacademic staff. Professors increasingly had to assume administrative functions, often at the expense of their research interests and occasionally of their teaching obligations as well. Perhaps the material resources accruing to these flourishing research institutes substantially weakened the professorial position within the university. The power of these institutional heads to hire and fire and to arrange research and teaching according to personal tastes was measurably increased, causing well-founded resentment.

Had the traditional principle of unity of research and instruction become an anachronism in the 1960s? The prime justification for the individualistic organization of the German university system, this unity was debated heatedly. In the classic system everything had been built around the professor as chairholder and director of an institute, as researcher and teacher, and as the organizer of both. The bulk of the academic profession still shunned disjuncture. To the contrary, they believed that considerable benefits derived from uniting research and instruction: scholars were given adequate financial means and personnel to carry out their research and to organize instruction via participation in research. Such assets were now being claimed by far larger numbers of academics than the traditional aristocratic few who had been at the center for almost a century.

Superimposed on these serious problems for the universities was the eruption of the student revolution of the late 1960s. Radical student groups turned university campuses into convenient battlefields for the pursuit of their campaign for political reform at home and abroad. The campuses provided relatively neutral territory for their campaigns because the principle of academic freedom inhibited police and authorities from interfering with student demonstrations and student strikes, even when they challenged established authority or resorted to limited "violence against property" in deliberate defiance of established law. Students usually justified these actions as attempts to make the "structures of power" become "manifest," thereby exposing the allegedly repressive nature of capitalist society. Overnight, universities were confronted by widespread student unrest—strikes, boycotts, protests, demonstrations, and sit-ins with which the authorities were unable to cope.

The objectives of the student revolution of the later 1960s actually had little to do with universities; their protests were directed at such worldwide issues as the Vietnam War, Western imperialism and the evils of the capitalist system. Nonetheless, the universities proved to be easy targets for radical criticism of the established order. Almost from the start, authority structures within the university system were exposed to severe attack, and the privileged position of the professors was singled out for vicious polemics. The majority of older scholars were understandably shocked and panic-stricken, which often caused them to overreact to the provocative student agitation; others preferred to compromise all the way. The junior staff, whose own interests were very much at stake, naturally took a more positive line toward radical student demands. The academic profession was therefore riven by severe internal conflict. The split between the conservatives and the progressives caused a rift throughout the entire body.

The chaotic events of those years and the outcome of the student revolution have been documented elsewhere. Immediate achievements faded rapidly, but long-term consequences for the academic system and for the status of the profession, particularly for its upper echelons, persisted. The student rebellion contributed to the dramatically diminished reputation of the academic profession. Although more blame was apportioned to students than to professors, the allegedly autocratic attitudes of the latter were nevertheless considered a major cause of the student unrest. Furthermore, government authorities now shed their hesitation about directly interfering with academic matters, even though it would certainly violate the state-respected, time-honored principle of faculty and university autonomy.

The general objective of government policies was to bring about university democratization, primarily by reducing professorial power and by giving a fair degree of codetermination of university affairs to the Mittelbau and to the students, and some share in this to the nonacademic personnel. The federal governments responded positively to the propaganda of the student movement and the junior staff voiced by the Bundesassistentenkonferenz. They acted on the naive assumption that once democratization was achieved and legitimate grievances had been attended to, the political troubles would disappear, and a well-functioning university system would gradually emerge. In this way the German "group university," a singular phenomenon in the Western world, came about. Here junior staff and students were given a substantial say in university affairs, at the expense of the professorial elite.[24]

Under these conditions the following earlier features of the university system came under attack:

- the monopolization by high-status full professors of all academic decision making (junior staff members had been granted only token representation on academic bodies).
- the autonomy of universities and faculties and their sole power to implement regulations for academic studies.
- the unity of research and teaching (or the principle of teaching via participation in research). Privileges deriving from this—the right to conduct both research and teaching, the access to research funds, the claim to a limited teaching load—were also demanded by other groups in all institutions of higher learning.
- the privileged status of universities and technical universities within the higher education system.

Strong political pressure to abandon the traditional hierarchical structure of higher education developed. Previously a sharp distinction had been maintained between universities and technical universities, and training colleges, polytechnics, schools of art, and other vocational training institutions. This demand for a reshuffling of the entire system was partly political in origin: the highly aristocratic posture of traditional universities was no longer acceptable; and academics who taught at "lesser" institutions should be accorded the same privileges and rights as members of the traditional academic community. This was argued primarily by the Social Democrats, but the CDU (Christlich-Demokratische Union) soon found there was much to be gained by backing such a policy, although a solid majority of university professors opposed this approach. Naturally, the professional interests of teachers at the Pädagogischen Hochschulen and the polytechnics also played a role in this; they clearly stood to benefit financially and professionally from obtaining the same status as university professors. Arguments for the abandonment of rigid barriers between the highest tier of the university system and the lower ones were also voiced, as this would create a more elastic system capable of accommodating more students as well as increasing social equality and improving opportunities for working-class students.

Demands for reform culminated in a plea for the creation of new comprehensive universities, bringing different institutions of higher learning together under one roof, where use of existing resources and staff would be more efficient.[25] In fields that trained teachers, for example, it was claimed that universities failed to provide courses in pedagogy. Education courses, strongly represented in teacher training colleges, were proposed, and elaborate legislation was sought to ensure that university students embarking on a teaching career were required to devote a substantial part of their studies to pedagogical subjects.

These appeals for university reform led the federal governments in the late 1960s to embark on two contradictory projects. Policies were designed to break the power of the Ordinarien and to introduce participatory democracy into the academic body. The underprivileged Mittelbau would be given a share in running the university and a share in the spoils of the professorial office—access to research funds; research assistants; use of secretarial facilities; and a share in the income derived from subsidiary-services associated with academic positions, especially in medicine. Privileges of professorial status were also extended to those faculty members whose primary responsibility was teaching, especially in teacher training colleges and polytechnics.

By broadening the old academic system simultaneously horizontally and vertically, more groups of academics were able to claim the traditional privileges associated with the conduct of research and instruction. But even the buoyant economy of the Federal Republic during the 1960s and early 1970s, with real growth rates around 4 to 5 percent, could not help the public exchequer meet the full cost of such expansion. The result was a shortage of research funds where they were most needed. The later 1960s and early 1970s witnessed the most dramatic change in the German academic system since the 1890s; the social status, legal position, and career prospects of academics were all deeply affected by reform legislation and were subjected to far-reaching changes. After 1945 the reconstructed system was simply unable to meet the new demands that emerged as a consequence of the dramatic increase in students and unbounded social change. The unity of research and instruction; the idea of education through participation in research; the organization of research and teaching by means of professorial chairs, each connected with small, autonomous research units and only loosely coordinated by the faculties: all now seemed to have been undermined.

Perhaps too much had been asked of the universities in terms of political ideals. Can a system of higher education ever provide equality of opportunity by giving everybody, at least in principle, access to higher education if they have completed the formal educational qualifications of the Abitur? Can greater equality among higher education institutions promote more effective research and teaching than good research facilities for a relatively few well-established scholars in the universities and Technische Hochschulen? Can university professors exclusively be blamed for the crisis, as the majority of the public and the governments were inclined to believe? In 1966 Professor Walcher, a physical scientist at Marburg University, wrote: "Our universities are subjected to revolutionary change not because they have been stricken by fundamental illnesses, but because demands are being made of them by modern society, which they do not possess the organized means to meet."[26]

If we take a closer look at the reform initiatives undertaken by the Länder governments since the late 1960s—particularly those begun under Social Democratic leadership—we see that they enacted new university legislation that fundamentally altered the legal base of the university system. Somewhat belatedly, in 1976, the federal governments also entered the scene with the so-called *Hochschulrahmengesetz*, which laid down general rules for university reorganization, although according to German constitutional law all university affairs are a Länder matter. Decisions by the Federal Constitutional Court established guidelines for university legislation that rendered some of the more radical elements of university laws obsolete. The battle for university legislation was long and bitter, with the professoriat making numerous appeals to the courts to defend its interests. Even today the new regulations continue to be most controversial, and some universities still have managed to avoid implementing them fully.

In addition to modifying university recruitment patterns for academics, the new regulations cut deeply into traditional institutional structures by affecting status, duties, and privileges, undercutting the traditional hierarchy within universities. The privileged position of the chairholders, the Ordinarien, was largely eradicated. The title *ordentlicher Professor,* which distinguished professors from associate professors, was abolished. Professorial chairholders no longer automatically retained control of the research apparatus associated with these chairs; control of the institutes, seminars, and laboratories was given in principle to the new Fachbereiche. (In practice, however, very little changed, because professors were then elected to these positions.) Even if the difference between chairholders and associate professors (or between C4 and C3 professors) was retained, the latter were given essentially the same corporative rights within the university. The Mittelbau, consisting of assistant professors, *akademische Räte, Kustoden, Hochschulassistenten* and *wissenschaftliche Mitarbeiter* were granted positions of greater independence within the system than they had previously enjoyed. But in fact they continued to be obligated to work closely with a professor and were still subject to the directives of their research-unit head. Legally, however, their responsibilities were solely to the Fachbereiche.

The original objective of this legislation—to break up the traditionally small units of teaching and research headed by a powerful professor—was not totally implemented; in many ways full professors managed to maintain privilege and influence. Nonetheless, legal control was transferred to the democratically elected Fachbereiche in which other groups, for example the Mittelbau and the students, were represented according to a specific ratio that varied from place to place, usually approximating *Drittelparität* (three-part equality). In the new Fachbereiche, taken over from traditional faculties, the professoriat can usually muster only one-third to one-half the vote, and the small elite group of chairholders are in a minority. Consensus can only be reached by winning over sections of the Mittelbau. Only in recruitment of research staff has the predominant influence of the professorial group been restored by a Federal Constitutional Court decision. But in fact reforms extensively increased the influence of junior staff at the expense of professorial power, not least because junior staff usually found it easier to compromise with student representatives than with professors.

The democratization of the university effected by these measures was hailed as a huge leap forward. The public assumed that wounds in the German academic system could be healed thanks to the cooperation of different groups within the university, including students. If the old authoritarian system of mandarin rule was indeed gone, the new "group university" had still to prove its effectiveness.

At present the reformed system has not yet been fully implemented as dictated by law. Traditional small units headed by full professors are still very much in evidence, though they rest on a more informal basis and are subject to Fachbereiche control. Further, the democratization of university bodies was somewhat fictitious because government authorities retained firm control over financial matters; democratization did not strengthen autonomy of the universities. They were even less able to decide on further developments, not only because it was difficult to reach consensus within the new representative bodies elected according to rather complicated suffrage regulations but also because governments retained the final say about all new academic positions. For the heads of the Fachbereiche and the newly elected *Rektoren* or *Präsidenten* of the universities, it has become a Herculean task to shift or restructure available academic resources to meet new challenges.

Internal democratization of university structures was accompanied by a sizable shift in control of academic affairs to outside, notably government, bodies. Further, multiplying committees and groups torn by struggles between various blocs, which had to operate according to complicated legalistic rule, put a considerable strain on all university personnel. Many first-rate academics, by preference, shunned involvement in university politics; they found it troublesome and unrewarding. In many instances Mittelbau representatives call the tune. Whether the Fachbereiche will thrive or be torn apart by internal strife will depend on the relations between the professoriat and the junior staff.

Today the negative consequences of the great reform era of the 1970s are underscored. Very few academics are satisfied with the existing state of affairs in German universities.[27] For some, the reforms did not go far enough, as they still permit the predominance, however veiled, of the professoriat; for others, the influence of the students and to some extent the influence of junior staff, on academic matters such as on appointments, the distribution of research funds, and the allocation of research assistants, appears highly detrimental. But the established manner of governing the universities by beneficial, patriarchal oligarchies of prestigious professors could not have survived in any case. Universities have become *wissenschaftliche Grossbetriebe* (knowledge factories) and cannot be administered as they had been in the nineteenth century. The just grievances of the junior staff and their claim that they were denied a voice within the university while doing a large share of the teaching and research have been almost entirely met. The present German university system may not last forever, but it is a base for gradually regaining a new consensus among the members of the academic profession—a necessary prerequisite for fruitful research and teaching.

Quantitatively, and in economic terms, the profession in general benefited substantially from the widespread reform of the 1970s. By 1981 there were about 127,000 persons employed in academic positions by institutions of higher learning, and a further 52,000 by research institutions and libraries affiliated with them.[28] Their income had risen slightly faster than that of other social groups. If they enjoy tenure, they are certainly quite well off. But the highest level clearly lost out in influence and status, and financially power shifted toward the Mittelbau at the expense of the traditional professoriat. For many years academic career prospects in the Federal Republic were extremely good, largely due to the founding of many new universities and other academic institutions. The underlying trends, however, point in the opposite direction, that is, toward a progressively weakening bargaining power for the profession. This is particularly true of the professoriat, which used to have more influence on purse string–holding university and governmental bodies. Finance ministries eliminated many formerly privileged academic positions within the civil service salary scale and often eradicated the special benefits available to leading academics.

This may be justified at a time when many young scholars seem to be having great difficulty finding a job at all, but the financial and institutional incentives to perform well and to embark on more research projects have been reduced considerably. Not only has it become more difficult to get funds to pursue research projects, but worse still, the new university bodies are not noticeably interested in promoting special projects by individuals; their interests lie in improving teaching conditions. Given their composition, these bodies are not suited to be the agencies that promote research inside universities, spreading funds evenly among all members of the Fachbereiche, regardless of academic distinction. And even if teaching has improved considerably, in part due to pressure by nonprofessional groups within the university, research achievement in universities cannot be considered impressive if measured by international standards. In this respect the new system still has to prove itself.

NORMALCY OR WELL-ADMINISTERED MISERY

Reform legislation of the late 1960s and early 1970s may have had many positive consequences, but it did not significantly relieve the mounting pressure of the rising tides of students. The new academic bodies found it repeatedly difficult to agree on suitable rules for courses of study; these *Studienordnungen* were intended to improve educational efficiency and give more effective guidance to students. But these attempts to develop an organizational solution to the crowding, undertaken with differing degrees of enthusiasm, were overruled by the sheer necessity of providing more facilities. The federal governments eventually solved the problem by passing temporary legislation that restricted admission to universities.

The introduction of *numerus clausus* in such sought-after disciplines as medicine, pharmacy, psychology, and German and English literature was actually a violation of various Länder constitutions, which stated that every citizen had the right to freely pursue an education if formally qualified to do so. Students brought many successful lawsuits against officials whose decisions refused them enrollment in a particular university. The Federal Constitutional Court decision of 18 July 1972 eventually legalized the policy of restricted access to universities, but with stringent conditions. Among them were the enforcement of full use of all existing facilities and the imposition of adequate measures to establish a fair system of access.

The Länder governments then took refuge in a very Teutonic, last-resort type of legislation, namely, the *Kapazitätsverordnungen* (capacity decrees), by which universities were forced to provide additional space for students. Existing facilities were stretched to the limit, and teaching capacity used to the full. Technically, this legislation was designed to meet the demands stipulated by decisions of the Federal Constitutional Court; actually, it amounted to massive government interference with the customary system of academic autonomy. For the first time the authorities imposed quantitatively stringent teaching obligations, differentiated according to type of class, and all new appointments were made dependent on actual teaching demand. Research was of little importance. Even worse, academic positions not apparently necessary to meet the obligations stipulated in the new Studienordnungen were eliminated. Simply put, teaching requirements became criteria according to which university departments were developed or cut back. The principle enunciating the essential connection between research and teaching was formally maintained, but in reality teaching, not research, became a predominant consideration in restructuring the university system.

The Kapazitätsverordnungen and similar regulations introduced to expand the capacity of the universities for the increasing numbers of students had some Kafkaesque consequences. The universities, to defend their staffs and their existing institutional structures, were naturally inclined to set low margins for actual teaching capacity; in some cases then the new legislation actually resulted in fewer student places. Direct governmental regulation and centralized control of academic staff activities were introduced on a grand scale. This merely strengthened the position of the bureaucracy, while faculty autonomy suffered a severe blow. The spectrum of academic teaching was distorted in favor of those fields most sought by students; more specialized or less popular disciplines inevitably suffered. This trend strengthened the tendencies toward provincialization of research and teaching. A decade later regulations initially introduced to create additional facilities for more students or to satisfy the demands of the courts to which appeals had been made were used in reverse fashion to restrict output of graduates, especially in those disciplines that produced teachers for the education system.

This type of legislation demonstrates that in Germany government influence on universities had risen considerably. Not only had the academic teaching load been raised to new levels, but the governments began to press universities to introduce new regulations pertaining to Studienordnungen in various disciplines and to intermediate examinations, hitherto unknown in the German tradition. They redefined the subjects to be covered in the final examinations, which decided the future employment (government service or the professions) of university graduates. Admittedly, many attempts came to naught. It turned out to be difficult to impose substantive regulations regarding subject-matter content of examinations; but universities were forced to abandon the traditional freedom of study for each student in favor of fairly rigid courses.

The academic profession has nonetheless largely managed to maintain its independent position even today, but at a cost. During the heyday of the reform era, politicians and governments agreed that universities would be unable to implement serious reforms themselves, that these had to be imposed upon them. To some degree this was true, but the new corporate bodies were even less able to agree on reforms and new study regulations than the old aristocratic faculties had been.

Unlike British and American universities, the German system had always been funded almost entirely by public monies from Länder governments. They do not receive any income from student fees (the nominal ones that existed earlier were abandoned in the 1950s); only very occasionally do they receive bequests from third parties. Traditionally, academic staff—certainly those in tenured positions—enjoyed all the privileges, and few of the disadvantages, of being civil servants. Customarily academics were given special status within the civil service; their salaries were fixed according to an elastic scale that allowed much individual variation; well-known scholars were often able to obtain good financial arrangements for themselves and to negotiate additional funds for their research units to pursue special research projects. In recent years these privileges have been largely abandoned, and it has become much more difficult, if not impossible, for individual scholars to negotiate the terms of their employment with university authorities and government. Here, as elsewhere, bureaucratization has triumphed; very little else considered negotiable is left.

The special status that permitted a higher degree of mobility and differentiation according to individual merit and research achievement within the academic profession has largely, though not entirely, disappeared. What remains is the very secure position, the substantial fringe benefits, and the prestige of membership in the civil service. Academics enjoy financial independence, inasmuch as they hold tenured office and are not subjected to financial pressure from third parties—an indirect guarantee of academic freedom. But an undoubted drawback of the system is the high degree of inflexibility within the staff structure: because all positions are itemized in the Länder budgets, universities are not free to rearrange positions—to downgrade them or upgrade them or freely shift them to other fields where they are most needed—without approval of government and, in principle, of Parliament. In this respect English and American universities, capable of operating quite freely within certain financial limits, are in a far better position than those in Germany. Compared to them, the German university adjustment to new research and development is more difficult. It is also more burdensome in Germany to cope with financial difficulties, because many simple methods of reducing costs are restricted. Problems in the system are due less to direct government influence—it is no stronger than in Britain or America—than to its relationship to a huge government apparatus that does occasionally make the universities less efficient and more difficult to administer.

One may regret this trend toward increasing bureaucratization of the academic system and rigid standardization of professorial status, without much attention given to academic achievement. One may also deplore the profession's failure to adjust in time to the changing conditions surrounding teaching and research. The transformation from the traditional *Gelehrtenuniversität*—the university of scholars—

to the *organisierte Grossbetrieb in Lehre und Forschung* (as Friedrich Ten-
bruch had put it) was a painful one.[29] Perhaps unavoidably, specific
individualistic features of the traditional German university system
were lost forever.

The consequences of reconstructing the system since the late 1960s
cannot yet be fully assessed. They were masked somewhat by the
relative abundance of financial resources and the continuing expansion during the 1970s. The spectacular growth of teaching and research facilities during those years did much to reduce internal conflicts. At the time few people anticipated this period of unmitigated
growth would come to a sudden halt within a few years. As late as
1974, some Länder governments still assumed they could afford a
major restructuring, for political reasons, of the academic system; they
established new comprehensive universities even though there was
no immediate need for additional teaching facilities. This policy required substantial additional financial outlays for at least one if not
two decades, much of which might have been saved by an adequate
expansion of existing institutions. Over the last five years, growth
has come to an abrupt halt, with very serious consequences, not yet
fully recognized, for the German academic community. Many achievements of the last twenty years have again been put in jeopardy, as
there are no longer sufficient financial resources to carry on with the
grand reform schemes initiated in the 1970s.

The symptoms of the present crisis are all too familiar; they are
shared by other nations. The Federal Republic of Germany suddenly
finds itself with a serious overproduction of university graduates not
likely to find employment in traditional professional fields at the same
time that the student population is still rising. (In a few years a substantial decline may be anticipated.) But the academic system itself,
which previously employed a considerable proportion of university
graduates, is shedding labor rather than taking on new graduates.
This is caused partly by a deliberate policy of cutting down the un-
employable surplus of graduates in future years. It would appear that
an entire generation of students who began their studies expecting
to automatically find employment in the professions, in teaching and
research, or in the civil service, has been grossly deceived. The high
degree of specialized professional training provided by German universities has turned out to be of doubtful advantage, inasmuch as
such training makes it more difficult for university graduates to find
employment in nonacademic jobs.

Repercussions on the academic profession are bound to be severe.
Those who hold tenured positions are in a comfortable position, but

for others the story is very different. The age structure of academics employed in institutions of higher education is massively distorted because a large percentage of present officeholders have been appointed only in the last fifteen years, and are likely to remain in these positions for many more to come. Only relatively few openings will become available through retirement or other natural causes in the next decade or so. Not until the 1990s will a larger number of professorial chairs and other tenured academic positions again fall vacant. By then an entire generation of young scholars, now in the early stages of an academic career, will be too old. The situation is made worse by the current policy of cutting jobs wherever possible in almost all disciplines, even though teaching loads are still rising. Further expansion will be required—despite a declining student population— if the present ratio of staff to students, considerably higher than those in comparable Western countries, is maintained. If no new positions are allocated, an entire generation of younger scholars stands almost no chance of ever obtaining permanent academic employment, however high their academic qualifications. This sorry state of affairs is bound to affect negatively the further development of research.

The underlying problems are perhaps even more difficult to solve. Seen in international perspective, the German academic profession is in good standing in terms of salaries, security of employment, fringe benefits, and resources for research. It operates on an elevated basis and enjoys a fairly high standard of living. The traditional high prestige of academics suffered but little during the turbulent 1960s and early 1970s. In only one respect are they less well-off than their colleagues in Britain and the United States: it usually takes a far longer time to obtain a teaching position at a university after a comparatively long period of training. We may see a rift developing between those who have regular employment and those, whose academic reputation may be very good, who do not.

This well-entrenched position of academics in the Federal Republic also causes difficulties: it disappoints an entire generation of younger scholars who had expected to obtain tenured positions in due course; it makes staff structures inflexible; it creates a comparatively high degree of bureaucratization; it fosters a decline in mobility and competition. Structurally rigid academic positions may well prove to be a major obstacle to mastering the problems caused by the present contraction. The civil-servant status of most scholars prevents such measures as early retirement, an option possible in Great Britain. Rigidly structured university jobs are a further disadvantage. Universities might cope better within a budget if internal autonomy permitted them to allocate positions and decide financial matters according to their own choices.

A high degree of bureaucratization reduces individual initiative and creativity. For a variety of reasons, both mobility and competition within the German university system have been declining. Universities no longer compete with one another for good students: students normally prefer to study at the university of their home region; and enrollment is very often arranged by bureaucratic procedure, the student having comparatively little choice. Far worse, competition among scholars for academic distinction has been gradually undermined. The traditional reward for academic distinction used to be calls to other universities, resulting in an improvement in salary and research facilities either at the new place or at one's own university. The new Fachbereiche dominated by members of the Mittelbau are usually little inclined to play the traditional game of offering positions to scholars already well-established elsewhere, however great their academic achievements may be. Nor are the Länder authorities particularly keen on playing this game themselves, in the understandable interests of keeping salaries down. Today there is no substitute for the traditional way of improving one's position in this manner. In the United States and elsewhere, distinguished scholars may well be rewarded in other ways by their home university for seniority or special achievement. No equivalents exist in German universities. Under these circumstances many academics tend to seek their fortunes outside.

These problems are aggravated by the vagaries of the recruitment system, which are all too often distorted by internal power struggles within the Fachbereiche. New bodies mostly favor insiders' groups over outsiders and usually prefer applicants considered to be in the mainstream of research. Politics have come back with a vengeance; the old doctrine that political persuasions ought not to play any role in academic decision making is ignored.

Standards of research in German universities have generally been declining when measured by international standards, the excellent research facilities notwithstanding. Loss of competitiveness within the academic system has had sad consequences. But although the German academic profession has just passed through a period of turmoil and upheaval, its research achievements still remain impressive. In spite of administrative structures, good or bad, the organizational principle at the core of the successful old German university system, namely, research carried out by small, informal groups of scholars and students, is being restored, albeit on an informal basis. Research funding is still available from third parties such as the

Deutsche Forschungsgemeinschaft, which perhaps counterbalances the influence of the Fachbereich that tends to distribute funds, personnel, and favors without regard to research achievement. The widespread fear that the universities might lose their role in promoting research to independent research institutes outside the university system, and in some cases to research institutes financed by industry, has not so far become a reality. Universities are still continuing to play a substantial role in research, and very likely will continue to do so even though the present state of affairs is somewhat bleak.

NOTES

1. The classic texts of Fichte, Schleiermacher, Steffens, and Wilhelm v. Humboldt on the philosophical foundations of the Prussian university system of Humboldt's time can be found in Anrich, ed., *Idee der Deutschen Universität und die Reform der Deutschen Universitäten.* A good historical survey of the German university is McClelland, *State, Society and University in Germany 1700–1914.*

2. This is demonstrated extensively for the first time by Pfetsch, *Zur Entwicklung der Wissenschaftspolitik in Deutschland 1750–1914.* See also Pfetsch, "Scientific Organisation and Science Policy in Imperial Germany 1871–1914," pp. 557–580.

3. Ringer, *Decline of the German Mandarins.*

4. Jarausch, *Students, Society and Politics in Imperial Germany.*

5. See Kaelble, "Chancenungleichheit und Akademische Ausbildung in Deutschland," pp. 121–149. See also Craig, "Higher Education and Social Mobility in Germany," pp. 219–244.

6. See Shils, "Power of the State and the Dignity of the Academic Calling in Imperial Germany," p. 587, translation slightly adjusted by the author.

7. See Bald, *Deutsche Offizier,* pp. 112 ff.

8. A prominent example is Dietrich Schäfer, whose background was working class. An active member of the Pan-German League, during World War I he became one of the most outstanding propagandists for global German war aims.

9. See, among others, Lindenlaub, *Richtungskämpfe im Verein für Socialpolitik;* vom Bruch, *Wissenschaft, Politik und Öffentliche Meinung.*

10. No satisfactory studies of university systems or their policies under National Socialism exist. Those available at present concentrate mainly on the period from 1932 to 1934 or on individual universities. General reassessments based on personal experience are found in Kuhn et al., *Deutsche Universität im Dritten Reich* and Abendroth and Heiber, eds., *Nationalsozialismus und die Deutsche Universität.* See also Adam, *Hochschule und Nationalsozialismus,* and more recently, Heinemann, ed., *Erziehung und Schulung im Dritten Reich,* and Hess, *Deutsche Universität 1930–1970.*

11. Especially for institutional changes, see Seier, "Rektor als Führer." The

failure of National Socialist Ernst Krieck to find acceptance for his ideas about National Socialist reform and permeation of universities is described in detail by Müller in *Ernst Krieck und die Nationalsozialistische Wissenschaftsreform.*

12. The spectacular failure of Walter Frank's endeavors to create at least the nucleus of a new National Socialist historiography is described in detail by Heiber in *Walter Frank und sein Reichsinstitut für Geschichte des Neuen Deutschlands.* See also the brilliant study by Werner, *NS-Geschichtsbild und die Deutsche Geschichtswissenschaft.*

13. See Beyerchen, *Scientists under Hitler.*

14. For this debate compare Heimendahl, ed., *Zukunft der Universität.*

15. See Schelsky, *Einsamkeit und Freiheit,* p. 276 ff.

16. See Wissenschaftliche Gesellschaft für eine Neue Deutsche Universität, *Aufruf zur Errichtung einer Neuen Deutschen Universität.*

17. Picht, *Deutsche Bildungskatastrophe.*

18. Dahrendorf, *Bildung ist Bürgerrecht.*

19. Hennis, "Germany," p. 7.

20. Peisert and Framhein, *Hochschulsystem in der Bundesrepublik Deutschland,* p. 22.

21. *Statistiches Jahrbuch 1983 für die Bundesrepublik Deutschland,* pp. 354–355.

22. A good example is Anrich, *Idee der Deutschen Universität.* Anrich had been one of the few active National Socialist academics before 1945.

23. *Empfehlungen des Wissenschaftsrats zum Ausbau der Wissenschaftlichen Hochschulen bis 1970,* pp. 320 ff.

24. See Hennis, "Germany," pp. 22 ff, for an analysis of some intended and some unanticipated consequences of introducing the Gruppenuniversität.

25. A useful analysis of the Gesamthochschulen is found in Cerych, Teichler, and Winkler, *German Gesamthochschule.*

26. See Heimendahl, *Zukunft der Universität.*

27. For two critical assessments of the reform policies see Schelsky, *Abschied von der Hochschulpolitik,* and Hennis, *Deutsche Unruhe.* For a positive assessment, see Nitsch et al., *Hochschule in der Demokratie.*

28. *Statistisches Jahrbuch 1983,* pp. 364–365.

29. Cf. Tenbruck, "Bildung, Gesellschaft, Wissenschaft."

BIBLIOGRAPHY

Abendroth, Wolfgang, and Helmut Heiber, eds. *Nationalsozialismus und die Deutsche Universität.* Berlin: de Gruyter, 1966.

Adam, U. D. *Hochschule und Nationalsozialismus: Die Universität Tübingen im Dritten Reich.* Tübingen: J. C. B. Mohr (Paul Siebeck), 1977.

Anrich, Ernst, ed. *Die Idee der Deutschen Universität und die Reform der Deutschen Universitäten.* Darmstadt: Wissenschaftliche Buchgesellschaft, 1956.

Bald, Detlev. *Der Deutsche Offizier: Sozial- und Bildungsgeschichte des Deutschen Offizierkorps im 20. Jahrhundert.* Munich: Bernard und Graefe, 1982.

Beyerchen, Alan D. *Scientists under Hitler: Politics and the Physics Community in the Third Reich.* New Haven: Yale University Press, 1977.

Cerych, Ladislav, Ulrich Teichler, and Helmut Winkler. *The German Gesamthochschule.* Paris: Institute of Education, 1981.

Craig, John E. "Higher Education and Social Mobility in Germany." In *The Transformation of Higher Learning 1860–1930,* ed. Konrad H. Jarausch, 219–244. Chicago: University of Chicago Press, 1983.

Dahrendorf, Ralf. *Bildung ist Bürgerrecht.* Hamburg: Nannen, 1965.

Empfehlungen des Wissenschaftsrats zum Ausbau der Wissenschaftlichen Hochschulen bis 1970. Bonn: Wissenschaftsrat, 1967.

Heiber, Helmut. *Walter Frank und sein Reichsinstitut für Geschichte des Neuen Deutschlands.* Stuttgart: Deutsche Verlags-Anstalt, 1966.

Heimedahl, Eckart, ed. *Die Zukunft der Universität: Lehre und Forschung oder Lehre und Verwaltung.* Munich: Nymphenburger Verlagshandlung, 1966.

Heinemann, Manfred, ed. *Erziehung und Schulung im Dritten Reich.* Teil 2, *Hochschule, Erwachsenenbildung.* Stuttgart: Klett-Cotta, 1980.

Hennis, Wilhelm. *Die Deutsche Unruhe: Studien zur Hochschulpolitik.* Hamburg: Wegner, 1969.

————. "Germany: Legislators and the Universities." In *Universities, Politicians and Bureaucrats, Europe and the United States,* ed. H. Daalder and E. Shils. Cambridge: Cambridge University Press, 1982.

Hess, Gerhard. *Die Deutsche Universität 1930–1970.* Neuwied: Luchterhand, 1968.

Jarausch, Konrad. *Students, Society and Politics in Imperial Germany: The Rise of Academic Illiberalism.* Princeton: Princeton University Press, 1982.

Kaelble, Hartmut. "Chancenungleichheit und Akademische Ausbildung in Deutschland." *Geschichte und Gesellschaft* 1 (1975): 121–149.

Kuhn, Helmut, et al. *Die Deutsche Universität im Dritten Reich: Eine Vortragsreihe der Universität München: Acht Beiträge.* Munich: Piper, 1966.

Lindenlaub, Dieter. *Richtungskämpfe im Verein für Sozialpolitik: Wissenschaft und Sozialpolitik im Kaiserreich, Vornehmlich vom Beginn des 'Neuen Kurses' bis zum Ausbruch des 1. Weltkrieges.* Wiesbaden: Steiner, 1967.

McClelland, Charles E. *State, Society and University in Germany 1700–1914.* Cambridge: Cambridge University Press, 1980.

Müller, Gerhard. *Ernst Krieg und die Nationalsozialistische Wissenschaftsreform.* Weinheim: Beltz, 1978.

Nitsch, Wolfgang, Ute Gerhard, Claus Offe, Ulrich K. Preuss. *Hochschule in der Demokratie: Kritische Beiträge zur Erbschaft und Reform der Deutschen Universität.* Berlin Neuwied: Luchterhand, 1965.

Peisert, Hansgert, and Gerhild Framhein. *Das Hochschulsystem in der Bundesrepublik Deutschland: Funktionsweise und Leistungsfähigkeit.* Stuttgart: Klett-Cotta, 1979.

Pfetsch, Frank R. "Scientific Organisation and Science Policy in Imperial Germany 1871–1914." *Minerva* 8 (1970): 557–580.

_____. *Zur Entwicklung der Wissenschaftspolitik in Deutschland 1750–1914.* Berlin: Duncker und Humblot, 1974.

Picht, Robert. *Die Deutsche Bildungskatastrophe.* Olten/Freiburg i. Br.: Walter, 1964.

Ringer, Fritz K. *The Decline of the German Mandarins: The German Academic Community, 1890–1933.* Cambridge, Mass.: Harvard University Press, 1969.

Schelsky, Helmut. *Einsamkeit und Freiheit: Idee und Gestalt der Deutschen Universität und Ihrer Reformen.* Reinbek b. Hamburg: Rowohlt, 1963.

_____. *Abschied von der Hochschulpolitik oder die Universität im Fadenkreuz des Versagens.* Gütersloh: Bertelsmann, 1969.

Seier, Helmut. "Der Rektor als Führer: Zur Hochschulpolitik des Reichserziehungsministeriums 1934–1945." *Vierteljahrshefte für Zeitgeschichte* 12 (1964): 105–146.

Shils, Edward. "The Power of the State and the Dignity of the Academic Calling in Imperial Germany: The Writings of Max Weber on University Problems." *Minerva* 11 (October 1973): 571–632.

Statistisches Jahrbuch 1983 für die Bundesrepublik Deutschland. Stuttgart: Kohlhammer, 1983.

Tenbruck, Friedrich. "Bildung, Gesellschaft, Wissenschaft." In *Wissenschaftliche Politik: Eine Einführung in Grundfragen ihrer Tradition und Theorie,* ed. D. Oberdörfer. Freiburg: Rombach, 1962.

Vom Bruch, Rüdiger. *Wissenschaft, Politik und Öffentliche Meinung: Gelehrtenpolitik im Wilhelminischen Deutschland.* Husum: Mattiesen, 1980.

Werner, Karl Ferdinand. *Das NS-Geschichtsbild und die Deutsche Geschichtswissenschaft.* Stuttgart: Kohlhammer, 1967.

Wissenschaftliche Gesellschaft für eine Neue Deutsche Universität. *Aufruf zur Errichtung einer Neuen Deutschen Universität.* Munich: Max Hueber, 1964.

3
The Academic Profession in France

Erhard Friedberg and Christine Musselin

Universities in France have always been only one part, and in many respects not the most important part, of a complex, compartmentalized system of higher education which comprises three main sectors: the *grandes écoles*, professional schools that train engineers, business executives, and officials of the higher civil service; a research sector built around the National Center for Scientific Research (CNRS), its sister institution INSERM for medical research, and other research institutions; and the university. The university sector is itself divided into two branches, one comprising the faculties of law and medicine, the other built around the faculties of science and humanities;[1] the training of teachers is its main task, and, as a by-product, the training of lower civil servants and other professionals.

This structural differentiation, which separates by institution the three principal functions fulfilled by a single university structure in other Western societies, did not come about as a result of recent trends toward more pronounced functional specialization in systems of higher education throughout the world. On the contrary, the three sectors in France are rooted in historical developments that partly originated in traditional recruiting patterns, especially in the higher civil service; they were also a response to perceived deficiencies in the university structure. And if recent trends, beginning in the sixties, tended to blur their differences by encouraging an increasing overlap of functions, the system still consists of three relatively autonomous sectors, each with its own power structures, modes of functioning, frames of reference, and distinctive institutional dynamics.

HISTORICAL DEVELOPMENT OF THE INSTITUTIONAL FOUNDATIONS

This fragmentation is highly significant for the structure of the academic profession in France, for it cannot be analyzed independently of its institutional bases. Indeed, its existence as a unified profession may legitimately be questioned on this ground—at least until further analysis proves otherwise. Before examining the present structure of the academic profession and discussing some of its current problems, we shall briefly show how historical developments affected each of the three sectors.

GRANDES ECOLES

Because of the predominant role that state entrepreneurship, in the Colbertist tradition, played in the economic development of France, the first grandes écoles were established in the eighteenth century as training centers for important government officials in the technical branches of the civil service, for example, in road construction, military matters, and mining. When the turmoil of the French revolution and its brief reign of terror shut down the old universities and institutions of higher learning, the need for competent, well-trained officials was all the more urgent for a nation still at war. This led to a reactivation and consolidation of the existing grandes écoles as well as the creation of new ones. The most illustrious of these were: the Ecole Normale Supérieure, created for training *lycée* teachers, which outgrew its original function and became the breeding ground for the intellectual and academic elite of France; and the Ecole Polytechnique, which was given and has retained the monopoly for recruitment to the technical corps of the higher civil service.[2] The Ecole Polytechnique provided the unattainable model for all the grandes écoles subsequently created in the engineering sector and others.

From the end of the Napoleonic era to World War I, the grandes écoles expanded rapidly. Their numbers increased from seven in 1816 to eighty-five in 1914, the expansion being particularly rapid after 1870, with seventy-eight schools founded between 1870 and the beginning of World War I. Considerable diversification paralleled this increase. Geographically, the grandes écoles radiated from Paris into provincial industrial centers; they were also ramified by the specific fields of engineering, architecture, business administration, and with the creation of the Ecole Libre des Sciences Politiques in Paris in 1871, public administration. After a slowing down that lasted until 1945, the growth and diversification of the sector again accelerated considerably in the economic and social modernization of France begun after World War II. Almost two-thirds of the present number of 300 institutions were created after 1945.

The pattern of this development has been to meet all demands and needs for professional and utilitarian training outside traditional law and medicine with the creation of new and often narrowly specialized institutions instead of new courses of study in the existing grandes écoles or in the universities.[3] As a consequence, the sector is now characterized by the extreme diversity, institutional fragmentation, and heterogeneity of its 300 independent schools. Training in the engineering professions is offered by 154 schools, 60 specialize in business, and 32 emphasize public administration and public management.[4]

A majority of these schools are state-financed, but many are either privately funded or financed by local chambers of commerce. In recruitment each is highly selective and restrictive; each functions with a relatively small permanent staff; each holds closely to tradition; and all are jealous of their prerogatives and autonomy. They are jointly administered by their directors and a controlling body of representatives of the financing authority and the alumni association, groups that always keep close watch on what happens to "their" school. Through this association the school cooperates with and remains closely related to the professional milieu from which it draws many of its teachers and in which most of its students will be placed.[5] In contrast, there is very little cooperation among these schools whether or not they are in the same field. The grandes écoles are fiercely competitive for good students, and more fundamentally, for a better ranking in the very stable hierarchy of prestige which implicitly structures this sector, strongly affecting student choice.

In short, this unusual sector, which traditionally has been, and in its more prestigious parts still is, the training ground for France's intellectual, administrative, and industrial elites, consists of autonomous institutions, with very little, if any, coordination among them. The Conference of the Grandes Ecoles, the only overall structure in the sector, has no real authority over its members. At best, it acts as a pressure group mobilized for the defense of the interests and the privileges of its members and the sector.

THE UNIVERSITIES

The peculiar status and position of universities in the French system may be better understood if we emphasize three major points. After the abolition of traditional universities during the French Revolution, "university" came to designate not simply institutions of higher education but the entire apparatus of secondary (lycée) and higher studies in various faculties. The complete public education establishment was thus merged into one large public corporation, created by Napoleon, on the model of a worldly order as opposed to a religious one, and was given a monopoly of awarding degrees. The most important was the Baccalauréat. It signified the ending of secondary schooling and automatically made accessible to the student the next level of education at the faculties of law, medicine, science, and humanities, which in turn awarded two diplomas, the licence and the agrégation. Thus secondary and university studies were closely linked. The entire system was structured around and tailored to the organization of national centrally administered exams, whose main purpose was to guard the entry to professional training for the medical and legal professions and for teaching in the natural sciences and the humanities.[6] With the possible exception of a few science faculties that developed applied research–oriented departments in conjunction with local industries in the last quarter of the nineteenth century, scientific training and research had a minor place here. Weisz has called this a structural inability to separate training for research and training for the liberal and teaching professions.[7]

A second major point is the difficult emergence of the university level, one capable of locally linking different monodisciplinary faculties and of insuring a minimum of coordination among them. Two major reform movements attempted to establish this organization and integration, but only partially succeeded. The first developed in the second half of the nineteenth century and achieved little. For the first time, the Law of 1896 formally established universities as public bodies; in reality it created little more than loose confederations of faculties that happened to be located in the same city. Their previous prerogatives were retained. The second movement, a late 1950s and 1960s development around very similar themes, was more successful largely because of the student movement of 1968.[8] The Loi d'orientation of 1968 laid down the basis for a new order in the universities: the faculty structure was formally dismantled and replaced by multidisciplinary units for teaching and research—unités d'enseignement et de recherche (UERs)—to be federated into universities that were then granted considerable pedagogical autonomy, but less financial independence. But structures die slowly in higher education. Even today, the faculty structure is still present indirectly: many UERs are identical with traditional faculties, and a major share of the sixty-seven universities in metropolitan France is still dominated by one or two of the old faculties. Only sixteen universities are truly multidisciplinary, ten others are partially so, and forty-one are dominated by one or two faculties in law, medicine, science, or humanities. Though the university president is an important intermediary between state authorities and basic teaching and research units, the universities as such are far from being a central, effective decision-making level.[9]

Understanding the nature of the French university system in terms of its centralized structure is a third factor. "Centralized," however, has had different meanings at different times. Traditionally, it implied a geographical base. Parisian universities held an overwhelmingly dominant position: there were more of them; their caliber was higher; the teaching profession was dominated by senior professors located mainly in Paris. A professorial nomination to a Paris faculty was considered the highest accolade in an academic career. Today this professorial network no longer exists in its original form. The university structure has itself become more polycentric. In many fields Parisian dominance is not as strong, quantitatively or qualitatively, as it once was.

Centralization also pertains to administrative and personnel affairs. In financial as in pedagogical matters—the definition and implementation of national curricula sanctioned by national degrees is an example—the state bureaucracy has retained considerable power and authority, and has regained, after 1968, even more. This makes it an indispensable partner for all initiatives taken at the university level. In personnel matters universities recruit and promote their staffs under the supervision of a central body that may intervene in university proposals. Conditions of access, statutory rules, salaries, and all other aspects of personnel management are run centrally by the state bureaucracy in bilateral negotiations with national unions. Such a unified personnel management system and its corollary, a united corps of civil servants, is probably the most accepted and thus the most resistant dimension of centralization in French universities, one that contrasts clearly with the decentralization that characterizes the grandes écoles.

THE RESEARCH SECTOR

Universities have clearly had difficulty making room for a formal system of graduate studies capable of producing teachers who also conduct research. In the past those who engaged principally in research were found in one institution and those who taught in another. Periodic weakness of the research function brought about the creation of a specialized institution responsible for both the funding and conducting of research.

Originally, research was limited to such special institutions as the College de France and the Museum of Natural Sciences. To overcome the research deficiencies of the faculty system, a new institution of graduate studies was created in 1868, the Ecole Pratique des Hautes Etudes. Divided into specialized sections whose members were freed from the teaching and examination duties that prevailed in the faculty structure in universities, they were commissioned to develop research and research training in their respective domains.

But the decisive impulse for the creation of a parallel institution for research came during and after World War I.[10] From 1901 a funding agency within the Ministry of Education was administered by a council of scientists. It was entrusted with the mission of raising and distributing funds for fundamental research programs proposed by university professors. The structure was perceived to be ineffective during World War I, and this perception helped bring about institutional innovations in both applied and fundamental research. In 1915 the Directorate of Inventions was created for applied research; it became the National Office of Scientific and Technical Research and of Inventions in 1922. An agency responsible for funding and development, it also sponsored its own research institutions. The notion of organizing basic research in a body composed of tenured public employees with its own permanent staff became more and more prevalent among scientists—especially among left-wing sympathizers in scientific circles—and led to the creation in 1930 of a new institution, the Caisse Nationale des Sciences (National Science Fund), which laid the foundation for today's research bureaucracy. It was administered de facto by a body of scientists who had informal decision-making power. They established funding procedures for projects and recruitment procedures for scholars who were to be freed from all teaching obligations for specified periods to concentrate on their research activities.

In 1935 all research funding was merged into the National Fund of Scientific Research, which continued to develop the policies of the National Science Fund and extended them to the applied sciences. In 1938 it became the National Center for Scientific and Applied Research (CNRSA); in turn, the CNRSA became the National Center for Scientific Research (CNRS) one and one-half years later. This move away from applied research was emphasized in 1941, when that section was dismantled. Since then, the CNRS has remained the central institution for fundamental research in all fields except medical and agricultural, even though in growing areas it coexists with specialized public research institutes.

The CNRS is administered by a directorate and an administrative infrastructure that has grown in size, complexity, and authority since its heroic beginnings. But actual decision making about research policy, funding, and personnel management (e.g., recruitment and promotion) is still in the hands of the scientific community whose representatives sit on national commissions structured by disciplines and whose advice is generally considered binding by the directorate. Research is actually conducted in decentralized institutes that depend on the centralized decisions of these commissions. Either associated with the CNRS (993 units) or integrated into it (339 units), the research institutes employ close to 10,000 permanent staff.

The CNRS is no longer responsible for all scientific research in France. In the fifties and sixties a growing number of independently managed research institutes were established; all publicly financed, today they specialize in such specific fields as space, atomic energy, and oceanography. This diversified sector of research institutes groups together over 6,000 researchers, making a total of over 16,000, a sum almost equivalent to 40 percent of university teachers.

Although this fragmentation of the academic community into three different sectors is basic for understanding the French academic profession, it should not be overemphasized. The three sectors have lately become more similar, not by interpenetration, as might be expected, but by internal diversification. Since 1945 universities have developed institutions whose mode of functioning, selective student recruitment, and autonomous management closely resemble the grandes écoles: engineering schools, university institutes of technology, and more recent professionalized curricula have been successfully established but have little to do with traditional university functioning. In some respects one might even speak of the beginnings of a fourth sector. Simultaneously, the grandes écoles and the universities have developed their research activities, either independently or in collaboration (including joint funding) with the CNRS. Reciprocally, the research units of the CNRS have been more closely associated with the organization of graduate courses, and its staff has taught classes aimed at training researchers.

The three sectors have thus developed a very similar dynamic of internal diversification that to some extent has brought their work closer together. An ambitious young professional in a university today would not dream of a successful career without conducting research. And, as we shall show, research as documented by publications is, next to seniority, the principal criterion for recruitment and promotion in most areas of the university, and in a growing number of grandes écoles as well. The converse is not quite as clear-cut: even today, an ambitious researcher may succeed very well in a career without teaching, but researchers are tending to take on more teaching duties in postgraduate studies.

This evolution of the content of work in the three sectors is not matched by significant increases in intersectoral mobility. Today a researcher will more readily accept some teaching in postgraduate courses or seminars, and a university professor may easily agree to do some teaching in a grande école. Similarly, research may now be conducted by CNRS members, by university teaching staffs, and by those in the grandes écoles. But all of them will do so while subject to their particular institutional conditions and career structures, which have remained separate, inducing intersectoral rigidities and barriers. As a general rule, one does not move from one sector to another; a career develops inside a sector. Intersectoral mobility between the university and the research sector, never very high, has actually declined during the last fifteen years: in 1967, 6.6 percent of researchers left the CNRS for the university sector; in 1976 only 2.9 percent did so.[11] Seen from the standpoint of statutory arrangements and career structures, fragmentation of the French academic profession into three separate sectors, each with its own institutional dynamic, is still very much a reality.

THE CURRENT SITUATION

After a description of career structures, including the very different growth patterns prevalent in each sector during the past twenty-five years, we describe the main characteristics of the academic profession in France today. Special emphasis will be placed on the university and research sectors, since no aggregate data are available on the grandes écoles. The reason for this is simple, and it points to a basic difference between the university and the research sector, on the one hand, and the grandes écoles on the other, a difference that ought to be kept clearly in mind. In the former a unified and national system of personnel management exists, whereas in the latter it does not; each grande école has its own system, thus adding to internal sectoral fragmentation.

CAREER PATTERNS

Located within different kinds of institutions, French academics are governed by different statutes. The disparities are widest among the grandes écoles. Here one finds teachers recruited and paid by the various ministries to which these schools belong, such as education, defense, industry, agriculture. Teachers may be gainfully employed by the chambers of commerce that run most of the management schools; they may also have direct contractual arrangements with the grande école for which they work. Extensive diversity also exists in the research sector: researchers belong to many different institutions attached to different sectors of the administration, though most have statutes and personnel procedures based on those of the CNRS. The university sector is also far from consolidated: even if personnel management is nationally unified, differences in statutes and career lines are important between disciplines, and an immense and confusing number of grades still exist despite the many attempts to simplify them.[12] Career patterns are too complex and varied to treat fully here; instead, we shall describe the major sectoral and subsectoral ones and remark on current tendencies.[13]

University Teaching. Common to all disciplines, the predominance of co-optation by peers all along the career line proves to be the principal characteristic of university teaching. Beyond this common feature, differences in career patterns between the disciplines are striking: the path to medicine, for example, must be distinguished from that to law or to the humanities.

The most important characteristic of the medical faculty is that its members, at all points in their careers, are both teachers and physicians. Teaching takes place in the most prestigious institutions in the health arena—public-sector hospitals. To become an assistant (*chef de clinique*) a candidate must first pass the highly selective resident internship examination; subsequently, he or she must find a position, by co-optation, in a Centre Hospitalo-Universitaire (CHU) with a two-year renewable contract. During this period the chef de clinique is expected to do research and to work as a doctor.[14] On the basis of research publications, an applicant may become *chef de travaux* (*maître assistant*). If this does not take place, the individual will leave the CHU after a certain period (it does not normally exceed eight years) to work in a general hospital or in the private sector. The passage from chef de clinique to chef de travaux and from chef de travaux to *professeur* occurs after the doctorat is decided on in the appropriate faculty council. University Council agreement is not necessary for these decisions. Such mechanisms promote local candidates, favor teachers who also do research (associated or not with INSERM, the medical research organization), and who have published in international journals.

To be recruited as an *assistant* in a law faculty the candidate, in principle, applies for a position in a specialty posted by the university.[15] The Commission de Specialité, a local council composed mainly of teachers working within that field in the recruiting university, will rank the candidates. After the candidate has been ranked first, the agreement of the University Council is then necessary.[16] Subsequently, two paths lead from assistant to professor. The quickest and the most prestigious is to write a doctorat and pass a rigorous competitive exam called the agrégation du supérieur. The top-ranked *agrégé* may choose among the universities having vacancies in the candidate's field. It is customary, however, that the initial teaching position not be in Paris. A young agrégé, if willing and if chosen by his colleagues, always starts a career in the provinces before "climbing" to Paris. The second road to the professorship is to begin as a maître assistant (roughly equivalent to instructor) and then follow a procedure identical to the agrégation pathway. For many years this was considered second class, used only by those who had failed the first route. And even now only a few travel on it: the main road to the professorship is still the agrégation.

A candidate who wishes a post as an assistant in a science or humanities faculty follows a track similar to that taken in the law faculties; promotions, however, are handled very differently. To become a professor—after a doctorat d'Etat has been written—or a maître assistant, an application must be made for a vacant position, published in the Bulletin Officiel, in a particular field. Candidates for recruitment, promotion, or transfer are examined by the Commission de Specialité, which chooses two to four candidates and ranks them. After agreement by the University Council, the national section of the Conseil Supérieur des Universités (CSU) in this field reexamines the candidates. Usually they will concur with the ranking by the Commission de Specialité and will forward the name of the first-ranked candidate to the Ministry of Education for nomination. When there is disagreement, the minister settles the matter: he may choose to follow the opinion of either the Conseil Supérieur or the Commission de Specialité, or he may order the procedure to start anew.

These differences among disciplines in recruitment and promotion procedures do induce different career patterns. Especially unlike are those of medicine and law, and humanities and sciences. In the former grouping, competitive examinations for recruitment and promotion have helped to regulate the growth and promotion of the assistant echelon. Procedures in the humanities and sciences, in contrast, seem to facilitate the recruitment and promotion of local candidates, even if, occasionally, the national section of the CSU acts as a moderator and refuses the local ranking because the candidate does not have sufficient scientific credentials.[17] In these disciplines the lack of competitive examinations to select assistants and the inability of local departments to resist pressures for tenure by staff working on a contractual basis have glutted career lines to a critical point, especially as a decreasing student population makes it difficult to argue for significantly increased teaching positions.

Important as these differences may be, at least two common points illuminate how the academic profession functions in the university sector. First, we note the weak influence of the university level (and its elected council) in appointment and promotion procedures in all three subsectors: the university as an institution, and the bodies that represent it, have little to say about who their future employees will be. Second, very little weight is given to the evaluation of teaching in career advancement. What is important is that the candidate already be part of the recruiting university or pass the competitive examination, and that he or she be engaged in research and have published. Teaching talent is a negligible criterion for promotion.[18]

CNRS. Unlike university practice, only the *directeurs de recherche*, the highest echelon in the CNRS career line, are tenured and appointed civil servants; the others are employed on state contracts. For the most part, however, all have enjoyed complete job security—an exception being *attaché de recherche*, the lowest echelon. The main differences from university practice, however, are the considerably more centralized appointment and promotion procedures. These are managed through forty-five national committees of elected CNRS researchers, and others, always including some university professors. A candidate for a position in the CNRS must apply by presenting a current research project and a list of previous research activities (*thèse de 3ème cycle*, publications, and the like). After having been interviewed, the candidates are ranked by the committee. Those ranked first are recruited according to the number of vacant positions. The new recruits usually begin as attaché de recherche and may stay in this grade for eight years. If they are not promoted by then, theoretically, they must leave. (This seldom occurs, as most attachés are promoted by this time.) Promotion is also decided on by the National

Committee and in principle depends on the candidate's research activities. No particular diploma is required for promotion, but it is useful to have the doctorat d'Etat. The individual research team or institute has relatively little influence during this procedure other than to attempt to mobilize as many members of the commission as possible in support of its candidates. The decision is the commission's, however, and positions or promotions are awarded not to research centers but to individuals who "own" them and can more or less do or go with them as they please.

Grandes écoles. Owing to the very deep fragmentation of this sector, the career pathways of its teaching staff are remarkably disparate. Appointment and promotion procedures and salaries vary greatly from one school to another. In some public-sector schools, appointment follows the successful passage of a competitive examination; thus a large part of the teaching staff will be tenured public servants of the ministry to which the school belongs. In private schools or in those financed by chambers of commerce, considerable leeway is left to each school to work out its own procedures and to tailor arrangements to individual cases.

The presence of part-time nonpermanent teaching staff is an important common characteristic of all grandes écoles. The ratio of permanent over part-time nonpermanent staff is very different in each school, but all rely to some degree on part-timers who are paid by the hour. Such an arrangement provides the schools with much greater organizational and employment flexibility. Common to the grandes écoles also, the directorates of individual schools are central decision-making bodies in all personnel matters: in no grande école, be it public, quasi-public, or private, may an appointment or a promotion be decided on without the agreement and the active participation of the school's director.

Undeniably, the contrast between the three sectors is striking. If decision-making power is located at the local level in the grandes écoles sector, the national level prevails in the CNRS and the research sector. In the universities the decision-making power is shared by the UER (faculty) and the national level. These organizational differences are in turn reflected in different growth patterns is the three sectors.

GROWTH PATTERNS OF THE ACADEMIC PROFESSION

The demographic explosion of the student population in the 1960s induced massive growth in the academic profession in all developed countries. France was no exception, as is shown in table 3.1.

TABLE 3.1

GROWTH OF THE FRENCH ACADEMIC PROFESSION IN THE UNIVERSITY AND
RESEARCH SECTORS, 1961 TO 1983

		Year	
Sector	1961	1970	1983
University	7,901	30,546[a]	39,549
Research	4,755	7,256[b]	17,528

SOURCE: Compiled from data published by J. L. Quermonne and the CNRS.[19]
NOTES: a. University institutes of technology omitted
　　　b. in 1967

In 1983 university teachers were five times more numerous than in
1961, their greatest period of growth (3.5 times) having occurred from
1961 to 1970. Researchers have quadrupled their numbers since 1961;
their increase, unlike that of teachers, has been fairly even during the
entire period. We have no overall figures for the grandes écoles sector,
but growth seems to have been more moderate.

Expansion brought about deep changes in the structure of the academic profession. Table 3.2 compares the distribution of personnel
by rank in the university sector between 1960 and 1982, and in the
research sector (CNRS) between 1965 and 1982. Though the data in
this table are difficult to compare and to interpret (some of the 1982
ranks have a meaning different from those of 1960), they clearly indicate a sharp increase of the middle ranks—the junior members—
in both the university and in the CNRS. This does not mean that the
members of the academic profession are becoming younger; on the

TABLE 3.2

DISTRIBUTION OF PERSONNEL IN THE UNIVERSITY SECTOR AND IN
THE CNRS, BY RANK, OVER TIME
(in percentage)

	CNRS				University		
Rank	1965	1970	1982	Rank	1960	1970	1982
Attachés	52.7	42.7	17.9	Assistants	38.7	47.3	31.8
Chargés	25.1	36.3	55.2	Maîtres-			
Maîtres	10.2 ⎱ 13.9	12.5 ⎱	21.4 ⎱ 26.9	assistants	15.9	25.9	40.1
Directeurs	3.7 ⎰	4.3 ⎰ 16.8	5.5 ⎰	Professeurs	45.4	26.8	28.1
Others	8.3	4.2 ⎰					

SOURCE: Compiled from data published by J. L. Quermonne and by the CNRS.[20]

contrary, the average age and the average seniority in the grade have tended to increase.

These general trends notwithstanding, growth patterns in the three sectors may be distinguished from each other; there are sharp differences among them as well as among units within each sector. In the grandes écoles, growth was controlled to some degree. Selection based on competitive entry examinations enabled this sector to limit rising entry demands far better than did the university. From 1962 the student population (including those in the *classes préparatoires*) only doubled, that is, the number of students increased at only one-half the rate found in the universities for this period.[21] Moreover, according to Magliulo, student population increased in the grandes écoles mainly because of an increased number of schools, although many opened their doors to women at that same time.[22]

The number of students per grande école has thus been stable or has grown only slightly. Although they maintain a very strong vocational orientation, many schools in the sector have widened their curricula and extended their activities to research, thereby inducing some growth in teaching staffs. But their usual and prevalent recourse to part-time faculty has enabled them to keep their full-time tenured teaching staff relatively small, and therefore to manage its growth much more smoothly. The institutional autonomy of each school was tremendously helpful in this regard.

Growth coupled with institutional diversification has been the tendency in the research sector. Though the CNRS still remains the basic institution for the French research establishment, it was stronger in 1962 than it is today. Over the years its staff has increased more slowly than did the research sector as a whole: personnel in the CNRS has been enlarged by a factor of 2.5 from 1962 to 1983 as compared to 3.7 in the entire sector. As a result the CNRS only represented 51 percent of all researchers in 1983, as against almost 80 percent in 1962. Institutional diversification in the research sector is the foremost reason for this shrinkage. Another reason is the development of associated research teams and laboratories in higher education whose members are teachers but whose subsidies come from the CNRS. Thus, although the CNRS has experienced rapid growth, the quantitative aspects of this growth in terms of career management are less acute than in the university sector.

In the universities, faculty increases were greatest in the humanities, next in law, and least in the sciences, the three fields that have been and still are the largest (table 3.3). The contrast becomes even clearer when we study the corresponding student-teacher ratios doc-

TABLE 3.3

INCREASE IN UNIVERSITY TEACHING STAFF BY DISCIPLINARY SUBSECTORS, 1960–1980

Year	Law		Humanities		Sciences		Health sciences	
	N	i[a]	N	i	N	i	N	i
1960	717	100	1,150	100	3,362	100	2,402	100
1970	3,227	450	6,722	584	11,170	307	9,327	388
1980	3,815	532	8,097	704	12,546	345	10,573	440

SOURCE: Compiled from data published by J. L. Quermonne.[23]
NOTE: a. Percentage increase from 1960 base.

umented in table 3.4. This ratio dropped continuously only in the humanities. In all other disciplines it rose again after 1970, the largest increases occurring in law and medicine. The peculiar career structures of these two fields combined with their ability to establish some clandestine selection procedures (e.g., highly selective examinations after the first year) to contain student numbers seem to have enabled a controlled growth of teaching staff.

As French universities have few entry barriers, they caught the full thrust of the enlarged student population: enrollments expanded by 400 percent. Universities tried to manage this in two ways, the first a traditional one: more teachers were hired in the standard fields of study. What had been done for 100 students would be done for 400.

This occurred to the greatest extent in the two years of university study leading to a degree called the DEUG (diplôme d'études universitaires générales), which, especially in law and humanities, are overcrowded. Such a traditional response complicated university management and created serious problems for the teaching staff. The second solution was the creation of new curricula oriented mainly

TABLE 3.4

NUMBER OF STUDENTS PER FACULTY MEMBER IN THE FRENCH UNIVERSITIES, BY DISCIPLINARY SECTOR, 1960–1980

Year	Law	Humanities	Sciences	Health sciences
1960	50	58	18	20
1970	46	34	10	14
1980	55	32	11	18

SOURCE: Compiled from data published by J. L. Quermonne.[24]

toward vocational training. These courses begin immediately after the baccalauréat for the university technological institutes (IUTs) and immediately after the DEUG for the new masters degree, such as the MST degree in science and technology and the MIAGE in computer sciences and management. These options replace or parallel the traditional curricula, but students always have the choice of returning to a traditional course should they decide not to seek employment immediately. The new structures especially pertain to the sciences, economics, business, and management, which are highly selective.[25] Generally they are successful.[26]

The recently created vocational curricula, together with the IUTs that employ both high school and university teachers and have a semiautonomous status within the university, indicate greater internal diversification in this sector. But these changes are still quite limited. The IUTs have not fulfilled quantitative expectations, and the new vocational curricula have followed the strategy of keeping numbers low to guarantee success in the job market.[27] The expanded student population generally continues to follow traditional university curricula; the old way is still considered the "noble road."

Present Structure of the Profession

As noted earlier, our data on the current organization of the academic profession will be restricted to the university sector and to one-half of the research sector, the CNRS; we have not been able to collect comparable data for the entire research arena or for the grandes écoles. Although about 57,000 individuals attached to universities and to the CNRS have provided us with information about present trends, we are not able simply to extrapolate these tendencies for the remainder of the academic community, especially for the grandes écoles sector.

In 1983 the university, with 39,549 teachers, loomed above the other sectors;[28] the research community had 17,528 researchers,[29] 8,657 of them working at the CNRS, and those grandes écoles belonging to the Ministry of Education had 2,400 teachers. This university predominance is also evident in the numbers of research units working within its limits. In 1980, 87 percent of the associated research teams and laboratories were housed in the universities, which employed 4,009 (46 percent) of the 8,657 CNRS researchers. An important part of the academic profession (researchers and teachers) is thus located in the universities, if not always financed and administered by them.

Today this population is much less concentrated in and around Paris than it was, even though Paris remains the main center for university teaching, and even more so for research. In 1982, 56 percent of CNRS researchers worked in Paris; of the 4,009 researchers working in research units associated with the CNRS located in universities, 46 percent were found in Paris. And to use yet another indicator, a majority of CNRS research units—*laboratoires propres*—always play a pilot role in research and are located in that city.

For university teachers Paris dominates less than it does for researchers; only 31 percent of teachers held positions there in 1980. They taught in only thirteen Parisian universities, however, as compared to fifty-six provincial ones, where 67 percent of all French students are found.[30] Parisian universities are admittedly much larger and more prestigious, but the provinces have been catching up, the rate varying from one discipline to another.

Not only is the academic profession still relatively Paris-based, it is also predominantly male. Only 25 percent of university teachers are women; this compares to the higher figure of 30.2 percent of researchers at the CNRS. The situation is even worse if we take into account position levels and disciplines. Humanities and health sciences in both sectors have the highest proportion of women; natural sciences are clearly dominated by men. (The health science and natural science areas are different from the area of medical research carried out in an autonomous research institute, not included here.) Moreover, and this is not surprising, the proportion of women decreases in all disciplines as one moves up the career ladder (table 3.5).

The most explosive feature of today's academic profession in France is its demographic structure. It is increasingly composed of older individuals. The average age of a university professor is forty-four, that of a CNRS researcher forty-one and rising steadily, although not equally across disciplines, ranks, and institutions (table 3.6).[31]

At the university, teachers in the humanities are the oldest for each rank; teachers in the law faculties are the youngest. In all disciplines the difference between the average age in the upper grades and the average age in the lower grades is about fourteen years. Moreover, the average age in the lower grades is quite advanced: thirty-six, or even forty-one, for an assistant in a humanities faculty. It is therefore not surprising to see that 37 percent of assistants in humanities and 28 percent of assistants in law hold a doctorat d'Etat or a thèse de 3ème cycle.[32] Since a master's diploma, in principle, is sufficient for these teaching grades, this clearly indicates problems in recruitment and promotion, a detailed discussion of which will follow in a later section.

The situtation in the CNRS is a bit brighter: individuals in the lower

TABLE 3.5

PERCENTAGE OF WOMEN RELATIVE TO RANKS AND DISCIPLINES IN THE
UNIVERSITY SECTOR AND THE CNRS

Rank	Law	University Humanities	Sciences	Health	Total
Assistants	31.8	41.4	29.9	30.3	32.0
Maîtres-assistants	21.7	38.6	22.3	44.7	30.1
Professeurs	7.9	16.6	7.3	6.0	8.7
Global	22.0	33.7	20.5	33.2	24.8

Rank	Humanities	CNRS Sciences	Life Sciences	Total
Attachés	39.3	28.5	42.0	34.8
Chargés	36.3	22.0	47.4	32.1
Maîtres	32.5	16.9	40.2	27.7
Directeurs	29.3	9.1	18.6	13.6
Global	35.8	21.1	43.4	30.2

SOURCE: From SEIS documentation and the *Rapport d'activité du CNRS 1981–1982.*

ranks of the CNRS career line are, on the average, younger than those in the lower ranks of university teaching; and the age differential between the attachés and directeurs de recherche is greater (twenty-three years) than in the university. But according to CNRS rules, researchers may not remain attaché more than eight years; their situation is therefore different from that of university assistants. Also,

TABLE 3.6

AVERAGE AGE OF UNIVERSITY TEACHERS AND RESEARCHERS AMONG
RANKS AND DISCIPLINES

Ranks	Law	University Humanities	Sciences	Health sciences	Total	CNRS	
Assistants	36	41	37	35	36	Attachés	31
Maîtres-assistants	42	46.5	43	44	43.5	Chargés	41
Professeurs	48	54	49	51	50	Maîtres	48
						Directeurs	54

SOURCE: SEIS documentation and *Rapport d'activité du CNRS 1981–1982.*

TABLE 3.7A

DISTRIBUTION OF RANKS AMONG DISCIPLINES IN THE UNIVERSITY SECTOR

Ranks		Law	Humanities	Sciences	Health sciences	Total
Assistants	N	1,700	1,766	3,467	5,206	12,139
	%	41.39	21.01	25.35	46.07	32.38
Maîtres-	N	1,251	4,530	6,910	2,255	14,946
assistants	%	30.46	53.88	50.52	19.95	39.86
Professeurs	N	1,156	2,111	3,300	3,840	10,407
	%	28.15	25.11	24.13	33.98	27.76
Total		4,107	8,407	13,677	11,301	37,492

SOURCE: From SEIS documentation.

the profession has a very peculiar distribution of ranks, with all career pyramids very bottom-heavy, as shown in tables 3.7A and 3.7B.

Here we see that a majority of university teachers are in junior ranks, and are maîtres assistants, its higher grade. This is true even in law and medicine where the high number of assistants is not significant; a larger proportion of them have not yet chosen an academic career and may drop out after some years of teaching either to become general practitioners or to enter the judiciary. Of those who have chosen a teaching career, 40 to 50 percent are in the middle ranks; full professors represent only one-fourth of the total teaching corps; medicine, whose share is one-third, is an exception.

The same pattern holds true for the CNRS, if we take the maître de recherche and the directeur de recherche to be the equivalent of full professor in the university system. The small number of attachés de recherche in the CNRS is noteworthy: numerous transformations

TABLE 3.7B

DISTRIBUTION OF RANKS AMONG DISCIPLINES IN THE CNRS

Attachés de recherche	N %	1,630 17.9		
Chargés de recherche	N %	5,025 55.2		
Maîtres de recherche	N %	1,952 21.4	N	2,452
Directeurs de recherche	N %	500 5.5	%	26.9

SOURCE: From SEIS documentation and *Rapport d'activité du CNRS 1981–1982.*

TABLE 3.8

AVERAGE ASSISTANT SENIORITY AMONG DISCIPLINES

Years of seniority in 1980	Law		Humanities		Sciences		Pharmacology		Total	
	N	%	N	%	N	%	N	%	N	%
5 years or less	490	30.8	673	30.9	880	21.7	226	46.4	2,269	27.3
6 to 10 years	720	45.3	1,004	46.1	1,335	32.9	153	31.4	3,212	38.6
11 years or more	381	23.9	502	23.0	1,843	45.4	108	22.2	2,834	34.1
Total	1,591		2,179		4,058		487		8,315	

of attachés positions into chargés positions substantially reduced the hiring of younger researchers.

Average seniority in both university and CNRS levels is high and rising. This is especially true for university assistants, as documented in table 3.8. Except for pharmacology, 70 percent of all assistants have been at their grade for more than six years. The situation is particularly dramatic in the sciences, where 45 percent of them have been in those positions for eleven years of more. Considering that the scientific disciplines alone employ more than one-third of the university teachers, the implications for new openings are evident. If the state of affairs in the CNRS seems to be somewhat less acute than in the universities, career prospects certainly are not bright in the next decade.

PROBLEMS AND DILEMMAS

The central problem of the academic profession in France today is related to the issues raised by its recent rapid growth. Aspects of that growth affect emerging quantitative problems; growth has also created qualitative consequences that alter the structure and the internal regulation of the profession. With the exception of the grandes écoles sector—a case apart—this rapid growth in universities and in the research sector has been little controlled or managed. It simply happened as an incremental, piecemeal answer to perceived situations of crisis. It first took the form of an overloaded student body after the university revolution of 1968. Massive union claims for integration of the permanent but untenured faculty followed. And by simply happening, it thoroughly disrupted the traditional modes of regulation and integration of the academic milieu, a milieu that has consequently become much more open and vulnerable to regulation from the outside, especially through bureaucratic procedures and through growing union interference and state bureaucracy. A discussion of these issues follows.

THE QUANTITATIVE CONSEQUENCES OF GROWTH

As a consequence of past growth the academic profession—again the exception is the grandes écoles—is increasingly threatened with blockage. The present no-growth period, with little promise of new positions or departures, has brought about the following serious bottlenecks in career patterns: bottom-heavy career pyramids in the universities and the CNRS, with junior grades predominating in all disciplines; small differences between the average age in lower and upper grades; and a high average seniority in the grades, especially the lower ones.

This situation is the direct consequence of massive recruitment waves that began around 1968 in the university and research sectors; the way this recruitment was carried out also affects the present situation. Responding to a series of factors (explosion of the student population, student unrest in 1968, belief in the expansion of science and higher learning as a prerequisite for societal growth), both sectors recruited masses of junior staff for regular positions and for temporary, contractual openings. To illustrate the suddenness and the tremendous scope of this intake, for example, 9,800 young assistants were recruited into the university sector between 1967 and 1971, that is, about one-third of the work force.[33] No similar research-sector estimates exist but without question the increase was equally huge, even though it did not occur at the CNRS directly. Individuals were recruited in a completely decentralized manner for different research units, according to the resources available from contracts. Here, too, recruitment was first on a temporary and contractual basis.

Thus in the early 1970s two coexisting populations doing very similar if not identical work did not enjoy the same statutory rights and privileges. The result was mounting pressures for the integration of the *hors-statut*—those outside the statute of the civil service. This integrative movement to give tenure or quasi tenure to all temporary staff on the public payroll began during the second half of the seventies, beginning with the universities and followed by the CNRS. It amounted in fact to a breach of regular recruitment and promotion procedures: the basic criteria were bureaucratic, not scientific—those who had been on the university or the public-sector research payroll for a certain period preceding a fixed date had a right to tenure; permanent positions were then created in previously temporary ranks. Thus the awarding of tenure became based on the bureaucratic criterion of years served. The new procedures did not bring fresh blood into the profession. They regularized the positions of those already in it; they discouraged recruitment because the absorptive capacity of the system had been saturated by waves of integration. The traditional channels of recruitment, through contract arrangement, were almost completely dried up.[34]

Frustration is one consequence of this situation. Career lines are completely clogged, and promotion for all those who expect it and anxiously wait is impossible. The important dividing line in the academic profession is increasingly horizontal; it cuts across disciplines and institutions. It splits the profession into two antagonistic camps: those in level B of the public service (the junior faculty and researchers, comparable to the *Mittelbau* in Germany), and those in level A (the senior researchers and full university professors). This crystallization and strengthening of horizontal solidarities according to bureaucratic criteria makes the academic profession open and vulnerable to unionization along these lines.

The second consequence is the older age of members of the profession. One solution employed frequently to solve career problems is yet another bureaucratic device, the *transformation de poste*—the upgrading of lower into higher positions without the creation of new lower positions. If this procedure does alleviate some of the corporatist pressures produced by the situation, it also halts recruitment, a step highly detrimental to the demographic balance and to the innovative potential of the academic profession. For the past three years the academic profession has been unable to recruit younger scholars; stop-and-go growth is feared.[35] According to Quermonne the forecast of annual retirement rates for university teachers will rise annually from 181 during 1981 to 1985 to 961 during 1996 to 2000.[36] This means that academia will experience another sharp growth pattern beginning in 1990 following the present blocked situation; after this a new no-growth period will ensue.

FROM OLIGARCHY TO BUREAUCRACY

One must go beyond mere numbers in discussing the present problems and dilemmas of France's academic profession (or professions).

Quantitative aspects are sometimes merely the expression of more basic changes in the social structure and the rules of the game in academia.

In a seminal paper that draws most of its material from the humanities but which is generally representative of the entire university and research sector, Terry Clark has shown that the academic profession outside the grandes écoles was traditionally structured by and regulated through the "cluster."[37] By this term he designates the informal networks linking the few less prestigious members of the teaching profession (in the provincial faculties, in secondary schooling, and so forth) to one or two central chairholders in Paris, mostly in the Sorbonne. In contrast to the "school of thought" characteristic of the German university system, the cluster was less organized and less centralized around the master. Nor was it concentrated in one location. A more dispersed and permeated network shaping the entire discipline, or perhaps a number of closely related disciplines, it was primarily founded on the capacity of the patron or patrons to control, organize, and further the careers of its members and their clientele. Through its patrons, the cluster stayed in close touch with the important officials in the state bureaucracy with whom all important matters concerning the discipline (and the corresponding faculty) were negotiated. The patrons mediated the influence of the state officials. They also mediated the influence of the scientific marketplace of ideas and persons, giving it only a minor role. The organizational infrastructure of the disciplines (professional associations, journals outside the control of the clusters, scientific gatherings) has always been and still is weak in France. Regulation of academia in France thus became based on the interaction of a small number of prestigious Parisian cluster leaders who maintained oligarchical control in their own fields by working with each other and with a small number of state officials.

This mode of regulation by the mandarins was much criticized but worked reasonably well. It completely collapsed under the combined thrust of quantitative growth, the consequences of the revolution in the universities in 1968, and the ensuing university reform. No alternative mode of regulation has taken its place: as Raymond Boudon has shown, French academia is still far from regulation through the organization of a scientific marketplace.[38] Although the traditional monopolistic structuring of disciplines by cluster leaders has been replaced by more polycentric and oligopolistic patterns that have opened up the profession to some extent, monopolistic attitudes and values still prevail and dominate. They cause intensive scientific infighting around territories and positions and are reflected in a very dogmatic and often unconstructive type of scientific debate and intercourse in France.

External forces have been filling the void; corporatist unionization, politicization, and growing bureaucratization are striking features of today's situation, moving French academia much closer than before to the state corner in Burton R. Clark's triangle of coordination, in which the three poles are market linkages, professional self-regulation, and state authority.[39] The weakness of what Clark has called the enterprise level is also a striking feature today. Between individual members of the academic profession and the national bureaucratic and statutory structure, there are few or no mediating institutional or organizational frameworks. Particularly in the research sector, we find highly centralized decision-making prerogatives that affect day-to-day management; a career system that protects the rights and privileges of individual researchers; and an atomization of the research profession, whose institutional structure is extremely weak. The situation is somewhat less extreme in the university sector. If the university president has become important, especially as an intermediary between the UERs and the central authorities, the university as an organizational and management unit remains very weak or nonexistent. In a study we are now conducting on the management of French and German universities, only the UER or the local faculty exhibit some autonomy and decision-making capacity.

The university reform of 1968, with its emphasis on more participation, especially of junior faculty members and of a large number of discontented permanent but untenured staff expecting to be integrated into the civil service, brought about the growing influence of the unions, which were able to make themselves heard on all levels. They were strongest on the national level where they exerted corporatist pressures and became privileged partners of the state bureaucracy, especially since the left-wing victory in 1981. At the same time union power was increasing, and partially because of it, the profession has become more politicized. Political cleavages and clusters have become more important in university decision making. This tendency, witnessed by many observers, has brought intense political infighting to some universities and has increased the influence of political, mostly union, affiliation in recruitment and promotion decisions.[40]

All these factors have prepared the ground for the growing bureaucratization of both the university and the research sectors. In the absence of legitimate selection criteria, and in the face of an overload of candidates, seniority is always a possibility and a tempting way out. Seniority and localism, that is, the tendency to hire local candidates; horizontal mobilization around statutory and political lines; and the ever-growing presence and weight of the state bureaucracy in the management of the profession have become the paramount features of the crisis situation today.[41]

CONCLUSIONS

Our line of argument has clearly denied the implicit assumption that one unified academic profession exists in France. We have shown that it is divided into three sectors, each with a different history, different career patterns, different institutional frameworks, and different traditions. Although each sector has developed internal dynamics of diversification that cause some convergence with the other major parts, all three are still very much separate, the greatest distance being between the grandes écoles and the other two sectors. A horizontal demarcation has to be added to these vertical ones, namely, the cleavage dividing university and research sectors along statutory lines—junior against senior staff—in a national context mediated by the unions and the state bureaucracy.

Finally, we hesitate to speak of *an* academic profession for a much simpler reason: in French nomenclature, the term—the concept—does not exist. Closest to a parallel conception is a reference to individuals who work in "university and scientific milieux." Without overestimating the importance of definitions and etymological issues, the looseness of the corresponding French concept is indicative of the way the academic life is perceived and lived. A person may be a scientist, a researcher, a university professor, an assistant or a maître assistant, but none of these individuals will say that he or she is a member of the academic profession.

NOTES

1. The *faculté de lettres* in France is not limited to the studies of literature; it encompasses all human and social sciences. Its equivalent in Germany would be the faculty of philosophy.

2. This was also true for many political leaders at the end of the nineteenth and the beginning of the twentieth centuries. Once entering the Ecole Normale Supérieure, it was difficult to tell where and how far one would land.

3. Gruson, *Etat Enseignant*, pp. 97–98.

4. These figures are drawn from Magliulo, *Grandes Ecoles*, p. 25. They differ from more conservative ones given by the Conference of the Grandes Ecoles:

154 engineering schools and 30 business schools are recognized by the conference and affiliated with it. This more conservative count is probably due to the very restrictive policy of recognition by the conference, which sees itself as the guardian of excellence in this sector.

5. For an analysis of the most prestigious technical grandes écoles and the role of the alumni associations, see Friedberg and Desjeux, *"Rôle de l'Etat et Fonctions des Grands Corps"*; and Crozier and Thoenig, "Grandes Ecoles dans le Système Social Français."

6. Prost, *Histoire de l'Enseignement en France 1800–1963*; Weisz, *Emergence of Modern Universities in France,* p. 212.

7. Weisz, *Emergence of Modern Universities in France 1863–1914,* p. 212.

8. The two reform movements resembled each other closely in their objectives and in their mythical reference to foreign models—the German university at the end of the nineteenth century and the American university in the fifties and sixties. See Drouard and Weisz, *Processus de Changement.*

9. Fréville, *Rapport au 1er Ministre de la Commission d'Etude,* p. 56.

10. See Blancpain, "Création du C.N.R.S.," pp. 751–797.

11. See Schwartz, *France en Mai 1981.*

12. For example, the term *agrégation* does not have the same meaning in law and medicine as it does in science and the humanities. In the former disciplines it designates a university examination to be passed to obtain the post of university professor. In science and the humanities, however, the same word designates some sort of postgraduate examination—a prerequisite for becoming a higher-salaried high-school teacher or an assistant or maître assistant in the university.

13. More detailed descriptions may be found in Cerych and Neave, "Structure, Promotion and Appointments of Academic Staffs in Four Countries," and in Sarrault, *Carrières de l'Enseignment.*

14. This is the terminology for *cliniciens.* The terms and the promotion "delcup" are rather different for the "fondamentalistes."

15. This also includes university faculties of economics, political science, and business.

16. The agreement of the Conseil Supérieur des Universités is not necessary; assistants in law are under the authority of the recteurs and not directly under the ministry.

17. So far we have no figures to prove this, but after interviewing 40 teachers as part of a recent research project at a French university, this seems to be the case.

18. This may change due to a new project for recruitment and appointment procedures: the national section of the CSU would first examine the candidates and then, the Commission de Specialité would subsequently choose among the list established by the CSU for each post. This, in principle, ought to weaken the power of local interests.

19. This is a compilation of data from Quermonne, *Etude Générale des*

Problèmes, p. 78, *Recherche Scientifique, 1958–1967,* and *Rapports d'Activité du CNRS.*

20. Ibid.

21. Ibid, p. 25.

22. According to Magliulo, in *Grandes Ecoles,* these schools are three times more numerous today than in 1945.

23. Quermonne, *Etude Générale des Problèmes,* p. 78.

24. Ibid., p. 78.

25. For example, the IUT at the University of Paris XII received 9,900 applications, but admitted only 600 students.

26. Even these institutes have their problems; see Cerych, "Implementation of Higher Education Reforms in Europe," and Boudon, *Effets Pervers et Ordre Social.*

27. Cerych, "The Policy Perspective," p. 245.

28. This figure includes the number of full professors, maîtres assistants, assistants (different ranks of assistant and associate professors) in the universities in 1982–1983, including the IUTs (technology institutes) but not the engineering schools in the universities (ENSI), which are considered part of the grandes écoles sector.

29. According to the Loi de France, *Rapport Pour la Loi de Finance Pour 1984,* with those researchers we have included the *ingenieur* grade directly below; actually many of them conduct research without being considered researchers.

30. See Fréville, *Rapport au 1ᵉʳ Ministre de la Commission d'Etude de la Réforme,* p. 11.

31. Table 3.6 includes all teachers who belong to the Ministry of Education, that is, university teachers, teachers in the 18 grandes écoles that depend on this ministry, and those who are part of the Collège de France, Ecole Normale Supérieure, and so on.

32. Quermonne, *Etude Générale des Problèmes,* p. 70.

33. Schwartz, *France en Mai 1981,* p. 248.

34. In social science the funding mechanisms have been profoundly affected. On a research contract funded by public money, it is not possible to pay salaries, and the permissible annual fees payable to the same person are strictly limited. In short, new people may not be employed on public research grants. Of course, there are ways to circumvent this regulation; but these have to remain semiclandestine and are in no way a substitute.

35. Quermonne, *Etude Générale des Problèmes,* and Schwartz, *France en Mai 1981.*

36. Quermonne, *Etude Générale des Problèmes,* p. 64.

37. T. Clark, "Patron et Son Cercle," pp. 19–39.

38. Boudon, *Effets Pervers et Ordre Social.*

39. Burton R. Clark, *Higher Education System.*

40. See Boudon, "French University Since 1968," pp. 106–107, and Bour-

ricaud, *Réforme des Universités en France et ses Déboires.* In our ongoing research, interviews show that most of the votes in the university council were taken purely on political grounds, irrelevant of the issues involved.

41. In such matters as the detailed allocation of research funds, authorization of new curricula, statutory rules for teaching and administrative personnel, the central administration in Paris has regained remarkable vigor in the last ten years.

BIBLIOGRAPHY

Altbach, Philip G., ed. *Comparative Higher Education: Research Trends and Bibliography.* London: Mansell, 1979.

Blancpain, Frédérique. "La Création du C.N.R.S.: Histoire d'une Décision Administrative." *Bulletin de l'Institut International de l'Administration Publique* 32 (October–December 1974): 751–797.

Boudon, Raymond. *Effets Pervers et Ordre Social.* Paris: PUF, 1977.

–––––––. "The French University since 1968." *Comparative Politics,* 10 (October 1977): 89–119.

Bourricaud, François. *La Réforme des Universités en France et Ses Déboires.* Brussels: Fondation Européenne de la Culture, 1977.

Boussard, Isabel, Marie-Jose Guedon, and Didier Wolf. "Les Institutions Universitaires Françaises: Situation Actuelle." *Notes et Etudes Documentaires,* no. 2424–2427. Paris: Documentation Française, 1977.

Centre National pour Recherche Scientifique. *Rapports d'Activité.* Paris, 1977–1978, 1979–1980, 1981–1982, January 1984.

Cerych, Ladislav. "The Policy Perspective." In *Perspectives on Higher Education: Eight Disciplinary and Comparative Views,* ed. Burton R. Clark, 233–248. Berkeley, Los Angeles, London: University of California Press, 1984.

Cerych, Ladislav, and Guy Neave. "Structure, Promotion and Appointments of Academic Staffs in Four Countries: Recent Developments." *Report of the Institute of Education for the Volkswagen Stiftung.* Paris: Institute of Education, 1981.

Clark, Burton R. *The Higher Education System: Academic Organization in Cross-National Perspective.* Berkeley, Los Angeles, London: University of California Press, 1983.

Clark, Terry. "Le Patron et Son Cercle: Clef de l'Université Française." *Revue Française de Sociologie* 12 (January–March 1971): 19–39.

Colcombet, Paul, and Guy Denièlou. "La Compétition des Grandes Ecoles," *Projet,* no. 140 (December 1979): 1227–1240.

Colloque National de Lyon. *Mission Nouvelles Pour les Universités.* Lyon: Presses Universitaires de Lyon, 1982.

Conference des Grandes Ecoles. *Les Grandes Ecoles Demain: Douze Propositions* Paris: C.N.G.E., 1981.

Crozier, Michel, and Jean-Claude Thoenig. "Les Grandes Ecoles Dans le Système Social Français." *La Jaune et la Rouge,* no. 238 (December 1968): 49–55.

D.G.R.S.T. *La Recherche Scientifique dans le Budget de l'Etat 1958–1967*. Paris: Progrès Scientifique, 1967.

Drouard, Alain, and George Weisz. *Processus de Changement et Mouvements de Réforme dans l'Enseignment Supérieur Français*. Paris: Editions du C.N.R.S., 1978.

Fomerand, Jacques. "Policy Formulation and Change in Gaullist France: The 1968 Orientation Act of Higher Education." *Comparative Politics* 8 (October 1976): 58–89.

Fréville, Yves. *Rapport au 1ᵉʳ Ministre de la Commission d'Etude de la Réforme du Financement des Universités*. Annexes. Paris: Documentation Française, 1981.

Friedberg, Erhard, and Dominique Desjeux. "Rôle de l'Etat et Fonctions des Grands Corps: le Cas du Corps des Mines." *Bulletin International d'Administration Publique* (1972): 226–242.

Gaudemet, Yves. "La Situation du Personnel de Universités." *Revue Française d'Administration Publique*, no. 14 (April–June 1980): 299–311.

Girod de l'Ain, Bertrand. "Institutions d'Enseignement Supérieur et Innovation Pédagogique." *Perspectives Universitaires* 1, no. 2 (1983): 76–83.

Grafmeyer, Yves. "Un Enseignement Supérieur en Quête d'Universités." In *Français, Que Etes-Vous?* ed. Jean Daniel Reynaud and Yves Grafmeyer, 421–434. Paris: Documentation Française, 1981.

Gruson, Pascale. *L'Etat Enseignant*. Paris: Mouton/Ehess, 1978.

Kosciusko-Morizet, Jacques. *La Mafia Polytechnicienne*. Paris: Seuil, 1973.

Lautman, Jacques. "Sur les Finalités des Universités," *Projet*, no. 140 (December 1979): 1209–1218.

Lisle, Edmond, Howard Machin, and Sy Yasin. *Traversing the Crisis: the Social Sciences in Britain and France*. London: Economic and Social Research Council, 1984.

Loi de France. *Rapport Pour la Loi de Finance pour 1984: Rapport Annexe sur l'Etat de la Recherche et du Développement Technologique*.

Magliulo, Bruno. *Les Grandes Ecoles*. Paris: PUF, 1982.

Ministère de la Recherche et de l'Industrie. *Hommes et Institutions. Actes du Colloque National*. Annexe 4. Paris: Documentation Française, 1982.

Mingat, Alain, and Jean Perrot. "Les Enseignants des Universités." *Consommation* 27 (January–March 1980): 73–90.

Organisation for Economic Co-operation and Development. *Les Politiques d'Enseignement Supérieur des Années 80*. Paris, 1983.

Peretti, André de. *Rapport au Ministère de l'Education Nationale de la Commission de la Formation des Personnels de l'Education Nationale*. Paris: Documentation Française, 1982.

Prost, Antoine. *Histoire de l'Enseignement en France 1800–1963*. Paris: Colin Armand, 1968.

Quermonne, Jean Louis. "Pour des Universités Autonomes." *Projet*, no. 140 (December 1979): 1188–1208.

———. *Etude Générale des Problèmes Posés par la Situation des Personnels Enseignants Universitaires*. Paris: Documentation Française, 1981.

Rémond, René. "Université: Une Loi en Trop," *Le Débat*, no. 25 (May 1983): 52–57.

Ringer, Fritz K. *Education and Society in Modern Europe*. Bloomington: Indiana University Press, 1979.

Sarrault, Muriel. *Les Carrières de L'Enseignement*. Paris: Editions Génération, 1984.

Schwartz, Laurent. *La France en Mai 1981: l'Enseignement et le Développement Scientifique*. Paris: Documentation Française, 1981.

"La Situation de l'Université en France, Dix Ans Après Mai 1968." *Esprit*, Special Issue, no. 276 (November–December 1978).

Suleiman, Ezra. "Higher Education in France: A Two Track System." *West European Politics*, no. 3 (October 1978): 97–114.

Van de Graaff, John H., Burton R. Clark, Dorotea Furth, Dietrich Goldschmidt, and Donald Wheeler. *Academic Power: Patterns of Authority in Seven National Systems*. New York: Praeger, 1978.

Weisz, George. *The Emergence of Modern Universities in France 1863–1914*. Princeton: Princeton University Press, 1983.

4
The Academic Profession in the United States

Walter P. Metzger

In 1980 the United States National Center for Education Statistics estimated that as many as 846,000 individuals were members of an instructional staff of an American institution of higher learning.[1] That number could have been lowered or raised by a different set of exclusions and inclusions. Had these census-takers seen fit to exclude graduate assistants and part-time faculty, their head-count would have dropped to around 460,000; had they included campus professionals who did not teach or do research and campus researchers who did not hold faculty appointments, their total would have soared to well above a million. By lumping together the 1,274 two-year colleges that awarded nothing higher than the associate degree with the 1,957 four-year colleges and universities that awarded nothing lower than the baccalaureate, they enlarged their survey; by ignoring the numerous correspondence schools, extension divisions, and training institutes that offered courses not creditable to degrees, they narrowed it. Following established protocols, these surveyors may have achieved methodical consistency at the price of a certain arbitrariness. Nevertheless, their in-and-out decisions did draw a defensible line between the American academic profession at its furthest reaches and the terrain of impinging but recognizably different occupations. Bearing in mind that the territory here included was not just the "central city" of full-time faculty in the regular ranks but a large "metropolitan area" with outlying suburbs, one may justifiably assert that the working population of the academic profession in this country transcends the adjective *large* and approaches the awe-filled word *colossal*.

Almost 80 percent of all academics in 1980 occupied positions that did not exist thirty years before. The 1950 census put the number of academics at 190,000. By 1960 the number had grown to 281,000; by 1970 to a whopping 532,000.[2] At the end of those two decades, the academic profession was almost three times larger than it had been at its start; in only one decade—the 1960s—as many new academic posts were created as had been accumulated since Harvard College, three and one-third centuries ago, appointed a president and five tutors to the first academic teaching staff assembled on these shores. In this century only the professions of accountancy, nursing, and engineering grew so lustily in so short a season, but they took off from much smaller bases. If their percentage increases were comparable, the absolute magnitude of their expansionary feats was not.

Although immensity was a late development, the American academic profession has exhibited a prospensity to grow for well nigh a century. In 1880 the United States Commissioner of Education counted only 11,500 faculty members in the entire country; thirty years later, there were three times as many.[3] Dwarfed by later enumerations, the 1910 figure of 36,500 may not seem very impressive today. But those who were on the academic scene in 1910 doubtless used a retrospective rather than a prospective yardstick, and by that measure the statistic was prodigal indeed. It signaled the conversion of an occupation that had hitherto been very sparsely populated into one that, however blessed, no longer conferred the distinction of rarity. From that time, to be an academic in America was to be one of a rapidly growing multitude. Despite momentary slowings during major wars and a downturn in the trough of the Great Depression,[4] the overall academic rate of growth between 1880 and 1960 doubled every fifteen years. The doubling of the American academic work force in only ten years—the demographic extravaganza of the 1960s— represented a dramatic acceleration of what had long been a galloping trend.

Why did this profession grow so fast, for so long, and in the recent past with such exuberance? How was it affected by its history of rapid, sustained, and then prodigious growing? Regrettably, no widely accepted theory is at hand to explain its growth dynamics, and no conventional procedure has been devised for relating the stimulants of growth to changes in its conduct and self-image. Growth in general has been closely studied, but growth in this (or in any other) particular occupation has not yet found its Paul Samuelson or Club of Rome.

This is not to say that academics are lacking in firm opinions about why and to what effect their profession grew. With regard to its quantum mechanics, they generally suppose that faculty growth responds to and is commensurate with student growth, that invariably the professional supply takes its orders from client demand. Those familiar with the statistical history of American higher education know that the number of academic students increased in step with the number of persons appointed to instruct them, and that the former actually outran the latter during the recent bonanza years.[5] Add to this striking historical parallelism the worried attention now paid to the downward trend in the number of persons of college age—the apocalyptic warnings of demographers that falling birthrates foretell declining enrollments in years to come, the prophylactic reactions of administrators who thin their faculties in anticipation of the predicted onset of that dread disease—and it becomes conventionally wise to assume that the size of the profession has one and only one determinant, the size of student enrollments.

As for consequences, the going consensus, similarly tinged with immediate worries, is that growth is the hallmark of professional glory, stagnation or contraction the badge of professional defeat. Recent statistical trends appear to back this view. Although the number of academics kept increasing throughout the 1970s, the rate of increase in that decennium fell to about a third of the historic one, and 70 percent of the increment was confined to the junior and part-time ranks, the marginal zones of the profession. Rare today is the academic old hand or acolyte who cannot give personal testimony of the hardships that come when growing stops. Veteran faculty members who keep track of the purchasing power of their paychecks, of the waiting time between promotions, of the quality of work amenities and supporting services, of their chances of getting a research project funded, can attest that the previous period of rapid expansion was attended by the furnishing of concrete benefits the next period largely snatched away.[6] Young and would-be faculty members can define, with poignant first-hand knowledge, the terms that have crept into the no-growth lexicon: the "folding chair" (the unrenewable appointment that lasts for a year and then expires); the "nontenure track" (the renewable appointment that precludes a status promotion, thus reviving the Calvinistic doctrine that good works can never earn salvation); the academic "gypsy" (the job-seeker in a casual labor market who travels everywhere but in the end gets nowhere).[7] American academics have long been noted for their progrowth biases; the current mood does not describe a new affection. What is new is that now, with their wistful remembrances of great times past, they tend to think of growth as a token of a once secure and since lost prosperity, and thus add it to all their other keepsakes of a golden age beyond recall.[8]

The central argument of this chapter is that there is more to be learned about the growth of the American academic profession, and more to be learned about this profession from its tale of growth, than those who wear weeds for the recent past suggest. As this tale is long, it is bound to be a causally complex one; a trend that perdures through a hundred years is most unlikely to be governed by a single variable. And the tale is likely to disclose growing pains as well as pleasures: the rapid growth of a profession, like a population boom in a society, can hardly have other than mixed effects. For those who seek to understand this phenomenon, the guiding slogan should not be "growing, growing, gone"—the refrain of inconsolable mourners—but a paraphrase of the warning in Galatians—"as a profession grows, so shall it reap."

SUBSTANTIVE GROWTH

Around the turn of the century, American academics commenting on their vocation were apt to dwell on the changes it had undergone within their lifetimes, for many within the span of their own careers. No changes struck them as more important than those that bore on the academizing of knowledge, and of these none received more attention than the enlargement of the academic curriculum, the expansion of the faculties' gnostic range.[9] From the perspective of 1900, the curricular history of the American professoriat in the nineteenth century had been constituted in two installments—a long, relatively inert "before" and a short, remarkably energetic "after," with the demarcation line roughly drawn by the outbreak of the Civil War. On the one side of that line, stretching back to the colonial period, stood the "old-time" or "antebellum" college, bastion of the traditional course of study, surrounded by the rubble of occasional but mostly futile challenges. Designed to raise up Christian gentlemen for the learned professions and public service, it was presumed to have provided a small set of stipulated courses centered on the classical languages and mathematics, with a sprinkling of natural science and a topping of moral philosophy—courses that, however, flavorless to the young, were deemed nutritious to their minds and souls. On the other side of that line, rising rapidly after Appomattox, stood the omniscient multipurpose universities, answering the call for a qualified and credentialed manpower from a host of white-collar occupations; the land-grant colleges, created by federal largesse to advance the neglected fields of agriculture and engineering; the remodeled liberal arts colleges, which rejected the old hegemony of the classics in favor of a more varied bill of fare. In the prewar setting, faculty members had been homogeneous: they had literally spoken the same languages (they had been universally proficient in Greek and Latin) and had figuratively spoken the same language (they had shared a common fund of knowledge imparted in a common didactic cause). In the postwar setting, faculty members tended to dissolve the old lingua franca into the vernaculars of specialty, and the old commonality of purpose into divergent and sometimes clashing aims. Whether the change was for good or ill was vigorously debated in fin de siècle journals. For some, it brought a new freedom, a new vitality, a new social relevance to the academy; for others, it represented the debasement of academic standards, the enthronement of vocationalism, the creation of intellectual chaos in the name of educational reform.[10] But few doubted that the academic profession in this country had been suddenly and irrevocably transformed by the diversification of its stock-in-trade.[11]

In some respects, as recent scholarship has shown, this view from the bridge of the late nineteenth century was a too foreshortened one.[12] When antebellum colleges at different stages of maturation are differentiated, and when their curricular decisions are arranged in patterns rather than treated as discrete events, it becomes clear that an appetite for substantive innovation was never missing from the American academic enterprise, even when it paraded under stand-pat flags.

By 1860 most of the nine oldest colleges in the country (those of the colonial or first generation)[13] had deviated considerably from their early-nineteenth-century curriculum, and some—notably Harvard, Yale, Columbia, and Pennsylvania—had acquired national reputations for their range of offerings. Of the thirty-six middle-aged colleges (those of the new nation or second generation, founded between 1789 and 1830),[14] a good many had added some new subjects to their original course of study, and a few—notably Union, Virginia, Amherst, and Vermont—had acquired regional fame for their diversity. Only the 136 youngest colleges (those of the Jacksonian or third generation, founded after 1830 and too readily cited by historians as *the* antebellum colleges) had failed as a group to compile a significant record of diversification. But some of these infants and adolescents in 1860 had a future of curriculum expansion before them which would make them the equal of their elders but which could not be credited to their antebellum accounts.

Most of the new subjects admitted to antebellum curricula were outgrowths of more inclusive subjects that had established their academic worthiness, had absorbed an abundance of new material, and had grown too plethoric to stay intact.[15] The workings of this process— it may be called the process of *subject parturition*—are best illustrated by the emergence of new academic sciences. The Copernican and Newtonian revolutions opened the colonial colleges to surges of fresh discoveries that flowed into two waiting vessels—natural philosophy and natural history. During the antebellum period, although no paradigms of comparable scope and power took American colleges by storm, factual findings incompatible with reigning theories entered to dissolve the conceptual cement in the old containers, and the intake was of such a volume that it could not be held within their bounds. The first subject to break away was chemistry, which assumed an independent existence in many older colleges by 1820; by 1840 geology was a recognizably distinct subject in many places; by 1860 astronomy, physics, and biology were beginning to exist on their own.[16] In the region of the curriculum that would later be called the social sciences, the parturitive process was at work as well, but was slower and had less clearly defined results. Here the matrix subject was moral philosophy;[17] the subjects swelling in embryo were political economy and political science; the incoming materials were the works of classical economists and the constitutional founding fathers. By 1860 political economy had emerged as a separate subject in several institutions, though it remained closely linked to its parent, and political science was just about to gain a separate lease on life.[18]

In addition curricular diversity was attained in the antebellum period through what may be called the process of *program affiliation*. In 1860 four-fifths of all academic institutions that awarded the bachelor's degree provided a liberal arts training and nothing else. But the other side of this statistic is that as many as one-fifth provided that and something more—a program designed to train novitiates for the learned professions of medicine, law, or divinity (a few "college-plus" institutions served the needs of all three). Thus there existed, along with the storied old-time college, a less memoralized old-time university, not in the English sense of that term (a cluster of colleges without professional appendages), nor in the German sense (a group of professional faculties empowered to award advanced degrees), but in the Scottish sense (a loose association of one or more professional schools with a college of general learning, each authorized to confer its own, usually first-level, degree). Aside from adding many new subjects in their own right, the professional schools served for a time as the seedbeds for new college subjects: thus chemistry owed its precocious entry into the college lineup to the prominent place it had achieved in the academic training of physicians.[19]

Finally, some subjects gained admission to the college course not by descending from a respected ancestor, but by overcoming an initially ignoble reputation. The slow-footed entry of modern languages provides a case in point. Originally the guardians of the college curriculum held that the only good academic language was a dead one; in the first half of the eighteenth century, they retreated from this linguistic necrophilia to the point of admitting English as the medium of instruction and as the fountain of belles lettres; in the later eighteenth century they went so far as to let in French, usually as a social accomplishment that could be acquired from a native speaker in after-hours for a special fee. Not until 1819 when Harvard appointed George Ticknor, a member of the avant-garde that trekked to Germany for advanced instruction, to the first American professorship in modern languages did word go out from a venerable college that teaching students how to read and speak a live foreign language was not tantamount to teaching them how to dance. Not until 1826 when Bowdoin College offered the young poet, Henry Wadsworth Longfellow, a similar post on the condition that he follow in Ticknor's footsteps, did a younger college concede that a polyglot curriculum could be a respectable one. Thereafter, one or more of the Romance and Teutonic languages would enter the college course lists with growing frequency, though not without antecedent argument and sometimes after blackballing efforts failed.[20] Another example of the operation of this process—let us call it the process of subject *dignification*—is afforded by the belated entry of technology. Long regarded as too practical and plebeian to belong in an academic program, the applied sciences and engineering were at last admitted in the late 1840s into the general course by a few state universities and into cognate schools set up by a handful of private colleges.[21] Generally, to get past the keepers of the college curriculum in this period, a subject that lacked an established pedigree had to have an esteemed first patron, an unusually well-prepared practitioner, or a segregated niche. But the fact to be emphasized is that it did get in, however slow the process of legitimation.

All in all, the historical record rebuts the view that two entirely distinct professions occupied the nineteenth century, the one replacing the other when the quest for new knowledge became the norm.

Yet the fin de siècle sense that major changes had lately occurred was not illusionary. Diversification did not begin in the Gilded Age; the bipartite vision needs corrective lenses. But diversification after the war did differ from antebellum diversification in several significant respects.

First, the academizing of new subjects speeded up dramatically, particularly after 1880. The acceleration of the parturitive process was especially marked in the once slow-moving social sciences: thus, while it had taken political economy all of eighty years to begin to emerge from moral philosophy, it now took economics (an old subject renamed and somewhat redefined) no more than a decade to give birth to a new subject called sociology.[22] In the natural sciences the gestation period grew noticeably shorter: thus biology, the still youthful spawn of natural history, delivered genetics and microbiology, and coalesced with border sciences to produce biochemistry and biophysics—all within the space of about a dozen years.[23] The other processes quickened too, and in so doing vastly increased their scope. Previously, program affiliation had been strictly confined to the learned professions. In the later period it extended its reach to embrace the latter's retinues and spinoffs—pharmacy, nursing, dentistry, veterinary medicine—and a variety of self-defined new professions—education, journalism, engineering in many subfields, social work, accountancy, and finance.[24] Subject dignification, which in the slowness of time had worked to elevate only several parvenus, now appeared to run amok. Not only were the techniques of pursuits aspiring to be professions readily granted the benefit of any doubt, but the knacks of the kitchen, the athletic field, the military parade-ground, the concert hall, the art studio, and the business office—competences once too lowly to be noticed—were raised to the stature of full-fledged academic fields.[25] Finally, as the subject of history blossomed forth from weak beginnings, a new diversifying process was set in motion. History had always been taught to collegians in America, consistently as a supplement to the classics ("Greek and Roman Antiquities"), occasionally as a supplement to theology ("Ecclesiastical History"). But except for the aborted efforts of Enlightenment planners and a short "false dawn" at antebellum Harvard, very little had been done to promote the temporal study of humankind when the time period came after the fall of Rome and the humans were neither biblical nor sacerdotal.[26] It was not until the eighth decade of the century that history was given leave to extend to modern Western societies (including the American) and some Eastern ones as well, and the process of *subject dispersion*—the spread of an academic subject beyond the era and locale in which it had initially gained acceptance—was allowed to operate at full force. By the end of the century, history (along with other dispersive subjects such as anthropology) had taken over so many times and territories that a person could sign up at an American university and practically see the world.[27] No doubt, even by the end of the century, there were keepers of particular curriculums who still held rather stiff-necked opinions about which subjects were academic and which were not. But within the system as a whole, hardly anything the intellectual world called knowledge and not very much of what the workaday world called skill was considered categorically beyond the pale.

The second distinctive feature of the new diversity was its institutional pervasiveness. During the postwar period, the once quite strong association between institutional age and curricular diversity fell apart. True enough, most of the first-generation private colleges grew into complex universities and thus continued to conform to the rule that venerableness and innovativeness went together. But most third-generation state universities did the same, and many second-generation private colleges, though outdistanced in the race to diversify, strove energetically to keep up. Especially out of step with the rule that age defies tradition and that youth must perforce succumb to it were the members of the fourth generation—the institutions, private and public, founded between 1865 and 1900. Within this teeming generation (it contained more than half of all academic institutions in existence at the end of the century) was a multitude of small denominational colleges that out of choice or necessity set a very Spartan table.[28] But the ranks of these newborns also included some of the most diversified institutions of the country: a dozen or so private universities breathed into life by tycoon wealth and immediately invested with infant vigor;[29] the half-dozen most ambitious women's colleges that sought to match the all-male colleges field for field if not course for course;[30] the sixty-five land-grant colleges that were either grafted onto state universities well provided with the arts and sciences or else allowed with "A & M" (agricultural and mechanical) independence to tack on technical courses to their initial classical line.[31] Needless to say, no single institution embraced everything that some institutions somewhere saw fit to teach. None could afford and few aspired to maintain a department-store curriculum, fully stocked. On the other hand, rarely would a subject be carried exclusively by institutions of a certain type. Curricular eclecticism, not curricular purity, was the order of the day. Thus in 1896, of the seventy-nine institutions giving instruction in electrical engineering, forty-six were institutes of technology or land-grant colleges, but the rest were a curious mélange that included Iowa Wesleyan, Catholic, Tufts, Washington, Princeton, and Yale. Military science was taught by all land-grant colleges, where it was legally required, and also by Baylor, Georgetown, Brown, and Yale, where it was not; domestic science was offered by state universities known for their "low" utilitarianism, and also by Clark and Chicago, reputed to seek the most exalted knowledge the fortunes of their founders could buy.[32] Diversification in its early phase, touching certain parts of the curriculum in certain institutional generations, may be said to have acted on the academic system; diversification in its later phase, vast in its curricular reach, affecting institutions in every cohort, sparing only the sectarian Lilliputs and a few New England holdouts, may be said to have defined it.

The new diversity stood for not only a faster influx of new subjects, but a warmer welcome to them after they arrived. The old-time college had had a refined capacity to grant visas to gnostic immigrants but not to accord them full citizen rights. One of the main reasons for its grudging hospitality had been its structural inflexibility. Since the shelf-space of its curriculum had been heavily stocked with prescribed goods and could not readily be expanded, a new arrival would inescapably pose a threat to the *Lebensraum* of existing subjects and would have to overcome their resistance before it could secure an equal niche. Ordinarily a well-born subject, for instance, a descendant science, fared well in these postadmission struggles. But a baser subject, such as engineering or a modern language, had often confronted an apparatus of invidiousness—inconvenient course hours, discounted degree credits, low faculty status—that kept it in an inferior place.[33] By the end of the nineteenth century, the habit of treating new subjects as in but not fully of the institution—we may call this *marginal diversification*—had grown appreciably weaker. It had not wholly disappeared. The slogan "all knowledge is created equal," though it gained some subscribers, did not secure so wide a hold that no mathematician would ever look down his nose at a statistician, no humanist would ever speak disparagingly of a social scientist, no theoretical physicist or biologist would ever sneer at colleagues engaged in designing machines or improving cows. But the structural supports for marginal diversification—the unyielding time frame, the mass of required courses, the paraphernalia of discrimination—did give way sufficiently to strip academic snobbery of its old organizational effectiveness. Solutions to curricular overcrowding were provided by the introduction of postgraduate training, which broke through the four-year ceiling of academic study, and by the gradual surrender of the colleges to the elective system—a dietary regimen that presented undergraduates with a wide display of course and gave them permission, broad if not unlimited, to order them à la carte.[34] One measure of the new equality instinct in the new diversity was the mounting percentage of bachelors' and first professional degrees awarded in fields that had not heretofore produced them. Between 1906 and 1910, only a quarter of those degrees (they constituted fully 95 percent of all degrees) were awarded in the humanities and arts, once the predominant yielders of degrees: the rest were awarded in the natural and social sciences, health, law, business, home economics, agriculture, and engineering.[35] If further proof were needed that the old prides and prejudices had retreated, it could be found in the bulk and format of the new academic catalogs. In these annual announcements of ever more sumptuous impending feasts, courses came to be listed numerically under departments listed alphabetically, as though to imply that all were of standard value, and none was the specialty of the house.

Seeking to explain the changes they were witnessing, a number of fin de siècle commentators fastened on the explosion of human knowledge as the master key. "As knowledge has grown," wrote Charles W. Thwing, a college president turned historian, "the course itself has grown. Every enlargement of the domain of knowledge has ultimately resulted in the enlargement of the academic field."[36] To William T. Foster, the author of a major study of the curriculum, the history of American colleges was the "record of institutions under conservative influences forced by the growth of human knowledge and the demands of an increasingly complex civilization to take up one subject after another."[37] Passed down from that era to our own, the "quantum-of-knowledge" explanation retains a strong empirical and logical appeal. By every telling indicator—the number of scholarly journals founded, the number of scientific papers published, the number of patents issued—the quantity of knowledge in existence grew by leaps and bounds after the Civil War.[38] This explanation makes sense not only as a tautology (knowledge that does not exist obviously cannot be academized) but also as a statement of probability (more knowledge is likely to be academized as more of it comes to exist). Nevertheless, it does not succeed as an explanatory passe-partout. The suggestion that the curriculum waited about, Micawber-like, for a windfall of a new knowledge to turn up is contradicted by the many instances in which a course of study was established on a small or precarious knowledge base. The land-grant colleges, for example, were created at a time when the horticultural sciences were at a stand-still, lying in the doldrums between the heralded but disappointing chemical researches of the 1840s and 1850s and the great genetic and biological breakthroughs of the 1880s and 1890s.[39] Not all processes of diversification took their impetus from fresh discoveries. It is clear that subject parturition did thrive on infusions of new knowledge (undoubtedly the works of Darwin and Spencer sped the emergence of academic social sciences), but it is doubtful that program affiliation always required that kind of nourishment (more than one of the new professions were living on a meager or borrowed substance when they first found academic homes), and it would appear that subject dignification fed much more on familiar skills and artistries than on scholarly advances or new scientific truths. Nor can it be said that a field of knowledge had merely to exist in order to be taken in. Courses in military science did not arrive when they did because the art of war had suddenly been invented; courses in music were not delayed because there had been nothing to listen to before Brahms and Wag-ner; courses in commerce did not increase from none to plenty because Americans after centuries of ignorance finally learned how to trade. The relationship between knowledge and the academy in the Gilded Age was not one of abundant giving and supine taking; it involved, rather, a heightened offering on the one side, and an altered policy of accepting and rejecting on the other. After giving the growth of knowledge its full due, one must still ask: Why did the academy in this period (and thereafter) reject so little and accept so much?[40]

Of the explanations for the new diversity which speak of the acad-emy in the active voice, one has gained the widest currency. It stresses the changes that came over the professoriat in this period, changes that made it more receptive to knowledge in sundry forms. Three changes are commonly cited as contributing to pansophist goals.

The secularization of faculty training. Traditionally, American faculty members had been largely trained in religious institutions. Even as late as 1870, an estimated one-quarter of all full-time faculty members in a sample of first- and second-generation colleges held bachelor of divinity degrees and were ordained or licensed, if not practicing, clergymen.[41] Of the lay remainder, impressionistic evidence suggests that a large percentage had pursued some theological study before settling on an academic career.[42] Moreover, with the exception of a small band of foreign scholars, nearly everyone teaching in an Amer-ican college, whether or not he wore the collar or had gone to a medical school to learn a science or to a law school to try that profession out, was a graduate of an American college—an institution that had served for centuries as the preparation ground, if not as the finishing school, for the nation's Protestant ministers. But by the end of the nineteenth century, the bulk of new academic appointees was being drawn from secular institutions. They came from European, mostly German, universities to which an army of Americans numbering in the thousands repaired, most of them (after 1870) for advanced instruction in non-theological subjects;[43] from American graduate schools, which had begun to take over from foreign universities the task of supplying the arts and sciences with trained recruits holding the increasingly requisite Ph.D. degrees;[44] from American professional schools, which were turning out teachers as well as practitioners for their expanding vocations; and, behind this, from American colleges which, though they still clung to compulsory chapel and in loco parentis rules, were cutting their remaining ties to their religious past. Meanwhile, the academic presidency, for ages a benefice of the clergy,[45] was falling into the hands of laymen, a trend that set in when Harvard unfrocked that office in 1869 and that reached a noted climax when Princeton followed suit in 1902.

The institutionalization of academic research. From the founding of the first colleges, the overriding duty of American professors had been to teach. On this score there had been no distinction between one professor and another, one type of institution and another. As late as 1869, Charles W. Eliot, on assuming the Harvard presidency, had asserted that "the prime business of American professors . . . must be regular and assiduous class teaching"; no one would have disagreed with this assertion. But thirty years later the same authority, on the eve of his retirement, was moved to declare that the appointment and promotion of professors at his institution depended as much on their "success as investigators" as on their teaching prowess.[46] Reflected in this altered expectation was the arrival in the interim of the American research university, first heralded by the founding of the Johns Hopkins University in 1876, and then confirmed by a file of ambitious imitators of which Harvard was one. By 1910 it was generally agreed that the two dozen private and public universities that composed the membership of the Association of American Universities (AAU) were the leading exemplars of this type. Outrivaling every other social agency as a patron of intellectual innovation, the research university took custody of the technical apparatus of modern science, the questing spirit of German scholarship, and the pick of the nation's scientists and scholars. Though hardly the typical American institution of higher learning, it quickly became the nation's cynosure institution of higher learning, and it served through the

magnetism of its presence to enlarge professorial ambitions and re-
define institutional success. For the academic practitioner to be called
to such a place was to be included among the chosen; for the academic
donor or president to establish or captain such a place was to perform
a crowning creative act.[47]

The organization of academic specialties. Between 1870 and 1900 nearly
every subject in the academic curriculum was fitted out with a new
or refurbished external organization—a learned or disciplinary association, national in membership and specialized in scope—and with
a new or modified internal organization—a department of instruction
made the building block of most academic administrations. These
were more than formal rearrangements of the campus workforce: they
testified to and tightened the hold of specialization in academic life.
The learned society provided, inter alia, a variety of vehicles for the
presentation, propagation, and criticism of research; awards, in the
forms of prizes and elective offices, to high achievers acknowledged
to be such by their peers; an informal employment agency for the
matching of job givers and job seekers in an increasingly impersonal
talent market; a community of cooperating competitors in special
fields that was sometimes torn by ideological conflicts but was imbued
with a strong consciousness of kind.[48] The intramural department
helped turn faculty members knowledgeable in a subject into resident
agents for far-flung disciplines; it became the means by which control
over academic appointments, which had already shifted in many institutions from the governing board to the president,[49] would shift
again (especially in the major universities) to faculty members in their
disciplinary formations;[50] it gave organizational support to the belief
that an American academic served two masters—not just the faculties
of the University of Wisconsin or Chicago but also the disciplines of
chemistry or history—a duality of allegiance that marked the rise of
academic professionalism in its modern form.[51]

It seems reasonable to suppose that each of these interrelated
changes favored a broader rather than a narrower course of study. A
faculty molded by the secular concerns of a graduate school or a new
professional school was less likely to gravitate to the subjects of the
traditional curriculum than a faculty composed of clergymen and of
laymen schooled to a large extent like clergymen. A faculty charged
with producing knowledge was more likely to be a venturesome consumer of it, to cycle back its own findings into the course of study,
to regard an old textbook as an outmoded one, than a faculty not
inducted into the research role. A corps of gnostic sponsors quick to
spot and plead the case for a new subspecialty was more likely to

arise within a faculty divided into departments of instruction than a faculty organized as a committee of the whole.[52]

But these likelihoods do not add up to the conclusion that changes in the character of academic personnel were responsible for the diversification of the postwar course of study. For one thing, the timings of these events did not precisely correspond. In most cases it took longer to remake a faculty than to remake a curriculum. Because the academic employment cycle was so long (the combination of tenure and an unspecified retirement age made thirty-, forty-, and even fifty-year incumbencies not unusual), and because the time that elapsed between training and practice in a rapidly changing profession could create large cultural lags (a senior professor in 1900 might well have received his formative education in a pietistic college in the 1870s), a significant residue of old-style faculties often attended the promulgation of new-style programs. Only a newborn institution had the congenital opportunity to assemble a faculty of *novi homines* at the outset. Even then it was an open question as to whether the faculty had been recruited to initiate a diverse curriculum or to implement one that had been ordained. For another thing, changes in the mindset of the faculties did not have as broad an incidence as changes in the range of offerings. The research university, though it had broad ripple effects, did not transform a teaching profession into a research profession overnight. Even a research university imposed heavy teaching duties on its faculty (though it might relieve its professors of some of the routine burdens of undergraduate instruction by employing graduate assistants). Even such an institution did not commit a vast amount of money to research (in that day science was at the Edison and not the Brookhaven scale of costs and could be sustained by small capital outlays and regular instructional funds). A fortiori, over the vast expanses of academe, there were countless diversifying institutions in which much less was done for research and in which the pure and simple pedagogue, if no longer regarded as exemplary, might still enjoy the status of the unexceptional. At most, changes in the training, role-set and organization of American faculties in this period reinforced a curricular trend that had its own momentum. These changes could not have been the necessary conditions for a modest amount of diversification, for this had been achieved before their influence had been fully felt. And these changes could not have been the sufficient conditions for pell-mell diversification, since they affected other Western professoriats without producing anything like the same result.

The assumption that changes in character of academic knowledge were caused by changes in the character of the men of knowledge also suffers from its failure to account for the circularity of causes and effects. If it can justly be said that secularization, research, and specialization gave impetus to curricular innovation, it can also be said— and with equal justice—that curricular innovation gave impetus to secularization, research, and specialization. That the causal arrow can be pointed the other way becomes clear when one examines the antecedents of any of these supposedly shaping forces. Take secularization, for example: child of the Protestant Reformation and its repeated aftershocks, the old-time college was by birth and declared intention a religious institution. Typically, it sought to provide an ambience of devoutness and sobriety, a welcome to quickenings of the religious spirit, a grounding in the fundamentals of religious learning that would not only equip the consecrated student for further study but would hold open for the undecided the option of a ministerial career.[53] It made a sedulous effort to reconcile science and religion, usually through the medium of natural theology, an irenic system that sought to vindicate Christianity by appealing directly to nature, and to pursue the study of nature by drawing from it proofs of God's design.[54]

Nevertheless, as recent studies emphasize, the typical old-time college was not institutionally religious in the furthest sense of that accordion word. It was not a theological seminary; it was not a tightly sealed claustral community; it was not a clerical corporation that barred the laity from key positions. Seldom did it impose articles of religious faith on its faculty (it never put its students to religious tests); only rarely was it directly governed by the ecclesiastic leaders of its founding sect or church.[55] Significantly, the more it diversified its curriculum, the further it tended to depart from a ne plus ultra religiosity. By and large, the colleges that absorbed the new sciences and that annexed schools of medicine and law were the ones that saw the percentage of pulpit-bound graduates decline and the percentage of nonclerical trustees and professors rise most sharply.[56] Ranked by five indicators of institutional religiousness—preseminarianism, reclusiveness, clericality, ecclesiasticism, and sectarianism—the most diversified colleges in 1860 (these were mainly the colleges of the first two generations) would fall significantly below any other institutions with which they might reasonably be compared. On most counts they were less religious than the third-generation colleges in 1860; on two counts (extent of clerical penetration and degree of student sequestration), they were less religious than they themselves had been in 1800; on three counts (percentage of students preparing for holy orders, percentage of faculty in cleric ranks, the use of doctrinal adherences as conditions of admission or appointment), they were less religious than Oxford or Cambridge, their contemporary beaux ideals. This is not to suggest that diversification was an original force, an uncaused cause. Had their religiousness been more otherworldly, the Harvards and Columbias, Amhersts and Vermonts, would not have sought out so many secular subjects. But the point is that, once they did reach out, they became worldlier still, and in far-reaching ways.

The second moral to be drawn from a review of antecedents is that the characteriological changes that occurred among American academics after the Civil War were gradual evolutions, not mutations. To the extent that the "changed personnel" hypothesis implies the contrary, it warps our understanding of the history of this profession. Like the growth of secularism, the rise of a research ethos had a long, facilitating prehistory. Only an uninformed bipartist would contend that research was never done by faculty members in the antebellum period, that no professor ever conducted a scientific experiment or led a geological expedition or collected flora and fauna or published his lectures in the form of books.[57] The facts are that scholarly and scientific publication had afforded an added source of income and an avenue to enhanced prestige to some academics in every era. What we perceive as postbellum novelties—the incorporation of research into the academic person's formal duties and the academic institution's explicit functions—were not spontaneously generated; they sprang from (and drew on) precurrent actions and motivations.

Similarly, academic specialization in the postwar period had important links to the past. It has been assumed by cultural historians that the antebellum climate of opinion was hostile to "narrow" experts and partial to the jack-of-all-trades.[58] This may be an accurate depiction of popular attitudes, but it is a misreading of academic attitudes, a further example of two-part conventionalism that historians would do well to discard. Generally speaking, academic leaders in the antebellum period, though committed to unspecialized student study, were not committed to unspecialized college teachers. For all their paeans to Renaissance man and Emerson's all-seeing scholar, they tended to suspect that breadth was not a substitute for mastery and that the know-it-all did not know enough. This attitude was exhibited in their tendency to narrow instructional assignments when they could. As early as 1767 the Harvard Corporation directed its tutors to stop teaching everything to one class of students as it marched from entry to graduation and to start teaching certain basic things to each wave of freshmen—to specialize, in short.[59] When they could, academic leaders strove to curtail the intellectual jurisdictions of their professors. Columbia's titular reductions during the antebellum period may be taken as a striking example of this tendency. Around the turn of the century, a Columbia professorship usually surveyed two vast dominions, for example, "Mathematics *and* Natural History." In one case, the professorship of "Natural History, Chemistry, Agriculture, *and* Other Arts Depending Thereon," a title conferred on Professor Samuel L. Mitchell in 1792, the conjunction *and* seemed to convey the infinite reach of the words *et cetera*. From that time on, however, Columbia proceeded to shrink such holdings. It first did so by refusing to let the most spacious claims be passed on to new appointees. Thus in 1802, when Mitchell retired from his position, the vast entitlements that went with it were retired also, and his successor had to rest content with a smaller area called "Chemistry and Experimental Philosophy." What was not done by partible inheritance was accomplished by divestiture, subdivision, and repossession. By 1830 the professor of moral philosophy had relinquished his stake in "Rhetoric" and "Belles Lettres"; by 1850 the multilingual empire of the "Modern Languages" had been broken up into the professorial duchies of "French," "German," "Spanish," and "Italian"; by 1860 the hallowed coupling of "Greek and Latin" had given way to two separate professorships, and a group of bounded estates— "Surgery" and "Midwifery" and "Obstetrics"—had been added when the runaway school of medicine returned.[60] To be sure, specialization in this era was not exactly the same as specialization in the next. Antebellum Columbia did not go in for overlapping jurisdictions: rather than intensive, its way of specializing was extensive—more subjects per faculty but one person per subject. Antebellum Columbia did not insist that a professor end up in the subject to which he had been initially appointed or for which he had been formally trained: its way of specializing had been cross-sectional rather than longitudinal. But these less developed ways of honoring expertise were more the products of size and the training system than the consequences of belief. It is a current axiom of social theory that the division of labor tends to become more refined as the tasks of that labor grow more complex, and it is a commonplace of current social observation that claims to omniscience tend to become less credible the further they are stretched. Postbellum academics were not the first of their tribe to obey these precepts; their forerunners did so also, but in a manner dictated by their means.

No explanation for the new diversity can be complete unless it takes account of an economic factor—the driving force of institutional competition under peculiarly American conditions. The potency of this force was often recognized by those who took part in curricular debates throughout the nineteenth century. And even when the participants preferred to argue about what knowledge is of most worth and what kind of education would be ideal, an awareness of the compulsions of economic competition lay just below the surface of their expressed concerns.[61]

Before the American Revolution, the so-called private college was a publicly assisted, publicly protected, sometimes publicly supervised institution.[62] With but one exception, no colonial colony permitted more than a single college to rise up within its borders; with local variations, each college formed a close (if not frictionless) alliance with the state to protect its territorial monopoly and (where the politics of religion permitted) to insure a flow of public subsidies. After independence this quasi-mercantilist system gave way to an open-market system, intensely competitive and all too open. The easing of college incorporation laws, the evangelical zeal for college-building, the college-wooing schemes of land speculators and town developers, the constitutional immunization of private colleges from state encroachments, all conspired to flood the country with wave after wave of new college enterprises. Although some of these new enterprises answered the unfilled needs of newly settled territories, many intruded on the overserved backyards of established institutions. Although student enrollments grew faster than the general population, they remained a tiny fraction of persons eligible by sex and age to attend a college, and their growth did not keep pace with the growth of the institutional population.[63]

Notably missing from the antebellum scene were the regulatory and rationalizing functions performed by state ministries of education, parliamentary committees, and royal commissions in other countries. Here, the federal government, which allotted public lands to the states to promote higher education but set no further conditions on their use, and the several states, which phased out their subventions to private colleges and kept their own universities on pauper rations, were not major supervisory or directive forces. Missing, too, were native counterparts of Oxford and Cambridge, ancient bodies of exceptional wealth with privileged ties to a ruling class. In this country there were a few trend-setting colleges, but none that possessed the political strength needed to impose a modicum of order, or the social luster needed to block pretenders and corner elites. Were it not for the fact that colleges in America sold their services to local and denominational constituencies rather than to random customers, and that social good, not profit, was the object of the sale, the academic economy in the early nineteenth century would have had all the earmarks of laissez-faire capitalism in the heyday of its ascendancy: a multitude of small self-directed firms vying for a limited and uncertain patronage; a market of easy access from which there could be, and often were, painful exits; a governmental unobtrusiveness that almost reached Manchesterian extremes.

This was not the kind of economic environment that encouraged curricular inertia. This point can be stated more emphatically: in this kind of economic environment diversification was a competitive necessity. A college wedded to a fixed curriculum would pass up the chance to improve enrollments by catering to heretofore neglected publics. A college that refused to match the added attractiveness of a rival would be in danger of losing ground by standing still. Indeed, so intense and endemic was the pressure to diversify in such a system that one may wonder, not why certain colleges did not practice the traditionalism they liked to preach, but why the spirit of innovating daring, one of the putative glories of free enterprise, did not burn more brightly among them all.

But they did have a rational ground for cautiousness. Adding a new subject to a curriculum meant adding a new person to a faculty, when its current members were unequipped or unwilling to teach that subject. Unless it could be achieved through faculty versatility, diversification entailed faculty expansion, and that was bound to give pause to these small (usually tiny), poor (often shoestring) academic firms. For colleges on austere budgets, the assumption of a relatively large and sustained salary expense in anticipation of a future payoff could never be undertaken lightly; indeed, it was not likely to be undertaken at all, unless a way could be found to hedge against a faulty market guess. And as it happened, hedging in the antebellum period became an increasingly difficult and constricted art.

One possible way to hedge would have been to shift the entrepreneurial risk of growth from the institution to its employees by requiring faculty members to earn all or most of their incomes from student fees. Fee compensation had long been practiced in the *Privatdozent* system in Europe, and it was entrenched in the academic professional schools in America, where it conformed to the norms of private practice.[64] But in this country it ran into growing resistance from college faculty members, who preferred the certainty of a fixed salary to the chancy returns from a student head tax, and the dignity of indirect payment to the status threat implicit in the direct purchase of their teaching skills.[65] By the end of the period, the fee system had practically disappeared from these central haunts, and had largely retreated from the undergraduate peripheries.[66] Ultimately a uniform system of salary payment would contribute to faculty expansion by removing one of its main impediments—the teacher loath to share his platform lest by doing so he be required to share his student commissions too. In the short run, however, the decline of the system of fee payment doubtless served as a deterrent to faculty expansion, engendering fiscal anxieties in institutions with very small margins for mistakes.

A second possible way to hedge would have been to confine expansion to entry positions that offered the lowest possible rate of pay. But the trend of the times was highly unfavorable to this method of risk reduction. At the beginning of the nineteenth century, the faculties of the first-generation colleges were equally divided between tutors and professors; thirty years later the professors in these institutions outnumbered the tutors about seven to one; thereafter, in all institutional generations, the tutor became a progressively less conspicuous, if not quite vanishing, breed.[67] The traditional workhorse of college instruction, the tutor had typically been a recent college graduate who paused at the lectern of his alma mater before venturing forth to his chosen (usually clerical) career. Although some tutors had stayed on and a few had earned the affectionate regard of students, in most instances tutors had cut an undistinguished and unhonored figure, and their academic work life, if not utterly brutish, had been laborious and short.[68] By contrast, the professor, who was generally older, better educated, more likely to be appointed without limit of time and to spend all of his time in college teaching (increasingly at the same institution), had come to be seen as an indispensable anchor to a faculty seeking a larger measure of campus authority, public recognition, and scholarly repute. In the history of the American academic profession, the eclipse of the tutor by the professor was a development of epochal importance. As the collective biographies of a number of faculties are beginning to show,[69] it served, among other things, to erode the in-and-out pattern of employment that degraded academic teaching, to raise the average age of academics and thereby dispel their look of callowness, to convert an occupation filled with transients into one that offered, and in time demanded, commitments to lifelong careers. But it did not serve the institutional hedger's purpose. In the long run it probably encouraged faculty expansion by reducing the rate of turnover and by requiring institutions to diversify by addition rather than by substitution. But in the pre–Civil War period, it probably had the opposite effect. Before intermediate ranks were widely introduced, the professorial vogue threatened to create top-heavy faculties and thus to increase the salary costs of growth.

The safest way to gamble on a new appointment would have been to do so on donated funds. Unlike the others, this expedient did remain in fashion. Some institutions did acquire endowments large enough to support new faculty positions before they appointed anyone to occupy them. Generally, these were the institutions that had been able to look to mother England for benefactions, that had turned out large numbers of alumni whose loyalties could be converted into generosities, and that were located in areas of the country graced with a large supply of potential donors—in short, the first- and (to a lesser extent) the second-generation colleges. But this was hardly an expedient that could put all fiscal fears to rest. Even the favored older colleges found themselves chronically pinched for venture capital: in 1860 the largest endowment (Harvard's) came to no more than a million dollars, and that was several times larger than the cohort average. All too often, a solicited gift would have to be used to pay off debts or cover ordinary operational expenses, that is, to subsidize the past, not the future.[70] And for almoners who were able to raise no more than pittances (the great majority of antebellum colleges), this form of hedging was simply out of reach.

All institutions relied on one mode of risk reduction that was not emboldening: to pay for expansion out of student pockets and to pay-only-as-you-go. Time and again the antebellum colleges would hold back on a desired appointment until their current enrollments were large enough to generate a tuition surplus or until prospective enrollments were so clearly sighted that a quick return on borrowed money was assured. Following the signals of student numbers was widely seen as the most prudent course. But neither the curriculum nor the faculty was likely to grow at a rapid pace when growth depended so directly on gate receipts in hand or on tightly timed payback calculations.

In most of its essential features, the open market system remained intact throughout the latter part of the nineteenth century (and well beyond). The academic institution birthrate did not begin to subside until the 1890s. In time the public sector was enlarged and a stronger federal presence was established, but governmental authority did not attempt at any level to tame the anarchy of institutional competition. Academic enrollments began to rise, but the major upsurge in demand would not occur until the following century. Diversification remained an institutional imperative; institutions wishing to diversify continued to face financial risks. Nevertheless, in one significant respect the academic economy did change its character during the latter half of the nineteenth century. Academic institutions found a way to assemble enormous work forces. In 1860 Harvard's teaching staff of forty-one was the largest in the United States. Within a thirty-year period starting in 1880, that number was substantially exceeded by middle-sized colleges, dramatically by the large universities. By 1910 the Johns Hopkins faculty had grown from 50 to 215; the Yale, Wisconsin, and Cornell faculties, starting with smaller rosters, ended up with 450, 520, and 750 members, respectively. In this period the unit size of faculties, heretofore limited to slow accretions, underwent a drastic change of scale.

Academic institutions did not throw caution to the winds at that time; rather, they finally discovered how to hedge their bets. To some extent, they were able to find safety in large numbers by creating subprofessorial ranks into which recruits could be inserted inexpensively. Between 1869 and 1908 the proportion of full professors in this country shrank from two-thirds to one-fifth, while the proportion of instructors and assistant professors rose from one-fifth to one-third. In research universities crowding of the lower ranks was even more pronounced: in 1908 three-quarters of the faculties of Harvard, Wisconsin, Yale, and California were instructors and assistant professors.[71] If the low-cost appointment was important, the prepaid appointment was essential in moderating the risks that attended growth. In this period vast amounts of money were injected into the capital reserves of academe. Lump-sum giving in the private sector attained new orders of magnitude: Ezra Cornell's gift of $500,000 in the 1860s equaled the total of all academic endowments at the opening of the nineteenth century; Johns Hopkins's bequest of $3,500,000 in the 1870s matched the endowment it had taken Harvard two and one-half centuries to amass; after another decade even these princely amounts would be overshadowed by the benefactions of a Rockefeller and a Leland Stanford.[72] Like the burgeoning of private donations, the rise in public appropriations signaled the desire of a country tuning up for industrial supremacy to enlarge and enrich a critical infrastructure. Not all the new money poured into academe went into financing faculty expansion. Some of it was expended on more complex administrations, on lusher campus homes and gardens, on more numerous student scholarships and fellowships, and on libraries and laboratories, once a minor and now a major cost of doing academic business. Nevertheless, a good part of the new money was used for expansionary purposes. It was hardly a coincidence that the eleven private AAU universities, which possessed fully 40 percent of the

$323,000,000 in total endowments piled up by 1910, were also the leading progenitors of new faculty positions in this period. To be sure, not all their intrepid growing was attributable to their growing rich. Some credit must also be given to the Napoleonic ethos of their presidents—the Daniel Coit Gilmans, Charles William Eliots, William Rainey Harpers—who seldom passed up an opportunity to annex a new field of learning or snag a distinguished scholar on the loose. But it may be said, apropos these notorious imperialists, that ethos without endowment would not have carried them very far.

One major consequence of large endowments and handsome appropriations was the lessened importance of student numbers as a regulator of faculty growth. It is true that, with but a few exceptions, all the AAU institutions did have very large student bodies. In 1910 the University of Chicago, with 6,681 students, had the largest academic enrollment in the country; the University of Minnesota came next, followed by the universities of Illinois, Michigan, Pennsylvania, Harvard, and Columbia. Several conclusions may be drawn from this conjunction of large student bodies and large teaching staffs. One is that immense enrollments and elite pretensions were not seen as incompatible in this period: the time had not yet come when an American university would gain more prestige from the selectivity than from the magnitude of its admissions. Another is that enrollments probably had to reach a certain critical mass before a university would massively enlarge its faculty. But, as the trend in student-faculty ratios suggests,[73] it would be wrong to infer from the double-size superiority of the AAU institutions that increases in enrollments preceded and authorized new hires. Among the private AAU universities, the number of students per faculty member dropped from 11.5 in 1880 to 7.8 in 1900, at which point it was far below the nation's average. This decline probably meant that these institutions were offering a much fuller panoply of subjects and a much larger faculty to teach them (largely though not entirely in their graduate divisions) than was warranted by the increased number of paying guests. In the next decade the number of students per faculty member rose slightly, to 8.5. Probably some concern for economies of scale, some desire to retreat from past extravagances, may be detected in this later upswing. But it is also reasonable to suppose that the earlier investment in diversity was beginning to pay off in enhanced enrollments—that the increased supply had stimulated an increased demand.

At the public AAU institutions, the trend in student-faculty ratios followed a somewhat different course. Relatively high in 1880 (12.1:1), it went even higher by 1890 (13.4:1). Conceivably, economy-minded legislators in western and midwestern states were inclined to translate a growing patronage, in part the consequence of a growing population, into heavier workloads for the faculty. But during the next two decades, the ratio declined to 12.9:1 in 1900 and to 10.7:1 in 1910. The most plausible explanation for this reversal is that, once the popularity of the leading universities in these states had been demonstrated and state pride in their reputations had been aroused, the public keepers of the purse became more willing to pay for the accoutrements that had given the major private universities their envied cachet, accoutrements that included a graduate school geared to teach small classes and a faculty hired to teach new things. Thus even in the public sector, where resource allocation could not wholly be divorced from student numbers, faculty growth and student growth were not precisely correlated.

We need a name for an increase in faculty numbers that stems much more from the absorption of new subject matter than from a growing clientele. For want of an existing term, I shall call it *substantive growth.* This kind of growth ought to be distinguished from that which proceeds primarily from a heightened demand for professional services: this I shall call *reactive growth.* To argue that the first type gained prominence in the postbellum period is not to suggest that the second type ceased to count. In this period the academic profession became more diversified because academic institutions became more capable of growth. But it did not grow solely because institutions became more diversified. The founding of new colleges and universities, the increase in the size of student bodies, the decline in student-teacher ratios—these also led to the swelling of faculty ranks. Still it may be said, without letting classification run away with truth, that professional and institutional growth became less dependent on student numbers and more dependent on novel contents in this period than they ever had been before.

REACTIVE GROWTH

And more than they would be thereafter. It takes no more than a glance at later American academic catalogs to perceive that diversification reached no stopping-point in the twentieth century. Just as one may ask where history and sociology, business and journalism, music and drawing were in the academic scheme of things a century and a quarter ago, so one may also ask where linguistics, high energy physics, and modern Arabic were seventy years ago, or computer science, space engineering, area studies, women's studies, Black studies, and urban studies thirty or fewer years ago. Nevertheless, a profound change in the dynamics of growth did take place in time. In the twentieth century substantive growth was overtaken and eventually submerged by growth of the reactive type.

Until late in the previous century, academic enrollments had been constrained by a variety of factors: the barring of women from most colleges and universities; the scant appeal of the dominant academic culture to non-Protestant, nonnative, and nonwhite Americans; an occupational structure that frequently made on-the-job training a rational alternative to extended formal schooling; the high ratio of tuition costs to disposable family income; the added expense to college students of being domiciled while they were being taught; the inadequacies of the primary and secondary school system. Even by 1880 these factors, though they had been eased, still worked to limit college-going to a tiny fraction (probably less than 3 percent) of the age-eligible population. In that year the American schooling system could be likened to a watercourse that was relatively unimpeded in its further reaches but filled with gaps and blockages in its early runs. At the point where a white male adequately primed for college sought admission to college-level studies it presented only a possible financial impediment. Before that point was reached, however, the course could be treacherous and disheartening. Most children embarking at the headwaters (the first grade of grammar school) did not get very far downstream before they left to get a job. Of those who stayed on to the next scheduled landfall (graduation from grammar school), not many had the means or desire to reembark, that is, to enter a secondary school, then likely to be a private academy that charged tuition. And not everyone who did go forward acquired the classical skills needed for college entrance examinations, although in some regions the college obligingly maintained a preparatory department to repair such lacks. Even by this late date the young in America crowded the banks, and, save for short early passages, mostly stayed clear of the river.

Between 1880 and 1930 important aids to navigation were installed in this school system's upper stretches. As compulsory school laws took effect, as the public high school replaced the private academy as the chief link between primary school and college, and as high school diplomas (or, in the Ivy League, passing scores on standard aptitude tests) were taken as adequate testimonials of ability to do college work, the passageways became better aligned and smoothed for heavier traffic.[74] That there would be heavier traffic was assured by the spread of coeducation (the female half of the population contributed more than a majority of high school graduates and would, by the end of this period, contribute 40 percent of all college students) and by the growth of diverse curriculums, which would give men and women alike a vocational reason to stay in school. By 1920 it could be argued, by 1930 it was beyond all argument, that of all schooling systems in the Western world, the American was the easiest to navigate.[75] Unlike most others, it did not fix the educational destiny of students at an early age through irreversible sorting procedures, did not assign them to middle schools that were either conduits to a university or cul-de-sacs, did not refuse any high school graduate a college berth someplace, if not in the place of his or her first choice. Thanks in large part to this ease of passage, the percentage of 18- to 21-year-olds in college rose from 4.8 in 1910 to 12.1 in 1930, and the total number of academic students rose from 335,000 to beyond a million.[76]

Still, even in 1930 a large majority of students did not stay the course. Especially marked was the amount of attrition in the middle channel: in that year fully two-thirds of all high school ninth-grade entrants failed to complete the twelfth grade. This dropout rate, low when pitted against the showing of teenagers in other countries, was high when measured against the possibilities of a particularly lenient system, and this was noted at the time. But it would have taken an indomitable optimist in 1930 to believe that a significant rise in the high school completion rate was imminent; indeed, it was generally thought to be impossible, given the prevailing distribution curves of diligence, ability, and desire. As it turned out, however, optimism would have made for better prophecy. During the 1930s, for the first time since it grew to mass proportions, the high school population gave signs it would become a perseverant one. But the end of that decade, more than half of all high school entrants were staying on to graduate; between 1930 and 1940 the ratio of high school graduates to all persons aged seventeen years rose from twenty to fifty-one— an astonishing ten-year jump.

At that time it was widely believed that high school students were not so much curing themselves of the habit of dropping out as taking refuge in the schoolhouse until the general economy improved and employers were more willing to take them in. But that supposition lost force when, during the prosperous next decade, the high school completion rate rose again—to 78 graduates out of every 100 starters, to 59 diploma-holders out of every 100 persons aged seventeen. It is plain that the rising barometers of persistence were not measuring an ephemeral preference but a basic change in social attitude, a new conviction that going through channels—at least through high school channels—was the thing to do. Critics could still protest that, of the factors responsible for this attitude, a suddenly aroused passion for learning counted less than the public's perception that better jobs were going to the longer schooled. Nevertheless, the new stay-in-school psychology, even if it did not reach yeshiva intensities, did reflect the revolutionary notion that a significant part of a human lifetime ought to be spent preparing for the rest of it in the presence of blackboards and amid the smell of chalk.[77]

How much of a lifetime should be thus spent? College enrollments rose during the depression years to an all-time high of 1,400,000. But this figure represented a retreat from the accustomed rate of growth and suggested that, after graduation, a great many high school students felt they had had enough. Was it to be regretted that a high school diploma was commonly regarded as a terminal degree? In the mid-1940s, a chorus of articulate voices began to argue that it was. Academic administrators, having seen their campuses denuded of students by war, urged that something be done to guarantee their presence in time of peace; sociologists, discovering blocks to upward mobility in a country that had outlived its frontier, looked to a more accessible college education as the key to more general advancement; educational economists, following a tradition that antedated Adam Smith but relying on new national accounting data, conceived of an increase in enrollments as a means of adding to "human capital" and as a stimulant to economic growth.[78] The point on which these advocates all agreed was that the primary cause of early quitting was not intellectual or motivational, but financial: Americans on middle and lower incomes simply could not afford to attend or stay in college. To accept this diagnosis was to know the remedy: let society, more generously than it ever had before, cover the cost of extensive voyaging.[79] After the war a major step was taken in this direction when Congress enacted the G.I. Bill of Rights for veterans, the largest academic scholarship program ever launched in the nation's history. At the same time many states began to expand their academic systems (in the northeast they built them up almost from scratch) so as to offer to larger numbers a cut-rate, tax-supported substitute for a private product that was going at an ever-rising price. The effect of these efforts to subsidize college costs was reflected on the tally sheets of campus registrars: by 1950 total academic enrollments had risen to 2,700,000, and almost a fifth of all Americans of college age were on the student rolls.

After this long history of facilitation, the 1950s would have witnessed a rise in enrollments even if nothing more were done to help them grow. But the 1950s did not coast on the momentum of past accomplishments. This was the decade in which the states planted two-year and four-year institutions at rational distances from one another to accommodate and regulate the student flow, in which graduate schools sprouted all across the land to provide a commensurate crop of teachers, in which the federal government began its first substantial funding of fellowships, dormitory construction, and research. Each move gave a boost to student numbers: the creation of a latticework of state colleges, by lowering tuition costs and offering room-and-board savings to commuters; the spread of graduate education, by lengthening student time in transit and thus increasing the number of souls en route; the federal programs of assistance, by easing the strain on institutional budgets with manna from an unwonted source.[80] (Looking back, one can see that this was the decade in which the old free-for-all market system finally gave up the ghost. For the first time, the birthing of new institutions became primarily a matter of public policy, the numbers of students and faculty in the public sector surpassed those in the private sector, and the central state became a force to be reckoned with, both as a rule-setter that made no exception for the academy and as a giver that insisted on compliance with the far-ranging conditions of its gifts.) At the end of this spirited decade, another record was set in an area where records were notoriously fleeting things: in 1960 academic enrollments stood at 3,200,000 and contained a quarter of all persons of college age.

Nevertheless, an alert observer might then have noted that the academic system was exhausting its own possibilities for further increase. High school attendance and graduation rates (roughly 90 and 70 percent, respectively) had begun to approach their possible or likely limits. The crossover rate—the percentage of high school graduates going on to college—had begun to stabilize (at approximately 50 percent) despite all efforts to convert personal into social costs (foregone earnings, a hidden personal cost, could not readily be passed on to society). Total enrollments in 1960 were only 20 percent higher than they had been a decade earlier—a sign that the tapwells were becoming less productive. All things being equal, these statistics predicted that the next decennium would show modest gains, and that in the not too distant future an end would finally be written to the epic American tale of enrollment growth.

The one flaw in that prediction was the assumption of ceteris paribus. Miraculously, an external source of invigoration—an unexpected upturn in the nation's birthrate, which had started in the early war years and had reached its peak at the end of the 1950s—entered to counteract the enervation of trends within. To some extent college enrollments had always relied on a growing population to sustain their buoyancy. But in the past, the rise in population had been heavily dependent on immigration, and it had taken time before even the beckoning Catholic colleges and the large municipal universities would receive the offspring of the foreign-born in numbers proportionate to their strength. What was different about population growth in this postwar period was that it came from natural increase, largely within a class that was acculturated to college, and that it supervened upon a huge, well-articulated school system, a society that regarded a higher education as everybody's birthright, and an economy that rewarded school persistence. Now acting on a succession of swollen birth cohorts, the high secondary school completion and crossover rates produced an astronomical number of enrollments by 1970: 6,600,000 undergraduate students, 900,000 graduate students, a 40 percent share of the population of relevant age. Capping a century of increase, this last enrollment spurt was seen by many as a portent of utopia, not as a temporary reprieve. Having seen the American system of higher education grow massive while others in the world were small, and become "mass" while others grew merely large, many observers could imagine, in the euphoria of autumnal growth, that it was on the verge of becoming universal.[81]

It is probably beyond the power of any recoverable data set to disclose just how many new faculty positions were created to meet the needs of this extraordinary student ingress, this most unpedestrian traffic. An academic post may have one aim set by its creator and a different aim fixed by its incumbent, or it may be designed from the beginning to straddle several goals. Nevertheless, the belief that the profession grew massively in this period in order to handle an overflow of subscribers and not to import new contents into curricula is, if not quantifiable, at least irresistible. In this period large spheres of faculty employment would have had no reason for being but for the pressure of enrollments. This was obviously true of state university branches set up in underserved areas to relieve the crowding of central campuses. Every faculty created de novo in Milwaukee, Portland, or Indianapolis for the purpose of replicating most of what was offered in Madison, Eugene, or Bloomington was a manifestation of reactive growth. And so too were the cadres of part-time teachers who were added to the university rosters in numbers frequently determined by a last-minute registration count. In this period a new didactic art form, welding the ancient technique of wholesale lecturing to the new technique of retail sectioning, was developed for batch instruction, and it created a market for a new kind of subaltern—the on-call, temporary section hand. Finally, in the burgeoning public sector, professional expansion was driven by enrollments even when its ostensible goal was substantive. During the postwar decades public academic institutions that had lagged behind the star universities of their states endeavored to catch up: teachers' colleges sought to be transmogrified into universities; lesser universities sought to acquire new specialities and research facilities; land-grant colleges sought to live down their "aggie" (agriculture) reputation by acquiring a fuller humanistic line. These efforts were reminiscent of those made at an earlier time, when diversification supplied the fuel for most faculty expansion. But there was a difference. Six and seven decades earlier, a state's premier university, serving a slowly rising student population, could be singled out for special favor without having to meet a rigid enrollment quota. Six and seven decades later, when many state institutions sought funds for upgrading and places had to be provided for the young in droves, rare would be the legislature, coordinating board, or state budget office that would not apply the politically popular and apparently Solomonic formula: so many dollars for improvement in return for so many students signed and sealed.

GROWTH AND CONSEQUENCES

Hypothetically, the faster a highly esteemed occupation grows, the less able it will be to fill its ranks with persons drawn from the privileged strata of society and the more closely it will come to reflect the social makeup of the general population. We have seen that the American academic profession grew much faster when it grew reactively than when it grew to absorb new subjects. To the extent that the foregoing hypothesis is true, a significant conclusion would follow: democratization was one of the consequences of the shift in this profession's mode of growth.

Up to a point this conclusion is confirmed by what is known about the changing social composition of the American professoriat over the last 100 years. In the heyday of substantive growth, the unity of this professoriat was fractured by its secular training and by its specialized commitments. But these were changes in the intellectual foreground; in the social and cultural background, very little change occurred. One reason was that a full traversal of the school system—a precondition of a faculty appointment—required fiscal and motivational resources that were unevenly distributed among ethnic groups and social classes. Another reason was that the most expansionary institutions were the patrician eastern universities (and the new universities patterned after them) where pride of caste and class commingled with a proclaimed concern for merit. Accordingly, prior to World War I, the academic profession took its membership from a relatively narrow band of society. A study of a thousand scientists in 1906 and 1910 revealed that they came mostly from Protestant professional merchant families and were overwhelmingly white and male.[82] As yet, the long history of the rejection of Jews and Catholics by faculty recruiters had not run its course. In 1904 the young Ludwig Lewisohn, a promising undergraduate majoring in English at Columbia, was advised by a member of his department not to seek a graduate degree in that subject, since as a Jew he was likely to be regarded by potential employers as too culturally alien—too *Wesenfremd*—to be offered an academic appointment. Lewisohn did not heed that advice, and it did turn out to be slightly overstated; he managed to land an instructorship in German (not English) at the University of Illinois.[83] But the bias it bespoke was real enough. Not until the 1940s would the Columbia English Department appoint a professor of Jewish origin, a "cultural alien" by the name of Lionel Trilling. True, Jews had been appointed earlier to the Columbia University Department of Economics. This *was* a career open to talents—provided the talents conformed to ancient stereotypes!

Professing in America remained socially and ethnically exclusive until it became a more common activity in the period following World War II. Studies of faculty social origins, especially those that draw on the massive survey of the Carnegie Commission on Higher Education initiated in 1969, show that significant changes did take place. Clearly, the profession had grown less biased with respect to class. Though the parents of newer members of the faculty were disproportionately drawn from higher educational, occupational, and income strata, the disparity between them and the parents of all workers had been significantly reduced.[84] The proportion of Jews in the profession, which had risen since the early 1920s, soared by the late 1960s to 12 percent of the whole profession and 20 percent of the contingent in higher-quality institutions. Catholics also made major gains, although they apparently remained, as Jews did not, less well represented in the entire profession and particularly in its elite component than they were in the population as a whole.[85] These studies did not conclude that all the disparities based on class and religious background had disappeared in the period of reactive growth. Academics from families of lower socioeconomic status tended to cluster in lower-status institutions; Jews did exceptionally well in the social sciences, biochemistry, law, and medicine, but relatively poorly in the humanities and history (they remained as rare among the earth scientists as they had been among the earth tillers in the Russian Pale).[86] Nevertheless, within a relatively short period, what had once been an Anglo-Protestant profession had become much more pluralistic. What had once been a bourgeois-genteel profession had significantly opened up. The explanation for this change has to go beyond the causal factors stressed by ethnic celebrators and modernization theorists. The vaunted Jewish love of learning does not explain the substantial Catholic accomplishment; the need for a meritocracy in an industrially advanced society does not account for the slowness with which the caste system was broken down. Although the quest for motives is always speculative, one may plausibly suppose that the lowering of opportunity costs and the ability to delay gainful employment had as much to do with the high persistence rates of Jewish students as did their tropism toward scholarly activities, and that the seller's market created by teacher shortages did more to wear away the older clannishness than the perceived dysfunction of ascriptive norms.

But the democratization hypothesis is not vindicated on every count. By 1970 the American academic profession, though it had ceased to be the property of one class and stock, had remained largely the property of one sex (it was roughly 80 percent male) and even more the property of one race (it was well over 90 percent white). To be sure, the numbers of women and blacks in academic positions had about doubled during the preceding decades of expansion. But their continuing underrepresentation, and especially their statistical deficits in the higher reaches, hardly testified to the power of a rising tide to float all ships. Even when jobs were plentiful and sometimes went a-begging, women remained far behind men in appointments to prestigious institutions, tenured positions, and high-rank departments (they remained heavily concentrated in nursing, social work, and education: the popular phrase "men of science" still had too much descriptive accuracy to be dismissed as a gender slur).[87] As for blacks, their numbers outside the predominantly black institutions remained so miniscule that they lent themselves more to anecdotal pointings than to census counts.[88] To what extent these lags can be attributed to a prejudiced profession rather than to an unfairer, unequal society is an issue, of interest to current analysts, which cannot engage us here. It need only be noted that gender and racial imbalances were not adequately corrected during the era of expansion, that they were, if anything, worsened by the principle of "last in, first out" which

guided the next period of retrenchment, and they were not significantly redressed by recourse to affirmative action, in part because the
force of law had to be pitted against the power of a grudging market
in what turned out to be an unequal contest. But the shadowy side
of the effulgent years of reactive growth is not without some glimmers
of hope for the future. A surge of incomers into an occupation in one
era ordains a surge of outgoers in a later era, the span being fixed by
the time it takes to complete the employment cycle.[89] Reactive growth
thus promises, as one of its delayed effects, a demographic windfall
in the form of massive retirements, and a second chance to revise the
occupation's social makeup. Although it is far from certain that group
disadvantages left standing in the initial thrust will be eliminated in
the distant aftermath, the hope of a partial rectification is held out by
the vast increase in the number of women (but, alas, not of blacks)
in the feeder pipelines of the graduate schools and by the recent
fanning out of women (and to some extent of blacks) into other heretofore closed professions.[90]

In a playful essay on the science of science, Derek Price makes the
point that nothing in nature or society expands exponentially forever.
Sooner or later, the number or the height or the size of things, after
growing at ever-greater rates for a while, enters a period of constraint
and approaches a stable ceiling. In statistical terms, the exponential
curve turns into a logistic one.[91] So it is with respect to fruit flies
multiplying in a bottle, and increases in the energy of particles released in an accelerator, and the improvement in the performance of
human artifacts, such as the speed of vehicles and the percentage
increases of the GNP. And so it would have had to be with respect
to faculty numbers: the expansion of the fifties and the sixties could
not have continued forever.

But it is not a fact of nature or society that every curve of growth
must reach its ultimate plateau and decline *abruptly*. Most cumulative
phenomena move slowly and more or less smoothly toward their
maximum, and thus leave time for those affected by them to adjust
to the changing slope. The last expansion of the profession, however,
did not subside in a gradual arc: rather, it decelerated sharply, like
the value of stocks in a panicked market or a speeding car braked to
avoid a crash. This brusque arrest could be attributed to the kind of
expansion it mostly was. Professional growth based on increments of
knowledge is hard to regulate from a central office: the unplanned
emergence of new subjects, the unpredictable turns of research, tend
to work against decisive cutoffs. On the other hand, one of the critical

facts about professional growth based on student numbers is its sus-
ceptibility to control by planning bodies. X number of students in the
channels can be seen as requiring Y number of openings in a faculty,
and by a ratio that can be precisely calculated, with numerator and
denominator measured to the nearest FTE (full-time equivalent). Naturally, a faculty that can be enlarged by such projections can also be
reduced by them. Even when the general skies were fair, a dip in one
year's freshman applications or even in one program's yearly regis-
trations at any particular institution had been able to produce the
minus signs that raised the issue of faculty redundancy. But only
when the overall picture darkened did the reductive potentials of this
arithmetic cease to be local and adventitious. Once the news was
carried from the Census Bureau to the schoolhouse that the baby
boom was over, that a host of contraceptive decisions made in a
multitude of private bedrooms in the 1960s would have adverse consequences for enrollments some years hence, the valves of faculty
employment began to be shut as tightly as once they had been opened
wide.

It is currently taken for granted that there *are* pivotal valves of
employment in this profession, and that officials not in the profession
are licensed to turn them on or off. But these mechanisms of control
and these controllers were not always in place in academia; they are
themselves among the consequences of reactive growth.

That no such mechanism of control attended the earlier way of
growing can be gathered from the following incident. In 1910 the
Carnegie Foundation for the Advancement of Teaching commissioned
Morris L. Cooke, a disciple of Frederick Winslow Taylor, the founder
of the school of scientific management, to study the modus operandi
of American colleges and universities and to recommend appropriate
reforms. Armed with the gospel of efficiency the Taylorites of that
period were promoting with religious zeal, Cooke visited Harvard,
Columbia, Toronto, Princeton, Wisconsin, the Massachusetts Institute
of Technology—some of the most rapidly growing institutions of that
period—and Williams and Haverford colleges, the less distended
school places of the well-to-do. Had he been a Puritan touring Roman
Catholic churches, the visitor could not have been more appalled by
the impieties he found. Everywhere he saw signs of sinful wasteful-
ness: a primitive system of accounting, a confusion of functions and
responsibilities, a tangle of customary procedures tied to no obvious
utility, an antiquated reliance on rule of thumb, the value of which
defied a clear rationale. In his report, which he titled, without em-

barrassment, "Academic and Industrial Efficiency," Cooke recommended a more orderly method of running universities: a strengthening of presidential authority in line with the managerial revolution then taking place in the realm of business; a functional division of labor that would relieve the faculty of administrative responsibilities for which it had no training and little skill; a hierarchic arrangement of authority that would put an end to "management by committee"—his name for departmental autonomy—and would replace government by the incapable—his opinion of a society of peers. Cooke's main recommendation was directed at the standard used to measure and evaluate academic work. He believed that faculty compensation should be geared to faculty production, and that faculty production should be determined by the number of hours spent by a teacher in the classroom multiplied by the number of occupied classroom seats.[92] What is striking about this episode today is not the philistinism of Cooke's approach (that no longer takes one by suprise) but the scornfulness of the academic response. One professorial conference called to consider Cooke's ideas concluded that a time measure of efficiency might be appropriately applied to the maintenance of buildings, but when applied to the teaching of Chaucer it was patently absurd. For awhile the Harvard faculty was requested to fill out time sheets; most refused to comply and the matter was quietly dropped.[93] If a commercial ethos did pervade these bastions of higher learning (as Thorstein Veblen went to the lengths of a book to argue),[94] it was not brought in by the cultists of scientific management, who could not gain a foothold either in the Ivy League establishments or in the public sector of academe.

It was not just professorial haughtiness that kept the Taylorites at bay. In 1910 American colleges and universities were so many tight little islands, each in many ways a law unto itself. Administratively, each was a discrete entity, with its own board of regents or trustees, its own president, its own capital funds and working budget. Legally, each was endowed by charter, constitutional rule, or statute with a vast amount of discretionary authority that extended to both the management of property and the treatment of personnel. Physically, each campus—compact, fenced in, usually sequestered—had the look of a foreign enclave, enjoying the privilege of extraterritoriality within the ambit of a larger civil state. Doubtless these institutions were more self-contained in appearance than in reality. With their commitment to growth, they were often in the position of trying to do more than they could immediately afford and of thus having to appeal, cap in hand, to legislators or donors. But their commitment to substantive growth spared them some of the loss of independence that goes with constant begging: in matters concerning academic knowledge, they were likely to impress the givers as being exceptionally in the know. Try as they might, the Taylorites of the period could not breach these enclosed and disconnected structures with their centralizing ideology of measured effort and hierarchical control.

In the course of time, and especially during the period of post–World War II expansion, American institutions of higher learning lost much of their discrete and insulated character. Some of this loss was caused by factors that had nothing to do with expansion. Once free to expand their boundaries as they saw fit within rural or small-town settings, many colleges and universities now found themselves engulfed by growing central cities and compelled to adjust their policies concerning land use to the intricacies of race relations and the vagaries of the politics of city hall. Once free to take in or thrust out students more or less at will, and to promote or discharge faculty members within the permissive terms of employment contracts, all colleges and universities now came under the constraints imposed by laws against discrimination, and the public ones had to abide by the free speech and due process requirements of the Fourteenth Amendment to the Constitution.[95] But nothing did more to "delocalize" academic authority than the drenching increase in student numbers.[96] In 1910 all but two states were content to let their major university, their land-grant college, their technical institutes, and their normal schools go their separate ways. By 1965 all but nine states brought these tax-supported institutions into coordinated or integrated statewide systems, headed by extramural central boards. Whether superstructure was a rational answer to supernumbers is debatable. It can be argued that no better way could have been found to insure an equitable and efficient distribution of public moneys on so great a scale. Or it can be argued that the bureaucratic imagination ran wild when California brought seventy-six junior colleges, eighteen state colleges, and a nine-campus university under the control of three governing boards, or when Wisconsin decided to crowd 135,000 students, 14,000 faculty members, and 10,000 other academic employees into one hippopotamic firm. But however these pros and cons are decided, there can be no doubt that the power to make policy decisions flowed from local campuses to central organs, and that the wrappers of organizational insulation were peeled away. When this happened something else occurred: the apostles of scientific management, now armed with the visions and vocabularies of courses in educational administration, finally found the vantage point from which to resume the academic

Kulturkampf that had been launched and rebuffed fifty years before. Hundreds of thousands teaching millions largely at public expense would have presented a tempting target for the enthusiasts of efficiency in any operational format. But it was the Brobdingnagian systems built up in the era of reactive growth that especially bid them welcome, hired them by the crowd to fill new bureaucratic offices, and in many cases invited them to take control.[97]

How, under different growth conditions, has the "profession" of the American academic fared? To answer this last and most inclusive question bearing on the influence of demography, one must first grapple with questions of morphology: In what form or forms is the academic profession constructed? Which part of its structure felt most keenly the impact of substantive and reactive growth?

Contemporary American academics belong to four occupational entities: to the field of higher education, to the institution that employs them, to a faculty within that institution and by extension to faculties in general, and to a particular discipline. Analysts commonly agree that only the last two entities plausibly define the boundaries of a profession. But they do not agree on which entity—the faculty or the discipline—is the major axis of academic professionalism, or on whether clashing, divided, or mutually reinforcing loyalties are felt by academics who belong to both.

From some perspectives any holder of a faculty appointment, simply by virtue of that appointment and irrespective of institution or specialty, belongs to a profession as binding and as unified (if not as legally privileged or politically powerful) as the profession that includes every doctor who obtains a license to practice or the profession that encompasses every lawyer who passes an examination for the bar. Such apparently is the view of respondents to opinion surveys who rank "professors," field and firm unspecified, high on the prestige scale of occupations; of students and parents who watch "the faculty" marching as a monolith in campus ceremonies; of legislators who treat academics as a class when they provide for collective bargaining in the public sector or raise the mandatory retirement age. And such apparently is the view of an army of educational researchers who rush to tell the quantitative truth about "academic man" undeterred by conceptual uncertainties. But many who make it their special business to assess the professional claims of callings tend to find something fragile or even fictive about this undifferentiated grouping. Although not of one mind about the societal value of "profession" (some regard it as a badge of honor, others as a bag of tricks),[98] they

are usually willing to confer that title on all or most academic specialties—the fifty-odd disciplines that inhabit a department of arts
and sciences somewhere on an American campus, the eighteen or so
vocations that reside in a school of professional training somewhere
in academe. But "One Big Profession for All," an image that causes
them no discomfort when applied to doctors and lawyers (or, for that
matter, to engineers, architects, or accountants) is apt to strike them
as problematic when applied to academic persons, as a claim to solidarity that laymen are wont to credit, but that connoisseurs have
reason to discount.[99]

Some of the discounters take their cue from indications that teaching, the one activity all faculty members have in common, counts for
less in their scale of values than research, the activity that ties them
to specific disciplines. Surveys of faculty opinion suggest that even
if the emphasis academics place on research varies according to the
type and quality of their institution, most of them—even those in
teaching-oriented institutions—deem it a more severe test of themselves to publish their ideas rather than to utter them, to submit to
the judgment of their peers rather than to the judgment of their
pupils.[100] Furthermore, it has been widely observed that disciplinary
knowledge is treated more solicitously and passed on more systematically than knowledge about teaching. Graduate programs that prepare academics for their careers notoriously consist of a major, a
minor, and a vacuum, the last referring to the time and care expended
on didactic theory or technique. The degrees that certify academics
for employment attest to their prowess as mathematicians, botanists,
or classicists, not to their competence as educators; indeed, even the
degrees awarded in education seldom provide a warrant of tested
pedagogic skill. Unlike the medical intern in a hospital who is closely
supervised by a mature practitioner, the academic journeyman is seldom placed in the hands of a master teacher; unlike the veteran lawyer
who gains eminence at the bar for his courtroom powers, the senior
professor at a university seldom receives his metier's highest prizes
for talents exhibited in class. And relatively rare is the faculty member
who joins a professional society or writes for a professional journal
whose prime aim is to perfect the teacher's art. On the assumption
that the activity one pays greater homage to defines one's stronger
affiliations, many observers conclude that the academic profession is
much less a unity than a congeries, and probably is unique in this
respect.

It is not only the perceived discrepancy between teaching and research that brings the existence of a unitary profession into question;

the structural consequences of specialization also raise ontological doubts. To some arbiters of professional entitlements, any occupation that may include on any work site an economist and a home economist, a fashion designer and a financial expert, a journalist and a jurisprudent, a physicist and a physical educationist, can hardly generate that community of interest, that common vocabulary of discourse, on which the communal feelings of professionals are thought to thrive. Diversity carried to such drastic lengths is presumed not only to engender internal fragmentation but to erase the distinction between the internal and the external within each fragment. The professions of architecture, journalism, and business may spend most of their time in extramural offices and use their academic schools as pieds-à-terre; the professions of clinical psychology, chemistry, and economics may shuttle between the university and private industry or private practice hardly conscious of which home is home; the professions of history, sociology, and English literature, though known for their academic addresses, may decide to camp out in the world when outer opportunities beckon and inner opportunities start to fade. And almost all of these partly in, partly out professions contain contingents of nonacademics who owe no allegiance to a teaching corps.[101]

Impressed by these signs of fragmentation, one educational sociologist, Donald Light, has flatly concluded that "the academic profession does not exist. . . . The academic man is a myth. . . . The professor as a distinct type in society" is an optical error.[102] Most sociologists are not such radical dissolutionists. But even those who use the definite article in describing this profession tend to agree that professionalism finds its major habitat not in the common room of the house of learning, but in its specialist wings and suites. To Talcott Parsons and Gerald Platt, the academic profession incarnates the core values of the disciplinary professions—cognitive rationality, functional specificity, the goal of sustained inquiry.[103] To Logan Wilson, teaching and research form a single professional role set that is best exhibited in major universities where they find their greatest compatibilities despite certain strains.[104] To Burton R. Clark, "e pluribus unum" takes the form of a hierarchy of academic cultures in which one, the culture of the discipline, overtops the rest.[105] Seldom do these theorists visualize the existence of two full-fledged, mutually supportive professions in the academic fold—the knowledge-seeking professions of the disciplines, whose members are drawn in large part from campus stations and organized into far-flung colleagueships, and a free-standing teaching profession of the faculties, composed of all academic staffs. This kind of double vision is obstructed by the general tendency to write off the faculties as a formless collectanea of professional alignments running in and out, or as weak competitors for the loyalties and energies of academics subject to powerful counterpulls.

But there are good empirical and logical reasons why full professional faith and credit should be extended to the comprehensive as well as to the partial entity. The fact remains that while all or nearly all academics teach, only a quarter of them account for what may deservedly be called research, and only a tenth of them account for nine-tenths of all scientific and scholarly publication.[106] And it remains a fact (evident to the close observer of the academic ego, if not always to the surface questioner) that academics do derive deep personal satisfaction from teaching well and are pained by student ratings and enrollments that tell them they do not. On its face, a universally shared activity fraught with emotional meaning for the participants is not markedly inferior to a narrowly engaged, albeit more highly regarded and rewarded, activity as a professional tie that binds. Nor is the body of academic teachers rendered a professional nullity by its haphazard approach to the science or art of teaching. No law of nature decrees that a profession must deploy knowledge strictly of its own creation or generate knowledge of a highly esoteric kind. Academic teachers draw much of their classroom expertise from the knowledge funded by their specialties, and they also acquire a special lore about the workings of academic institutions and the norms of academic citizenship. To hold that they are too unknowing to constitute a true profession is to favor one of a number of tenable gnostic requirements, not to state an ineluctable truth.

Nor is it self-evident that academics are too closely identified with their specialties to form more ecumenical attachments. True, these attachments do not receive the precursory assistance provided by the other professions. Studies show that future academics tend to elect a discipline before they opt for teaching, in contrast with doctors and lawyers, who reverse this order in their early socialization.[107] Usually, legal contrivances are not employed to induce academics to make broad and then narrower connections: appointed to an institution rather than licensed by the state, and appointed simultaneously to both a department and a staff, they do not undergo the examinational trials and sequences that attach other professionals to a general field before they can make more refined commitments.[108] But each profession has its own instruments of integration, and the instruments of the academic profession—a common employment status giving rise

to common irritations and insecurities, a high degree of collegial interaction within the occupational setting—may atone for conventional
lacks. Even more questionable is the assumption that the fealties of
academics are so fixed and limited that they can be devoted to the
part only by being subtracted from the whole. If this were true, the
most ardent devotees of the broad profession would be homebodies
detached from any discipline, and disciplinary notables would be
singularly uninvolved with local or national faculty affairs. No doubt
this kind of compensatory affiliation does occur, but few familiar with
the hydraulics of academic loyalty would say that it occurs with decisive frequency. Indeed, it may more often be the case that professional loyalty, like love, languishes for want of objects and expands
with opportunities for practice.

The second logical implication of this argument puts it to a critical
test. If commitments to a specialty are to be made at the expense of
the totality, then it would follow that substantive growth, which created and sustained the professions-in-the-disciplines, was the ne-
mesis of a viable profession-across-the-disciplines, and has been so
ever since it began in earnest around a century ago. A fixed-sum
psychology, to which many subscribe without much evidence, translates into a historical thesis that can be tested.

Do the findings of educational historians support the logic of an
argument that so trenches on their domain? Not explicitly and directly:
despite the vast amount that has been written about American academics, no full-scale history of the academic profession in this country
has yet appeared.[109] But those who have examined its past in bits and
pieces do seem, in a roundabout way, to have taken sides. Apart from
the few revisionist scholars who have fixed their attention on this
subject, historians have generally taken for granted that there was no
faculty profession before the specialties became professionalized, that
is, before the closing decades of the nineteenth century.[110] To find no
evidence of a profession in a period that lasted several centuries is
not tantamount to concluding that a faculty profession did not come
to pass. But the assumption that it did not do so when it had the
field entirely to itself does lend color to the argument that the whole
always suffered from a lifelessness that was simply underlined by the
later vigor of the parts.

This consensus as to timing raises an intriguing question: If not a
distinct profession, what was the occupation of academic teaching
prior to the era of rapid substantive growth? It cannot be said to have
been merely an adjunct to the clerical profession. Even when the
clerical and academic callings most overlapped, the one never wholly

subsumed the other. Unlike contemporary dons at Oxford and Cambridge, American professors and tutors in the seventeenth and eighteenth centuries, clerical though they were or aimed to be, were not vested with church livings by their colleges, were not required to remain in holy orders while they accepted their positions, were not required to relinquish their positions in order to assume the pastoral role.[111] And the growing proportion of nonclergymen on the faculties during the antebellum period made the separateness of these callings yet more evident and complete. Should the occupation of academic teaching be considered the upper floor of the occupation of school teaching? On balance, this conceptualization fails as well. It is true that many antebellum faculty members taught school at some point in their lives—during their own college years to pay their bills, after graduation as a stopgap measure until they found their true careers, occasionally during academic service to man their college's preparatory departments. It is also true that an initially large (though rapidly shrinking) percentage of antebellum college students were of what we would call high-school age.[112] But probably in every era, and certainly after the tutor began to be eclipsed by the professor, membership in an academic faculty carried with it an aura of public respect and a degree of institutional independence seldom vouchsafed teachers in schools for the lower grades. And teachers in schools for the lowest grades suffered the status infirmities of the feminine gender to add to those of transience and poor pay.

Was, then, the occupation of academic teaching a sui generis nonprofession, a distinguishable form of educated labor but otherwise nondescript? One is at liberty to think so, but only if one is prepared to use an anachronous definition of the term *profession*. If, to qualify as a profession, an occupation must be composed of members who are to the "nth" degree credentialed, who are appointed and promoted strictly on merit, who are quick to adopt the latest fruits of science, who enjoy a large measure of autonomy or an exclusive jurisdiction over an area of acknowledged expertise, who operate on a broad national or international stage, then arguably the earlier American professoriat would not qualify. But neither would the earlier clergy, lawyers, or doctors in England or America, since they seldom presented parchment testimonials of a long and arduous preparation for their work, were not immune to favoritist or nepotist practices, were not exceptionally innovative, were often tied to particularist sects or cults, and did brook commands from organizational superiors and external powers. Yet they have been dubbed professional even by quite finicky judges.[113] On the other hand, if to qualify as a profession an occupation has to be composed of members who attain the highest level of formal education available at that time, who espouse even if they do not invariably honor the injunction to grant rewards according to "worth not birth," who preside with benign intent over a vital sphere of human concern, who devote all their working time to one pursuit and, increasingly, who follow that pursuit all their working lives, and who perform intellectual tasks that are more discretionary than routine, then the earlier American professoriat would qualify, and by a comfortable margin.

Arguments that can be won by definition are not very interesting arguments. But arguments that can be lost by definition may carry clarifying concepts down with them to defeat. It would illuminate a rather murky history to affirm that a faculty profession did exist—for decades and perhaps for centuries—before the specialist professions came on the scene. But it was a certain kind of profession, a *traditional* rather than a *modern* one. This is a distinction worth preserving: if one asks no more of a profession than that it evolve to the limits of its type, one will not be inclined to tax it for lacking the properties of something else.[114] The traditional faculty profession would never produce the hyphenated academic—the teacher-specialist—caught (and liberated) in a double bind. It would never acquire extramural clients—the business enterprise and the public agency purchasing academic expertise—to go with the intramural client, the student seeking tutelary enlightenment. It would never foster a national association of professors or furnish other strong connections among faculties in all locales. But it would beat pivotal elements of professionalism into a rising cake of custom. It would derive from a string of campus religious controversies a demonology of high-handed trustees and a martyrology of dissenting professors that would give academic freedom a sustaining folklore.[115] It would secure the rudiments of academic tenure by instituting professional appointments for unlimited terms.[116] It would lay the groundwork for collegial governance by creating informal partnerships between the paterfamilias-president and the faculty who were once his senior sons but who were gradually raised to a higher status.[117] And by the end of the antebellum period, it would harbor tendencies—the diversification of curriculums, the specialization of teaching, the sprouting of cosmopolitan avant-gardes—that foretold its ultimate demise.

The traditional profession of the faculty was both the seedbed of the professions of the specialties and their direct and vicarious beneficiary; that it was also at times a reluctant giver and taker is a point to be noted but not exaggerated. The older presence gave the emerging new professions the gift of a long collective memory concerning matters professorial; a sense of academic work as *Beruf* that associated learnedness with the state of blessedness; an internalized, if not codified, service ethic; and on a different plane, an initial supply of recruits. The new professions, in turn, gave their precursor new powers and ambitions that would transform it: a blossoming sense of class importance based on the conquests of modern science; a multiplicity of clienteles that made it harder for campus administrators to judge the quality or fix the tempo of a faculty's performance; a rationale for academic freedom that rested more on the functional need for unfettered inquiry than on the quirks of the religious conscience; a rationale for academic tenure that sought to prevent, through judicial processes in dismissal cases, the retrogression of scientific subjects into branches of lay morality. The interplay between a faculty profession long established and the specialty professions late in coming created the bivalent modern academic profession, a result better pictured by the biologist's concept of synergism than by the gamester's concept of zero sum.

One event provides a striking illustration of this interaction. In 1915 the American Association of University Professors (AAUP) was founded by a group of distinguished scholars at leading research universities—John Dewey, E. R. A. Seligman, and Franklin Giddings at Columbia; Roscoe Pound at Harvard; Richard T. Ely at Wisconsin; and Arthur O. Lovejoy at Johns Hopkins, who wrote the "Call" that launched the venture and who framed the organization's guiding principles. In the precipitating announcement, Lovejoy noted that "the university teacher is professionally concerned with two distinct, though related, interests." One set of interests, the advancement of knowledge in a specialty, was being served by the disciplinary societies, but the second set of interests, rising from the membership of professors in the legislative bodies of local institutions and also possessed of societal significance, had not yet found an instrument for "authoritative expression" and "collective action." It was to provide a vehicle for these shared concerns that the recipients, all highly placed academic scholars, were urged to rally around.[118] The belief that the general interest was as "professional" as the specialized interest was so deeply etched in the minds of these founders that they seldom bothered to defend it. No question about whether academic teaching met all the indicia of professionalism arose to trouble them; no vision of disintegration caused by specialties shook their faith in the integrity of the whole. And they would leave this immunity to skepticism as a legacy to those who followed them. In the coming years the motto "There is one faculty profession and the AAUP is its prophet" would be ceaselessly chanted by the mullahs from their mosque in Washington, D.C.

It is not surprising that the founders of the association should have modeled the new society on the learned societies in which some had been prime movers and all were still active participants. Their provision for a revolving leadership of elected officers who would serve as volunteers pro bono, for a president likely to have attained scholastic honors that would shed glory by reflection on the whole society, for a membership that was initially honorific (and would for years be modestly selective)—all bore the stamp of what was for them a familiar model. But it is surprising that the leading figures in the disciplinary associations should have gone to the trouble of building a transdisciplinary one. In Great Britain and in Germany at the same time, the major thrust toward an all-faculty organization came not from the academic stars but from the lowly junior professors and assistants who banded together to demand a living wage and some small voice in running their universities. The fact that this initiative was assumed by the academic elite in this country points to the special context in which the call for professional unity arose. Here professors were not members of autonomous guilds or of a high and privileged stratum of the civil service; they were employees of lay governing boards in private and public institutions. Here the senior faculties, unlike most of their foreign counterparts, did not cope with external threats to guild prerogatives posed by a bureaucratic monarchy or an established church, but with more interior perils: a president who was the deputy of a lay governing board, an administrative apparatus that was accountable to the president, a tradition of governing en famille that could be turned into a regime of petty tyranny. The attempt to build up the defenses of the broad profession was not a whimsical display of civic consciousness on the part of a secure professoriat; it was a natural response to a general condition of subordination, intensified by a new sense of group amour propre. For warding off the Gothic contention of certain boards that professors were nothing but hired hands, no better talisman could be found than to claim they were members of a profession and entitled to all the dignities and courtesies this term implied. For persuading presidents and trustees to agree to self-denying ordinances, no stronger argument was at hand than to assert that professional rights entailed professional responsibilities and that the faculty, recognized as a profession, would take steps to police itself. For defending faculties endangered by forces within the gates at a time when the law afforded few protections, no better weapon could be forged than a national organization of professors, whose expressions of opinion would sound "authoritative" and whose actions would be of a "collective" sort.

Credit the expansion of the faculties in this period with producing fresh disquiets that gave Lovejoy and company cause to act. Far from creating a sense of summer throughout the American professoriat, the changes brought about through substantive growth ushered in for many faculty members a winter of discontent. Three kinds of discontents were voiced in the early planning sessions that looked to the founding of an ecumenical association. Some members complained that the growing demand for productive scholars was outrunning the supply of able candidates: to them, growth raised the specter of attenuation. Some believed that attacks on academic freedom, especially in the newly formed and controversial social sciences, were masquerading under innocent labels: to them, growth fostered administrative repression and dissimulation. And some feared that domineering presidents at the helm of expanding universities were trampling on faculty prerogatives: to them, growth encouraged executive usurpation.[119] Of the three possible organizational objectives prefigured in these complaints, the first—improvement of the quality of the faculties—was destined to bulk larger on the agendas of the AAUP than on its record of accomplishment. Qualitative improvements involved subjective judgments that were difficult to second-guess and almost impossible to standardize, and which touched on a variety of issues, such as the content of graduate training and the value of the Ph.D., which had already been seized by the learned societies and other bodies and were contingent on supply-demand factors in the labor market which the rhetoric of uplift could not affect. It was the other growth-related action programs—faculty defense and faculty governance—which would consume the energies and establish the reputation of the AAUP, not least because they did yield to general principles, were not in the protective care of the learned societies, and could be acted on by local chapters in individual institutions and by the national body, ordinance by ordinance, case by case. In these two areas the association would become the philosophic, adjudicative, and avenging arm of the profession-across-the-disciplines. Over the years, it would count among its significant achievements the extension of the concept of academic freedom to include extramural utterances or civil liberties; the revision of the rules of tenure to eliminate permanently temporary appointments regardless of rank, and to provide for academic due process in dismissal cases; the development of formulas of faculty participation in academic governance; the impartial investigations of alleged infractions of academic freedom and tenure, and the public exposure of verified violations; a number of pacts with administrative associations on a wide range of professional issues; and the use of its experience and good offices to advise administrators on personnel practices and to resolve disputes between administrators and faculty members before they flared.

With social theorists who define away the significance of the broad profession, with historians who presume it has no deep roots, with all who imply that it was withered, not strengthened, by the impact of substantive growth, this chapter has taken issue. But these arguments against the diminishers and nullifiers do not imply that it is nowadays hale and hearty. On the contrary, they concede that it was badly battered by the subsequent onset of reactive growth and that it is now gravely troubled and divided.

Starting from almost zero in the mid-1960s, a growing number of American academics during the next decade and a half became members of academic unions. By September 1981, 737 campus units—around one-quarter of the total—were under collectively bargained contracts.[120] According to surveys of faculty opinion, the idea of faculty unions became increasingly acceptable, even popular, in this period. To the question of whether collective bargaining had a place in academe, 59 percent of a representative sample of respondents answered affirmatively in 1969 and 72 percent in 1976. To a stronger question, "Do you yourself favor collective bargaining?" a smaller but sizable majority answered yes in 1976.[121] Clearly something new had happened under the academic sun.

At no time in its first fifty years of existence had the AAUP taken a formal position on the social value of trade unionism. (Probably, if its predominantly liberal members had been polled, they would have appeared readier than the general population in every era to characterize the American labor movement as a progressive force.) At no time during that long history had the AAUP issued a pronouncement on the unionizing of professionals outside academe. (Probably its members would have thought such a move incongruous, as professional unions had been such a rarity before the mid-1960s.) Nevertheless, for all its reticence on these broader issues, the AAUP had never been at a loss for words on the specific issue of faculty unions. During the half-century in which its deepest traditions were laid, it had consistently declared that unions were not suitable for academic professionals and that a professional society of academics should not join a union or comport itself as one.

This is not to say that it had been indifferent to the material well-being of academics, the interest unions claim to advance. It had not, however, been willing to concede that in union there was needed strength. During the early decades it had been content to rely on appeals for higher salaries by publishing tearful stories about professors who were floating their institutions on their own impoverishment. In the late 1950s it began to conduct annual surveys of the pay scales of faculty members, broken down by rank and type of institution, in the hope that the emulative instincts of universities—their desire to keep pace with the Joneses ahead of them, not behind them—would have an elevating effect. And indeed, during the next decade a significant rise in real academic incomes did take place, helped along (though hardly caused) by the publication of the AAUP's reliable comparative statistics. The task of gathering and broadcasting this provocative information was placed in the hands of the Association's Committee Z on the Economic Status of the Profession. That committee owed its last-place letter, as Committee A on Academic Freedom and Tenure owed its alphabetical supremacy, to the timing of its establishment. But these designations may also be interpreted as revealing symbols. In the priorities of the association, the issue of faculty compensation did not rank as high as the issue of faculty freedom and tenure. All AAUP leaders thought professors ought to be better paid (it is hard to imagine that all AAUP members did not think so too), but it was part of their professional credo to assert that the highest satisfactions came from intrinsic, not extrinsic, rewards. Further, the association believed that, while the protection of the academic freedom ought to be universalized and the rules of academic tenure standardized, decisions affecting academic compensation ought to be individualized (i.e., largely based on merit judgments), contrary to the wage philosophy of union bargainers who preferred the objective standard of stepped rewards for seniority and percentage increases across the board.

The clash between professional society and professional union went beyond the issue of remuneration; it involved divergent definitions of academic power relationships. With a tirelessness that betokened a root belief, the AAUP had proclaimed from its inception that faculty employment differed categorically from all other employments, even from other professional employments. It had devised a nomenclature to fit this claim to specialness: trustees were not proprietors but stewards, presidents were not bosses but administrators, professors were not employees but appointees, akin to judges on the federal bench. Aimed primarily at the philistine utterances of lay authorities, the AAUP's claim to specialness was no less at odds with the industrial imagery of union organizers who referred to faculty members as workers and to trustees and presidents as managers able in the last analysis to demonstrate who was boss. The principle of governance advocated by the AAUP went under the caption of "shared authority." Put forward as an alternative to outright faculty control (a syndicalistic notion that the AAUP had rejected in its natal period) and to administrative autocracy (the regimen it believed it had been put on earth to counter), shared authority held charms for generations of AAUPers, not just for the faculty senates and joint committees it effected, but for the flattering self-portrait it conjured up. It suggested that professors were the partners, not the minions, of those who signed their checks; that professors and presidents carried out different functions on at least the same plane of importance; that a latent community of interest existed among the three estates that needed only the right interconnecting mechanisms to be made manifest and put to work. "Collective bargaining," though it might accept some of the practical devices of "shared authority," appeared to rebuke and even ridicule these symbols. Its assertion that the best way to a reliable agreement was through arm's-length negotiations between two unentangled parties working toward a legally binding contract appeared to imply that there was an inherent disharmony of interests, that agreement by consensus was unreliable, and that professors with administrative responsibilities were more often double agents than connecting links.[122]

These oppositions could be seen even more clearly in the long history of interorganizational hostility. In 1916 the American Federation of Labor set up an affiliate called the American Federation of Teachers (AFT) to organize teachers on every tier. For half a century thereafter, the successes of the AFT were to be limited to public school teachers in the larger cities; not one academic faculty would select it as a bargaining agent. Still, the presence of a tough kid in a nearby neighborhood coveting its own turf had made the leaders of the AAUP uneasy. In the very early years, when the AFT, to gain an academic foothold, proposed a merger with the professors' organization, Lovejoy replied that the independence of the AAUP as an institution and the credibility of academic freedom as a neutral principle would be compromised by such a partisan alliance.[123] In the 1930s when a unit of the AFT flayed the association for not rising to the defense of threatened campus radicals, the leaders of the AAUP declared that it would not rush to judgment in such cases and would not endorse the principle of "my co-worker right or wrong."[124] By the eve of the great expansion, much had gone into shoring up the AAUP's conviction that, in academe if nowhere else, professionalism was professionalism, unionism was unionism, and never the twain should meet. And it carried this conviction into the boom years.

But not for long thereafter. At its 1972 convention, the AAUP voted "to pursue collective bargaining as a major additional means of realizing the Association's goals in higher education." If ever in the life of an organization a policy reversal may be labeled fateful, this one deserves that tag.[125]

What led to this volte-face? The reader of the record of the two-year debate that culminated in that decisive resolution will find few members asking the AAUP to abandon the crucial tenets of its faith. Indeed, those who favored the adoption of collective bargaining were firm in pledging that it would add to the weaponry of the association without compromising its theology or identity. In the debate two important camps of opinion, in some ways philosophically at odds, joined forces to overcome resistance. One regarded a willingness to compete in collective bargaining elections as an unfortunate organizational necessity. Although an immense union army had not yet appeared, a number of veteran leaders, themselves not dissatisfied with the status quo, were persuaded that such an army would soon materialize and that the association would suffer grave defections if it let unchallenged rivals take command. The other regarded the entry of the association into negotiations over the terms and conditions of faculty employment as an unqualified organizational desideratum. Critical of the association's supposed elitism, this group of somewhat less seasoned leaders, as populist as they were unionist at heart, welcomed engagement, feeling it would answer the needs and address the problems of the underprivileged rank and file. These two groups, however, were not entirely ill-matched bedfellows. They agreed on one major point: the American professoriat was changing, and in a direction that made it less susceptible to the AAUP's traditional appeals.

That shared perception had some foundation in reality. Many of the academic institutions that had recently undergone reactive growth had become, to a large degree, less professionlike, less readily distinguishable from places where the ordinary working life is staged. This could be said of the mushrooming community colleges, whose programs ranged over almost every vocational and avocational endeavor and whose personnel were drawn from almost every walk.

And it could also be said of the newly founded or newly enlarged state colleges and multicampus universities, whose aims were considerably more academic, but whose size and structures, origins and ambiences, worked against professional distinctiveness. Universities created by legislative fiat to teach and to hold a student torrent, universities made massive in a jiffy in line with encompassing master plans, were not given time to acquire and develop a strong professional esprit. Academics who found themselves not in sodalities but in systems, academics who saw the locus of effective power shifting from the campus to the statehouse or superboard, were likely to feel that they were beset by forces that professional manners were too tame to influence and professional procedures too weak to reach. In this milieu it became easy to forget what there was about an academic institution that set it apart from other establishments. A campus unit conceived as a branch office in a statewide complex charged with carrying out instructions from a central source was likely to become too Westinghouse in look not to be treated as Westinghouse in fact. A faculty brought into being by quantitative inputs and evaluated by quantitative outputs was likely to perceive no vast difference between itself and other bureaucratized white-collar cadres under similar regimes.

Nor was it only when and where it reached its peak that reactive growth fostered a slide to ordinariness. It would also do this by coming suddenly to an end and by hurtling the academic system into the tactics of retrenchment. Brought into academe in mounting numbers to give instruction at piecework rates, the part-time faculty member bid fair to become the very model of the modern academic nonprofessional.[126] Consigned to hopelessness by tenure quotas and nontenure tracks, legions of junior professors came, served, and inescapably went, like so many caterers to a birthday party or a fancy ball. Perhaps the greatest blow to the claim to specialness was delivered by the firing of tenured professors, not individually for cause with due procedures, but by administrative directive by reason of "financial exigency," or "program-reduction," grounds that permitted the summary dispatch of many professors.[127] In the past, faculty purges had been rare and had almost always been precipitated by state governing boards or governors who treated academic posts as party spoils. In the late seventies, on the downside of the academic business cycle, mass academic removals were occasioned by a patronage problem of another sort—a drop in tax appropriations or in student numbers—and could thus purport to be as passionless and nonpartisan as layoffs from an automobile factory with declining profits or declining sales. (Indeed, these terminations actually were called "layoffs," a term new to the academic lexicon if not to the parlance of blue-collar industry.) Not even during the Great Depression, when the academic economy had failed after a period of less hefty growth, had institutions acted on the premise that professors could be dropped when work was slack and recalled when orders started coming in, or that bottom-line considerations warranted the volatile employment practices of private enterprise.[128]

It would be going further than the complexities of academic life allow to contend that the weakening of faculty professionalism was solely responsible for the strengthening of faculty unionism. Professors choosing to be represented by a union did not often say and did not customarily believe they were voting profession down when they voted collective bargaining up. Some faculty members opted for a union on the assumption that very narrow economic issues would be bargainable and that everything else would remain in place. Some faculties organized defensively, either to hold their own against organized blue-collar workers on their campuses or to keep pace with other organized faculties within a multicampus frame. But it can hardly be denied that academics became more favorably disposed toward unionism the more they were convinced that adhering to old professional verities was rather like guarding an empty shrine. To many, unionism did seem to represent a movement on behalf of faculty members in a direction that had already been irresistibly taken by the system. When professional decisions were already made by outsiders, it did not seem unusual to ask public employee relations boards to define the voting unit of a faculty or to appeal to external arbitrators to settle campus disputes. When professors were subject to massive market threats, it did not seem inappropriate for them to mass together to gain market power, and it was not utterly inconceivable that in case of an impasse they should strike.

For all this, those who voted in 1972 to change the course of the AAUP made two significant miscalculations: faculty professionalism did *not* expire and faculty unionism did *not* sweep the field. In those parts of the sytem where reactive growth had been contained and where its aftereffects were not extreme, the old sense of professional distinctiveness survived. In fact, even in the swollen public sector it never received a coup de grace. It continued to draw strength from a variety of sources: from the human desire to ennoble work, from status demands and expectations that stemmed from long and costly training, from the efforts of enlightened administrators to preserve it as a valuable resource, and above all, from commitments to the disciplinary professions which, even in environments hostile to the broad profession, managed in many cases to remain intense. As it happened, fewer academics were as willing to vote for a union in a campus election than they were on a survey questionnaire. Despite the decision of the National Labor Relations Board in 1969 to extend the protective features of the Wagner Act to collective bargaining in private colleges and universities (a decision that would stand until it was overruled by the Supreme Court in 1980),[129] a number of faculties in the private sector turned down unionism when they had a chance to vote for it, and an overwhelming majority were so opposed to it that they would not muster the card-signing 30 percent necessary to call a referendum. Even in the public sector, where an increasing number of states passed facilitating legislation, the prophecy of the opinion surveys was not wholly vindicated. Most faculties in the flagship state universities either formally rejected collective bargaining or kept it from coming up as an electoral option. What had loomed in the early seventies as a coming tidal wave turned out, after a decade of experience, to be a large but spotty outflow, mostly inundating the lower-lying regions of academe: the junior colleges (they constituted two-thirds of all unionized campuses), quite a few state colleges gathered into massive systems, the campus spores of certain major universities, and a small number of large private universities in which the relations between faculties and administrations were especially tense.

The AAUP spirit lives; the question is whether it will live in the AAUP. In 1972 the organization opted for a policy change that it hoped would fortify and expand its membership while leaving its essence much the same. Today, although it is too soon for a final reckoning, the close observer would have to agree with the poet Robert Burns that the "best laid schemes o' mice an' men gang aft a-gley." Collective bargaining seems not to have attracted more members than it has repelled. No doubt the AAUP would not now have most of the members who belong to the eighty-eight campus units, for which it is the exclusive bargaining representative, if it had remained a professional organization like the American Medical Association or the American Bar Association. But the AAUP's modest successes on this front— modest because it has frequently lost out to its competitors and now is sole bargaining agent for only a minority of all unionized faculties— are offset by hemorrhaging defeats on another. Since 1972 the AAUP's strength in research universities and the more selective colleges (once its greatest strength) has been eroded. In part the reasons for the decline centered on hostility to the idea of collective bargaining and to the high dues caused by the expense of collective bargaining. By current reckoning, the total membership of the association, which stood at 90,000 prior to the climactic vote, has since diminished by about one-third.

The moral of unanticipated consequences is drawn by more than this discouraging arithmetic. The venture into collective bargaining has created a crisis of organizational identity that may be more anguishing to AAUP leaders than the shrinking membership base. At the moment of decision, few AAUP leaders had suspected that a local chapter running in a tight election would prefer to combine with a union rival than to permit the antiunion forces to divide and conquer; fewer still had foreseen that once precertification mergers became acceptable, postcertification mergers (the incorporation of established external unions into the AAUP as partial dues-paying affiliates) would come to pass; and none imagined that the heads of these outside bodies, representing blocs of dues payers many thousands strong, would be elected to the inner councils of the AAUP where they could affect its policies and protect their organizational interests. Yet all this turned out to be, if not an inescapable dynamic, at least the outcome the AAUP permitted the momentum of unionism to gather. The AAUP owes most of its recent gains in membership to a half-dozen or so one-sided corporate marriages—to its joint ventures with its long-rejected suitor, the AFT, and (to a lesser extent) with the premier organizer of teachers in grades K through 12, the National Education Assocation, whose primary academic holdings lie in the community colleges. These arrangements, whatever short-term fiscal good they do, have the ultimate effect of making the AAUP less the master of its own house. In their current forms these ventures pressure the association to play the union game by others' rules, and they make it vulnerable to threats by paying inside-outsiders they will withdraw if they are displeased, to turn it into a field of battle between two allies who happen to be deadly foes.

That the functions of collective bargaining would be harmoniously folded into the established government of the association was a hope many years ago; only an outvoted minority had some presentiment of the dual structure that has actually emerged. Today, a collective-bargaining faction, united by their frontline experience in the union trenches and by the belief that they do not receive the power and respect they deserve, battle for control of the AAUP with a diminishing old guard they call, not euphemistically, "Committee A types" or "traditionalists." There does exist, on the one side, a desire to recapture the credibility and éclat of the old association and, on the other, a desire to fulfill the promises of 1972 despite the batterings of events. Yet there is much distrust between the Collective Bargaining Congress, which has elaborated the rudiments of a second government and bids fair to dominate the first, and the stand-patters, who fear that the professional society will be transformed into an ordinary trade union. This creature of substantive growth, now adrift in the eddies of reactive growth, longs to unify and renew itself, but does not yet know quite how.

NOTES

Since 1984, when this essay was written, the AAUP has given heartening signs of healing its internal divisions and to some extent of reaffirming its independence.

1. U.S. Department of Education, *Digest of Educational Statistics 1982*, p. 107.

2. U.S. Bureau of the Census, *Historical Statistics*, p. 284. See also Harris, *Statistical Portrait of Higher Education*, p. 335.

3. U.S. Bureau of the Census, *Historical Statistics*, p. 383.

4. Willey, *Depression, Recovery and Higher Education*, pp. 17–34.

5. U.S. Bureau of the Census, *Historical Statistics*, p. 383.

6. Calculated in constant dollars, average faculty salaries were 92 percent higher in 1965 than in 1950—a remarkable gain since they were no higher in 1950 than in 1912, a depressingly lofty achievement when compared with the 2 percent loss sustained during the seventies. Bowen, "Faculty Salaries," p. 69; AAUP Committee Z, "Annual Report," p. 4. The decline in academic amenities can be reckoned only impressionistically. Metzger, "American Academic Profession in 'Hard Times,' " pp. 25–65.

7. Stern et al., "Status of Part-time Faculty," pp. 29–39; Tuckman et al., "Part-Timers and the Academic Labor Market," pp. 184–195; Thompson and Sandalow, "On Full-Time Non-tenure-Track Appointments," pp. 267–273; Van Arsdale, "De-Professionalizing a Part-Time Teaching Faculty," pp. 202–216.

8. The 1950s and 1960s had their seething side as well. See Metzger, "Crisis of Academic Authority," pp. 568–608.

9. For this period, academics' opinions about their vocation have been canvassed with helpful thoroughness by Veysey, *Emergence of the American University*. I depart from my informed guide by discerning a common theme—a broad acceptance of the recency and irrevocableness of an academic knowledge revolution—running through their articulations of clashing educational ideals.

10. Among the most outspoken enthusiasts for curricular diversity were presidents of midwestern state universities; see Draper, *American Education*. Among its most vocal opponents were academic men of letters in patrician private universities; see Babbitt, *Literature and the American College*. But, as

Veysey points out, academics were divided on this issue in all regions, in many disciplines, and in institutions of different types.

11. Although some commentators drew periodizing lines within, rather than between, the prewar and postwar periods, most did suppose that the war, which traumatized the nation, formed the key partition in academic intellectual life. See the typical line-drawing of Snow, *College Curriculum*, p. 15. Only recently have historians passed over the Civil War seam to create intervenient boundaries. See Rudolph, *Curriculum*; Guralnick, "American Scientist in Higher Education," pp. 90–137.

12. Bequeathed to later generations, this sense of a bifurcated past was incorporated into the mental landscapes of historians of American higher education. Not everyone who benefited from years of further scholarship and added hindsight turned every nineteenth-century development into a two-act play. But most who dealt with the academizing of knowledge, like Christian chronologists concerned with a more immense occurrence, did accept the fundamental premise that the story was divided into a "B.C." and an "A.D.," separated by one momentous advent. See Schmidt, *Liberal Arts College*, and *Old-Time College President*; Butts, *College Charts its Course*; Storr, *Beginnings of Graduate Education*; Ross, *Democracy's College*. During the last several decades, a group of revisionist scholars have challenged what they take to be a false dichotomy dressed up as history. More than a nuanced disagreement with the conventional time-zones of previous historians, their dissent from the notion that the intellectual resources of academics were spare and frozen until Armaggedon became a memory compels a reconsideration of almost every heirloom belief concerning the history of the American academic profession. For summaries of their main findings and contentions, see McLathlan, "American College in the Nineteenth Century," pp. 287–306; Herbst, "American College History," pp. 256–266; Sloan, "Harmony, Chaos and Consensus," pp. 221–251.

Many of these historians have a polemical aim: to rescue the supposedly calumniated antebellum college from its supposed calumniators—the leaders of the university movement in the late nineteenth century who blackened its name to promote their rival causes, and the university-trained historians of the twentieth century who credited the latter's tainted testimony because they were ideologically partial to the winning side. Insofar as older historians did believe that the antebellum college curriculum was puerile and impoverished, or that its classroom instruction was invariably uninspired and uninspiring, or that its curriculum was inhospitable to science, the revisionists may be credited with slaying stereotypes. (See Daniels, *American Science in the Age of Jackson*, Guralnick, *Science and the Ante-Bellum College*, McLathlan, "Choice of Hercules," pp. 184–206; Smith, "Apologia pro Alma Mater," pp. 125–153.) Further, to the extent that their precursors fancied that the old academic order collapsed at the first bugle blast of the grey and blue, their efforts to show that denominational colleges flourished long after the Civil War and that a residuum of old-style professors tarried long in Eliot's new-style Harvard supply a needed corrective. (See Potts, "American Colleges in the Nineteenth Century," pp. 363–380; McCaughey, "Transformation of American Academic Life," pp. 219–334.) This paper is influenced by their insistence that the antebellum college had considerable intellectual vitality and that a new postwar academic order did not spring up at once, in full command and with a scant inheritance.

But a redemptive mission can blind the missionary. Like others who write to rescue the reputation of an institution, some revisionist authors have tended to be too selective in what they chose to notice—the expansiveness of the antebellum curriculum but not its rigidities and limits; the best but not the worst examples of antebellum pedagogy and parietal control. And like other innovative historians who fancy that their predecessors were sunk in error, some members of this school tend to exaggerate the originality of their own assertions. The partisan impulse in this revisionism, and its occasionally overcocky and self-righteous air, leave many readers, including the present author, unpersuaded that it has uttered the last corrective word. What it has done is to reopen what had been regarded as settled questions. It has pumped new life into the question of when curricular diversification in fact began; it has impelled us to ask in what respects the modern academic profession is continuous or discontinuous with its premodern past. In short, a new inquisitiveness has arisen in this much-worked field, and this may turn out to be revisionism's greatest gift.

13. Although it has not yet caught the fancy of historians, a breakdown of antebellum colleges into a number of generations—three is a warrantable and a convenient, though not an incontestable, number—has much to recommend it. In a country undergoing swift territorial, cultural, and economic changes, colleges born in the same era and acquiring roughly the same longevity (by a certain date) were likely to share other attributes as well. Not to sort out the infant, adolescent, and mature colleges in the antebellum period is to risk making ambiguous periodical comparisons. Thus some historians have assumed that American colleges advanced toward curricular diversity in the late eighteenth century, only to retreat to exiguous offerings in the early nineteenth century, and to inching changes thereafter. But proof of a "great retrogression" (Richard Hofstadter's much quoted phrase) cannot be adduced from the offerings of second-generation colleges, which were too new in the early part of the nineteenth century to have owned a significant tradition and too young to be said to have regressed. Signs of retreat must be found, if possible, in the actions of first-generation colleges, which alone derived from their age and natal circumstances a chance to depart from a richer past (Hofstadter, *Academic Freedom in the Age of the College*, pp. 209–222; Metzger, *Development of Academic Freedom in the Age of the University*, chap. 1). It should be noted, however, that the logical and empirical advantages of a generational typology do not extend beyond the antebellum period. Afterward, as we shall see, the birthdates and life spans of institutions become

weak predictors of curricular diversity and most other institutional characteristics.

14. These and subsequent counts refer to those colleges in each generation that survived to 1860. They are derived from Tewksbury, *Founding of American Colleges and Universities*. Getting reliable figures on the nonsurvivors is a formidable task. Tewksbury's estimate that 81 percent of all colleges founded in the antebellum period folded by the end of the nineteenth century has fostered the impression among historians that the institutional birthrate in the antebellum period had been incontinent and, as a consequence, that the death rate had been extremely high. This impression is strongly challenged by revisionists, who calculate that no more than 20 percent of colleges founded before 1860 expired by that date. Naylor, "Ante-Bellum College Movement," pp. 261–274; Burke, *American Collegiate Populations*, pp. 11–51. The gross discrepancy between these estimates may be attributed to different cutoff dates, to Tewksbury's incomplete and inaccurate reporting, and above all, to differences in definition. Taking the number of college charters issued as his denominator, the older scholar necessarily included in his numerator many institutions that had never opened their doors or that had collapsed before they received any students; limiting his base to colleges in actual operation, Burke necessarily excluded all miscarriages, abortions, and neonate departures, and thus reduced the mortality rate. In any case, it is impossible to tell from either compilation or from the accessible sources how the nonsurvivors stood in the matter of curricular diversity. Burke's more thorough exhumations do not indicate whether they died from an overdose of rash experiments or from an obstinate devotion to a classical curriculum that lost its popular appeal. In this respect the nonsurvivors must be treated as academic unknown soldiers—too pathetically laid to rest to be forgotten, but too anonymous to be described.

15. As used here, a "subject" is a body of knowledge identified in academic titles or catalog captions as the substantive domain of a professor or as the primary content of a course. It covers a larger area than a "topic," which may be identified by a chapter heading in a textbook or an item mentioned in a course description; it is qualitatively different from a "discipline," which has a social as well as intellectual dimension in that it refers to a community of practitioners within and outside the academy who derive their occupational identity from it and who secure career advantages by improving its efficacy and repute. In the antebellum college there was a greater diversity of topics than of subjects and a greater diversity of subjects than of disciplines. (Indeed, it can be argued that the latter, because of the rudimentary development of departments and the thinness of the networks of scholarly communication, hardly existed at all.) The growth and academization of disciplines has received much scholarly attention. See Ben-David and Collins, "Social Factors in the Origins of a New Science," pp. 451–465; Kohler, "History of Biochemistry," pp. 275–318; Merton, *Sociology of Science*; Oleson and Brown, eds.,

Pursuit of Knowledge in the Early Republic. The growth and academization of subjects has not yet become a target of sustained inquiry, though it is a crucial part of the story of diversification.

16. Guralnick, *Science and the Ante-Bellum College,* pp. ix, 62 ff; Wilson, "Emergence of Geology as a Science in the United States," pp. 416–437; Kevles, *Physicists;* Daniels, ed., *Nineteenth Century American Science.*

17. Moral philosophy was a course prescribed for juniors and seniors from the middle of the eighteenth century to the Civil War. The primary aim of this capstone course was to provide a moral basis for society apart from, not in opposition to, that supplied by scriptural authority; its characteristic method was to apply a set of ethical principles, rooted in the facts of human nature, to the full range of social institutions; its intellectual root was the faculty psychology and realistic epistemology of the Scottish Enlightenment, together with the Anglican tradition of prudent piety (Sloan, *Scottish Enlightenment*). This subject was nothing if not tenacious. Its standard textbook, written by William Paley in the eighteenth century, continued to be prescribed by Harvard and Yale until the 1840s, by Dartmouth and Rutgers until the mid-1850s. Nor did it sink in prestige as it gradually gave rise to progeny: throughout the antebellum period, it remained in the hands of the most esteemed members of the faculty, usually college presidents, who were thought to be the best repositories of its practical wisdom and eternal truths. The air of changelessness that seemed to hang over the old-time college can in no small part be attributed to the durability of this centerpiece. That was a false impression: the curriculum of the old-time college was changeable and ever-changing. But it is true that curricular changes in the sphere of social values came more slowly than those in the sphere of material nature.

18. Smith, *Professors and Public Ethics;* E. R. A. Seligman, "Early Teachings of Economics," pp. 283–320; Haddow, *Political Science in American Colleges and Universities.*

19. For recent discussions of professional education in antebellum settings, see Haber, "Professions and Higher Education in America," pp. 346–352; William Johnson, "Education and Professional Life Styles," pp. 185–207; Naylor, "Theological Seminary in the Configuration of American Higher Education," pp. 17–30. Useful renderings of the historical details may be found in Norwood, *Medical Education;* Pound, "Law School," pp. 472–507.

20. Bagster-Collins, "History of Modern Language Teaching," pp. 49–64.

21. Cohen, "Science in America," pp. 167–189; Chittenden, *History of the Sheffield Scientific School,* 1, pp. 37–91.

22. Laughlin, "Study of Political Economy in the United States," app. 1, pp. 143–151. The movement from the study of social topics within the subject of economics to sociology as a separate discipline was accelerated by ideological conflicts within economics. Cf. Church, "Economists Study Society," pp. 18–90. A broader analysis of the acceleration of parturitive growth in the social sciences is in Bryson, "Emergence of the Social Sciences from Moral Philosophy," pp. 304–323.

23. Garland Allen, "Transformation of a Science," pp. 173–210.

24. The story of how the new professional schools changed the character of American universities still remains largely to be told. For an overview of the details, see Mendenhall, "Scientific, Technical and Engineering Education," pp. 533–592; for Eliot's pioneering efforts to integrate academic professional education into the administrative structure of the host institution, see James, *Charles W. Eliot*, 1, pp. 265–293.

25. To this author's knowledge, no one has attempted to write a synthesizing history of the institutionalization of these subjects, once regarded as below the salt. Discrete accounts may be found in Eels, "First Degrees in Music," pp. 35–40; Jack Morison, *Rise of the Arts on the American Campus;* Hunt, *Life of Ellen H. Richards;* Knepper, *History of Business Education in the United States;* Leonard and Afflack, *Guide to the History of Physical Education.*

26. The slowness with which the discipline of history was released from its original time and space constraints cannot be charged to a popular prejudice against modern history: the Puritans, after all, had written their own sagas with no sense that such works were too contemporary. There was something about the process of subject dispersion not present in the process of subject parturition which made the makers of curricula shy away from it. To admit one science born of another was to diversify at a modest pace regulated by the rate of fresh discoveries. To let history run free over globe and calendar would have been to diversify by annexing pockets of knowledge already there, and thus to change at a potentially excessive speed. That history became, after 1880, one of the American academy's fastest growing disciplines suggests that the once potent fear of uncontrolled dispersion had come to be assuaged. See Adams, "Study of History in American Colleges and Universities"; Holt, *Historical Scholarship in the United States.*

27. "Extent of Instruction in Anthropology in Europe and the United States," pp. 910–917 and "Teaching of Anthropology in the United States," pp. 211–216. To guard against a hardening of the categories, it should be mentioned that anthropology does not exemplify the dispersive process only. Insofar as it emerged from the study of human races and from departmental links to zoology and sociology, it may be said to be an example of parturitive growth. Insofar as the first campus anthropologists were curators of museum collections, it may also be considered part of the process of subject dignification. Differentiated for the purpose of analysis, these processes were not mutually exclusive.

28. Potts, "American Colleges," pp. 363–380.

29. A few of the start-from-scratch, exceptionally well-endowed fourth-generation universities exercised some curricular restraint and suffered no loss of prestige for it. Johns Hopkins and Clark won admiration for the quality of their faculties, not for the diversity of their offerings. But most of the others did advertise the idea that a multifarious curriculum, if it did not guarantee institutional fame, was an indispensable precondition of it. Stanford set the standard for envy and emulation when it entered the world decked out with

Latin, Greek, mathematics, physics, inorganic chemistry, German, Romance languages, American history, civil engineering, mechanical engineering, vertebrate zoology, cryptogramic biology, and education, and then, as if to clothe an infant nakedness, added organic chemistry, astronomy, ethics, geology, European history, physical training, freehand drawing, the art of writing, and horticulture during its first two years. Elliot, *Stanford University.*

30. The feminist movement of the nineteenth century provided an important impetus to the diversification of academic curriculums. Although some colleges had admitted women before the Civil War, their admission did not signify integration: even at pioneering Oberlin, women had to demonstrate their capacity to take courses routinely open to men. It was the women's college, a post–Civil War institution, that paved the way to a gender-blind curriculum. Vassar College, for example, by insisting that it was a college, and not a female seminary, and that science and humanities did not stand for masculine and feminine, used the diverse curriculum as an instrument and a symbol of women's rights. See Boas, *Women's Education Begins.*

31. Rosenberg, *No Other Gods,* pp. 135–172; Smith, " 'Cow College,' " pp. 299–310.

32. U.S. Commissioner of Education, *Annual Report, 1896–97.*

33. For an example of prolonged post hoc discrimination, see Tyack's discussion of the treatment accorded modern languages by antebellum Harvard. *George Ticknor and the Boston Brahmins,* pp. 85–128.

34. Pierson, "Elective System," pp. 165–174.

35. Harris, *Statistical Portrait,* p. 318.

36. Thwing, *History of Higher Education in America,* p. 300.

37. Foster, *Administration of the College Curriculum,* p. 21.

38. Machlup, *Production and Distribution of Knowledge,* pp. 162–167; Price, *Science Since Babylon,* chap. 5.

39. Rossiter, *Emergence of Agricultural Science,* chap. 2.

40. The academic side, even when it became relatively unselective, did reject many things. No institution or system of higher learning is a warehouse in which everything known to everyone is stored. Much of what passes for knowledge in someone's opinion will be excluded by the academy because it is judged to be trivial, or because it is judged to be false, or because it is simply too hidden or inaudible—too removed from the circuits of communication that wind through colleges and universities—to be judged at all. Possibly, the total amount of "knowledge" excluded by the academy exceeds the total amount included in every era and at every level of accumulation.

41. Kennedy, "Changing Academic Characteristics," pp. 35–37. In this sample the faculties had been almost 100 percent clerical in 1800, and over 50 percent clerical in 1830; the 25 percent figure in 1870 was a point on what had been a plunging line.

42. The extent to which the preparatory experiences of lay college faculty converged with that of their clerical brethren becomes more apparent when one goes beyond the catalog listing of degrees to the schooling data contained

in autobiographies and biographies. In such sources one finds, for example, Alteus Crosby, a Dartmouth professor of Greek (who would enter the Kennedy count as "lay"), spending two years at a theological seminary before dropping out to accept an academic post, and Mark Hopkins, Williams's long-lived clerical president, dabbling in law and medicine after completing his theological studies and before applying for ordination.

43. The overwhelming majority of the 9,000 to 10,000 Americans who studied in Germany between 1815 and 1914 did so after 1870. Although throughout this period more Americans were registered in the philosophical than in the theological faculties, it was only after 1870 that this preference became overwhelming. See Diehl, *Americans and German Scholarship*, pp. 50–59; Herbst, *German Historical School in American Scholarship*.

44. Mounting numbers of American students attending American graduate schools—only 198 in 1871, over 6,000 by 1900—attest to the growing popularity of a stay-at-home alternative to the pattern of withdrawal and return. John, *Graduate Study in Universities and Colleges*, pp. 9, 19.

45. Schmidt's count of 262 ministers out of a total of 268 antebellum presidents has long served as a benchmark of the extent of clerical domination of that office. *Old-Time College President*.

46. Eliot, *Educational Reform*, p. 27; *University Administration*, p. 93.

47. Leading works that treat the history of research universities are Veysey, *Emergence of the American University*, and Oleson and Voss, eds., *Organization of Knowledge in America*. Excellent histories of particular research universities supplement these comprehensive efforts. Cf. especially Curti and Carstensen, *University of Wisconsin*; Cheyney, *History of the University of Pennsylvania*; Morison, ed., *Development of Harvard University*; Solberg, *University of Illinois*. But surprisingly little has been done to assess the influence of these famous universities on the aspirations and self-images of the broad academic profession.

48. In part as a reflection of the newly awakened interest of historians in the subject of professionalism, histories of the disciplinary societies have been issuing forth in a steady stream. Among recent works that place them in a social and ideological context are Haskell, *Emergence of Professional Social Science*; Kohlstedt, "Formation of the American Scientific Community"; Furner, *Advocacy and Objectivity*.

49. Although governing boards in certain church-related colleges and state universities in the South and West continued to take the initiative in faculty appointments, the principle of lay forbearance had taken hold in the greater places. In 1910 a survey of all twenty-two institutions in the AAU disclosed that, with but one exception, the governing boards did no more than ratify the president's nominations; see Van Hise, "Appointment and Tenure of University Professors," pp. 51–55. The further shift of power from the president to the faculty had also occurred in those places, but less uniformly. The departmental authority could propose, but the central authority would dispose, and there were many opportunities for collision between the inferior

right of suggestion and the superior right of final choice. Still, the 1910 survey indicated that departments in major universities had gained a close-to-dis-cretionary power over junior appointments and that presidents had largely made it their custom not to act on senior appointments without the concur-rence of affected departments.

50. The American department of instruction has been closely studied by educational sociologists, but it has not yet been taken in hand by historians. As a result, more is known about how it currently functions as a campus lobby (Clark and Youn, *Academic Power*), as a unit of production (Hagstrom, "Inputs, Outputs and the Prestige of Departments," pp. 375–397), and as a determinant of academic quality (Peterson, *Organization of Departments*) than about how it evolved from earlier forms. The empirical groundwork for a developmental study has been laid by Veysey, *American University*, who offers a panoramic view, and by studies of particular departments in particular places (Dinar, "Department and Discipline", pp. 514–533; Darnell, "Emer-gence of Academic Anthropology at the University of Pennsylvania," pp. 80–92).

51. See below for a discussion of the academics' dual professional alle-giance.

52. Historians have just begun to pay attention to the role of faculty mem-bers in this period as identifiers and endorsers of new academic subjects. This is not to say that they have just begun to note the sponsorial activities of individual professors. How Edward Tichener transformed psychology from a philosophical to a biological subject at Cornell, how William Graham Sumner fought to establish the bone fides of sociology at Yale, how Franz Boas put modern anthropology on the map at Columbia and elsewhere, have been amply documented (Boring, *History of Experimental Psychology;* Murchison, *History of Psychology in Autobiography;* Starr, *William Graham Sumner;* Darnell, *Readings in the History of Anthropology*). But on such analytic questions as what American professors had to gain by speaking up for new subjects, if their commendatory judgments counted for more than those of presidents or out-siders, and why they were more active than their foreign counterparts in accepting parvenu fields of learning, historians have just begun to make a dent. The historical sociologist Joseph Ben-David has made significant inroads on the last question in "Universities and the Growth of Science in Germany and the United States," pp. 1–36. He believes that the American depart-ment—stratified by rank but heavily populated by senior professors, large and ever eager to grow larger—was a much better instrument for the rapid academizing of new subjects than the German chair-plus-institute format, in which the full professor reigned as a seigneur over an entire field of learning and was surrounded by subordinates and assistants. The comparative point seems well taken. Such disciplines as psychoanalysis and statistics did find it harder to crack the German system, where academic chieftains tended to define new subdisciplines as potential rivals, than the American system, where a collectivity of equals tended to welcome them as reinforcements. But

Ben-David does not indicate why the more open form was established in the United States, except to suggest that Americans studying in Germany mistook its hierarchic arrangement for a more egalitarian one and imported that misperception when they came home. This is not a persuasive explanation: attempts were made to establish departmental headships in America on the German plan, but they did not succeed, at least not in the arts and sciences. Something more fundamental than the use of a misdrawn blueprint has to account for the triumph in this country of the roomy departmental form.

53. Burritt, "Professional Distribution of College and University Graduates"; Burke, *American Collegiate Populations*, chap. 4.

54. Bozeman, *Protestants in an Age of Science;* Hovenkamp, *Science and Religion in America: 1800–1860.*

55. Naylor, "Theological Seminary," pp. 17–30; Allemendinger, *Paupers and Scholars*, chaps. 3, 5; Potts, "American Colleges," pp. 363–380.

56. Buritt, "Professional Distribution of College and University Graduates"; McGrath, "Control of Higher Education in America," pp. 256–272.

57. Guralnick, "American Scientist in Higher Education," pp. 127–128.

58. Higham, "Matrix of Specialization," pp. 3–18.

59. Samuel Morison, *Three Centuries of Harvard, 1636–1936,* p. 90.

60. Columbia College, *General Catalog, 1784–1894,* pp. 84–152.

61. The strong emphasis in the following pages on institutional means rather than on faculty mentalities is not meant to suggest that curricular decisions were untouched by pedagogical and ideological considerations. But historians of American higher education have imputed so much causal power to ideas that an emphasis on economic calculation is needed for a more balanced picture. See Hall, "Veritas et Pecunias." To some extent economic historians have offered correctives to the overdominating ideational approach. In general, however, they have been more interested in exploring the macro side of educational finance—the levels of American investment in education, the proportion of the national product invested in human capital, the opportunity costs of formal schooling—than in the microissues involved in decision making by academic firms. See Fishlow, "Nineteenth-Century American Investments in Education," pp. 418–436; Solmon, "Estimates of the Costs of Schooling," pp. 431–481; Soltow and Stevens, "Economic Aspects of School Participation," pp. 222–243. Harris, *Economics of Harvard* and Foster, *Economic History of Harvard College* are noteworthy exceptions, but these works have not been followed up by the economic studies that would tell us wherein Harvard was and was not unique.

62. Whitehead, *Separation of College and State.*

63. Educational historians have long relied on the analyses of antebellum college enrollments made by two contemporaries—President Francis Wayland of Brown (*Report to the Corporation*) and President F. A. P. Barnard of Columbia (*Some Statistics of Collegiate Education*). Both concluded that the antebellum colleges were unable to secure more than an unduly small and declining share of males of college-going age and both called for curricular changes

that would enhance the weak and waning popularity of these institutions. Lately, revisionist historians have challenged the validity of their data (and the perceptiveness of historians who have relied on them) with a fervor that seems disproportionate to the seriousness of the mistakes; see Potts, "Curriculum and Enrollments," pp. 88–109; Potts, "Students and the Social History of American Higher Education," pp. 317–327; Burke, *American Collegiate Populations*, chap. 2. Undoubtedly, the statistics gathered by the older amateur demographers leave much to be desired. Barnard, for example, concentrated on the New England colleges but gave the false impression that he was covering all the colleges; he excluded college students in nonliberal arts programs and thus understated their total number; he included immigrants in the base population and thus inflated the number of age eligibles who stayed away. Burke's brighter statistical conclusions—that "the liberal arts colleges, although narrowing the age of their students, experienced a fourteen-fold increase in enrollments in six decades," and that the percentage of white, college-age males in college doubled during those sixty years—must be accepted as counterweights to the presidents' doomsday account (Burke, *American Collegiate Populations*, p. 54). But Wayland and Barnard were not egregiously off the mark. Even after revisionist recalculation, it appears that only a tiny fraction of potential college-goers went to college. The largest college in 1860 had only 400 students; in the midwest and the south, the number ranged from 25 to 80 students, and the 16-fold increase in student numbers has to be reckoned against the 20- to 30-fold increase in the number of institutions (depending on how one calculates decreases). Educational leaders in this period had good reason for pessimism, even if they did not get their numbers straight.

64. The abolition of the fee system in academic medical and law schools would occur in the postbellum period. At bellwether Harvard, Charles W. Eliot cast it out by shifting control of medical school finances from its proprietor-like professors to the corporation treasurer and by converting law school professors from part-time to full-time employees (James, *Eliot*, pp. 100–101). Changing the method of faculty compensation in professional schools was not a small technical issue. It was part of a larger effort to integrate professional education into the administrative structure and academic norms of the university. It permitted the "academized professionals"—the teachers in the professional schools—to share the occupational concerns of the "professionalized academics"—the teachers in the arts and sciences departments—while they retained certain distinctive work styles and extramural attachments. It was a step toward the building of a unitary academic profession.

65. Occasionally, the reversion from a salary to a fee system was urged by an academic president on the grounds that it was the only way to improve faculty compensation. But even when it was touted as potentially more enriching, this kind of proposal was likely to arouse strong opposition from college faculties. See Bronson, *History of Brown University*, pp. 159–169.

66. In some instances the fee system served as an instrument of marginal diversification. At the beginning, the Yale School of Applied Chemistry had been forbidden to give instruction to any student in the college proper or use college funds to support its work. For some years, the faculty acted like franchisers on a lease arrangement: they subsisted entirely on student fees, paid the corporation rent for its facilities, and had the privilege of advertising in the college catalog but not of awarding diplomas or degrees. Before the end of the antebellum period, however, an equalizing trend set in: the students of what was to be called the Sheffield Scientific School were permitted to earn a special B.A. degree and—a critical step—their professors were placed on salary after a separate endowment had been secured. Chittenden, *History of the Sheffield Scientific School*, 1, pp. 37–91.

67. Finkelstein, "From Tutor to Specialized Scholar," pp. 99–121.

68. Wilson Smith paints a rosier picture of the longevity, maturity, and respectability of the tutor at eighteenth-century Harvard than have most observers of that species in other habitats. But this was Harvard—and Harvard can never safely be taken as a proxy for other institutions. "The Teacher in Puritan Culture," pp. 394–411.

69. Finkelstein (see above) pulls together most of the work that had been done to 1983 on the collective biographies of American academics in the eighteenth and nineteenth centuries. This latter body of work is small and spotty. It includes: Carrell, "American College Professors, 1750–1800"; Tobias, "Old Dartmouth on Trial"; Cruetz, "Evolution and Professionalization of Academics at the University of Michigan"; McCaughey, "Transformation of American Academic Life: Harvard University 1821–1892." The paucity to date of such career-line studies should remind quantitative historians of the world that waits to be conquered by their survey and computer skills.

70. Burke, *American Collegiate Populations*, pp. 49–53.

71. Marx, "Composition of University Staffs," p. 609, and "The Problem of the Assistant Professor," p. 35.

72. Brubacher and Rudy, *Higher Education in Transition*, pp. 373–375.

73. These student-faculty ratios have been computed from the U.S. Commissioner of Education *Reports*, a not infallible source, but one whose fallibilities are consistent enough to yield a reliable trend.

74. The leading work on college admissions policies is Wechsler, *Qualified Student*. The seminal analysis of the smoothing of the passageways and the increased flow of travelers is by Trow: "Democratization of Higher Education," pp. 231–262. See also Trow, "Reflections on the Transition from Mass to Universal Higher Education," pp. 1–42.

75. Subtle retreats and advances in this heroic story of enrollment growth should not be overlooked in the course of its rapid telling. For example, though the absolute number of persons going from high school to college increased in this period, the percentage of high school graduates doing so actually declined between 1890 and 1940. The reason is simple: when secondary education was an elite system, it sent almost half its graduates to

college because it was set up to do so; as it became a mass system, it sent on a diminishing fraction of its graduates (until the low point of 10 percent was reached in 1940). But thereafter, a third transformation took place: the mass system produced an increasing percentage of college-bound graduates until (by 1960) it reached the figure attained in 1890. Ferris, *Indicators of Trends in American Education*, p. 109; Trow, "Second Transformation of American Secondary Education," pp. 144–160.

Some of the increased amount of traveling came from the growing reluctance of school authorities to hold the low achievers back. In the early twentieth century, a quarter of the elementary and high-school populations were over the normal age for their grades. Some overage students were late starters, but most were retarded in school because they did not deserve promotion according to the standards then in force. In time the system made promotion almost automatic: by 1960, only 2.4 percent of the students in elementary schools and only 8 percent in high schools were counted as grade-retarded. Folger and Nam, *Education of the American Population*, p. 7.

76. These and subsequent census data are taken from U.S. Bureau of the Census, *Historical Statistics of the United States*, Harris, *Statistical Portraits of Higher Education*; and Ferris, *Indicators of Trends*.

77. For a review of public opinion surveys that document this sea change in public attitudes toward extensive education, see Jaffe and Adams, "College Education for United States Youth," pp. 269–283.

78. After World War II attempts by economists to measure the impact of schooling on human capital and economic growth became increasingly sophisticated. This branch of economics took impetus from three landmark studies: Denison, *Sources of Economic Growth*, which attributed the rate of increase in total output over the rate of increase of capital and labor inputs to the growth of skill and knowledge; Schultz, *Economic Value of Education*, which argued that expenditures on education, heretofore seen as consumption costs, ought to be treated as income-yielding investments; and Becker, *Human Capital*, which estimated that investments in schooling were justified by lifetime monetary returns, even when putative returns on alternative investments are factored in. Not every economist, and certainly not every friend of higher education, agreed that these were the weightiest arguments that could be made on behalf of broader schooling (see Solmon and Taubman, eds., *Does College Matter?*). But it is doubtful that the political leaders of the nation would have made higher education such a lavishly favored enterprise if its advocates claimed it merely sustained cultivated tastes, human values, and a civic spirit.

79. If a single document may be credited with reorienting the nation's educational agenda, it was the six-volume report of the Truman-appointed president's commission entitled *Higher Education for American Democracy*, which called for the immediate abolition of all barriers to educational opportunities, these barriers being defined as poverty and discrimination, not as a lack of personal motivation or ability.

80. The propulsion of the first Russian satellite into space in 1957 helped

propel the federal government, under the rubric of national security, into heretofore unventured skies: financial aid to students, to public and private institutions, to academic libraries and laboratories, and so on. Although it may not have initiated the academic build-up in this period, the Cold War did play an important role in overcoming constitutional and other objections to the central state as a major academic force.

81. See McGrath, ed., *Universal Higher Education*.

82. Cattell, "Statistical Study of American Men of Science," pp. 699–707 and "Further Statistical Study of American Men of Science," pp. 633–648.

83. Benjamin, "Ludwig Lewisohn and the Lost Generation," pp. 17–24, 27.

84. Crane, "Social Class Origin and Academic Success," pp. 1–17.

85. Lipset and Ladd, *Jewish Academics in the United States*, pp. 92–93; Steinberg, *Academic Melting Pot*.

86. Lipset and Ladd, *Jewish Academics in the United States*, pp. 92–95. See also Wuthnow, "Is There an Academic Melting Pot?" pp. 7–15; Greeley, "On 'Is There an Academic Melting Pot?' " pp. 218–219.

87. Solmon, "Women in Doctoral Education," pp. 299–332; Graham, "Women in Academe," pp. 1284–1290; Johnson and Stafford, "Earnings and Promotion of Women Faculty," pp. 1099–1123.

88. Logan Wilson, *American Academics, Then and Now*, p. 57.

89. Any shortening of the average academic employment cycle brings closer the day when the original tide will drain away; conversely, any extension postpones this reflux. In every period, the average length of the employment cycle is determined by the average starting age, which subsequent policies cannot affect, and the average leaving age, which current policies can indeed affect. Thus the 1982 act of Congress that forbade the mandatory retirement of professors before the age of 70 (most institutions had set that age at 65) had the effect of lengthening the cycle. But governmental policies are not always determinative. Professors do not retire only when they must; they also retire when they wish, and an institution may, through a varied repertory of options for voluntary early retirement, be the abettors of that wish.

90. There is no assurance that positions vacated by retiring professors will be kept open for replacements. Having learned in recent years to retrench, the academic budget keepers may not be inclined in later years to replenish. But if they are likely to be more parsimonious in the 1980s and 1990s than they had been in the 1950s and 1960s, they are not likely to be as tightfisted as they had been in the 1970s. When professors fall away one by one—by a heart attack, by the lure of private industry—an institution may be irresistibly tempted to save money by expunging posts. But when, following the inexorable laws of demography, professors start to retire in droves, and when whole departments are threatened with decimation, the stronger institutional urge will probably be to hunt for new incumbents, not to shorten the roster and pile up savings.

91. Price, *Little Science, Big Science*, pp. 4–22.

92. Cooke, "Academic and Industrial Efficiency," pp. 1–64. Limitless and humorless, Cooke would have applied the gospel of efficiency to academic research as well as to academic teaching. Believing that "few workers can be at their maximum of efficiency unless their work is subject to fairly constant, intimate and impartial review," he proposed that a research board be established in every university to pass on the "expediency of undertaking any given project" and of eliminating those that were "a waste of time" (p. 32). Cooke became a target of derision in certain quarters, but he was not a sport. Efficiency expert William Harvey Allen stirred up academics in Wisconsin by conducting a similar survey and making similar recommendations (Allen, *Efficient Democracy*). And the rationalizers gained considerable success in the lower schools (Callahan, *Education and the Cult of Efficiency*).

93. Webster, "Scientific Management and Academic Efficiency," pp. 416–417; *The Nation*, "The Efficiency Nostrum" (editorial), pp. 49–50; Curti and Carstensen, *University of Wisconsin*, 2, pp. 272–275.

94. Veblen, *Higher Learning in America*.

95. See Finken, "Toward a Law of Academic Status," pp. 575–602 and Van Alstyne, "Cracks in the 'New Property,' " pp. 445–490, for examples of contributions to a field of legal commentary that hardly existed in the days, not necessarily halcyon, when personnel practices of academic institutions had not been subject to close judicial scrutiny, let alone to legal suits that posed constitutional questions.

96. The phenomenon of "delocalization" is analyzed in Metzger, "Academic Freedom in Delocalized Academic Institutions," pp. 1–33.

97. Taylorism would later be elaborated by strategic planning, computer technology, systems analysis, and institutionalized research, sophistications that would make the simple formulas of Cooke seem as archaic as the self-confident rebuttals of his opponents. See Hydeband, "Technocratic Administration of Higher Education."

98. Until comparatively recently, expert opinion was undivided in regarding "profession" as a badge of honor. The archetypal expression of the belief that it is an accolade is Flexner's *Is Social Work A Profession?*, pp. 2–22. In time, Flexner's view that this designation had to be awarded parsimoniously lest it be trivialized and debased and that an occupation had to have all the ennobling stigmata set forth on the checklist in order to earn a passing grade, gave way among sociologists to a preference for less demanding inventories and for the use of intermediate categories—semiprofession, quasi profession—that would grant an occupation a silver medal until it was ready to earn the gold. See Goode, "Community Within a Community," pp. 194–200; Moore, *Professions*; Wilensky, "Professionalization of Everyone?"; Etzioni, *Semi-Professions*. In the late 1950s a group of sociologists, chafing at what they saw as acquiescent and apologetic trends within their disciplines, began to unmask the hidden motives behind professionalism, which they took to be a lust for power and unbridled greed. The less extreme debunkers conceded that a neurologist had to know a lot about the nervous system in order to

vend what he knew at immodest prices, that an obstetrician had to be able to accomplish safe deliveries to reduce his patients to a state of abject dependency. The more extreme in this camp contended that neurologists, obstetricians, and the like gained their self-seeking ends not by knowing more but by *seeming* to know more: indeed they came close to denying that the term *profession* had any objective meaning at all (Hughes, *Men and Their Work*, p. 44). But even those who did not believe that everything was done with mirrors were ready to agree that the preeminence of the professions in modern societies rested on considerable symbolic huckstering. In these circles a shorthand version of social change came to pass as sufficient history: whereas lineage had once established effective claims to deference, political power, and good life chances, and then wealth in time had supplanted lineage, now something was supplanting wealth: an ingeniously wrought and plausibly presented occupational mystique (Habenstein, "Critique of 'Profession' as a Sociological Category"; Larsen, *Rise of Professionalism*). Although it did not go uncontested in the American scholarly community, this devaluation of the title of profession was by no means limited to an eccentric tendency in sociology: it cropped up and became the prevailing view in many disciplines, including history (Wiebe, *Search for Order*), legal studies (Auerbach, *Unequal Justice*), political science (Gilb, *Hidden Hierarchies*), psychiatry (Szaz, *Myth of Mental Illness*) and American studies (Bledstein, *Culture of Professionalism*). Lacking a history of antiprofessionalism that could stand shoulder to shoulder with Hofstadter's history of anti-intellectualism (the two "antis" overlap but they are not identical), one must guess as well as one can about why it arose with so much force when it did. But no one who would try to winnow causes can neglect the effect of professional expansion in this period. It seems reasonable to suppose that the professions, where they greatly increased their numbers, lost some luster to their growing commonness; that professional services came to be so lavishly provided that they engendered universal expectations that were bound to be disappointed; and that professionals became so ubiquitous in society and so prominent in government that no one could aim a critical arrow at a social institution or a public policy without piercing professional flesh. See Metzger, "What is a Profession?"

99. "Experts" on the structure of the academic profession may be found in many fields, but they are most prominent in the sociology of the professions and the sociology of higher education. Both are relatively new subdisciplines. Although the professions were of interest to Max Weber and Emile Durkheim, their systematic study by sociologists did not begin until 1939, when Talcott Parsons launched a prolonged attempt to describe their strategic position in modern industrial societies ("Professions and Social Structure," pp. 457–467). Similarly, although higher education had concerned the founders of modern sociology, the first book-length sociological study of the academic profession did not appear until 1942 (Logan Wilson, *Academic Man*) and this was not followed by a comparable study of a non-American professoriat until 1971 (Halsey and Trow, *British Academics*). The newness of these fields may account

for the vast amount of intellectual effort they still invest in discovering the hallmark attributes of professionalism and for the conceptual blurriness that still attends their efforts to define the salient features of academic professionalism.

100. Finkelstein, "Three Decades of Research on American Academics," pp. 195–202; Light, Marsden, and Cori, *Impact of the Academic Revolution on Faculty Careers*, pp. 3, 12–31; Lewis and Ryan, "Professionalization and the Professoriate," p. 283.

101. Gouldner, "Cosmopolitans and Locals," 1, pp. 281–306; 2, pp. 444–480; see also Blau, *Organization of Academic Work.*

102. Light, "Structure of the Academic Profession," pp. 12–14.

103. Parsons and Platt, *American University*, pp. 103–129. See also Parsons and Platt, *American Academic Profession.*

104. Wilson, *Academic Man*, pp. 6, 114.

105. Clark, *Academic Culture*, pp. 2–8.

106. Fulton and Trow point out that only 4 percent of the respondents to the massive 1969 Carnegie questionnaire said that their interests lay very heavily in research as opposed to teaching, whereas another 20 percent said "both, but leaning to research." It is immediately clear that judged by its staff's self-conceptions, the American academic system as a whole is primarily a teaching system (Fulton and Trow, "Research Activity," pp. 32–33). To be sure, a majority of this faculty sample were teachers in four-year and junior colleges where teaching held the highest priority. But only half the respondents in the high-quality research universities identified themselves primarily as researchers; at all levels of the system, teaching played a crucial part. See also Blackburn, "Careers for Academics and the Future Production of Knowledge," p. 33; Hammond, Mayer, and Miller, "Teaching versus Research," pp. 682–690.

107. Dunham, Wright, and Chandler, *Teaching Faculty in Universities*, pp. 22–25, app. 4; Parsons and Platt, *American Academic Profession*, pp. v–19. Evidently, academics who wind up in teaching-centered institutions tended to form a cathexis to teaching before they identified with a specific field. See Eckert and Stecklein, *Job Motivations and Satisfactions of College Teachers*, pp. 72–76.

108. A licensed profession generally appears to onlookers and experts alike as a single profession with interior subspecialties. Not requiring a license to practice (a Ph.D. is not a license but a certificate; a license in medicine or law is not required for academic practice in those fields), academic teaching does not lend itself to this kind of structural description by cognoscenti, though it may be so defined by the casual public. Its fundamental structure would not have become so much an object of controversy if all academics took general qualifying examinations and then sat for their history or chemistry boards.

109. Very few historians have lamented this lacuna; few, indeed, have taken public notice of it. (An exception is McLathlan, "American College in the Nineteenth Century," p. 298n.) Until recently, the contributions of trained

historians to this subject may be described as massive in detail and rich in flavor, but thin in concept and bare of theory. Generally, they did not study academic faculties as such: they wrote histories of universities, histories of higher education, histories of academic intellectual trends—and thus covered a great deal more; or they wrote biographies of scholars and college presidents, accounts of dramatic campus incidents, colorful vignettes of campus life—and thus covered a good deal less. Even to this day, the vast bulk of scholarly writing on faculty members as professional workers is over the signature of social scientists, especially sociologists, not historians (Finkelstein, "Three Decades of Research on American Academics"). Consequently, while many studies pay their ritual respects to history in an opening paragraph or chapter, few add a time perspective intrinsic to the analysis and not just tacked on. Contemporary research on the academic profession still very largely turns out to be research on contemporary academic professionals, a monument to the living if not the quick.

110. Jencks and Riesman, *Academic Revolution*, p. 6; Shryock, "Academic Profession in the United States," pp. 32–70; Content, "Emergence of the American Professor," pp. 430–434. The revisionist effort to predate the *faculty* profession is still in its infancy (see n. 62). Where there have been attempts to reset the clock, they have generally involved the origins of the *disciplinary* professions. Daniels, "Process of Professionalization in American Science," pp. 151–166; Reingold, "Definitions and Speculations," pp. 63–77; Bender, "Science and the Culture of American Communities," pp. 63–67. Discussions of the issue of periodization—that hardy perennial of historical discourse—leave the impression that professionalization is a field-specific process that strikes at academics as a by-product, and not a more general process that may originate within the academic pursuit itself.

111. Engel, "From Clergyman to Don."

112. Thomas, "Changes in the Age of College Graduates," pp. 150–171; Burke, *American Collegiate Populations*, pp. 103–105.

113. Reader, *Professional Men*; Johnson, "Education and Professional Life Styles," pp. 185–207; Rothstein, *American Physicians in the Nineteenth Century.*

114. The ideal-typical characteristics of a traditional profession are laid out in a classic and still influential work: Carr-Saunders and Wilson, *Professions.*

115. Hofstadter, *Academic Freedom in the Age of the College.*

116. Metzger, "Academic Tenure in America," pp. 111–135.

117. Beach, "Professors, Presidents and Trustees."

118. *Science*, "National Association of University Professors," p. 458.

119. Metzger, "Origins of the Association," pp. 229–237.

120. *Chronicle of Higher Education*, September 1981.

121. Ladd and Lipset, *Professors, Unions and American Higher Education*, p. 12; Ladd and Lipset, *Chronicle of Higher Education*, 26 January 1976.

122. Brown, "Collective Bargaining in Higher Education," pp. 1067–1082; Lewis and Ryan, "American Professoriate and the Movement Toward Unionization," pp. 139–164; Kadish, "Theory of the Profession," pp. 120–125. Bier-

stedt and Machlup, "Representation of Economic Interests," pp. 232–234. As late as 1966, the AAUP joined with the American Council on Education and the Association of American Governing Boards to formulate a statement on shared authority that gave professors some voice in every sphere of governance and a predominant say in matters of professional concern. Although the 1966 statement did not explicitly disavow collective bargaining, it was obviously put forward as an alternative to the adversarial relationship throught to be implicit in collective bargaining. "Joint Statement on Government of Colleges and Universities," *AAUP Policy Statements and Reports*, pp. 105–110.

123. Lovejoy, "Annual Message of the President, 1919," pp. 21–28. Through the quarter century in which he served the association as its éminence grise, Lovejoy maintained this position. See "Professional Association or Trade Union?" pp. 410–415.

124. AAUP, "Report of Committee A," p. 132.

125. AAUP, "Council Position on Collective Bargaining," pp. 46–61.

126. Van Arsdale, "De-Professionalizing of Part-Time Teaching Faculty," pp. 202–216.

127. The number of mass dismissals for financial reasons has not yet been quite as large as the tidings of the *Chronicle of Higher Education* might lead the quick reader to suppose. Many cuts in tax appropriations were absorbed by institutions without dismissals; some dismissals were threatened by institutions as defensive maneuvers to head off cuts; at times, the clouds of a shortfall quickly gathered and just as quickly dissipated—a weather pattern not uncommon in the realm of public finance. Nevertheless, there has been plenty of reliable bad news in these weekly bulletins of disaster. Consider, within the academic year 1982–1983, the following events: University of Louisville (37 full-time faculty removed, 11 of them tenured professors); Northern Michigan State (19 tenured and tenure-track faculty members cast out); Western Oregon State (16 faculty members removed, three-quarters from tenure slots); State University of New York at Brockton (53 faculty members, including 37 with tenure, laid off).

128. Stroup, Van Gliessen, and Zirkel, "Deficits, Declines, and Dismissals," pp. 4–41.

129. U.S. Supreme Court, NLRB v. Yeshiva University, 444 U.S. (1980).

BIBLIOGRAPHY

Adams, Herbert Baxter. "The Study of History in American Colleges and Universities." *Bureau of Education Circular of Information*, No. 2. Washington, D.C.: Government Printing Office, 1887.

Allen, Garland. "The Transformation of a Science: T. H. Morgan and The Emergence of a New American Biology." In *Organization of Knowledge in Modern America, 1860–1920*, ed. Alexandra Oleson and John Voss, 173–210. Baltimore: The Johns Hopkins University Press, 1979.

Allen, William Harvey. *Efficient Democracy.* New York: Dodd, Mead, 1912.

————. *Self-Surveys by Colleges and Universities.* Yonkers-On-Hudson, New York: World Book, 1917.

Allmendinger, David. *Paupers and Scholars: The Transformation of Student Life in Nineteenth-Century New England.* New York: St. Martin's, 1975.

American Association of University Professors. "Report of Committee A." *AAUP Bulletin* 23 (February 1937): 103–108.

————. "Council Position on Collective Bargaining." *AAUP Bulletin* 58 (Spring 1972): 46–61.

————. "Annual Report on the Economic Status of the Profession, 1982–1983." *Academe* 69 (July–August 1983): 3–8.

————. "Joint Statement on Government of Colleges and Universities." *AAUP Policy Statements and Reports.* Pp. 105–110. Washington, D.C., 1984.

Auerbach, Jerold S. *Unequal Justice.* London and New York: Oxford University Press, 1976.

Babbitt, Irving. *Literature and the American College.* Boston: Houghton Mifflin, 1908.

Bagster-Collins, E. W. "History of Modern Language Teaching in the United States." In *Studies in Modern Language Teaching,* ed. E. W. Bagster-Collins. 49–64. New York: Macmillan, 1930.

Barnard, F. A. P. *Analysis of Some Statistics of Collegiate Education.* New York: Columbia University Press, 1870.

Beach, Mark B. "Professors, Presidents and Trustees: A Study of University Governance, 1825–1918." Ph.D. diss., University of Wisconsin, 1966.

Becker, Gary. *Human Capital: A Theoretical and Empirical Analysis with Special Reference to Education.* Princeton: Princeton University Press, 1964.

Ben-David, Joseph. "Universities and Growth of Science in Germany and the United States. *Minerva* 7 (1968–1969): 1–36.

Ben-David, Joseph, and Randall Collins. "Social Factors in the Origins of a New Science: The Case of Psychology." *American Sociological Review* 31 (August 1966): 451–465.

Ben-David, Joseph, and Abraham Zloczower. "Universities and Academic Systems in Modern Societies." *European Journal of Sociology* 3 (1962): 45–84.

Bender, Thomas. "Science and the Culture of American Communities: The 19th Century." *History of Education Quarterly* 16 (Spring 1976): 63–77.

Benjamin, Robert. "Ludwig Lewisohn and the Lost Generation." Ph.D. diss., Columbia University, 1973.

Bernard, F. A. P. *Analysis of Some Statistics of Collegiate Education.* New York: Columbia University, 1870.

Bierstedt, Robert, and Fritz Machlup. "Representation of Collective Interests: Dissenting Statement." *AAUP Bulletin* 52 (Summer 1966): 232–234.

Blackburn, Robert. "Careers for Academics and the Future Production of Knowledge." In *The Academic Profession,* ed. Philip Altbach and Sheila Slaughter. Philadelphia: The Annals of the American Academy of Political and Social Science, 1980.

Blau, Peter. *The Organization of Academic Work.* New York and London: John Wiley, 1973.

Bledstein, Burton. *The Culture of Professionalism.* New York: Norton, 1976.

Boas, Louise S. *Women's Education Begins: The Rise of Women's Colleges.* Norton, Mass.: Wheaton College Press, 1955.

Boring, Edwin. *History of Experimental Psychology.* 2d ed. New York: Appleton-Century-Crofts, 1950.

Bowen, Howard R. "Faculty Salaries, Past and Future." *Educational Record* 49 (Winter 1968): 9–21.

Bozeman, Theodore Dwight. *Protestants in an Age of Science: The Baconian Ideal and Antebellum Religious Thought.* Chapel Hill: University of North Carolina Press, 1977.

Bronson, Walter C. *The History of Brown University, 1764–1914.* Providence, R.I.: Brown University, 1914.

Brown, Ralph. "Collective Bargaining in Higher Education." *Michigan Law Review* 67 (March 1969): 1067–1082.

Brubacher, John S., and Willis Rudy. *Higher Education in Transition: A History of American Colleges and Universities, 1636–1968.* New York: Harper and Row, 1968.

Bryson, Gladys. "The Emergence of the Social Sciences from Moral Philosophy." *International Journal of Ethics* 42 (1931–1932): 304–323.

Burke, Colin B. *American Collegiate Populations: A Test of the Traditional View.* New York: New York University Press, 1982.

Burritt, Bailey B. "Professional Distribution of College and University Graduates." *Bureau of Education Bulletin of Information.* Washington, D.C.: Government Printing Office, 1912.

Butts, R. Freeman. *The College Charts Its Course: Historical Conceptions and Current Proposals.* New York: McGraw-Hill, 1939.

Callahan, Raymond E. *Education and the Cult of Efficiency: A Study of the Social Forces That Have Shaped the Administration of the Public Schools.* Chicago: University of Chicago Press, 1962.

Carrell, William D. "American College Professors, 1750–1800." *History of Education Quarterly* 8: (Fall 1968): 289–305.

Carr-Saunders, A. M., and P. A. Wilson. *The Professions.* Oxford: Clarendon, 1933.

Cattell, J. McKeen. "A Statistical Study of American Men of Science. 2." *Science,* n.s. 24 (30 November 1906): 699–707.

——. "A Further Statistical Study of American Men of Science." *Science,* n.s. 32 (4 November 1910): 633–648.

Cheyney, Edward Potts. *History of the University of Pennsylvania, 1740–1940.* Philadelphia: University of Pennsylvania Press, 1940.

Chittenden, Russell H. *History of the Sheffield Scientific School of Yale University, 1846–1922.* Vol. 1. New Haven: Yale University Press, 1928.

Church, Robert L. "The Economists Study Society: Sociology at Harvard,

1891–1902." In *Social Sciences at Harvard, 1860–1920*, ed. Paul Buck, 18–90. Cambridge, Mass.: Harvard University Press, 1965.

Clark, Burton R. "Academic Culture." Higher Education Research Group Working Paper, No. 42. New Haven: Yale University, March 1980.

Clark, Burton R., and Ted I. K. Youn. *Academic Power in the United States.* American Association for Higher Education. *Research Report*, No. 3. Washington, D.C., 1976.

Clarke, F. W. "The Appointment of College Officers." *Popular Science Monthly* 21 (June 1882): 171–178.

Cohen, I. Bernard. "Science in America: The Nineteenth Century." In *Paths of American Thought*, ed. Arthur M. Schlesinger and Morton White, 167–189. New York: Collier's, 1962.

Columbia College. *Officers and Graduates of Columbia College: General Catalogue, 1784–1894.* New York: Columbia College, 1894.

Content, Robin. "Emergence of the American Professor." *History of Education Quarterly* 14 (Fall 1974): 430–434.

Cooke, Morris Llewellyn. "Academic and Industrial Efficiency: A Report." Carnegie Foundation for the Advancement of Teaching. *Bulletin*, No. 5. New York, 1910.

Crane, Diana M. "Social Class Origin and Academic Success: The Influence of Two Stratification Systems on Academic Careers." *Sociology of Education* 42 (Winter 1969): 1–17.

Cruetz, Allan. "From College Teacher to University Scholar: The Evolution and Professionalization of Academics at the University of Michigan, 1841–1900." Ph.D. diss., University of Michigan, 1981.

Curti, Merle, and Vernon Carstensen. *The University of Wisconsin: A History. 1848–1925.* 2 vols. Madison: University of Wisconsin Press, 1949.

Daniels, George H. *American Science in the Age of Jackson.* New York and London: Columbia University Press, 1968.

————. *Nineteenth Century American Science: A Reappraisal.* Evanston, Ill.: Northwestern University Press, 1972.

————. "The Process of Professionalism in American Science: The Emergent Period, 1820–1860." *Isis* 58 (Summer 1976): 151–166.

Darnell, Regna. "The Emergence of Academic Anthropology at the University of Pennsylvania." *Journal of the History of the Behavioral Sciences* (January 1970): 80–92.

————. *Readings in the History of Anthropology.* New York: Harper and Row, 1974.

Denison, Edward F. *The Sources of Economic Growth and the Alternatives Before Us.* Committee for Economic Development. Supplementary Paper, No. 13. New York, 1962.

Diehl, Carl. *Americans and German Scholarship: 1770–1870.* New Haven and London: Yale University Press, 1978.

Dinar, Stephen J. "Department and Discipline: The Department of Sociology at the University of Chicago, 1892–1920." *Minerva* 13 (Winter 1975): 514–533.

Draper, Andrew. *American Education.* Boston: Houghton Mifflin, 1909.

Dunham, R., P. S. Wright, and M. O. Chandler. *Teaching Faculty in Universities and Four-Year Colleges, Spring 1963.* Washington, D.C.: U.S. Office of Education, 1966.

Eckert, Ruth E., and John E. Stecklein. *Job Motivations and Satisfactions of College Teachers: A Study of Faculty Members in Minnesota Colleges.* Washington, D.C.: U.S. Office of Education, 1961.

Eels, Walter Crosby. "First Degrees in Music." *History of Education Quarterly* 1 (March 1961): 35–40.

"The Efficiency Nostrum" (editorial). *The Nation* 96 (16 January 1913): 49–50.

Eliot, Charles W. *Educational Reform: Essays and Addresses.* New York: Century, 1898.

———. *University Administration.* New York: Houghton Mifflin, 1908.

Elliott, Orrin L. *Stanford University: The First Twenty-Five Years.* Stanford, Calif.: Stanford University Press, 1937.

Engel, Arthur J. "From Clergyman to Don: The Rise of the Academic Profession in Nineteenth Century Oxford." Ph.D. diss., Princeton University, 1975.

Etzioni, Amitai. *The Semi-Professions and Their Organization.* New York: The Free Press, 1969.

"Extent of Instruction in Anthropology in Europe and the United States." *Science,* n.s. (1899): 910–917.

Ferris, Abbott L. *Indicators of Trends in American Education.* New York: Russell Sage Foundation, 1969.

Finkelstein, Martin J. "Three Decades of Research on American Academics: A Descriptive Portrait and Synthesis of Findings." Ph.D. diss., State University of New York at Buffalo, 1978.

———. "From Tutor to Specialized Scholar: Academic Professionalization in Eighteenth and Nineteenth Century America." *History of Higher Education Annual* 3 (1983): 99–121.

Finken, Matthew. "Toward a Law of Academic Status." *Buffalo Law Review* 22 (1972): 575–602.

Fishlow, Albert. "Levels of Nineteenth-Century American Investments in Education." *Journal of Economic History* 26 (December 1966): 418–436.

Flexner, Abraham. *Is Social Work A Profession?* New York: New York School of Philanthropy, 1915.

Folger, John K., and Charles B. Nam. *Education of the American Population: A 1960 Census Monograph.* Washington, D.C.: Government Printing Office, 1967.

Foster, Margery S. *"Out of Small Beginnings . . ." An Economic History of Harvard College in the Puritan Period 1636–1712.* Cambridge, Mass.: Belknap, 1982.

Foster, William T. *Administration of the College Curriculum.* Boston: Houghton Mifflin, 1911.

Fulton, Oliver, and Martin Trow. "Research Activity in American Higher Education." In *Teachers and Students: Aspects of American Higher Education*, ed. Martin Trow. New York: McGraw-Hill, 1975.

Furner, Mary O. *Advocacy and Objectivity: A Crisis in the Professionalization of American Social Science*. Lexington: University of Kentucky Press, 1975.

Gilb, Corinne L. *Hidden Hierarchies: The Professions and Government*. New York: Harper and Row, 1966.

Goode, William J. "Community Within a Community: The Professions." *American Sociological Review* 22 (1967): 194–200.

Gouldner, Alvin W. "Cosmopolitans and Locals: Toward an Analysis of Latent Social Roles." *Administrative Science Quarterly* 2 (December 1957): 281–306; 3 (March 1958): 444–480.

Graham, Patricia. "Women in Academe." *Science* (25 September 1970): 1284–1290.

Greeley, Andrew. "On 'Is There an Academic Melting Pot?': Comment." *Sociology of Education* 50 (1977): 218–219.

Guralnick, Stanley A. *Science and The Ante-Bellum College*. Philadelphia: American Philosophical Society, 1975.

_____. "The American Scientist in Higher Education." In *The Sciences in The American Context: New Perspectives*, ed. Nathan Reingold, 90–137. Washington, D.C.: Smithsonian Institution Press, 1970.

Habenstein, Robert W. "Critique of 'Profession' as a Sociological Category." *Sociological Quarterly* 4 (Autumn 1963): 291–300.

Haber, Samuel. "The Professions and Higher Education in America: A Historical View." In *Higher Education and the Labor Market*, ed. Margaret S. Gordon. New York: McGraw-Hill, 1974.

Haddow, Anna. *Political Science in American Colleges and Universities: 1636–1900*. New York: Octagon Books, 1969.

Hagstrom, Warren O. "Inputs, Outputs and the Prestige of University Departments." *Sociology of Education* 44 (1971): 375–397.

Hall, Peter Dobkin. "Veritas et Pecunias: The Historical Economy of Education." Higher Education Research Group Working Paper, No. 3. New Haven: Yale University, December 1975.

Halsey, A. H., and Martin A. Trow. *The British Academics*. Cambridge, Mass.: Harvard University Press, 1971.

Hammond, P. E., J. W. Mayer, and D. Miller. "Teaching Versus Research: Sources of Misperceptions." *Journal of Higher Education* 40 (1969): 682–690.

Harris, Seymour. *Economics of Harvard*. New York: McGraw-Hill, 1970.

_____. *A Statistical Portrait of Higher Education*. Carnegie Commission on Higher Education. New York: McGraw-Hill, 1972.

Haskell, Thomas. *The Emergence of Professional Social Science: The American Social Science Association and the Nineteenth Century Crisis in Authority*. Urbana: University of Illinois Press, 1976.

Herbst, Jurgen. *The German Historical School in American Scholarship: A Study in the Transfer of Culture*. Ithaca, N.Y.: Cornell University Press, 1965.

———. "American College History: Re-examination Underway." *History of Education Quarterly* 14 (1974): 259–266.

Heydeband, Wolff. "The Technocratic Administration of Higher Education." Unpublished manuscript.

Higham, John. "The Matrix of Specialization." In *The Organization of Knowledge in Modern America, 1860–1920*, ed. Alexandra Oleson and John Voss, 3–18. Baltimore and London: The Johns Hopkins University Press, 1979.

Hofstadter, Richard. *Academic Freedom in The Age of The College.* New York: Columbia University Press, 1955.

Holt, W. Stull, ed. *Historical Scholarship in the United States, 1876–1901.* Baltimore: Johns Hopkins Press, 1938.

Hovenkamp, Robert. *Science and Religion in America: 1800–1860.* Philadelphia: University of Pennsylvania Press, 1978.

Hughes, Everett C. *Men and Their Work.* Glencoe, Ill.: The Free Press, 1958.

Hunt, C. L. *The Life of Ellen H. Richards.* Washington, D.C.: American Home Economics Association, 1942.

Jaffe, Abe J., and Walter Adams. "College Education for United States Youth: Attitudes of Parents and Children." *American Journal of Economics and Sociology* 23 (July 1964): 269–283.

James, Henry. *Charles W. Eliot: President of Harvard University.* 2 vols. Boston: Houghton Mifflin, 1930.

Jencks, Christopher, and David Riesman. *The Academic Revolution.* Garden City, N.Y.: Doubleday, 1968.

John, Walton C. *Graduate Study in Universities and Colleges in the United States.* Washington, D.C.: Government Printing Office, 1935.

Johnson, G. E., and E. P. Stafford. "The Earnings and Promotion of Women Faculty." *Journal of Political Economy* 85 (December 1977): 1099–1123.

Johnson, William R. "Education and Professional Life Styles: Law and Medicine in the Nineteenth Century." *History of Education Quarterly* 14 (Summer 1974): 185–207.

Kadish, Sanford. "The Theory of the Profession and Its Predicament." *AAUP Bulletin* 58 (June 1972): 120–125.

Kennedy, Sister Mel. "The Changing Academic Characteristics of the Nineteenth Century College Teacher." Ph.D. diss., St. Louis University, 1961.

Kevles, Daniel J. *The Physicists: The History of a Scientific Community.* New York: Knopf, 1977.

Knepper, Edwin G. *History of Business Education in the United States.* Bowling Green, Ohio: Edwin G. Knepper, 1951.

Kohler, Robert E. "The History of Biochemistry: A Survey." *Journal of the History of Biology* 8 (1975): 275–318.

Kohlstedt, Sally. "The Formation of the American Scientific Community: The American Association for the Advancement of Science, 1848–1860." Ph.D. diss., University of Illinois, 1972.

Ladd, Everett C., and Seymour M. Lipset. *Professors, Unions and American Higher Education.* Berkeley: Carnegie Foundation for the Advancement of Teaching, 1973.

————. "Survey." *Chronicle of Higher Education* (26 January 1976).

Larson, Magali S. *The Rise of Professionalism: A Sociological Analysis.* Berkeley, Los Angeles, London: University of California Press, 1977.

Laughlin, J. Laurence. "The Study of Political Economy in the United States." *Journal of Political Economy in the United States* 1 (December 1892): 1–19, 143–151.

Leonard, Fred E., and George B. Afflack. *A Guide to the History of Physical Education.* Philadelphia: Lea and Febiger, 1947.

Lewis, Lionel S., and Michael N. Ryan. "Professionalization and the Professoriate." *Social Problems* 24 (December 1976): 283–297.

————. "The American Professoriate and the Movement Toward Unionization." *Higher Education* 6 (1977): 139–164.

Light, Donald. "Introduction: The Structure of the Academic Profession." *Sociology of Education* 47 (Winter 1964): 2–28.

Light, Donald, L. R. Marsden, and T. C. Cori. *The Impact of the Academic Revolution on Faculty Careers.* Washington, D.C.: American Association for Higher Education, February 1973.

Lipset, Seymour M., and Everett C. Ladd, Jr. "Jewish Academics in the United States: Their Achievements, Culture and Politics." Reprint. *American Jewish Yearbook* (1971): 89–128.

Loughlin, L. Lawrence. "The Study of Political Economy in the United States." *Journal of Political Economy* 1 (December 1892): 1–19, 143–151.

Lovejoy, Arthur O. "Annual Message of the President." *AAUP Bulletin* 5 (November–December 1919): 10–40.

————. "Professional Association or Trade Union?" *AAUP Bulletin* 24 (May 1938): 410–417.

McCaughey, Robert. "The Transformation of American Academic Life: Harvard University 1821–1892." *Perspectives in American History* 8 (1974): 239–334.

McGrath, Earl J. "The Control of Higher Education in America." *Educational Record* 17 (April 1936): 259–272.

————. *Universal Higher Education.* New York: McGraw-Hill, 1966.

Machlup, Fritz. *The Production and Distribution of Knowledge in the United States.* Princeton: Princeton University Press, 1963.

McLathlan, James. "The Choice of Hercules: American Student Societies in the Early 19th Century." In *The University in Society,* ed. Lawrence Stone. Vol. 2. Princeton: Princeton University Press, 1974.

————. "The American College in the Nineteenth Century: Toward a Reappraisal." *Teachers College Record* 80 (December 1978): 287–306.

Marx, Guido. "The Problem of the Assistant Professor." *Journal of Proceedings of the Association of American Universities* 11 (1910): 17–47.

————. "Composition of University Staffs." In *Cyclopedia of Education,* vol. 5, p. 609. New York: Macmillan, 1913.

Mendenhall, T. S. "Scientific, Technical and Engineering Education." In *Monographs on Education in the United States,* ed. Nicholas Murray Butler, pp. 533–592. Albany, N.Y: J. B. Lyon, 1900.

Merton, Robert. *The Sociology of Science*. Chicago: University of Chicago Press, 1973.

Metzger, Walter P. *Development of Academic Freedom in the Age of the University*. New York: Columbia University Press, 1955. Originally published as Richard Hofstadter and Walter P. Metzger. *Development of Academic Freedom in the United States*, part 2.

———. "Origins of the Association: An Anniversary Address." *AAUP Bulletin* 47 (Summer 1964): 229–237.

———. "Academic Freedom in Delocalized Academic Institutions." In *Dimensions of Academic Freedom*, ed. John H. McCord. Urbana: University of Illinois Press, 1969.

———. "Crisis of Academic Authority." *Daedalus* 99 (Summer 1970): 568–608.

———. "Academic Tenure in America: A Historical Essay." In AAUP/AAC Commission on Academic Tenure, *Faculty Tenure: A Report and Recommendations*. San Francisco: Jossey-Bass, 1973.

———. "The American Academic Profession in 'Hard Times.' " *Daedalus* 104, Vol. II. (Winter 1975): 25–65.

———. "What is a Profession?" Program of General and Continuing Education. *Seminar Reports* 3, 1975.

Moore, Wilbert E. *The Professions: Roles and Rules*. New York: Russell Sage Foundation, 1970.

Morison, Jack. *Rise of the Arts on the American Campus*. New York: McGraw-Hill, 1973.

Morison, Samuel Eliot, ed. *The Development of Harvard University Since the Inauguration of President Eliot, 1869–1929*. Cambridge, Mass.: Harvard University Press, 1930.

———. *Three Centuries of Harvard 1636–1936*. Cambridge, Mass.: Harvard University Press, 1936.

Murchison, Carl. *A History of Psychology in Autobiography*. 4 vols. Cambridge: Clark University Press, 1930–1952.

"A National Association of University Professors." *Science*, n.s. 39 (27 March 1914): 458.

Naylor, Natalie A. "The Ante-Bellum College Movement: A Reappraisal of Tewksbury's *The Founding of American Colleges and Universities*." *History of Education Quarterly* 13 (Fall 1973): 261–274.

———. "The Theological Seminary in the Configuration of American Higher Education: The Ante-Bellum Years." *History of Education Quarterly* 17 (1977): 17–30.

Norwood, William F. *Medical Education in the United States Before the Civil War*. London: Oxford University Press, 1944.

Oleson, Alexandra, and Sanford C. Brown, eds. *The Pursuit of Knowledge in the Early Republic: American Scientific and Learned Societies from Colonial Times to the Civil War*. Baltimore and London: The Johns Hopkins University Press, 1976.

Oleson, Alexandra, and John Voss, eds. *The Organization of Knowledge in Mod-*

ern America, 1860–1920. Baltimore and London: The Johns Hopkins University Press, 1979.

Parsons, Talcott. "The Professions and Social Structure." *Social Forces* 17 (May 1939): 457–467.

Parsons, Talcott, and Gerald M. Platt. *The American Academic Profession: A Pilot Study.* Cambridge, Mass.: Harvard University Press, 1968.

———. *The American University.* Cambridge, Mass.: Harvard University Press, 1973.

Peterson, Marvin. *The Organization of Departments.* American Association for Higher Education Research. Report No. 2. Washington, D.C., 1970.

Pierson, George W. "The Elective System and the Difficulties of College Planning, 1870–1940." *Journal of General Education* 5 (April 1950): 167–174.

Porter, Noah. *The American Colleges and the American Public.* New Haven: Charles C. Chatfield, 1870.

Potts, David B. "American Colleges in the Nineteenth Century: From Localism to Denominationalism." *History of Education Quarterly* 11 (Winter, 1971): 363–380.

———. "Students and the Social History of American Higher Education." *History of Education Quarterly* 15 (Fall 1975): 317–327.

———. "Curriculum and Enrollments: Some Thoughts on Assessing the Popularity of Ante-bellum Colleges." *History of Higher Education Annual* 1 (1981): 89–109.

Pound, Roscoe. "The Law School." In *Development of Harvard University Since the Inauguration of President Eliot, 1869–1929,* ed. Samuel E. Morison. Cambridge, Mass.: Harvard University Press, 1930.

Price, Derek J. De Sola. *Science Since Babylon.* New Haven: Yale University Press, 1961.

———. *Little Science, Big Science.* New York: Columbia University Press, 1963.

Reader, William J. *Professional Men: The Rise of the Professional Classes in Nineteenth Century England.* London: Weidenfeld and Nicholson, 1966.

Reingold, Nathan. "Definitions and Speculations: The Professionalization of Science in America in the Nineteenth Century." In *The Pursuit of Knowledge in the Early American Republic: American Scientific and Learned Societies from Colonial Times to the Civil War,* ed. Alexandra Oleson and Sanford C. Brown, Baltimore: The Johns Hopkins University Press, 33–69.

Rosenberg, Charles E. *No Other Gods: On Science and American Social Thought.* Baltimore: The Johns Hopkins University Press, 1976.

Ross, Earle D. *Democracy's College: The Land Grant Movement in the Formative Stage.* Ames: Iowa College Press, 1942.

Rossiter, Margaret W. *Emergence of Agricultural Science: Julius Liebig and the Americans, 1840–1880.* New Haven: Yale University Press, 1975.

Rothstein, William G. *American Physicians in the Nineteenth Century: From Sects to Science.* Baltimore: The Johns Hopkins University Press, 1972.

Rudolph, Frederick. *Curriculum.* San Francisco: Jossey Bass, 1977.

Schmidt, George P. *The Old-Time College President*. New York: Columbia University Press, 1930.

———. *The Liberal Arts College: A Chapter in American Cultural History*. New Brunswick, N.J.: Rutgers University Press, 1957.

Schultz, Theodore W. *The Economic Value of Education*. New York: Columbia University Press, 1963.

Seligman, E. R. A. "The Early Teachings of Economics in the United States." In *Economic Essays Contributed in Honor of John Bates Clark*, ed. J. H. Hollander. New York: Books for Lybrans Press, 1927.

Shryock, Richard. "The Academic Profession in the United States." *AAUP Bulletin* 38 (Spring 1952): 32–70.

Sloan, Douglas M. *The Scottish Enlightenment and the American College Ideal*. New York: Teachers College Press, 1971.

———. . "Harmony, Chaos and Consensus: The American College Curriculum." *Teachers College Record* (Fall 1971): 221–251.

Smith, Wilson. *Professors and Public Ethics: Studies of Northern Moral Philosophers Before the Civil War*. Ithaca, N.Y.: Cornell University Press, 1956.

———. "The Teacher in Puritan Culture." *Harvard Educational Review* 36 (1966): 394–411.

———. " 'Cow College' Mythology and Social History: A View of Some Centennial Literature." *Agricultural History* 44 (July 1970): 299–310.

———. "Apologia pro Alma Mater: The College as Community in Ante-Bellum America." In *The Hofstadter Aegis: A Memorial*, ed. Stanley Elkins and Eric McKitrick. New York: Knopf, 1974.

Snow, Louis F. *The College Curriculum in the United States*. New York: Teachers College Press, 1907.

Solberg, Winston U. *The University of Illinois*. Urbana: University of Illinois Press, 1968.

Solmon, Lewis C. "Estimates of the Costs of Schooling in 1800 and 1890." *Explorations in Economic History* 7 Supplement (Summer 1970): 531–581.

———. "Women in Doctoral Education: Clues and Puzzles Regarding Institutional Discrimination." *Research in Higher Education* 1 (1973): 299–332.

Solmon, Lewis C., and Paul J. Taubman, eds., *Does College Matter?* New York: Academic Press, 1973.

Soltow, Lee, and Edward Stevens. "Economic Aspects of School Participation in Mid-Nineteenth Century United States." *Journal of Interdisciplinary History* 8 (Autumn 1977): 222–243.

Starr, Harris E. *William Graham Sumner*. New York: Henry Holt, 1925.

Steinberg, Stephen. *The Academic Melting Pot*. New York: McGraw-Hill, 1974.

Stern, Carol Simpson, Jesse Choper, Mary Gray, and Robert J. Wolfson. "The Status of Part-Time Faculty." [Report] *Academe* 67 (February–March 1981): 29–39.

Storr, Richard J. *The Beginnings of Graduate Education in America*. Chicago: University of Chicago Press, 1953.

Stroup, Stinson W., Nan Van Gliesson, and Perry A. Zirkel, "Deficits, Declines, and Dismissals." Washington, D.C.: ERIC Clearinghouse on Teacher Education, February 1982.

Szasz, Thomas. *The Myth of Mental Illness*. New York: Harper and Row, 1979.

"The Teaching of Anthropology in the United States." *Science,* n.s. 15 (1902): 211–216.

Tewksbury, Donald C. *The Founding of American Colleges and Universities Before the Civil War*. New York: Teachers College Press, 1932.

Thomas, W. Scott. "Changes in the Age of College Graduates." *Popular Science Monthly* 63 (1903): 159–171.

Thompson, Judith, and Terrance Sandalow. "On Full-Time Non-tenure-Track Appointments." *AAUP Bulletin* 64 (September 1978): 267–273.

Thwing, Charles F. *A History of Higher Education in America*. New York: D. Appleton, 1906.

Tobias, Marilyn. "Old Dartmouth on Trial: The Transformation of the Academic Community in Nineteenth Century America." Ph.D. diss., New York University, 1977.

Trow, Martin. "The Second Transformation of American Secondary Education." *International Journal of Comparative Sociology* 2 (September 1961): 144–160.

———. "The Democratization of Higher Education." *European Journal of Sociology* 3 (1962): 231–262.

———. "Reflections on the Transition from Mass to Universal Higher Education." *Daedalus* 99 (Winter 1970): 1–42.

Tuckman, Howard, and Jaime Caldwell. "The Reward Structure for Part-Time Teaching Faculty." *Journal of Higher Education* 50 (November–December 1979): 745–760.

Tuckman, Howard, Jaime Caldwell, and William Voger. "Part-Timers and The Academic Labor Market of The Eighties." *American Sociologist* 13 (November 1978): 184–195.

Tyack, David B. *George Ticknor and the Boston Brahmins*. Cambridge, Mass.: Harvard University Press, 1967.

U.S. Bureau of the Census. *Historical Statistics of the United States: Colonial Times to 1970*. Washington, D.C.: Government Printing Office, 1975.

U.S. Commissioner of Education. *Reports*. Washington, D.C.: Government Printing Office, 1870–1932.

U.S. Department of Education. *Digest of Educational Statistics 1982*. Washington, D.C.: Government Printing Office, 1982.

U.S. President's Commission. *Higher Education for American Democracy*. Washington, D.C.: Government Printing Office, 1948.

U.S. Supreme Court. NLRB v. Yeshiva University. 444 U.S. Washington, D.C.: Government Printing Office, 1975.

Van Alstyne, William. "Cracks in the 'New Property': Adjudicative Process in the Administrative State." *Cornell Law Review* 62 (1977): 445–490.

Van Arsdale, George. "De-Professionalizing a Part-Time Teaching Faculty." *The American Sociologist* 13 (November 1978): 212–216.

Van Hise, Charles R. "The Appointment and Tenure of University Professors." Association of American Universities. *Journal of Proceedings and Addresses* 12 (November 1910): 51–55.

Veblen, Thorstein. *The Higher Learning in America: A Memorandum on the Conduct of Universities by Businessmen.* New York: B. W. Heubsch, 1918.

Veysey, Lawrence R. *The Emergence of the American University.* Chicago: University of Chicago Press, 1965.

Wayland, Francis. *Report to the Corporation of Brown University on Changes in the System of Collegiate Education.* Providence, R.I.: 1850.

Webster, Arthur Gordon. "Scientific Management and Academic Efficiency." *The Nation* 9 (2 November, 1911): 416–417.

Wechsler, Harold S. *The Qualified Student: A History of Selective College Admission in America.* New York: John Wiley, 1977.

Whitehead, John S. *The Separation of College and State: Columbia, Dartmouth, Harvard and Yale, 1776–1876.* New Haven: Yale University Press, 1975.

Wiebe, Robert. *Search for Order, 1877–1920.* New York: Hill and Wang, 1967.

Wilensky, Harold L. "The Professionalization of Everyone?" *American Journal of Sociology* 70 (1964): 137–158.

Willey, Malcom W. *Depression, Recovery and Higher Education: A Report of Committee Y on the American Association of University Professors.* New York: McGraw-Hill, 1937.

Wilson, Leonard. "The Emergence of Geology as a Science in the United States." *Journal of World History* 10 (1967): 416–437.

Wilson, Logan. *Academic Man.* New York: Oxford University Press, 1942.

———. *American Academics, Then and Now.* New York: Oxford University Press, 1979.

Wuthnow, Robert. "Is There An Academic Melting Pot?" *Sociology of Education* 50 (January 1977): 7–15.

PART II
DISCIPLINARY AND
INSTITUTIONAL CONTEXTS

5

The Academic Estate in Western Europe

Guy Neave and Gary Rhoades

Two features of academia in Western Europe condition change in higher education systems: its internal organization and its national nature. External forces such as governments, political parties, trade unions, and economic and demographic trends have impact. But equally important is the way academia is organized and how it interacts with those external forces bearing down on higher education. Academia helps both to structure its organizational setting and to determine the work done in it.

As elsewhere, academia in Western Europe is fragmented by disciplinary identity and specialization and by its location in different institutional sectors within the overall system of higher education. But an additional fault line characterizes it in Continental Europe, setting it apart from its fellows in the United Kingdom and the United States: the deep rift between junior and senior staff, between the largely untenured assistant class and the full professoriat. Such ranks are found in British and American academia, but they are not a basis of separate organization. They do not spawn polarized groups of academics that separately represent their interests within or outside the academy to the public central administration or legislative bodies.

This rift in Continental academia may be attributed to the chair-faculty structure predominant until the late 1960s in most Western European universities.[1] This structure is inherently hierarchical, with potential divisions of interest among academics of different ranks. It was based on a system of patronage in which members of the non-

professorial class remained highly dependent on individual chairholders not merely for admission into academia but also for advancement once inside.

The demographic explosion of the early 1960s coupled with the
runaway demand for higher education exposed and exacerbated these
underlying tensions. The rising tide of new students heightened tensions in two ways: it increased the teaching load borne by nonprofessorial staff, particularly assistants; and it unbalanced the "ecology
of academia" by the rapid growth in that same staff, brought in to
teach the ever-rising influx of students. If chairholders still wielded
power and influence, expansion in the lower ranks placed a severe
strain on their patronage networks. And, no less important in molding
the expectations of younger academics, nonprofessorial positions expanded far faster than the professorial posts to which many had
aspired. Expansion also profoundly changed nonprofessorial posts.
In a stable academic ecology these had been a species of protracted
apprenticeships that, with the fullness of time and suitable backing,
would lead to professorial status. When the ecological balance was
upset, however, a new subclass began to assume a permanent status,
and the traditional process of socialization into academia became
strained. Historically, such socialization took place through a master-
apprentice relationship. Proliferation in the lower ranks of university
teachers meant either that such a process became more attenuated or
that for many junior staff it was lacking.

Such tensions were deeply embedded in many of Western Europe's
academic bodies. They contributed to and shaped the course of change
in universities. In an attempt to secure tenure or advancement, certain
sectors of nonprofessorial academia looked toward trade unions, reas-
serted their links with political parties, or formed associations inside
the university directly affiliated with these institutions outside.
Through them, and at times allied with students, they sought to bring
pressure on external political and governmental agencies for university reform. They sought in the new world of the political process to
rebalance the hierarchy of forces in the old world of academia. The
rise of student activism in the late 1960s contributed in no small
measure to this development.

The house of academe was divided against itself. This division
brought about a remodeling of its university home and a redistribution
of power within it. In many university systems the structures of internal management were either "modernized" or "democra-
tized,"depending on one's inclination. The chair-faculty structure was
uprooted and replaced by new basic units of organization. Formally,

nonprofessorial academics were given a greater say in university affairs. These changes were not simply the product of external intervention by the legislator. They were driven by factions of nonprofessorial malcontents in academia.

But attempts by governments to introduce change in universities cannot rely on playing one group inside academia against another. In the academy, as in law, circumstances alter cases; divisions are not always prominent. A second feature of Western European academia has inhibited governmental efforts to promote certain kinds of change in higher education. In mainland Western Europe, academia is not a profession. It is an estate, whose power, privileges, and conditions of employment are protected by constitutional or administrative law. As such it is linked directly to the state and is distinctly national in orientation. The house of academe is riven with factions when the agenda involves the distribution of internal privilege and power, but on matters involving the place, privileges, purpose, and mission of academia in society—and by extension, the university—corporate solidarity very quickly replaces internecine feuding. Nonprofessorial staff in the late 1960s were not so much engaged in recasting the national purpose and place of the institution in which they worked;[2] rather their objective was to share in the power and privileges enjoyed by chairholders.

From the late 1960s, governments in Western Europe struggled to reorient and redirect the work of universities. They have attempted to "vocationalize," "industrialize," and "regionalize" university education, and generally make it "more relevant" to perceived national priorities. Academics of all ranks moved to block or impede these reforms.[3] The driving force behind their resistance to change was the desire to preserve the relatively homogeneous and national character of university education. Government proposals were perceived as detrimental to the public status of academe and the university as national institutions. Divided though it is, academia in Western Europe still conceives itself to be a national estate.

These two central characteristics of academia in mainland Europe— the junior-senior faculty rift and the close relationship to the state— are discussed in the following pages. We analyze European chair-faculty structure and contrast it with organizational patterns in British and American academia. Subsequently, we examine two variants of the ideal typical chair-faculty model. In the next section we venture more deeply into the academic estate in Western Europe, focusing on its national dimension and historical origins and on the cultural assumptions underpinning its development. In two following sections we relate these organizational characteristics to academia's role and stance in promoting and inhibiting change in university systems. Due to its fissures, academia brought about major change in the structure and governance of universities. Despite its internal divisions, it also held at bay governmental efforts at bringing about fundamental change in the work of universities.

These sections may be viewed as case studies of how academia responds to issues it regards as central. The academic body is not a monolithic entity. On the contrary, its internal schisms and alliances— quite apart from its mésalliances—are as shifting as they are kaleidoscopic. Patterns of academic organization are important in understanding the denizens of the academic world and their actions. The way the academic animal enacts a role is profoundly influenced by the internal organizational environment in which he or she evolves.

THE SEATS OF DIVISION

Forms of work organization, and the social relations they embody— between employer and employee, master and apprentice, or strata of professional colleagues—have embedded tensions. Academia is no exception. Generally, two patterns of organization prevail at the lowest decision-making units.[4] We focus on the chair-faculty structure, contrast it with the department-college structure, and identify its historical origins, referring to some of its variants. Special attention is drawn to inherent tensions within the chair-faculty structure which potentially can divide academics into polarized, conflicting groups.

The chair-faculty structure dominated in Western Europe through the 1960s. It was replaced in varying degrees by a department "electoral college" structure different in several ways from the department-college structure, the hallmark of American academia. One major difference is that the electoral college structure rests on the principle of constituent, corporate interests. Organized on the basis of rank in the academic career ladder, each constituency is formally represented in all university decision-making organs according to a nationally prescribed formula.[5] Unlike the American college structure, there is no collegium. British academic organization supplies still another type that combines elements from chair-faculty and department-college models.

Two Ideal Types: The Chair-Faculty and Department-College Structures

In the chair-faculty mode the salient feature is its attachment of overwhelming weight to the independence and personal authority of individual chairholders—the professors. Around this figure academic work is organized. Although a large share of work is actually done by subordinate academic staff, it is managed by the professor. Chairholders are the "local expression" of a discipline or a field. So strong is their autonomy that Continental European universities have been described as "associations of independent practitioners."[6]

Independent though they are, chairholders are neither isolated nor freestanding. They are joined in faculties that serve diverse functions: as vehicles for coordination between professors; as units that oversee broad areas of academic work, for example, theology, law, medicine, arts, or philosophy; and as a fount of professorial self-government.[7]

Nevertheless, faculties are a source of horizontal linkage, not of vertical control: they are dominated from below by the chairholders. Though they have power, faculties are not part of a vertical hierarchy above the chair. In fact, the dean of the faculty is elected by the professoriat and the deanship is largely an honorific post.[8]

Professorial power and independence derive from privileges, resources, and facilities that the state confers on the chairholder. Such resources, individually designated, are also the sinews of an authority over subordinates so absolute that professors are rulers over "private fiefdoms."[9] The medieval metaphor is apt since the origins of the chair-faculty structure are traceable directly to medieval guilds. Professors are the masters, and the subordinate academic staff serve either as their apprentices or, in a slightly less humble station, as their journeymen.[10] In either case the relationship is based on a very high degree of dependency, often for extended periods.

Commentators on chair-faculty structures have tended to emphasize its inbuilt rigidity and its lack of adaptive capacity in the face of changes and expansion in knowledge.[11] But its inflexibility extends into social relations between professorial and nonprofessorial academic staff. The institutionalization of the latter's total dependency with the former's unalloyed power had the potential to deeply divide academia into conflicting groups. Historically, social relations may have been stable. But under specific circumstances they could erupt into conflict over the distribution of academic privilege and power. They could also foster the development of academic orders whose interpretations of the academic enterprise were antithetical. If, in the realm of knowledge, the chair-faculty structure gave rise to a fragmentation and balkanization of disciplines, so too did it lead to fragmentation inside the work structure, polarizing interests along the dimensions of formal rank and official status.

The department-college structure is, by contrast, based on a group of colleagues, rather than an individual, as the basic working unit.

Even in Britain, where the chair-faculty structure runs parallel to a departmental organization, chairholders possess neither the privileges nor the powers of their Continental counterparts. Academic work is organized and managed by the department, not by the individual chairholder.[12] Such an arrangement permits some measure of collegiality to be built into the basic operating unit. In the United States this is pushed further. Department heads rotate. This practice further disperses power among many academics instead of concentrating it in one permanent chairholder or head.[13]

In department-college structures nonprofessorial academics are neither powerless nor dependent on an individual chairholder. Their probationary period is not as extended as it is in Continental Europe, and they need not bank on a chairholder to be granted tenure by a department.[14] Nonprofessorial staff members participate actively in departmental life, not as complete equals nor as complete dependents. "The department spreads responsibilities and powers among a number of professors of similar senior rank and more readily allows for some participation by associates and assistants." The department-college structure provides the opportunity for more collegial interplay between academics of different ranks.[15]

Between the department and the university stands an intermediate grouping that links departments. Though terminology varies in the United States, this body is typically known as the college.[16] It has considerable power over departments, which derives from its allocation and control of resources and its involvement in decisions about academic work.

Colleges in an American university differ from faculties in Continental Europe because they have a powerful administrative framework. Heads of colleges—deans—are appointed from above, not elected from below, and colleges, unlike faculties, sit above departments as part of a vertical hierarchy.[17] The head of a department is thus accountable to the college; in Europe the chairholder is not responsible to the faculty in the same manner. If the faculty stands as a voluntary association of professors, acting only on the authority of this same group, the college in the American university occupies a separate administrative position over and above academics, and is endowed with its own powers of initiative.

The college structure engenders a sense of immediate solidarity among all ranks of academic staff, setting them apart from, sometimes in opposition to, a bureaucracy.[18] The collegium is reinforced in that it sets over against academic staff a competing nonacademic, bureaucratic force. Such an organizational model stands in sharp relief to

Continental European universities, where the faculty acts as the long arm of the basic unit, the chair, rather than as its potential rival.

BRITAIN: A MIDPOINT

The college model in America drew considerable inspiration from the clusters of colleges in Oxford and Cambridge, striking examples of an inclusive collegium where all academics participate equally in college governance. But it tends to be an atypical form of organization, even in Britain, and is rarely emulated by other British universities. The more usual pattern brings together chair organization with departmental structure, which is overlaid by faculties, not colleges.[19]

Despite variations among universities, there are qualities common to both British faculties and their fellows in Continental Europe. If, from an organizational perspective, they stand above the department, still they do not constitute a hierarchy of vertical control. Faculties operate more as intermediary and advisory bodies, responding to initiatives coming from elsewhere in the system—mainly from professors who make up the faculty and who, through it, elect the dean.[20]

In one important respect, however, British faculties are different from those on the Continent. They are not freestanding, autonomous, exclusive academic guilds, as were the French faculties in the nineteenth century. British faculties are part of a university governmental structure that has independence and power and which, from the earliest times, has also included nonacademics who had considerable influence—a feature serving to strengthen a common identity among academics.

The British system then stands midway between European and American structures, linking a departmental structure to a modified version of the chair-faculty system. Yet in terms of the social relations it fosters, it is closer to the American pattern. The British department has effective power over individual chairs and professors; it thus constrains how much autocratic power may be exercised by the chairholder over nonprofessorial colleagues. Since the department provides an inclusive collegium, tensions among the ranks of academics are less pronounced. The British faculty unit further contributes to a sense of academic solidarity.

VARIANTS OF THE CHAIR-FACULTY PATTERN

University systems of Western Europe and their chair-faculty patterns of work are diverse. Our discussion centers on those variations in France and in the Federal Republic of Germany. We do not pose them as basic models, although the latter did exercise no small influence over academic work organization in Dutch, Danish, Norwegian, and Swedish universities, and the former had a similar influence on Spanish and many Latin American universities.[21] Here we simply note the interplay between historical and institutional forces that give rise to these variations in the chair-faculty structure. Despite these variations, the central theme holds: embedded in the social relations of these structures are potentially divisive tensions between professorial and nonprofessorial academic staff.

French faculties were more freestanding than their German counterparts. Before implementing the Higher Education Guideline Law of 1968, M. Edgar Faure, then France's Minister of Education, suggested that before that time separate universities did not exist in France.[22] Strictly speaking, he was incorrect. In 1896 the largely self-contained faculties had been united into individual universities, thereby reviving an institution abolished by the French Revolution of 1789. But M. Faure did not entirely err because that decree remained largely unobserved. The *faculté* remained the highest organizational grouping; hence only deans of faculties existed, not university presidents. Professors alluded to themselves as *professeurs à la faculté* rather than—as Anglo-Saxon expectations might suggest—*professeur à l'université*.[23] In fact "l'université" did not mean a single establishment. It referred to the entire public secondary and higher education system and its personnel.[24] *Les amis de nos amis sont parfois de faux amis!*

By contrast, German faculties had always been part of a university structure of governance. The deanship in a German faculty was a powerless office, but the *doyen de la faculté* was not.[25] Even so, the powers of the German faculty as a corporate body were not inconsiderable. Though often subject to negotiation with central authority, it supervised the filling of vacant chairs, and also took an active part in granting the Habilitation degree. In both instances the faculty mitigated the particularistic domination of individual professors.[26]

No less important was the formal independence of German universities vis-à-vis public authorities. In France the faculty played only a part, and perhaps not the major one, in filling professorial vacancies.[27] If individual institutions lacked control over their professorial nominations, this was compounded by the presence of the *Agrégation*. Comparable in importance to the German Habilitation, the Agrégation is a centralized state examination, administered neither by a single professor nor by a single faculty. Simultaneously, it was a symbol of national excellence and institutional weakness. If faculties were autonomous in relation to individual universities in France, this autonomy was restricted by their links with centralized agencies. The German faculties, on the other hand, derived strength both from their controlling role inside universities and from the autonomy universities enjoyed in teaching and research.

Differences between the two countries are also visible within the chair structure. France and Germany are substantially different in the patterns of dependency this structure engendered. This dissimilarity reflects the diverse ways in which professorial power was developed and exercised. The two variants on the chair model have been described as the "cluster" pattern in France and the "apprenticeship" pattern in Germany.[28]

The French cluster pattern rested on the influence individual chairholders exercised over the careers and fortunes of their students and disciplines. Clusters were composed of a dozen or so individuals, generally including *lycée* teachers, members of research institutes, and chairholders in provincial universities. These individuals were grouped as supplicants around a *patron*—an eminent chairholder more often than not based in prestigious Parisian faculties. The elements of the cluster penetrated across institutions; the cluster reflected, by its form of social grouping, the essential centralization of the higher education system and also of French political, intellectual, and cultural life.[29]

The power of patrons over their clusters was a function of linkages with elite academic institutes, research bodies, crucial agencies regulating the outer frame of higher education, and with the central administration. Particularly significant was the cluster's strength as an instrument of patronage and as a distributor of blessings for which all honor and ambition contend. Clusters acted as a substitute for national disciplinary associations or professional bodies, which in Germany, Britain, and the United States stand as key vehicles for building and advancing an academic career.

The power of the German chairholder drew on different sources: prime among them was his position as director of a research institute that, if affiliated with the university, was under the chair's sole charge. Control over a research institute also meant command of substantial research funds and other facilities furnished by the state.[30] As director of the institute, the chairholder was intellectual and administrative master of a local grouping, creating thereby a school of thought that had a particular, highly localized, spatial existence.[31] The French cluster was diffuse, dispersed across various institutions and sectors of the education system; it included other chairholders as well as select graduates. In Germany, on the other hand, the subordinates of the chairholder were local apprentices—students, and assistants.

The cluster and apprenticeship models involved different degrees and types of dependency. In France such feudal ties could often be lifelong. In Germany, however, the apprentice, when he had served out his indentures and gained the coveted Habilitation, could reasonably expect to become a professor in turn, moving to another university and setting up his own power base.[32] The relative freedom of German universities from state interference made it somewhat easier for new professors to set up power bases than, for instance, in France. The authority of the professor in Germany, then, was much more circumscribed, being limited largely to the individual university where he held his post.

These variations in the structure and operation of the chair-faculty system were differences of degree, not of kind. Both are qualitatively different from the American department-college structure. True, there were marked differences in the length and severity of dependency embedded in the French and German chair-faculty structures, but dependency there was. In both cases academics were found in separate camps, distinguished by vastly differentiated powers and privileges, and in both cases the all-powerful chairs, unfettered by the faculties, highlighted such differences.[33] Such working arrangements contained a latent conflict among different academic orders—among power holders, power seekers, and those for whom power became unattainable. If the chair was a seat of power, it was also potentially a seat of division in academia in many Continental Western European universities.

THE NATION AND THE ACADEMIC ESTATE

In both Great Britain and the United States academia is assumed to be a profession. This is not the case in the majority of Western European countries. There is no sense of its being a part of one of the "liberal professions" such as medicine or law.

As a corporate entity, academia in Western Europe does not lend itself to translation into terms equivalent to the Anglo-American concept of an academic profession. In French there are two terms: one has a juridical overtone; the other has connotations of an invisible "intellectual college" that extends far beyond the university as an institution. *Les corps universitaires* (the university corporations) is a legal designation used in conjunction with the now defunct Conseil des Corps Universitaires (a national body responsible for academic appointments and promotions under the Giscardian administration). It does not link with the concept of a "profession," but rather appears to equate academia with *les corps d'état*—those technical and expert services of central government which include *le corps de mines* (engineering services) and *le corps enseignant* (the national teaching body). The second term, *le milieu universitaire et scientifique*, is more broad-ranging, embracing an intellectual caste both within and outside the university. It does not include the liberal professions but encompasses an invisible college whose frontiers are vague and fluctuating. Academia is deemed to be part of the intelligentsia, without presuming that all denizens of higher education are intellectuals, or that all intellectuals are to be found in higher education.

The terminology is no clearer in other European languages. In German the nearest equivalent is *Korporationen der Professoren,* a term closely aligned with the medieval guild. It does not include middle ranks of academics *(Mittelbau)* who are not formally professors. In Dutch the terminology is even more imprecise. *Wetenschappelijk Lid* merely describes individuals involved in scientific-academic activities, and might include those in upper academic secondary schools. As with the French and German terms, there is no direct and explicit identification with the liberal professions. No collective and generic term denotes academia as Anglo-Americans define it.

In part the difficulty of equivalence lies in the distance of British and American academia from the central state. In those two countries the academic profession is identified principally through its independence of the state. The control and certification of those entering it is handled not by the state but by the profession as a whole or by the individual disciplines. And academia has a professional ethic, with powers of sanction and reward for those infringing on or endorsing it.[34]

Academia in Western Europe does not share all of these characteristics. By statute, academics are civil servants, not independent professionals. Members of the state service, in their middle-to-upper ranks they are designated as such—*fonctionnaires, Beamten, Amtenaaren.* Entry to academia is regulated not by an independent profession, but by competitive, state-validated examinations.

Thus the problem of terminology goes far beyond the technicalities of translation or language. It reflects a fundamental difference in the place and status of academics in Britain and the United States as against their colleagues in Western Europe.

In the absence of a generic term for academia in the European context, and to remind ourselves of differences that exist, academia in Western Europe will be referred to as an academic estate rather than as an academic profession.[35] Academia has never held the status of an estate to the same degree as did the clergy, nobility, or burgesses in feudal times. But it did have important analogous functions within the cultural domain.

The use of the term *estate* is appropriate from another view: it defines academics by institutional position. European terminology tends to ignore this dimension.[36] European terms are not sufficiently inclusive or exclusive: they do not include all teachers in institutions of higher education. At the same time they comprise more than just that populace. By calling academia in Western Europe an estate, we place it on a footing similar to its Anglo-American counterpart; in both systems academics are defined by employment in institutions of higher education.

The notion of an academic estate, advantageously, does not imply independence from the central state. Integration with state service is a salient feature of academia in Europe, where academia has a national perspective.[37] The academic estate tends to be a national body, looking toward the center for confirmation of senior appointments and for the perceived role of the university. The commitment to serving the immediate community, though strong in public rhetoric and in debates among international organizations, is in practice ancillary, where it exists at all.[38]

Seen from this view, academia in Britain and America is unusual because it dichotomizes "cosmopolitans" and "locals"—those who are seen as operating nationwide and those whose commitments tend toward their immediate institution or locality. This split is less pronounced among British academics, who, though not part of a state service as such, nevertheless see themselves as members of a national profession.[39] Despite this cosmopolitan professional orientation, British academics tend to be highly involved in and committed to their local institutions. The United States provides the extreme case of localism. Large sections of American academia are locals in professional orientation, work, and commitment; they are not members of a national body associated with central government service. Nor, with the possible exception of those in research universities, are they members of a national profession.

Such distinctive differences in the profile of the academic estate in Western Europe are not merely contemporary in nature. They are deeply embedded in the historical development of higher education.

THE ORIGINS OF THE ACADEMIC ESTATE

The rise of the modern university in Western Europe is largely contemporaneous with the rise of the central bureaucratic state in the eighteenth and early nineteenth centuries.[40] The explicit move to identify the university with state service, legally and professionally, through the education of civil servants is part of a long process that emerged in Sweden during a thirty-year period beginning in the 1740s. A similar development took place in Austria during the reign of Josef II (1741–1790). The Humboldtian reforms of 1809–1810 together with the establishment of the Napoleonic Université Imperiale in 1811, stand as markers along this same road.[41]

The role of universities, however, was not limited to providing the pool of capable individuals from which the highest offices of the land would be filled. In such countries as France, Belgium, and Italy, the state university stood as the bulwark of secular national pluralism against the claims of religious hegemony advanced by the Catholic Church.[42] In these countries, where development of national identity was divorced from religion, the academic estate enjoyed distinct political status as the symbol of secular rationalism. This in turn derived from the broader cultural and political mission conferred on the university as a repository of scientific, rational inquiry set against the proponents of revealed knowledge. Yet even in Sweden, Prussia, and the Netherlands, where religion was incorporated into nationalism, the state possessed a firm cultural dimension reflected in the perceived standing of academia. In varying degrees, then, European universities were charged with an explicit cultural and political function. From a structural viewpoint the relationship between the state and the academic estate rested on three pillars: a monopoly in awarding certificates and degrees leading to state service; an elaborate, formal legal framework; and an explicit cultural mission.

In German, French, and Italian education systems, the state awarded certificates giving access to high honor and preferment at two levels. The first was located at the end of academic secondary schooling, in the forms of the Abitur, the Baccalauréat, and the Maturità, all state-validated, national qualifying exams. The second level, a point at the end of some period in higher education—in the Staatsexamen, in Germany, or in the various national diplomas in France and Italy—were qualifications underwritten by the state. The Staatsexamen is directly associated with public service employment and stands apart from such academic degrees as Magister, Doctor, or the Habilitation. Similarly, in France and Italy, national diplomas are distinguished from certificates awarded by individual universities. The former are validated and awarded by the state, which also accredits the individual institution teaching them. Since the state underwrites their quality, national diplomas generally are held to be superior in quality and far more prestigious than those awarded by a particular establishment. Clearly, they are considered to be so by private-sector employers.[43] Such national diplomas are the imperative prerequisite for any applicant seeking a post in public employment; hence the academic estate and the central administration are linked by these certificates that lead on to state service.

Academia is also linked to the state because academics are themselves civil servants subject to laws, decrees, ordinances, and directives that lay down both framework and detailed legislation not only in the public life of the estate but also in many areas considered by Anglo-American academics to be part of the private life of that body.[44] In addition to the usual issue of public accountability for finance and expenditure, such matters as requirements for certification, procedures for appointments, conditions of eligibility for academic posts, conditions of service and those for promotion, are all subject to formal national legislation. The academic estate employs various stratagems to operate and interpret these regulations to its advantage, but formal compliance is required. Universities in Western Europe tend to be state institutions as well as public corporations, and are subject to public and administrative law.[45]

Popular justification for this legal corset reveals the extent to which the academic estate is seen as part of the services of the nation. To European eyes the positive aspects of this legalism are threefold. First, formal bureaucratic control by central administration over selection and appointment to tenured posts is a means of upholding universalistic criteria for judging merit and advancement; the state acts as the ultimate protection against corporate reproduction and the rise of a new nobility.[46] Second, it maintains both the quality and the institutional homogeneity of establishments in a given segment of the higher education system. Third, it is a means of upholding national unity through ensuring the formal equality of provision and service among universities.[47]

The academic estate was linked to the state in another way: through its role as an instrument of cultivation and nation building. Today institutions of mass culture are located outside the university, but earlier when the formal relationship between academia and the state was being defined, the university occupied a central role in shaping national culture. Universities performed a vital role in asserting, legitimating, and perpetuating a country's claim to nationhood.[48] The concept of a *mission civilisatrice*—of culture as an assimilative agent that underpins linguistic, political, and administrative homogeneity—or of its German counterpart, the *Kulturstaat*—a common culture binding together, defining, and even transcending political boundaries—were supremely important. They not only expressed a desire for cultural normalization; they also stood as manifestations of a unity far deeper than that imposed through conquest by kings and armies. In the nineteenth century, the cultural centrality of the university was no less important than its economic centrality in the mid-twentieth.

Nineteenth-century Europe saw the imposition of national norms in the educational domain, in which values were transmitted and institutionalized away from the church and toward the school. The universities trained and nurtured the nation's political and administrative elites and supplied the elite corps of teachers. In teaching and research—and above all in the humanities—they fostered the basic values of political socialization for future citizens in a diluted form through the school curriculum. Finally, they deepened the legitimacy of the state through the writing of its history and through study of the national language.

The cultural centrality of the university not only defined the place of the professor within it but was itself reflected in his standing in public life. Individual status and organizational form were intertwined. Within the university and outside it, the professor occupied a key position in this national edifice. In the extreme case of Prussia, for example, *Kulturtrager* (the guardian of civilization) was appended to his title. But throughout Western Europe professorial stature, power, and patronage dominated. The professor's repute—especially in those countries influenced by the German model—derived from his dual role as master of his specialty inside the university, and from his position, always symbolic but at times in fact, as upholder of the nation's culture and its excellence.[49]

The professoriat enjoys a comparable standing neither in the United Kingdom nor in the United States. This can be attributed to the nature of universities and the patterns of academic organization in those countries.

A HOUSE DIVIDED AGAINST ITSELF

Within the academic estate divisions among different orders—professors, middle ranks, assistants—brought forth radical changes in internal university authority and governance.[50] Between 1968 and 1975 traditional models of authority in many university systems found themselves under severe challenge. Some crumbled. Others, such as those in Belgium and the United Kingdom, survived with minimal, if any, change.

In this period the cosmology of Europe's academic universe underwent drastic revision. The Ptolemaic notion that academia revolved around the chairholder and the faculty structure gave way to a more chaotic concept of power sharing that some have compared to Leibnitz's theory of a monadic universe.[51] The chair-faculty system of management and authority was replaced by a participant corporatist model, rooted in the collective authority of differing interest groups. These interest groups were not integrated in a collegium that previously had been embodied in the faculty system. Nor were they confined to the university. In many countries—the Netherlands, France, Italy, and the Federal Republic of Germany—such interest alignments inside academia extended outside through affiliation with trade unions and political parties—a process that fragmented authority still further.

Prior to the uproar of 1968, the chair-faculty structure was under strain, but it was not under direct challenge. Yet by 1975, with pressure from junior staff, students, and trade unions, the polity had intervened to bring about root-and-branch reform in academia's internal organization. The French Higher Education Framework Law of 1968 marked the start of this development. With the exception of medicine, which remained under the guidelines drawn up in 1958, the faculty structure was demolished and replaced by new decision-making units, each a unit for education and research (UER). Three years later, similarly wide-ranging changes in the management structure of the Dutch academic estate were enacted—though nominally on an experimental basis. Today the shocks that spread from the epicenter at Paris have not yet entirely ceased. In Greece the June 1982 law remolded both structure and function at the institutional level and within the academic body. In Spain the August 1983 University Reform Act was couched in a similar spirit. The academic estate was stratified among various ranks and power was dispersed away from the faculties.[52]

The conflict and outright hostility that accompanied these changes revealed how broad the gulf was between the party of order and the party of movement, an alignment that tended to split academia, with senior professorial staff against largely untenured junior staff. By and large, the former regarded such change as symbolizing the sleep of reason, and the measures themselves as the monster that, inevitably, such sleep must bring forth. For the lower ranks, the reforms resembled the righteous blast of the trumpet that brought the walls of academia tumbling down together with the feudal power of the professorial barons.

By forcing the intervention of the polity, junior staff successfully challenged, and in some cases brought about the demise of, the chair-faculty model. But if the tide of reform still flows strongly on the periphery of the Continent, there are signs that the center now faces an ebb. The battle over power, authority, governance, and the structures that uphold them in the academic estate is not finished. In the Federal Republic of Germany and the Netherlands, for example, the harsh economic climate and the need, once again, to protect excellence and achievement point toward a delicate and circumspect restoration of professorial power.[53]

The house of academia remains divided, and in its internal division each order continues to appeal to friends and allies in the polity. The recent petition of full professors (left and right wing) to the President of the French Republic, in a despairing effort to prevent the ravages of his Minister of Education M. Alain Savary, is a dramatic illustration of this general process.[54]

Struggles for authority within the academic estate in Europe were not rooted primarily in political disagreement among its different orders. Instead, they sprang from structural and demographic pressures that led to an "ecological imbalance" in the estate—an imbalance that not only affected the ratio between senior and junior staff but went far deeper into the process of socialization into academic values. Such a breakdown in the system of transmitting academic values posed a direct threat to the chair-faculty structure. And it led junior staff to seek a solution to their condition inside academia by calling in the polity to redress patterns of authority and governance within the university itself.

THE DEVELOPING ECOLOGICAL IMBALANCE

Academia is a repository of organizational forms and relationships that reflect "past rationalities." The rediscovery—others might say the persistence—of the guild model of academic behavior is perhaps the most obvious. Its presence has been identified and analyzed in systems as different as Britain, Italy, and Sweden. This "inner organization" may be traced back in various ways, to the University of Paris in the fifteenth century.[55]

The incorporation of academia into state service in Western Europe did not alter this inner environment. Academia was deluged with all sorts of regulations that defined its role and responsibilities by legal and, in some cases constitutional, instruments, and at the same time strengthened faculty structure and chairholder status. This formal "exterior environment" served to protect and give expression to another relationship, key to the chair-faculty edifice. The master-pupil bond between chairholder and graduate assistant may be seen from two perspectives: first, as another enduring form of academic organization, which continued in academia long after it disappeared from other sectors of society; and second, as a system of enculturation into academic values and as an initiation into the various disciplinary cultures inside the university.[56] As a prime instrument of socialization into academia, the master-pupil relationship was crucial for reproduction of the academic estate.

The estate in Western Europe was effectively endowed with a dual nature: on the one hand, it was formally bureaucratized in such procedures as appointment, examination, and promotion; on the other, in its private life it still exercised an ethic and comportment closely aligned with the corporatist guild mentality.

The balance between the external frame and the internal environment was extremely delicate. Both professorial authority and the master-pupil model of academic socialization—the inner environment—depended on factors in the external frame. Some of these were not directly under the control of university authorities, but rested on those legal and constitutional arrangements governing the linkage between secondary and higher education. In short, stability in the inner environment of academia was dependent on the screening function of the academic upper secondary school, on its ability to limit numbers passing from school to university, or alternatively, on its ability to reorient or "cool out" all save the most brilliant and persistent.[57] Universities in Britain and the United States, by contrast, selected at the point of entry and could therefore regulate student demand in keeping with their resources, academic or financial. In France, the Federal Republic of Germany, and Italy, however, holders of the Baccalauréat, the Abitur, and the Maturità had a legal, constitutional right to a place in higher education. Universities there could not select at the point of entry, though they did resort to an often drastic process of weeding out at various points in undergraduate study.[58]

Starting in the late 1950s, the secondary education system in Western Europe, far from limiting demand for higher education, effectively increased it, sending it onward and upward.[59] Student enrollments spiraled. Between 1959–1960 and 1970–1971, overall student numbers

TABLE 5.1

Enrollments and Growth Rates in University-Type Establishments in
Western European Countries 1959–1960 to 1978–1979[a]
(in thousands)

Country	1959– 1960	1964– 1965	1966– 1967	1968– 1969	1970– 1971	1975– 1976	1978– 1979
Belgium	29.2	42.4	53.8	—	75.1	83.4	89.3[b]
Growth rate	100	145.2	184.2	—	257.2	285.6	305.8
France	201.1	434.0	—	—	682.6	840.0	870.7
Growth rate	100	215.8	—	—	339.4	418.1	433.0
Great Britain	104.0	138.7	—	211.5	235.3	268.7	295.9
Growth rate	100	133.4	—	203.4	226.3	258.4	284.5
Italy	243.3	354.5	449.7	—	709.8	960.2	996.2
Growth rate	100	145.3	184.8	—	291.7	394.7	409.5
Netherlands	37.7	61.8	82.5	—	103.4	120.2	137.4
Growth rate	100	163.9	218.8	—	274.3	318.8	364.5
Sweden	31.5	61.4	82.5	—	120.2	110.0	—
Growth rate	100	194.9	261.9	—	381.9	349.2	—
West Germany	189.1	246.8	266.6	—	407.1	675.3	756.9
Growth rate	100	130.5	140.9	—	215.3	357.1	400.3

Notes: a. full-time under- and postgraduate
   b. 1977–1978

Sources: OECD, *The Development of Higher Education 1950–1967*, vol. 2, table 2, p. 23.

   Cerych, Colton, and Jallade, *Student Flows and Expenditure in Higher Education 1965–1979*, table 1, pp. 36–37.

more than tripled in France and Sweden and reached almost the same rate of expansion in Great Britain, Italy, and the Netherlands. By the end of the following decade—1979 to 1980—student numbers were four times their level of two decades earlier in Italy, France, and the Federal Republic of Germany. They had reached three times that level in Belgium and the Netherlands and had risen by just under three times in Great Britain (table 5.1).

Growth in the Academic Estate

Developments in the academic estate paralleled the path of Europe's universities away from an elite system of cultivation toward a mass system of training. Increases in student numbers brought increases in staff. Continental European universities lacked the capacity to regulate the growth of academic staff as well as student enrollment. Between 1960 and 1970, the academic estate in France, Italy, and West Germany grew by 348, 365, and 323 percent, respectively. In Britain,

TABLE 5.2

EXPANSION OF FULL- AND PART-TIME ACADEMIC BODY IN WESTERN
EUROPEAN COUNTRIES 1960–1961 TO 1979–1980

Country	1960–1961	1965–1966	1970–1971	1973–1974	1975–1976	1978–1979	1979–1980
Belgium	3.515[a]	4.563	7.878[b]	—	—	—	—
Growth rate	100	144.8	250.0	—	—	—	—
France	8.131	—	28.319	37.602	38.142	41.978	—
Growth rate	100	—	348.3	462.5	469.1	516.3	—
Great Britain	12.929	18.375	26.904	—	31.381[c]	—	33.300
Growth rate	100	142.1	208.1	—	242.7	—	257.6
Italy	4.980	7.804	18.215	—	30.279	—	—
Growth rate	100	156.7	365.7	—	608.0	—	—
Netherlands	—	8.429	12.953	—	14.782	—	—
Growth rate	—	100	153.6	—	175.3	—	—
Sweden	3.400	4.500	7.000	8.000[d]	—	—	—
Growth rate	100	132.4	205.9	235.3	—	—	—
West Germany	15.552	—	50.227	—	58.305	—	—
Growth rate	100	—	322.96	—	374.9	—	—

NOTES: a. 1960/1961   b. 1971/1972
        c. 1975/1976   d. 1973/1974

SOURCES:

Belgium: Verhoeven in Shils and Daalder, *Universities, Politicians, and Bureaucrats,* table 7, p. 142.

France: Salmon in Shils and Daalder, *Universities, Politicians, and Bureaucrats,* table 3, p. 77.
"Evolution du Ministère de l'Education Nationale: Elèves, Etudiants Enseignants." *Cahiers de l'Avenir de la France,* No. 1.

Great Britain: *Statistics of Education,* vol. 6, *Universities,* 1967, table 56, p. 101; 1970, p. 77; 1979, table 25, p. 53.

Italy: Giglioni, *Baroni e Burocrati,* table 1.5, p. 34.

Netherlands: Daalder in Shils and Daalder, *Universities, Politicians, and Bureaucrats,* table 2, p. 180.

West Germany: Peisert and Framhein, *Systems of Higher Education: Federal Republic of Germany,* table 6, pp. 68, 69.

Belgium, and Sweden, though expansion was less substantial, it was no less marked—208 percent, 250 percent, and 206 percent (table 5.2)

Overall growth rates, however, hide substantial changes in the increase of the various strata within academia, particularly in the junior ranks. Table 5.3 illustrates the growth rate among junior staff—that group of academia that, like Louis Chevalier's nineteenth-century Parisian working class, changed from being a *classe laborieuse* to a *classe dangereuse* in the course of a decade.[60] Junior staff expanded substantially in all countries for which we have information, and particularly so in Belgium, France, and Italy.[61]

In what way did an increased junior staff affect the overall balance

TABLE 5.3

JUNIOR STAFF GROWTH RATE IN WESTERN EUROPEAN COUNTRIES
1959–1969 TO 1979–1980[a]

Country	1959– 1960	1964– 1965	1969– 1970	1975– 1976	1979– 1980	Base Number
Belgium	100	154.1	332.2	—	—	1445
France	100	—	330.8	441.2	371.4	4056
Great Britain	100	134.4	202.3	218.9	225.2	9152
Italy	100	174.8	403.2	602	—	3052
Sweden	100	127.3	225.6	288.2	—	1575
Netherlands	—	100	158.0	156.2	—	6285

NOTE: a. Belgium: junior staff = assistants
France: assistants and others
Great Britain: junior lecturers/lecturers, and others
Italy: assistenti di ruolo
Sweden: assistant level
Netherlands: junior staff as designated by Daalder
SOURCES: derived from sources cited in tables 5.1 and 5.2.

of the strata or the orders of the academic estate? Table 5.4 shows the proportion of all university staff represented by junior ranks for the period 1959–1960 to 1979–1980.

In all countries except Great Britain, the growth of academia during the 1960s involved a disproportionate increase in junior staff, even though data for individual countries show considerable variation. Though there is an element of statistical artificiality in our categories, the junior order already constituted an absolute majority in Britain, the Netherlands, and Italy, a substantial minority in Belgium and Sweden, and almost half of academia in France at the start of the decade and before the onset of expansion. By 1970 they were the majority group in academia.

Britain is odd man out. Compared to the academic estate in countries with a similar population size (France and Italy, for example) members of the British academic profesion are far more numerous. Moreover, the proportion of junior staff relative to the entire academic population fell steadily throughout this period.[62] This suggests that promotion and interrank mobility was greater in the British academic profession than in the Continental European academic estate.

Britain then was successful in maintaining the ecological balance in academia, and in improving on it steadily. In part this came about because the inner environment in Britain's academic profession controlled certain dimensions in the external frame: nomination for posts,

TABLE 5.4

PROPORTION OF JUNIOR STAFF IN THE UNIVERSITY-SECTOR TEACHING BODY
IN WESTERN EUROPE 1959–1960 TO 1979–1980
(in percentages)

Country	1959–1960	1964–1965	1969–1970	1975–1976	1979–1980
Belgium	41.1	48.8	60.9	—	—
	of 3,515	of 4,563	of 7,878	—	—
France	49.9	—	52.9	46.9	38.03
	of 8,131	—	of 25,356	of 38,242	of 39,639
Great Britain	70.8	67.7	68.8	63.8	61.8
	of 12,929	of 18,375	of 26,904	of 31,381	of 33,300
Italy	61.3	68.4	67.6	60.8	—
	of 4,986	of 7,804	of 18,125	of 30,276	—
Sweden	46.3	44.6	50.8	56.7	—
	of 3,400	of 4,500	of 7,000	of 8,000	—
Netherlands	—	74.6	76.7	76.2	—
	—	of 8,429	of 12,953	of 14,782	—

SOURCES: derived from sources cited in table 5.1.

conditions of advancement, and the creation of new posts, among
other factors, were not part of the formal bureaucratic overlay of
national ministerial control that characterized the European academic
state.

In continental Europe academia not only faced a massive influx of
junior staff but had to rely on formal national and bureaucratic procedures to ensure mobility, procedures it might initiate but did not
ultimately control. The academic estate was not utterly deprived of
advancement and promotion—an important internal safety valve. But
if one takes the growth rate of junior orders and the balance between
senior and junior staff, it is arguable that a high degree of blockage
in interrank mobility existed. When promotion did come, it came later
and in a more panic-stricken manner. In France, for example, the
growth of the middle ranks (maîtres assistants) from 1968 to 1978–
1979 was as indecent as it was rapid (from 5,426 to 14,742), an as-
tounding development, as in 1960 a mere 500 were on the rolls. A
similar phenomenon prevails in Italy in relation to the *professori in-
caricati*, parallel figures in the academic firmament, who also rose from
earth in large numbers: 2,370 in 1969–1970 and 6,668 by 1975–1976.[63]

Such promotion spurts indicate not only that the external environment of the academic estate lay under government control but also
that the government appeared well aware of academia's internal ten-

sions and sought to alleviate them by accelerating promotion for a class that, once laborious, had now become politically dangerous as well.

FROM A CLASSE LABORIEUSE TO A CLASSE DANGEREUSE

In Western Europe the transformation of higher education from an elite to a mass institution was purchased at the price of equally massive expansion in junior staff. If such expansion altered the quantitative balance between the senior (tenured) and the junior (substantially untenured) orders of the academic estate, what impact did it have on the qualitative relationships between the two? Was the authority of the chairholder over junior staff already under attack before the onset of the "events of May"? Did the challenges posed by student unrest merely provide a heaven-sent occasion for the junior orders to throw down the gauntlet to professorial authority? Or was it, on the contrary, the final factor in a long-drawn-out drifting apart of the two orders, the origins of which lie deep within the recesses of academe? In seeking answers to these questions we need to pay attention to the ways that developments affecting the public life of academia also affected its private life.

The collegium of chairholders was the organizational heart and symbol of unity of corporate professorial authority. It existed alongside another, less visible but no less powerful collegiate linkage between senior orders of the academic estate and their aspirant junior counterparts. The "parallel collegium" operated vertically across ranks rather than horizontally among members of the full professoriat. But it was no less important in maintaining professorial authority and in simultaneously governing the expectations of the assistant class.

This vertical collegium rested on the notion—sometimes a reality, at other times existing simply by force of myth—that all orders of academia were engaged in both teaching and research. Archaic though it may appear, the apprenticeship model performed two functions that were vital to the cohesion and identity of academia. It created a bond of common identity and interest between junior and senior staff, offsetting the horizontal collegium of professorial authority with an equal and no less powerful collegium of colleagues who, despite differences in age and rank, were each engaged in seeking truth. It was also the prime agency of induction and socialization into academia.

Research was not simply a matter of acquiring techniques of analysis or the accumulation of knowledge and judgment. It was also the

vehicle for the passage of values—some explicit, others unspoken—
from master to pupil. It was central to the perpetuation of academic
cultures and to the common identity among ranks and orders of
academia.[64] Research combined with teaching (or its ritual invocation)
distinguished academia from schoolmastering, which was confined
to the simple joys of teaching. The collegium of chairholders was
bonded by the shared responsibilities and authority of coevals. The
invisible collegium that underwrote a joint commitment to research
held together different orders of academia—senior, middle, and junior.

In such countries as France, the Netherlands, and the Federal Republic of Germany, expansion of the academic estate did not entirely
dissolve the vertical collegium, but it did weaken it. For a substantial
subsection of the assistant class it had become largely irrelevant. Other
agencies began to play a crucial role in the socialization of junior staff
and in shaping their attitudes and perceived role in the university.
These agencies primarily reflected external society, particularly then-
current student ideologies. They also showed the willingness of junior
staff to organize formally into bodies identified less with academia
than with the trade union movement. That this weakened the internal
linkage between junior staff and the professoriat reflected the fragile
hold the academic estate had over its external environment.

In Britain, by contrast, if there were tensions in the "key profession"
in the late 1960s, they did not take the form of younger staff seeking
pro rata representation or fragmenting the guild into formal and separate electoral colleges. Two factors operating in its internal environment, plus the high degree of de facto control it exercised over its
external frame, afforded greater strength to the British academic
profession's maintenance of a traditional method of socialization into
academic values. When expansion began in the early 1960s, British
academia was a large body relative to French and Italian counterparts.
And its internal governance rested on a collegium far wider than those
of professorial rank alone. By regulating student numbers, academia
in Britain exercised indirect sway over its own financial underpinning.[65] And since governments were willing to maintain a student-
staff ratio of approximately 9:1, the British academic profession
wielded equally efficacious control over staff members as well. This
was compounded by the profession's control of internal promotion
without the need to apply to central administration for confirmation
or nomination.

Conditions were not as favorable in most Continental European
countries. There the academic estate controlled its exterior frame in

a manner highly circumscribed by law and regulation. It could regulate neither student entry nor junior staff intake—this regulation was a ministry task. In addition to this were the sparse membership rolls of the academic estate before expansion. Spiraling student enrollments meant a premium was placed on recruiting graduates capable of instructing undergraduates. This made it difficult to create new academics (and maintain the supply) through the master-pupil system; socialization through research training is a protracted business. The solution was to engage a subclass within the junior staff whose responsibilities were limited to teaching, and who were usually on year-to-year contracts.

This situation in no way excluded the continued production of future academics by the time-honored method of sitting at the master's feet. But it meant that a substantial and growing number of junior staff were brought into the academic estate who had not undergone this rite of passage. The European university's path toward a mass clientele created a second route on the fringes of the academic estate, running parallel to the long-established vertical collegium. This second track differed fundamentally from the first and was only weakly associated with research training. In the minds of academia and government its sole raison d'être was the need for instructors.

This further stratification of the academic estate distinguished explicitly between those for whom the vertical collegium and eventually careers at the highest level were still viable, and those for whom neither was. By removing the research linkage, it also gave rise to a group within the instructor class that had no common interest in or formal connection to a chair-faculty system. Cut off from the privileges and rewards offered to those at the top of the estate of which they were only marginally a part, the instructor "subproletariat" recast authority in terms of naked, arbitrary power. Dependent though the apprentice academic had been on his guild master or his patron for advancement, he nevertheless could expect his training to bring him the qualifications necessary for that advancement, and with it the coveted status of civil servant—the Continental equivalent of tenure. The instructor class, by contrast, could look forward to none of these. Heavy teaching loads took up all the time needed for research that would lead to qualification. Within the formal canons of academia, instructors were not eligible for advancement and even less for tenure. Their lot was, or appeared to many to be, that of the eternal drudge who labored without reward.

In a situation reminiscent of the relation between the French nobility and the bourgeoisie on the eve of the 1789 revolution, a substantial part of the instructor class saw itself as powerless inside academia and aggrieved by the rest of the academic estate.[66] They sought to remedy their condition by appeals to more weighty interests outside. The rise of this semipermanent, untenured assistant class revealed how tenuous the estate's control was, even over its private life.

If they were isolated in the private life of the academic estate, that portion of the instructor class not part of the chairholder's patronage nexus was not segregated within the university. Against the vertical collegium that linked professors and junior staff through research, they brought to bear a countervailing linkage based on teaching.

In the social movements of the day this opposing power took various self-conscious forms. They revealed a "counter" or "alternative" culture that sought legitimacy, not merely by opposing academia's "high" culture, but from its claim to represent within the university a cultural pluralism found outside in the rapidly expanding youth culture of the 1960s.[67] This linkage was not entirely rhetorical. To be sure, it made for amusing slogans during the carnival atmosphere of May 1968: (*La jeunesse au pouvoir, Sus à la gérontocratie pédagogique*, and others less printable). Yet these appeals to age-group solidarity between younger instructor graduates and undergraduate students could not disguise certain similar interests for both parties. Together, they were affected by the deteriorating physical conditions (the most spectacular was overcrowding) accompanying the transition to mass higher education, especially in France, Italy, and the Federal Republic of Germany.[68] Both shared in the growing distance, physical and hierarchical, between the lower orders and chairholders. And both graduate instructors and undergraduate students necessarily sought redress for their grievances via political negotiation rather than through the academic process: the decision to grant civil servant status to a category of personnel depended not on academia but on national policy determined by central administration; and improvements in facilities, resources, and personnel allocation were the purlieu of the same agency. This reflected national bureaucratic power over academia's external environment, and academia's weakness in not mastering those vital frame factors that affected its physical working conditions.

By seeking redress outside the academic estate, the assistant class altered its status from a laborious to a dangerous class. Accompanied by an emerging critical ideology with which to justify its claims, it disrupted the inner environment of the academic estate. Assistants and students rose to political militancy accompanied by an ideology fundamentally hostile to the value system underlying not only the chair as symbol of academic authority but also the apprenticeship model of induction into academia. This ideology contained two major strands: first, a neo-Marxist critique of the university as a social institution; second, a concept of students as consumers of knowledge rather than as privileged members of an elite, with certain rights, not liberties.[69] Despite differences understood only by their particular adepts, these two positions agreed broadly on substantive issues. Both presumed the right of students to decide what ought to be taught— to have some say, if not the decisive one, over shaping the curriculum, determining the modes of evaluation, and, in certain instances, deciding the type of research the university should accept. For Marxists, and the German Sozialistischer Deutscher Studentenbund (SDS) in particular, such claims stemmed from the moral right of "workers" (students and junior staff) to control the means of (knowledge) production based on an industrial analogue of worker-management relations transferred to the university setting.[70] For "consumerists," the responsibilities of the "producers" (professors) was to supply knowledge deemed "relevant" or "necessary" by "consumers" (students).

These claims struck at the heart of the academic estate's private life. In so doing they also struck at the chair-faculty structure that symbolized professorial authority. In bringing into the groves of academe notions derived from labor movement history and industrial relations, which cast students and instructors as workers united against the arbitrary authority of professors as managers or intellectual capitalists, this ideology predicated a conflict model of relations. It also sought to take control over knowledge content away from those of proven excellence and achievement (the essence of the master-pupil relationship), and put it in the hands of the "counter collegium"— those who learned and those who taught. Thus the offspring of Marx, like their sire, stood Hegel, and the professorial hierarchy to boot, on their respective heads.

ACADEMIA AND UNIONIZATION

The challenge to the authority of the chair-faculty structure inside academia was accompanied by attempts by junior staff to link with such outside organizations as trade unions, political parties, or both. This move, found in the Netherlands, France, Italy, and the Federal Republic of Germany, was not universal. In Britain and Sweden, for instance, the established bodies representing the interests of academia as a corporate whole remained intact. Though differing in organization, public status, and membership, both the Association of University Teachers and the Sveriges Akademikers Centralorganisation Statsjantemannens Riksforbund continued, largely unchallenged, their roles as main channels of communication with the public and the polity.[71]

In those countries where, among the junior orders of the academic estate, the drive to unionize took place, one can distinguish between those, such as the Federal Republic of Germany, where this process was also accompanied by the emergence of counterorganizations inside academia nominally independent of union organization outside, and those, such as France, where the organization of oppositional power inside was an extension of official union penetration into the university.[72]

In the Federal Republic of Germany the emergence of an organization to counter professorial power in the heartland of academia took the form of the Bundeassistentenkonferenz (BAK). Set up in 1968, the BAK, as its title implies, was a national federation supportive of the junior order. Its nomenclature alone suggested that it had been created as a deliberate counterweight to the West German Rectors Conference—one of the more powerful agencies in higher education.[73]

The political platform of the BAK included three main issues: first, the restoration of education through research; second, the establishment of an integrated system of higher education embracing universities, teacher training establishments, and high professional schools (*Fachhochschulen*); and third, the abolition of the Habilitation as the prerequisite for professorial status. The common factor was the desire to improve career security and chances of promotion, either by removing barriers to research or by large-scale systematic reorganization that would set the BAK's membership on the golden road to chairholder status.

Organization inside academia paralleled attempts to increase political weight outside. Here the initiative was not entirely one-sided. The development of a subclass without formal research responsibilities was looked on by schoolteacher trade unions with no little rejoicing. Recruitment by teachers' unions from the instructor class not only increased membership, it presented an opportunity for them to increase credibility by tapping into the vicarious prestige of higher education. Such considerations prompted the largest teachers' union in West Germany—Gewerkschaft Erziehung und Wissenschaft—to regularly champion the assistant class during debates over reorganization of higher education around the Hochschulrahmengesetz and its aftermath.[74]

In France, Belgium, Italy, and the Netherlands, junior staff tended to avoid the creation of separate professional associations inside academia. Their approach involved the establishment of political groupings that reflected similar allegiances outside. Their goal was less to seek improvement by appeal inside the academic estate so much as to bring pressure to bear on it directly from outside through the political process.

In Belgium untenured assistants sought to pressure the government into granting them tenure through allying with the two major trade union federations, the Algemeen Christelijk Vakverbond and the socialist Algemeen Belgisch Vakverbond.[75] A similar tactic was seen in France. French assistants tightened up their links with the left-wing Syndicat National de l'Enseignement Supérieur (SNESup). SNESup offered substantial negotiating advantages not only on its own but as one of the forty-odd organizations that comprised the Federation de l'Education Nationale, an umbrella organization that coordinated the grievances and claims of the entire corps enseignant (teaching body) and communicated them to government and Parliament. If SNESup never managed to bring together an absolute majority in French academia, its weight in the public arena was not to be underestimated. Christian Fouchet, a former minister of education, once remarked wryly that the French teaching body "was more numerous than the entire Red Army."

That the junior orders in France, like the assistant class in Germany, identified with the national teaching corps, rather than with the university, was not entirely fortuitous. The alliance sprang from both the tasks and location of the instructor class in the university. Confined to undergraduate teaching, its members saw greater similarity between their condition and that of organized primary and secondary-school teachers than they did with the corps from which it was largely excluded.

This alliance pattern is also visible in Italy.[76] It brought national trade union federations to the negotiations about structuring higher education and defining conditions of employment, and it gave the assistants a firm organizational base outside academia from which to continue to press claims on the government, to effect change in academia's private life. Demands for more posts, more guaranteed hours (many assistants in France were paid by the number of hours they taught), and more promotions from the ranks of the precarious were part of the regular academic year in France and Italy.

This affiliation increased the pressure to which governments acceded; it had other consequences as well. Since organized labor now acted as a channel of negotiation for one segment of the academic estate, it also considerably influenced how "participation" and "democracy" were defined inside academia. The formal stratification of the academic estate into electoral colleges for internal decision making and governance drew heavily from various forms of worker participation current or under discussion in industry.

The clearest examples of the application of industrial relations concepts to this domain are found in France and the Federal Republic of Germany. The concept underlying the 1968 Higher Education Framework Law in France was that of *co-gestion* (joint managerial responsibility).[77] In West Germany the notion of *Mitbestimmung* (worker coresponsibility) emerged in attenuated form in the 1976 Hochschulrahmengesetz. It gave rise to the notion of the *Gruppenuniversität* (the university of grouped interests) in contrast to the *Ordinarienuniversität* (the university governed by professors).

Pressure from junior academics and students on the polity resulted in another layer of formal bureaucratic rationality, located not in the external environment but in its heart. It replaced the organic unity of the guild by a system of stratified representation of interests—middle and junior orders of staff, students, and in certain instances, technical staff and ordinary employees. Such arrangements justified to the hilt the accuracy of W. S. Gilbert's aphorism, "When everybody's somebody, then nobody's anybody."

Reorganization of Authority in Academia

The reorganization of academic authority restrained and reduced professorial power. The chair-faculty system was replaced by other basic decision-making units—the *unités d'enseignement et de recherche* (UERs) in France, the *Fachbereiche* in Germany, and the *Vakgroepen* in the Netherlands. But pressure for change was not universally successful, nor did it have the same objectives in all instances.

The Belgian reforms of 24 March 1971 expanded the participating constituency on the board of directors *(conseil d'administration)* of a university. But professors enjoyed a built-in majority on grounds of superior knowledge. Chair and faculty structures remained intact; faculty subgroups, though present, were confined to debating the tedious issues of teaching techniques. Similar changes in participant groups on faculty councils in Italy essentially left the structure and the professorial authority system untouched. But a second phase of reform has called for a subdivision of the faculty structure into departmental decision-making units based on a system of tripartite representation—one-third students, one-third tenured and untenured assistants, and one-third senior, tenured staff.[78]

The tripartite principle of representation took root elsewhere—in Austria, West Germany, Sweden, and the Netherlands. But it was not always accompanied by changes in the faculty system, as illustrated by the Austrian University Reorganization Act of 1975. Nor was it limited to changing participation patterns inside the academic estate, as evident in the Swedish University Reform Act of 1977, which extended the participant constituency to bodies external to the university.[79]

Formally, the French Higher Education Framework Law of 1968 provided for the participation of "external personalities." But this remained, by and large, a dead letter. On paper the chair-faculty structure was replaced by a series of hierarchically arranged councils, starting from the university council and passing through the academic council (*conseil scientifique*), and down into the basic decision-making unit, the UER council. The key to the vexed issue of representation in all three bodies was a complex system of electoral colleges that determined the number of places to be assigned to each interest on a specific council. In all, French reforms identified seven specific interest groups, from which the academic estate was partitioned into three strata—full professors and readers (*maîtres de conference*), lecturers (*maîtres assistants*), and junior lecturers (*assistants*), together with those of indeterminant state (*autres enseignants*).[80]

But arrangements set forth by the legislator do not always remain in the form that decrees ordain. In France, for example, the establishment of UERs (now changed by the 1984 Higher Education Guideline Law to UFR—*unités de formation et de recherche*) seems little more than the chameleon of the faculty structure that changes its color to the shade of the legislative fig leaf.[81] Some have argued that the effect of the 1968 reforms was to draw power upward into the hands of university presidents; at the same time they note that neither university presidents nor UER directors had much power over the academic staff (or over teaching, research, hiring, or promotion).[82]

Legislation and change may have reduced the ostensible and in some cases the real power of the chairholder by distributing responsibility across broad-based participating constituencies. It may have satisfied junior staff and removed students from the streets. But it also transferred the conflict back inside academia. In the Netherlands, for example, junior staff continued to press home their advantage and to override those safeguards on professorial appointments and on research that the 1971 Wet op de Universitaire Bestuurleiding had set down.[83] In France and the Federal Republic of Germany, attempts to reverse the fortunes of war came from a different source—the professoriat. What could be lost on the boulevards of Paris and the streets of Länder capitals could be regained in the anterooms of the Bundesministerium für Bildung und Wissenschaft.

The press for reform by junior staff could indeed be met by technical measures, by enhanced formal representation at the institutional level, and by the occasional largesse of ministerial announcements that advanced some junior staff to middling ranks. But in higher education systems regulated by central administration, professorial power and influence is not limited to the institutional level. It is found also in individual access to highly placed key officials, parliamentarians, ministers, and important national committees, research agencies, and policy-determining bodies. There is much to suggest that professorial power, diminished at the institutional level, regrouped and consolidated itself at the commanding heights from whence the higher education system is controlled.

Two episodes in France and the Federal Republic of Germany hint at this reassertion of professorial power at the system level. First, the aptly named Loi Sauvage (the savage, or wild-man law) of 21 July 1980 restored the number of seats reserved for professors on French university councils to 50 percent of the whole, cut those set aside for students to 15 percent, and reduced those for instructors to a risible 5 percent. At the same time the qualifications for tenured status were tightened. Second, in the Federal Republic, the return of a Christian Democrat coalition has seen moves to limit the rights of nonprofessorial staff to participate in rectorial elections and to examine Ph.D. theses, a symbolic though significant change in the 1976 Hochschulrahmengesetz.[84] If two measures do not a trend make, they suggest that the reality of professorial power is more multidimensional than its expression at the institutional level.

Operating styles of academic estate orders—the junior collectivist and public, the senior individual and private—are radically different. But each in its own way has been instrumental in shaping the house of academe. The internal division and fragmentation of the academic estate simply shows how differently each order seeks to wield it.

THE NATIONAL ESTATE AND THE REFORM OF ACADEMIC WORK

Changing the internal management of universities was not the only task undertaken by governments in Western Europe. They also aimed to alter the work and role of higher education in general and the university in particular. Changes in university governance structures had arisen largely from internal rifts in the academic estate, but they in no way invalidated its self-perception as a national body. Measures that involved redirecting the work and the role of universities posed what academia regarded as an inadmissable threat to its status. Efforts by governments to assign new goals and priorities to academia as a corporate whole found themselves blocked. An estate that demonstrated spectacular disunity on one issue could, on others, give proof of an equally disconcerting obduracy. The stances of the French and West German academics are especially illuminating examples of this capacity.

ATTEMPTS TO VOCATIONALIZE THE UNIVERSITY

The transition of European universities from elite to mass institutions in the 1960s paralleled a shift in their underlying paradigm. From being an institution devoted to cultivation, the university came to be perceived by governments as an instrument for economic expansion.[85] The paradigmatic shift in no way denied the centrality of the institution; it merely transferred such centrality from the task of cultural unification to that of ensuring the nation's economic growth and vitality.

In the early and middle 1960s such a change in priorities did not alter the historic role of universities in supplying qualified manpower to the state and to medicine and law. Economic expansion led to growth in the provisions of the welfare state and thus possibly increased the importance of this traditional occupational nexus.[86] Nevertheless, though vocational in the sense that they selected for occupations and granted credentials, universities in Western Europe tended neither to be geared toward the private-sector labor market nor to concern themselves with practical training.

By the mid-1960s, after the upsurge of student militancy, certain governments, including the French, West German, British, Norwegian, and Swedish, began to look at linkages with the non-public-sector labor market. Initially, efforts (especially those in France, Britain, and Norway) concentrated on the nonuniversity sector, emerging in institutional form in the university institutes of technology, the polytechnics, and the regional colleges. In part this stemmed from the same demographic pressure that had poisoned relations between senior and junior orders of the academic estate. But such policies were also driven by the feeling that, on their own, universities were not adequate to meet changes in the non-state-sector labor market.[87]

Governments also developed a sense that reform, intended to link higher education to the private-sector labor market (hitherto confined to the nonuniversity sector), perhaps ought to be extended to universities. For example, in West Germany, on the one hand the bottleneck at the transition from school to higher education, caused by growth in student numbers, resulted in the imposition of *numerus clausus*—selective entry to certain oversubscribed courses. On the other hand, the linkage between higher education and the state-sector labor market had broken down. In France massive growth in student enrollments also led to a glut of arts and science graduates and a marked decline in employment opportunities in the state sector, particularly in teaching.[88]

Thus in both the Federal Republic and in France, a more matured strategy directed at changing the university's function and long-term goals ran alongside emergency measures altering internal governance. In Germany this strategy culminated in the 1976 Framework Act for Higher Education (Hochschulrahmengesetz) and the thrust to set up new comprehensive universities (*Gesamthochschulen*). In France it took the form of the "second-cycle" (years three and four of university study) reform of the same year. Both, in their own manner, aimed at redirecting the work of universities.

One intent of the proposal to set up comprehensive universities and to publish the Hochschulrahmengesetz was to improve the "technocratic efficiency" of West Germany's higher education system.[89] Suggestions that university education ought to be more practical and more in keeping with manpower needs and skills of the private sector had been aired as early as 1967 in a report to the Baden-Württemberg Ministry of Culture by the sociologist Ralf Dahrendorf.[90] Dahrendorf recommended three-year university programs (not the more usual six or seven) with special weight on teaching rather than research. The proposal to uncouple the close relationship between universities and research was further advanced by reorganizing the university along comprehensive lines.

First presented by the federal minister of education in 1970, the Gesamthochschule policy had two consequences: it set the stage for the Hochschulrahmengesetz, and it triggered the drafting of detailed framework planning by six of the eleven Länder.[91] It called for a merger among the various types of higher education institutions, university and nonuniversity. The idea was to form establishments bringing together classical functions of universities with more practical preoccupations of higher technical colleges (Fachhochschulen), linking academic research and training to professional practice. Adaptation to economic change would be facilitated by institutional integration and curricular reform. Integration would presumably enhance mobility between academic education and vocational training tracks, provide parity of esteem among different institutions, and increase educational opportunity. Technocratic policy aims were married to democratizing plans.[92]

By contrast, French reform strategy espoused a purely technocratic approach, undiluted by considerations of educational opportunity. Changes in the second cycle in 1976 were the last phase in a policy dating from 1973 when the first cycle (years one and two) was revamped and the diplôme d'études universitaires générales (DEUG) was introduced as a degree leading to "practical" employment. As the DEUG developed, it turned out not to be a "terminal qualification" (in the ambiguous terminology of legislators) so much as an intermediate diploma.[93]

The main objective of second-cycle reforms was to extend the vocationalization (*professionalisation*) deeper into the university curriculum.[94] The licence was redesigned as a one-year degree after the DEUG, and was to be more practically oriented than it was as a three- or four-year purely academic program. Similarly, the maîtrise was conceived as a one-year program (consecutive to the licence) which, in certain instances, would involve scientific and technical training for a specific occupation. Both proposals contained, imprudently perhaps, provisions for selective entry. Educational efficiency was emphasized, not educational opportunity.[95]

In both the Federal Republic of Germany and in France, then, government policy toward higher education was organized around a specific form of vocationalization. Such policy aimed at linking the curriculum directly to skills in certain private-sector jobs. In officialdom vocationalization was seen as a remedy to shortcomings in university–labor market relationships. Though universities were linked to a particular "protected labor market" of state service, their training was neither specialized enough nor sufficiently based on practice. The historic role of the university had been to provide a screening and credentialing mechanism for the state sector rather than to furnish specific training for such jobs.[96]

The new vocationalism sought to alter the type of knowledge imparted by universities, emphasizing skills and shifting undergraduate attention toward the private sector. Such changes were immensely important, historically and sociologically. They uncoupled the university from its raison d'être of the past two centuries—namely, to prepare duly qualified entrants for state employment. Such a policy struck at the aspirations of many students, particularly those seeking posts in schoolteaching. By the same token, it appeared to menace both the status and identity of the academic estate, since the state labor market was associated with honor and security.[97]

THE DEAD LETTER OF REFORM

For the supporters of reform the Hochschulrahmengesetz rang exceedingly hollow. Even if it stipulated that the higher education system ought to be reorganized on the comprehensive model, the six establishments worthy of the comprehensive label, already in place, antedated the legislation and enrolled no more than 10 percent of the university population.[98] The comprehensive university, like the mule, begat no offspring; and given the current economic climate, the situation probably will not change.

Even in Nordrhein-Westfalen, where five comprehensive universities were created, the state was unsuccessful in dividing the *Land* into *Gesamthochschulregionen* that would incorporate existing universities.[99] The comprehensive universities were not part of a successful comprehensive strategy; they were isolated additions to the existing university framework.

Moreover, these new additions to the ranks of German higher education have experienced "academic drift" toward traditional patterns of teaching and research, symbolized by their assumptions of "Universität" in their names. A "practical emphasis" among these comprehensive universities is really solidly established only at Kassel.[100] Evidently, attempts to reform university education in the Federal Republic show that passage into the statute book is no guarantee of success.

The reforming impulse in France fared no better. Reviewing efforts in this direction, one scholar has suggested, "It was much ado about nothing."[101] The enactment of the decrees of 1976 remained, at the institutional level, largely a dead letter. Some curriculum changes had been carried out prior to these exercises planned on paper. But confined to certain establishments mainly specializing in business studies and administration, their impact on the rest of French higher education was minimal.[102]

Just how little was achieved may be seen from the objectives set out in the new Higher Education Guideline Law of 1984. Universities were called upon to "enhance the nation's scientific and cultural de-

velopment," exhorted "to help reduce social and cultural inequalities," and encouraged "to contribute to employment policy and regional development."[103] If the 1976 reforms had succeeded, there
would have been no need to repeat the message.

THE ACADEMIC ESTATE: A NATIONAL SERVICE IN RESISTANCE TO CHANGE

In both the Federal Republic of Germany and France, attempts at
reform have gone little further than their formal publication. Enactment has not been accompanied by implementation. In higher education implementation depends ultimately on the will and cooperation
of academia. Neither was forthcoming. Those who lose the battle at
the formulation and adoption phase of reform may live to fight on at
the stage of implementation, a tactic academia often efficaciously employs. A decade of research has shown just how impervious higher
education systems can be to external pressure, partly because of their
"bottom-heavy" nature and the consequent difficulties this presents
to both political and ministerial authorities in the exercise of effective
control.[104]

Reforms do not have to be killed off by strident opposition; inaction
and inertia are just as effective. Success in carrying out comprehensive
university reform required the compliance of the German academic
estate in actively promoting, or at least agreeing to, the integration
of their universities with technical colleges. This was not to be. The
established universities, and even those new ones with radical reputations, were opposed to this move.[105] They did not lobby state
governments to block the framework legislation; opposition was carried out privily within their own universities, and was successful in
quickly undermining the implementation process.

When the comprehensive university was first broached as an idea
in the earlier part of the decade, no active opposition emerged. Indeed, the authoritative West German Rectors Conference put forward
its own proposals, though later it slid into tacit opposition to comprehensivization. The Gesamthochschule policy had various aims,
some of which academics supported. Junior staff approved its egalitarianism—not only the intended increased access to higher education, but more important, the reduced hierarchy among academic
staff.[106] The professoriat opposed it. On this score the comprehensive
reform fell afoul of the battle for status and privilege within academia.

Nevertheless, both junior staff and professors were broadly united
in condemning the particular stress the Gesamthochschule policy laid
on the work-manpower function, the technocratic aims.[107] For in-

stance, the BAK did not endorse the shortening of study programs or the idea that such programs ought to concentrate on instruction and practical training in place of academic education and research. That such efficiency-oriented reforms were basically unattractive to university academics as a whole is reflected in their opposition to such measures in two other contexts. The proposal to shorten study time had been aired in 1970 by the Wissenschaftsrat (Science Council) and was unearthed again in 1978. Both times strong opposition from within the universities led to its elimination.[108]

If the academic estate in the Federal Republic had little influence on policy formulation regarding the comprehensive university issue, academia's role in implementation was decisive and negative.

In January 1976 the French government presented the outlines of the second-cycle reform. Opposition was neither quiet nor slow in developing. The strikes and demonstrations that broke out lasted until the summer—far longer than the events of May 1968, to which it was inevitably compared. Students formed the mass of strikers, but protests were organized by faculty unions that, like the Duke of Plaza Torro, "led their forces from behind." As in the Federal Republic, so in France, the academic estate, senior and junior orders all, attacked the proposals mainly where closer links between the university and the economy were anticipated.[109] Opposition was no less vehement over vocationalizing courses than it was over the participation of outside representatives of industry in planning committees that would draw up the new courses.

But it was not the more spectacular acts that undermined the reform so much as the covert resistance of academia at the phase of implementation. The government placed the initiative for planning and construction of new programs at the institutional level. Submissions were subsequently to be approved by special commissions nominated by the secretary of state for higher education and by the Conseil National de l'Enseignement Supérieur et de la Recherche—a national committee with responsibility for validation and accreditation of university courses. Lack of enthusiasm among most ranks of university staff was equaled and occasioned by the lack of incentive given by central administration. Rather than setting aside additional finances, the government pushed for a redeployment of existing resources. The new programs were not supplementary to the old; they were to replace them.[110]

As in Germany, French academics had little influence on the formulation and adoption of the proposed reforms. But their massive noncompliance stymied implementation.

RESISTANCE TO CHANGE: ITS ROOTS IN ACADEMIA

The academic estate, despite its internal divisions, has its own perception of self and status. On balance, academics regard themselves as members of a national body in the service of the nation—a view reinforced by central-government control over issues in the external environment.[111] Opposition to reform in the Federal Republic of Germany and France had this common feature, though different orders sometimes resisted from differing motives: namely, that change, as presented by the polity, boded fair to alter either their perceived standing (chairholders) or the standing they aspired to (younger staff).

The thrust of the two reforms discussed above was to assign a new mission to the university, to link it to the nation's economic well-being. Such an economic connection had justified university growth since the early 1960s. But the economic association of university and nation did not alter the national nature of the university's mission, nor did it introduce major curricular reform. On the contrary, the policy of growth in the earliest part of that decade rested on the time-honored formula of "more of the same." The economic rationale could easily fit in with the idea, retained from the nineteenth century, that the university performed a culturally unifying role in the nation.[112] When students looked to the state labor market in increasing numbers, they added a further dimension to established practice.

The collapse of the state labor market in the early 1970s altered this. From that point governments turned their attention, with varying degrees of determination, first to the private sector of the labor market and second to the linking of universities with the economic life of the region.[113] Such policies ran counter to the academic estate's self-perception as a national entity.

The regionalization of the university was profoundly antithetical to the French estate. Regional requirements of manpower and skills are not homogeneous. If universities have a regional commitment, that commitment demands differential responses, different types of courses. So regionalization threatened certain aspects of academia's prestige structure contained in the institution of "national diplomas." Teaching national diploma courses carries no small kudos, and French academics have demonstrated a continued desire to achieve this honor.[114]

Denationalization of France's academic estate also threatened to increase the administrative and social distance from the capital and central administration and also the distance from the privilege and power that come from association with that political and intellectual pole. Since the last years of the seventeenth century, Parisians have looked on the provinces with horror tinged with amusement. To be provincial is to be boorish and second rate. To be regional is not even that. In their opposition to regionalization, French academics were a faithful reflection of the prejudices of their country's elite.[115]

Academics also feared that the new policies would create differentiation and give rise to a pecking order of institutions—a major change from the formal legal situation in which, on paper at least, all were on an equal footing. With the new policies some establishments might be obliged to emphasize a particular type of research, others to stress teaching. Like their French counterparts, German academics of all orders opposed the downplaying of the research function. For it would be tantamount to reducing professorial status to something akin to a superannuated schoolmaster—as many university academics regarded their Fachhochschulen counterparts. Assistants feared that such a policy could cut them off from any hope of advancement into the prestigious realm of research. The BAK continually proposed that all institutions of higher education have a scientific orientation, and that all academics have an equal chance to pursue research as well as teaching.[116]

Given their strong academic prejudices, the vocationalism of the reform policies was distasteful to all orders of the academic estate. In their world prestige lay in both national and academic models of university education. This view derives from the early cultural and social history of European education systems at school and university levels. Traditionally, a fundamental dichotomy existed between education and instruction; the former was noble, intended to develop the whole person, to create cultivation and grace and to mature the mind. The latter was less noble: reduced in scope and intended simply to equip the bulk of the population with appropriate vocational skills. These distinctions are mirrored in the structure of Europe's education systems: the gymnasium and lycée are favored, elite establishments geared to *Allgemeinbildung* and *culture générale,* and the *Hauptschulen* and *cours complementaires* are more vocational. Similar distinctions penetrated into postsecondary education as nonuniversity institutions emerged.[117]

Antivocationalism in German and French academia was not simply a cultural holdover from the time the university's purpose was the free and unfettered pursuit of knowledge and cultivation. It was one of those deeply rooted values that served to identify academia's claims to superior status. So the notion that German university teachers ought to "instruct" was not only a derogation from the classical ideology of research and education through research passed down from the time of Alexander von Humboldt; it was also a derogation in terms of school-based hierarchies. The objection that many academics raised vis-à-vis such proposals as the "Dahrendorf plan" (it would make university studies *Schulisch*—school-like) could not have been more devastating.[118] The intensity of wide-ranging academic opposition to vocationalism showed it to be an assault on the identity and essence of academia and university work.

Regionalization and vocationalization called forth the resistance of the academic estate. This frustrated policy and set at nought the best-laid plans of bureaucrat and legislator and revealed the power of the academic estate. But such power is effective only in certain circumstances: first, when opposition is broadly consensual in all ranks, even though motives differ; second, when reform places initiative for implementation inside the inner environment of academia rather than with the exterior frame; and third, when the issues at stake are perceived by all sections of academia to call into question those fundamental values that underlie its corporate standing and identity in society as a whole, as a national body. The defense of such interests had far more priority than the internecine feuding over internal governance and structures of participation. It is one thing to rebuild one's dwelling. It is another to have the town hall forcibly order its relocation and reconstruction. To this axiom the house of academe was no exception.

CONCLUSION

Academia, like Proteus, has many guises. The manifold perception of its various facets, each in its various perspectives, contribute to understanding the total picture. Some observers attach importance to the unique nature of academic work. Others emphasize the concomitants of working within different institutional sectors of higher education.[119]

In this essay we have been concerned with two additional dimensions that have special significance in understanding academia in Continental Europe and in distinguishing it from its British and American counterparts: the fissures that split the orders of academia, stemming in large part from the chair-faculty structure of academic organization—fissures dividing senior tenured professors, nonprofessorial but tenured middle ranks, and the junior largely untenured assistant class; and the self-perception of European academia as a national body, an academic estate.

How these two dimensions bear on European academia and condition its role in change and reform in higher education is evident from the two cases we have explored. The first revealed the polity's accommodation to pressure from within academia to put its house in order. The second involved pressure from the polity to impose reform on academia. Measures introduced by governments to redistribute the balance of authority among various constituencies inside academia, principally along the lines of formal ranking in the academic hierarchy, corresponded to the wishes of many university teachers. On paper at least, such measures were largely successful. But the polity's bid to alter the work and role of universities and the academic estate, to regionalize and vocationalize them, were largely unsuccessful. Lacking support from academics, even the most strenuous efforts at change by German and French governments remained ineffective.

These changes were precipitated largely by developments outside the system of higher education: in burgeoning student enrollments, in corresponding prodigious growth in junior academic staff, and in a glut of under- and unemployed university graduates brought about by the inability of state labor markets to absorb the expanded supply of graduates. Such external pressures were the common lot of industrial countries in the 1960s and 1970s. But the way academia, whether profession or estate, met them was not.

In part this differential response was caused by differences in public control, accountability, and governance, which constitute regulatory mechanisms in the higher education–polity relationship. We have alluded to this as the outer frame of academia; it acts as a bureaucratic overlay, penetrating into the inner environment of that body.[120] The location and penetration of this overlay occupies a different position in the relationship between university and polity in Continental Europe than it does in either the United States or Great Britain. In the former it tends to reside with the central administration, in the ministries of education or higher education. Penetrating downward from central authority to institution, it coordinates from the top down. By contrast, in the United States and to some extent in Great Britain, the structure occupying a functionally similar position is contained within the institution and acts as an extension upward between academia and the polity.

Important though the outer frame is, it is only one aspect of the complex linkages that tie academia together. The other aspect is represented by the inner environment, which in turn is profoundly influenced by patterns of work organization and the depth of the fissures dividing academic orders in Continental Europe. If, conceptually, inner environment and outer frame appear as separate dimensions in European academia, in practice they are closely related.

In Continental Europe, reform in the authority structures of the university reflected the inability of the chair-faculty structure to take sufficient initiatives at the institutional level to prevent the accumulation of discontent. Academia in those countries had little control of, and even less latitude to maneuver within, the outer frame of bureaucratic control. Remedies for discontent were sought nationally, and issues were fought at that level.

But it is too simple to suggest that bureaucracy in Continental Europe was simply a stultifying force that prevented flexibility in academia: it also acted as a vehicle by which reform was proposed, if not disposed, and it sought to head off accumulation of discontent inside academia. Further, we do not suggest that bureaucracy in Continental Europe was a leviathan, running roughshod over a helpless academia. In focusing on the divided house of academe, we did not declare that a divided house falls because of pressure from the polity. Instead, we suggested that some members of a divided house can pressure the polity and use it as an ally to bring about change. We further demonstrated that academia is not bereft of power when the ultimate responsibility for reform lies in the heartland of the inner environment, especially when the polity attempts to impose reform that is seen as a fundamental threat to academic values and to academia as a national estate. Refusal to take on a policy designed to promote the vocational commitment of the university showed the extent to which academia is capable of exercising control over its own house.

NOTES

This paper was written when Guy Neave was a visiting scholar at the Center for Studies in Higher Education at UC Berkeley and when Gary Rhoades was a postdoctoral research scholar in the Comparative Higher Education Research Group at UCLA. Comments and criticism from Martin Trow and Burton R. Clark have brought clarity where obscurity might have prevailed. We acknowledge their support and our gratitude. Gary Rhoades wishes to acknowledge the assistance of the National Institute of Education, whose funding enabled him to undertake the research for this paper.

1. Here we are concerned only with academia inside the university; in the nonuniversity sector academic organization tends to differ from the chair-faculty structure. In Great Britain, for example, academic organization in

polytechnics largely rests on formal rank hierarchy. For similar divisions in the French system, see chap. 3 of this volume. Here we focus on the university *stricto sensu*. See Becher, Kogan, and Embling, *Systems of Higher Education*.

2. This generalization applies only on balance; for some of the more ideologically motivated nonprofessorial malcontents, it was not true.

3. Neave, "University and the State in Western Europe"; "Strategic Planning and Governance in French Higher Education"; and "Higher Education and Regional Development"; Premfors, "Regionalization of Swedish Higher Education"; Lane, Westlund, and Stenlund, "Bureaucratisation of a System of Higher Education"; Bladh, "Trends Towards Vocationalisation in Swedish Higher Education"; and Cerych and Sabatier, *Great Expectations and Mixed Performance*.

4. See Van de Graaff et al., *Academic Power*. Also see Burton R. Clark, *Higher Education System*.

5. However, not each stratum or ranking is formally represented as a separate interest. Some have been folded into others or combined with them. In France there are seven ranks of academics; only three are formally represented constituencies.

6. Burton R. Clark, *Academic Power in Italy*, p. 78; Ben-David, *Centers of Learning*, p. 17.

7. This must be distinguished from academic self-government since nonprofessorial academics have no voice in faculty deliberations. Faculties tend to be exclusive collections of professors.

8. Van de Graaff et al., *Academic Power*.

9. Burton R. Clark, *Higher Education System*, p. 114.

10. Rashdall, *Universities of Europe in the Middle Ages;* Reeves, "European University from Medieval Times"; and Verger, *Histoire des Universités Françaises.* In the Middle Ages "master" and "professor" were synonymous. See Baldwin, "Introduction."

11. Burton R. Clark, *Higher Education System*, p. 186–188.

12. Van de Graaff, "Great Britain."

13. A chairholder in Britain is often a department head, a permanent position.

14. In Britain almost 90 percent of probationers are granted tenure after three to five years. See Williams, Blackstone, and Metcalf, *Academic Labour Market*, p. 108. In the United States the tenure decision usually comes after six years. A far smaller proportion of candidates achieves this status, though variations exist among disciplines, institutions, and over time. See Cartter, *Ph.D.'s and the Academic Marketplace*. See also Finkelstein, *American Academic Profession*.

15. Burton R. Clark, *Higher Education System*, p. 108. This does not occur in all departments. The spirit of collegiality between junior and senior colleagues must sometimes shine by its absence.

16. Burton R. Clark, "United States." This refers to such units as the College of Arts and Sciences or the College of Fine Arts. Professional units at this

level are called schools; for example, law school, medical school, school of engineering.

17. Some universities have college-level bodies composed of and controlled by academics who work with the administration in a species of dual structure. Such bodies traditionally have been limited to full professors and are more exclusive than inclusive.

18. Inherent tensions exist in the department-college structure, but the major one tends to be between academic staff and campus or systemwide administration. This is reflected in the unionization pattern in American academia: all academics, regardless of rank, are grouped against a common foe. However, unionization does tend to differentiate academics by institutional sector. For example, academics at California state universities are unionized; academics in the University of California system are not.

19. Rudolph, *American College and University*; Perkin, *New Universities in the United Kingdom*; Moodie and Eustace, *Power and Authority in British Universities*. Though the new universities in Britain sought to renew the medieval legacy by remodeling the lower levels of department and faculty by boards of studies or schools, these structures tend to operate like the predominant department-faculty structure. See also Beloff, *Plateglass Universities*.

20. Van de Graaff, "Great Britain"; Moodie and Eustace, *Power and Authority in British Universities*.

21. Villanueva. "Spain."

22. Salmon, "France: the Loi d'Orientation and its Aftermath."

23. Zeldin, "Higher Education in France, 1848–1940."

24. Ringer, *Education and Society in Modern Europe*.

25. This occurred in part because a deanship in Germany was an annually rotating position, whereas the doyen may have sat in splendor for as long as a decade at a time, a practice consistent with the independence and autonomy of French faculties. See Van de Graaff, "Federal Republic of Germany"; Van de Graaff and Furth, "France."

26. For example, a departing professor had little formal influence over the choice of his successor. The Habilitation not only gives the right to lecture independently within the university, it is also the sine qua non of full professorial status. Craig, *Scholarship and Nation Building*.

27. Before 1939 perhaps the most important part in filling professorial vacancies was played by the permanent section of the Higher Council for National Education (Conseil supérieur de l'Education Nationale) in conjunction with the Consultative Committee for Public Higher Education. After 1944 this function was performed by the Consultative Committee of the Universities. See Minot, *Quinze Ans d'Histoire des Institutions Universitaires*.

28. See Terry Clark, *Prophets and Patrons*. Any dichotomous typology, such as chair-faculty versus department-college structure, obscures important variations. Within France the cluster pattern exists in law faculties but does not operate as intensely as it does in arts and science and, particularly, medical faculties.

29. Terry Clark, *Prophets and Patrons;* Van de Graaff and Furth, "France."

30. Terry Clark, *Prophets and Patrons;* Van de Graaff, "Federal Republic of Germany"; Van de Graaff and Furth, "France"; and Hennis, "Germany." Such research benefits were not automatically accorded to chairholders in France. They were obliged to get outside funds usually from centralized research organizations such as the National Center for Scientific Research (Centre national de la recherche scientifique).

31. Terry Clark, *Prophets and Patrons;* Friedberg and Musselin, "Academic Profession in France," chap. 3 of this volume. The French patron also influenced the discipline; even within this informal and dispersed structure, cluster members were expected to organize their work to test and elaborate the basic hypotheses in the patron's oeuvre.

32. Terry Clark, *Prophets and Patrons.* This comparison ought not be carried too far. Many French cluster members held posts in establishments other than those of their patron; this may have diluted the dependency level compared to the German apprentice, who relied almost totally on his master during those years spent working with and under him.

33. Since this work organization pattern persisted for centuries without incident, without an outbreak of hostilities between these two latent groups, evidently some elements of these structures cushioned and counterbalanced such disparities, for instance, the shared commitment to research.

34. In the United States a recent example of the sanctions encountered by one who is perceived to have violated this ethic is revealed in the controversy surrounding the work of a historian, David Abraham. See *Chronicle of Higher Education,* 6 February 1985.

35. This definition is similar to Smelser's in "Growth, Structural Change, and Conflict in California Higher Education," and is founded on the institutional position of academics. But Smelser distinguished among various academic estates according to position within the system: lower division (undergraduate) students, graduate students, teaching assistants, assistant professors, deans, chancellors, members of board of trustees, full-time research staff, and other groups. The definition we use refers only to teaching staff in institutions of higher education, whether professorial or nonprofessorial, tenured or nontenured.

36. If the university professor refers to his Fachhochschule colleague using the same title he accords his coeval it is often annoying to the former and frustrating to the latter.

37. Neave, "Regional Development and Higher Education."

38. Centre for Educational Research and Innovation, *University and the Community;* Neave, "University and the Community."

39. Gouldner, "Locals and Cosmopolitans"; Halsey and Trow, *British Academics;* Perkin, "Academic Profession in the United Kingdom."

40. Craig, *Scholarship and Nation Building.* Earlier, monarchs sought to turn aside proto-universities and to link them directly with training court officials. See Kamp, "Autonomy for Servicing Societies."

41. Svensson, "State and Higher Education"; Gruber, "Higher Education and the State in Austria." Many sociologists and historians tend to see the Humboldtian and Napoleonic reforms as the beginning of the university–modern bureaucratic state association. See Archer, *Social Origins of Educational Systems;* Kuenzel, "State and Higher Education in the Federal Republic of Germany." This view is tenable only as long as one looks at France and Germany. The Humboldtian and Napoleonic measures stand as the end of a process whose origins can be traced to Sweden from the 1740s to the 1770s and to the Austria of Josef II.

42. Geiger, "Universities and the State in Belgium"; Malintoppi, "Italy."

43. Malintoppi, "Italy"; Neave, "France."

44. For a discussion of the public versus the private life of universities see Trow, "Public and Private Lives of Higher Education."

45. Kuenzel, "State and Higher Education in the Federal Republic of Germany." Religious foundations are an exception. See Geiger, *Private Sectors.*

46. In certain countries, particularly Scandinavia, familial academic dynasties are not unknown. See Conference des Recteurs Européenes Bulletin d'Information, "On the Perils and Rewards of Boldness."

47. Neave and Jenkinson, *Research on Higher Education in Sweden.*

48. Ringer, *Education and Society in Modern Europe;* Craig, *Scholarship and Nation Building.* Such fields as history, classics, and to some extent, philology, were instrumental in reasserting a claim to nationhood in such countries as Italy, Belgium, and the German states, which were previously divided, occupied, or both. See Kohn, *Idea of Nationalism.*

49. For the role of the professor as a figure of "total status" see Burton R. Clark, *Academic Power in Italy.* For a less kind but illuminating view of university intellectuals as political figures, see Thibaudet, *Republique des Professeurs.*

50. French ladder ranks distinguish between *maîtres assistants* and *assistants,* roughly the equivalent in Britain to lecturer and junior lecturer and in the United States to assistant professor and instructor. The former may be tenured, the latter is rarely so; this has not prevented some individuals from being assistants for up to eleven years, on a year-by-year renewal. In 1978 the Ministry of Higher Education placed a time limit of no more than five years on the period in which assistants could hold such a post and attempt to become qualified, to reduce the servitude if not the grandeur of such appointments.

51. Lane, "Power in the University."

52. Daalder, "Netherlands"; Strathopoulos, "New Greek Law"; Villanueva, "Spain."

53. See German University Affairs, "Commission Presents Results" and "Partial Revision"; Ministrie van Onderwijs en Wetenschappen, *Beleidsvoornemens.*

54. Neave, "Strategic Planning and Governance in French Higher Education."

55. Burton R. Clark, *Academic Power in Italy;* Lane, "Power in the University"; Becher and Kogan, *Process and Structure in Higher Education;* Verger, *Histoire des Universités Françaises.*

56. Becher, "Cultural View."

57. See Burton R. Clark, " 'Cooling-Out' Function in Higher Education."

58. Burton R. Clark, ed. *School and the University.*

59. See Burton R. Clark, ed. *School and the University.* The first signs of change in the social demand for higher education emerged in the late 1950s in Sweden; by the early 1960s they began to alter quantitatively as well as qualitatively the articulation between secondary and higher education throughout Western Europe. Generally, some 5 percent of the relevant age group entered higher education at the start of the decade, a figure which, by 1970, became 12 to 13 percent. See Cerych, Colton, and Jallade, *Student Flows and Expenditure in Higher Education, 1965–1970.* The situation was made more complex in the latter 1960s and early 1970s when the Italian government (1969) and the Belgian government (1973) initiated a policy of multiple validity for school-leaving diplomas (*omnivalence des diplômes*). Essentially, this measure involved making all high school certificates, including those from technical schools, valid for a place in higher education. This had two consequences. It first removed an important element in the school-based screening process by opening up higher education to a new group of students who previously did not have access to the university. Second, it accelerated student demand for higher education, which already was growing rapidly.

60. Chevalier, *Classes Laborieuses et Classes Dangereuses.*

61. In Sweden, Britain, and the Netherlands they increased markedly but less rapidly. The fall in numbers in France over the period 1975–1976 and 1979–1980 is the result of the government's introduction of a rapid promotion policy for this order of the academic estate. Cross-national comparison raises severe methodological difficulties. Junior staff may be defined differently in each country, or certain categories—"lecturer" in Britain, for instance—may cover both the callow and the highly qualified, the aged respectable and the unqualified. Ladder ranks are also apt to change their designation over time, a development noticeable in Britain and France. For France, see Friedberg and Musselin, "Academic Profession in France," chap. 3 in this volume.

62. Student-staff ratios in British universities are particularly favorable compared to their Continental equivalent. In 1970 the student-staff ratio in Great Britain was 8.3:1. In Belgium it was 9.5:1; in Sweden, 17.2:1. By contrast, in France and Italy it was 24.1:1 and 38.9:1 (derived from tables 5.1 and 5.2). This calculation does not include part-time staff or students, nor does it discriminate between the very different ratios of various disciplines. Probably they err on the optimistic side, particularly in such countries as France and Italy that have a significant proportion of part-time staff. Were this to be taken into account, the contrast might be even more stark.

63. Salmon, "France: the Loi d'Orientation and its Aftermath." Giglioni, *Baroni e Burocrati.*

64. See Becher, "Disciplinary Shaping of the Profession," in this volume, chap. 6; Rothblatt, "Bearers of Civilization"; and Thelander, *Forsknarsutbildning som Traditionsformedling.*

65. Neave, "Elite and Mass Higher Education in Britain"; Trow, "Defining the Issues of University Government Relations." University finance in Britain was based on student numbers, and student financing was dependent on having been selected by academia for a place.

66. In the classic Tocquevillian situation, which bred revolution in France in 1789, one estate has partial access to the activities and rewards of another or does very similar work, but it is denied access to the full rewards of the higher estate. See de Tocqueville, *Old Regime and the French Revolution;* Smelser, "Growth, Structural Change, and Conflict in California Higher Education, 1950–1970," p. 67.

67. Webler, "Student Movement in Germany."

68. Sontheimer, "Student Opposition in West Germany."

69. Kuiper, "How Democratic is a Dutch University?"

70. On the SDS in Germany, see Hennis, "Germany."

71. In Sweden junior academics did not organize into separate bodies because major trade union organizations already enjoyed a legitimacy in discussions about national academic policy dating from the 1950s, if not before, and because secondary-school teachers, who were hired during the higher education expansion in the early sixties, actually enjoyed an enhancement of their previous status. In Britain, though a junior faculty–trade union alignment was attempted, it was a small minority movement. The modified chair-faculty structure and the countervailing constraints on professorial power at the department level were largely instrumental in preventing the buildup of tension between junior and senior orders within the British academic profession. See Hennis, "Germany." The AUT acted as a nonpolitical, professional association of university teachers. See Perkin, *Key Profession,* and "Academic Profession in the United Kingdom," chap. 1 in this volume. The representative association for Swedish academics was a broad-bottomed union federation operating on behalf of professionals, civil servants, and people with academic degrees. See Premfors and Ostergren, *Systems of Higher Education: Sweden.*

72. The two are not mutually exclusive, as the example of the Federal Republic of Germany shows. But to draw conceptual lines between them perhaps clarifies the concept.

73. Peisert and Framhein, *Systems of Higher Education: Federal Republic of Germany.*

74. Council of Europe, "Federal Republic of Germany."

75. Verhoeven, "Belgium."

76. Malintoppi, "Italy."

77. Bourricaud, "France."

78. Verhoeven, "Belgium"; Malintoppi, "Italy"; Council of Europe, "Italie."

79. Premfors, "Regionalisation of Swedish Higher Education"; and Lin-

densjo, "Högskolereformen en Studie i Offentlig Reformstrategi." The Swedish situation was somewhat different. Though student unrest was present and had been instrumental in ushering in the change, basic alterations to the chair-faculty structure had been introduced in a long-drawn-out series of reforms dating from the late 1950s. See Premfors and Ostergren, *Systems of Higher Education: Sweden;* OECD, *Reviews of National Policies in Education: Sweden.* The 1977 reforms were the last step in a coherent strategy for structural and management innovation that ended the model of university power Sweden imported from Germany—the *Ordinarienuniversität.*

80. Salmon, "France"; Minot, *Quinze Ans d'Histoire des Institutions Universitaires.*

81. For this point see Friedberg and Musselin, "Academic Profession in France," chap. 3 in this volume, and Patterson, "French University Reform."

82. Salmon, "France."

83. Daalder, "Netherlands."

84. Minot, *Quinze Ans d'Histoire des Institutions Universitaires;* Akademischer Dienst, "Hochschulverband."

85. Svensson, "State and Higher Education."

86. Zeldin, "Higher Education in France, 1848–1940." See also Ringer, *Decline of the German Mandarins;* Suleiman, *Politics, Power, and Bureaucracy in France;* Ben-David, *Centers of Learning;* and Neave, *Nouveaux Modèles d'Enseignement Supérieur et Egalité des Chances.*

87. Neave, *Patterns of Equality;* Weizsäcker, "Hochschulstruktur und Marktsystem."

88. See Lohmar and Ortner, *Doppelte Flaschenhals,* for a collection of articles on the "dual bottleneck." On the German labor-market linkage see Peisert and Framhein, *Systems of Higher Education: Federal Republic of Germany.* By the end of the 1970s, only 25 percent of higher education graduates found jobs in the public sector. See Teichler, "Recent Developments in Higher Education in the Federal Republic of Germany" and *Arbeitsmarkt für Hochschulabsolventen.* On France see Geiger, "Second-Cycle Reform and the Predicament of the French University"; Levy-Garboua and Orivel, "Inefficiency in the French System of Higher Education." Arts and science faculties had the largest enrollments and had long been geared to "internal reproduction"—educating people to staff the state school and university systems as well as the state administrative apparatus. See Boudon, "French University Since 1968."

89. Kuenzel, "State of Higher Education in the Federal Republic of Germany."

90. Peisert and Framhein, *Systems of Higher Education: Federal Republic of Germany;* Cerych, Neusel, Teichler, and Winkler, *German Gesamthochschule.* But Dahrendorf's prime interest was the expansion of educational opportunity, hence the title of his book, *Bildung ist Bürgerrecht* (Education is a Civil Right). Moreover, he believed reform sprang not from economic necessity, but from the need to ensure democratic evolution. See Mushaben, "Reform in Three Phases."

91. Cerych, Neusel, Teichler, and Winkler, *German Gesamthochschule.* A ministerial, not a federal government statement, this was a nonbinding declaration.

92. Peisert and Framhein, *Systems of Higher Education: Federal Republic of Germany;* Cerych, Neusel, Teichler, and Winkler, *German Gesamthochschule;* Kuenzel, "State of Higher Education in the Federal Republic of Germany."

93. Cohen, *Elusive Reform.*

94. See the chapter on France in this volume for a discussion of the makeup of study groups to design the courses. The presence of "outsiders" (like industrialists) attests to the government's desire to ensure that practical concerns were not ignored.

95. Geiger, "Second-Cycle Reform and the Predicament of the French University" and Cohen, *Elusive Reform.* This was one basis of strong student opposition to the measures. Some faculties previously practiced de facto selection, but the reforms threatened to make selection de jure. Students feared "juridical creep" of selection across the university.

96. Crozier, *Bureaucratic Phenomenon*, p. 239. French university education was overwhelmingly theoretical, giving little attention to experience. By vocationalization the government in part meant having university students put on *stages* in private enterprises (like the British sandwich courses, *stages* in France refers to periods of practical experience through job placement, interspersed with periods of coursework at the university). Even at the summit of French higher education, the grandes écoles do not provide specialized training in the sense of narrow skills-oriented study. But many do have students serve on stages. See Suleiman, *Politics, Power, and Bureaucracy in France* and "Myth of Technical Expertise." See also Millot, "Social Differentiation and Higher Education."

97. Neave, "The Dynamic of Integration in Non-Integrated Systems of Higher Education." There is a very strong anti-industrialist ideology among wide swathes of the academic estate. See, for example, Ringer, *Decline of the German Mandarins.* But the motives as well as the form this ideology takes tend to derive from differing assumptions in junior and senior staff. Gearing university studies to the private sector devalued or downgraded university education. See Patterson, "Governmental Policy and Equality in Higher Education," for the argument that the 1976 second-cycle reforms in France amounted to "junior collegizing" French universities.

98. Peisert and Framhein, *Systems of Higher Education: Federal Republic of Germany.* See also Cerych, Neusel, Teichler, and Winkler, *German Gesamthochschule.* According to Cerych et al., the four comprehensive establishments set up in Bavaria "in no way correspond to even the most modest definition of this new organizational form" (p. 15). One other comprehensive institution, the *Fernuniversität,* is effectively a counterpart of the British Open University.

99. See Cerych, Neusel, Teichler, and Winkler, *German Gesamthochschule.*

100. Gesamthochschulen in Nordrhein-Westfalen are designated "Uni-

versität." Unlike the Gesamthochschule Kassel in Hessen, they have been accepted as full members of the German Research Association in recognition of the academic, discipline-oriented work they do. See Cerych, Neusel, Teichler, and Winkler, *German Gesamthochschule,* pp. 32–33.

101. Salmon, "France: the Loi d'Orientation and its Aftermath," p. 92.

102. Cohen, *Elusive Reform,* p. 122. More students are choosing professionally oriented programs of study. See Furth, "New Hierarchies in Higher Education"; Bienaymé, "New Reform in French Higher Education." But changes in student preferences bear little correspondence to those of academic staff.

103. Bienaymé, "New Reform in French Higher Education"; Neave, "Strategic Planning and Governance in French Higher Education."

104. Cerych, "Higher Education Reform"; Bladh, "Trends Towards Vocationalisation in Swedish Higher Education." See also Burton R. Clark, *Higher Education System.*

105. Cerych, Neusel, Teichler, and Winkler, *German Gesamthochschule,* pp. 40–41.

106. Ibid., pp. 45, 47. For the details of the Bundesassistentenkonferenz comprehensivization plan see Federal Conference of University Assistants, *Kreuznacher Hochschulkonzept,* and "Integrierte Wissenschaftliche Gesamthochschule." A major concern of this plan was junior staff status and their work. See also Peisert and Framhein, *Systems of Higher Education: Federal Republic of Germany,* p. 121.

107. Mushaben, "Reform in Three Phases." By 1976 various academic associations representing left to right and junior staff to professors opposed the Gesamthochschule policy. See Mushaben, "The State v. the University." The earlier support in academia was mostly very general. For instance, in the early 1970s university committee resolutions generally supported the Gesamthochschule policy. But nowhere was the policy of integrating existing universities with technical colleges supported in practice. See Cerych, Neusel, Teichler, and Winkler, *German Gesamthochschule,* p. 42.

108. The Science Council dropped the idea in 1970 when visits to forty-five universities revealed heavy opposition. See Peisert and Framhein, *Systems of Higher Education: Federal Republic of Germany,* p. 119. Similar proposals in 1978 also encountered widespread and strong opposition by university academics. See Teichler, "Recent Developments in Higher Education in the Federal Republic of Germany," p. 166.

109. Boudon, "French University Since 1968." Staff and students were hostile to the reforms from different motives. For students the main sticking point was selection for admission to these new courses. For staff an additional factor was the vocational character of the proposed programs.

110. Geiger, "The Second Cycle Reform and the Predicament of the French University"; Cohen, *Elusive Reform.* In part the government did not provide additional resources because they wished to prevent universities from devising new courses simply as add-ons.

111. Neave, "Higher Education and Regional Development," and "Regional Development and Higher Education."

112. Neave, *Patterns of Equality*. Centre for Educational Research and Innovation, *University and the Community*.

113. Neave, *Strategic Planning and Governance in French Higher Education*.

114. See our earlier discussion of national diplomas. See also Neave, "France," and "Higher Education and Regional Development"; Fomerand, "French University"; Bienaymé, *Systems of Higher Education: France*.

115. Mme. de Sevigné, *Letters of Madame de Sevigné*. It is common reading in France, and until the sixties, this was one of the classic texts in most French lower secondary schools.

116. See Peisert and Framhein, *Systems of Higher Education: Federal Republic of Germany*, p. 121. See also our earlier discussion of the BAK.

117. The noble notion of education is linked with academic education. The distinctions between academic and vocational models are so marked that the status hierarchy is dichotomous rather than continuous. Academic institutions are on a different, more prestigious, plane than vocational institutions. If a university becomes practically and vocationally oriented, it is threatened with a step down the hierarchical ladder; this loss of status could even mean falling off the edge of the world or being relegated to a lower stratum of existence.

118. See Peisert and Framhein, *Systems of Higher Education: Federal Republic of Germany*, p. 119–121. These plans generated the strongest opposition from academics. The similar intention of the French government to promote "instruction" is evident in the renaming of the UERs to UFRs: Unités d'enseignement et de recherche (education and research) are to be renamed unités de formation de recherche (training and research).

119. Burton R. Clark, *Higher Education System*; Ruscio, "Many Sectors, Many Professions," chap. 8, this volume. In the United States observers examine colleges of letters and science as opposed to professional schools. For example, see Halpern, "Professional School in the American University," chap. 7, this volume.

120. The ways it does so depend largely on its precise internal elements. We have suggested that such elements are not merely budgetary and financial, but also extend to nominations to posts, confirmation of advancement, and conditions of service.

BIBLIOGRAPHY

Akademischer Dienst. "Hochschulverband: Forderungen zur Änderung des Hochschulrahmengesetzes." Bonn, 10 May 1983: 15.

Archer, Margaret. *The Social Origins of Educational Systems*. Beverly Hills, Calif.: Sage Publications, 1979.

Baldwin, John W. "Introduction." In *Universities in Politics: Case Studies from the Late Middle Ages and Early Modern Period*, eds. John W. Baldwin and Richard A. Goldthwaite. Baltimore: Johns Hopkins University Press, 1972.

Becher, Tony. "The Cultural View." In *Perspectives on Higher Education: Eight Disciplinary and Comparative Views*, ed. Burton R. Clark. Berkeley, Los Angeles, London: University of California Press, 1984.

Becher, Tony, and Maurice Kogan. *Process and Structure in Higher Education*. London: Heinemann, 1980.

Becher, Tony, Maurice Kogan, and Jack Embling. *Systems of Higher Education: United Kingdom*. New York: International Council for Educational Development, 1977.

Beloff, Michael. *The Plateglass Universities*. Rutherford, N.J.: Fairleigh Dickinson University Press, 1970.

Ben-David, Joseph. *Centers of Learning: Britain, France, Germany, United States*. New York: McGraw-Hill, 1977.

Bienaymé, Alain. *Systems of Higher Education: France*. New York: International Council for Educational Development, 1978.

―――――. "The New Reform in French Higher Education." *European Journal of Education* 19, no. 2 (1984): 151–164.

Bladh, Agneta. "Trends Towards Vocationalisation in Swedish Higher Education." Monograph 16. Group for the Study of Higher Education and Research Policy, University of Stockholm, 1982.

Boudon, Raymond. "The French University Since 1968." *Comparative Politics* 10, no. 1 (1977): 89–119.

Bourricaud, François. "France: the Prelude to the Loi d'Orientation of 1968." In *Universities, Politicians, and Bureaucrats*, ed. Hans Daalder and Edward Shils. Cambridge: Cambridge University Press, 1982.

Cahiers de l'Avenir de la France. "Evolution du Ministère de l'Education Nationale: Elèves, Etudiants et Enseignants." No. 1. Paris, 1984.

Cartter, Allan. *Ph.D.'s and the Academic Marketplace*. New York: McGraw-Hill, 1976.

Centre for Educational Research and Innovation. *The University and the Community: The Problems of Changing Relationships*. Paris: OECD, 1982.

Cerych, Ladislav. "Higher Education Reform: the Process of Implementation." *Educational Policy Bulletin* 7, no. 1 (1979): 5–21.

Cerych, Ladislav, and Paul Sabatier. *Great Expectations and Mixed Performance: The Implementation of Higher Education Reforms*. Stoke on Trent, England: Trentham Books, 1986.

Cerych, Ladislav, Sarah Colton, and Jean-Pierre Jallade. *Student Flows and Expenditure in Higher Education 1965–1970*. Paris: European Institute of Education and Social Policy, 1981.

Cerych, Ladislav, Åyla Neusel, Ulrich Teichler, and H. Winkler. *The German Gesamthochschule*. Amsterdam: European Cultural Foundation, 1981.

Chevalier, Louis. *Classes Laborieuses et Classes Dangereuses: Le Mouvement Social à Paris Pendant la Premiere Moitie du 19 Siècle*. Paris: Plon, 1969.

Chronicle of Higher Education. "Brouhaha over Historian's Use of Sources Renews Scholars' Interest in Ethics Codes." 29 (6 February 1985): 1, 9.

Clark, Burton R. "The 'Cooling-Out' Function in Higher Education." *American Journal of Sociology* 65, no. 6 (1960): 569–576.

––––––. *Academic Power in Italy: Bureaucracy and Oligarchy in a National University System*. Chicago: University of Chicago Press, 1977.

––––––. *The Higher Education System: Academic Organization in Cross-National Perspective*. Berkeley, Los Angeles, London: University of California Press, 1983.

––––––. "United States." In *Academic Power: Patterns of Authority in Seven National Systems*, by John H. Van de Graaff, Burton R. Clark, Dorotea Furth, Dietrich Goldschmidt, and Donald Wheeler. New York: Praeger, 1978.

Clark, Burton R., ed. *The School and University: An International Perspective*. Berkeley, Los Angeles, London: University of California Press, 1985.

Clark, Terry Nichols. *Prophets and Patrons: The French University and the Emergence of the Social Sciences*. Cambridge, Mass.: Harvard University Press, 1973.

Cohen, Habiba S. *Elusive Reform: The French Universities, 1968–1978*. Boulder, Colo.: Westview Press, 1978.

Conférence des Recteurs Européenes Bulletin d'Information. "On the Perils and Rewards of Boldness." *CRE Information* 62 (1983): 87–95.

Council of Europe. "Federal Republic of Germany: Higher Education Legislation and Student Unrest." *Council of Europe Newsletter* 5, no. 77 (1977).

––––––. "Italie: Relance de la Réforme Universitaire." *Council of Europe Newsletter* 2, no. 77 (1977).

Craig, John E. *Scholarship and Nation Building: The Universities of Strasbourg and Alsatian Society, 1870–1939*. Chicago: University of Chicago Press, 1984.

Crozier, Michel. *The Bureaucratic Phenomenon*. Chicago: University of Chicago Press, 1964.

Daalder, Hans. "The Netherlands: Universities Between the 'New Democracy' and the 'New Management.' " In *Universities, Politicians, and Bureaucrats*, ed. Hans Daalder and Edward Shils. Cambridge: Cambridge University Press, 1982.

Dahrendorf, Ralf. *Bildung ist Bürgerrecht*. Hamburg: Nannen, 1965.

Department of Education and Science. *Statistics of Education*. Vol. 6, *Universities*. London, 1967, 1970, 1979.

Federal Conference of University Assistants. *Kreuznacher Hochschulkonzept, Reformziele der Bundesassistentenkonferenz*. Bonn, 1968.

––––––. "Integrierte Wissenschaftliche Gesamthochschule." In *Die Schule der Nation*, ed. Klaus von Dohnanyi. Düsseldorf: Econ, 1971.

Finkelstein, Martin J. *The American Academic Profession*. Columbus: Ohio State University Press, 1984.

Fomerand, Jacques. "The French University: What Happened After the Revolution?" *Higher Education* 6, no. 1 (1977): 93–116.

Furth, Dorotea. "New Hierarchies in Higher Education." *European Journal of Education* 17, no. 2 (1982): 145–152.

Geiger, Roger L. "The Second-Cycle Reform and the Predicament of the French University." *Paedagogica Europaea* 12, no. 1 (1977): 9–22.

————. "The Universities and the State in Belgium: Past and Present Dimensions of Higher Education in a Divided Country." Higher Education Research Group Working Paper, no. 29. New Haven: Yale University, 1978.

————. *Private Sectors in Higher Education: Structure, Function, and Change in Eight Countries.* Ann Arbor: University of Michigan Press, 1986.

German University Affairs. "The Commission Presents Results: Suggestions for a Reform of University Structures." Vol. 29, no. 2 (1984).

————. "A Partial Revision: Federal Minister Wilms Wants Swift Measures." Vol. 29, no. 2 (1984).

Giglioli, Pier Paolo. *Baroni e Burocrati.* Bologna: Il Mulino, 1979.

Gouldner, Alvin W. "Locals and Cosmopolitans." *Administrative Science Quarterly* 1, no. 2 (1957): 281–306; 444–480.

Gruber, Karl-Heinz. "Higher Education and the State in Austria: An Historical and Institutional Approach." *European Journal of Education* 17, no. 3 (1982): 259–271.

Halsey, A. H., and Martin Trow. *The British Academics.* London: Faber, 1972.

Hennis, Wilhelm. "Germany: Legislators and the Universities." In *Universities, Politicians, and Bureaucrats*, ed. Hans Daalder and Edward Shils. Cambridge: Cambridge University Press, 1982.

Kamp, Norbert. "Autonomy for Servicing Societies." Dossier of the VIIIth General Assembly of the Standing Conference of Vice-Chancellors, Rectors, and Presidents of the European Universities. Athens: Conference des Recteurs Européenes, 1984.

Kohn, Hans. *The Idea of Nationalism: A Study of its Origins and Background.* New York: Macmillan, 1961.

Kuenzel, Klaus. "The State and Higher Education in the Federal Republic of Germany." *European Journal of Education* 17, no. 3 (1982): 243–258.

Kuiper, R. J. "How Democratic is a Dutch University?" In *A Decade of Change*, ed. A. Armstrong. Guildford, England: Society for Research into Higher Education, 1979.

Lane, Jan-Erik. "Power in the University." *European Journal of Education* 14, no. 4 (1979): 389–402.

Lane, Jan-Erik, Anders Westlund, and Hans Stenlund. "Bureaucratisation of a System of Higher Education." Report of the Department of Political Science, University of Umea, 1981.

Levy-Garboua, L., and F. Orivel. "Inefficiency in the French System of Higher Education." *European Journal of Education* 17, no. 2 (1982): 153–160.

Lindensjo, Bo. "Högskolereformen en Studie i Offentlig Reformstrategi." Summary in English. Stockholm Studies in Politics, no. 20. Department of Political Science, University of Stockholm, 1981.

Lohmar, Ulrich, and Gerhard E. Ortner, eds. *Der Doppelte Flaschenhals—Die*

Deutsche Hochschule Zwischen Numerus Clausus und Akademikerarbeitslosigkeit. Hannover: Schroedel, 1975.

Malintoppi, Antonio. "Italy: Universities Adrift." In *Universities, Politicians, and Bureaucrats,* ed. Hans Daalder and Edward Shils. Cambridge: Cambridge University Press, 1982.

Millot, Benoit. "Social Differentiation and Higher Education: The French Case." *Comparative Education Review* 25, no. 3 (1981): 353–368.

Ministrie van Onderwijs en Wetenschappen. *Beleidsvoornemens: Taakverdeling en Concentratie Wetenschappelijk Onderwijs.* 'sGravenhage: O & W, 1983.

Minot, J. *Quinze Ans d'Histoire des Institutions Universitaires, Mai 1968–Mai 1983.* Paris: Ministrie de l'Education Nationale, 1983.

Moodie, Graeme, and Rowland Eustace. *Power and Authority in British Universities.* Montreal: McGill-Queens University Press, 1974.

Mushaben, Joyce Marie. "The State v. the University: Juridicalization and the Politics of Higher Education at the Free University of Berlin, 1969–1979." Ph.D. diss., Indiana University, 1981.

————. "Reform in Three Phases: Judicial Action and the German Federal Framework Law for Higher Education of 1976." *Higher Education* 13 (1984): 423–438.

Neave, Guy. *Patterns of Equality.* Windsor, Berks: NFER, 1976.

————. *Nouveaux Modèles d'Enseignment Supérieur et Egalité des Chances: Perspective Internationales.* Luxembourg: Commission des Communautes Européenes, 1978.

————. "On Wolves and Crises." *Paedagogica Europaea* 13, no. 1 (1978): 11–33.

————. "Higher Education and Regional Development: An Overview of a Growing Controversy." *European Journal of Education* 13, no. 1 (1979): 207–231.

————. "Regional Development and Higher Education." *Higher Education Review* 11, no. 3 (1979): 10–26.

————. "The Dynamic of Integration in Non-integrated Systems of Higher Education." In *The Compleat University,* ed. Ulrich Teichler, Harry Herrmanns, and Henry Wasser. New York: Schenkman, 1983.

————. "The University and the Community: a Critique." *Studies in Higher Education* 9, no. 1 (1984): 87–90.

————. "The University and the State in Western Europe." In *The Future of Higher Education,* ed. David Jacques and John Richardson. London: NFER-Nelson, 1985.

————. "Strategic Planning and Governance in French Higher Education." *Studies in Higher Education* 10, no. 1 (1985): 5–18.

————. "Elite and Mass Higher Education in Britain: a Regressive Model?" *Comparative Education Review* 28, no. 3 (1985): 347–361.

————. "France." In *The School and the University: An International Perspective,* ed. Burton R. Clark. Berkeley, Los Angeles, London: University of California Press, 1985.

Analysis and an Evaluation. Stockholm: Almqvist and Wiksell International, 1983.

Organisation for Economic Cooperation and Development. *The Development of Higher Education, 1950–1967.* Paris, 1970.

————. *Reviews of National Policies in Education: Sweden.* Paris, 1980.

Patterson, Michelle. "French University Reform: Renaissance or Restoration?" In *University Reform,* ed. Philip G. Altbach. Cambridge, Mass.: Schenkman, 1974.

————. "Governmental Policy and Equality in Higher Education: The Junior Collegization of the French University." *Social Problems* 24, no. 2 (1976): 173–183.

Peisert, Hansgert, and Gerhild Framhein. *Systems of Higher Education: Federal Republic of Germany.* New York: International Council for Educational Development, 1978.

Perkin, Harold. *Key Profession: The History of the Association of University Teachers.* London: Routledge and Kegan Paul, 1969.

————. *New Universities in the United Kingdom.* Paris: OECD, 1969.

Premfors, Rune. "The Regionalization of Swedish Higher Education." *Comparative Education Review* 28, no. 1 (1984): 85–104.

Premfors, Rune, and Bertil Ostergren. *Systems of Higher Education: Sweden.* New York: International Council for Educational Development, 1979.

Rashdall, Hastings. *The Universities of Europe in the Middle Ages.* 2d ed. Oxford: Oxford University Press, 1936.

Reeves, Marjorie. "The European University from Medieval Times." In *Higher Education: Demand and Response,* ed. W. R. Niblett. San Francisco: Jossey-Bass, 1970.

Ringer, Fritz. *The Decline of the German Mandarins: The German Academic Community 1890–1933.* Cambridge, Mass.: Harvard University Press, 1969.

————. *Education and Society in Modern Europe.* Bloomington and London: Indiana University Press, 1979.

Rothblatt, Sheldon. "The Bearers of Civilization." Center for Studies in Higher Education Occasional Paper, no. 28. Berkeley: University of California, 1982.

Rudolph, Frederick. *The American College and University.* New York: Knopf, 1962.

Salmon, Pierre. "France: the Loi d'Orientation and its Aftermath." In *Universities, Politicians, and Bureaucrats,* ed. Hans Daalder and Edward Shils. Cambridge: Cambridge University Press, 1982.

Sevigné, Marie de Rabutin-Chantal. *Letters of Mme de Sevigné to Her Daughter and Her Friends.* London: Routledge, 1937.

Smelser, Neil. "Growth, Structural Change, and Conflict in California Higher Education, 1950–1970." In *Public Higher Education in California,* ed. Neil Smelser and Gabriel Almond. Berkeley, Los Angeles, London: University of California Press, 1974.

Sontheimer, Kurt. "Student Opposition in West Germany." *Government and Opposition* 3, no. 1 (1968): 49–65.

Strathapoulos, Michael. "The New Greek Law: Structure and Function of Higher Education Institutions." *CRE Information* (September 1984).

Suleiman, Ezra. *Politics, Power and Bureaucracy in France.* Princeton, N.J.: Princeton University Press, 1974.

———. "The Myth of Technical Expertise." *Comparative Politics* 10, no. 1 (1977): 137–158.

Svensson, Lennart. "The State and Higher Education: A Sociological Critique from Sweden." *European Journal of Education* 17, no. 3 (1982): 295–306.

Teichler, Ulrich. *Der Arbeitsmarkt für Hochschulabsolventen.* Munich: Saur, 1981.

———. "Recent Developments in Higher Education in the Federal Republic of Germany." *European Journal of Education* 17, no. 2 (1982): 161–176.

Thelander, Jan. *Forsknarsutbildning som Traditionsformedling.* Department of History Report, no. 3. 2d ed. Lund, Sweden: Lund University, 1980.

Thibaudet, Albert. *La Republique des Professeurs.* Geneva: Slatkine Reprints, 1979.

Tocqueville, Alexis de. *The Old Regime and the French Revolution.* Garden City, N.Y.: Doubleday Anchor Books, 1955.

Trow, Martin. "The Public and Private Lives of Higher Education." *Daedalus* 2 (1977): 113–127.

———. "Defining the Issues in University Government Relations—an International Perspective." Center for Studies in Higher Education Occasional Paper, No. 27. Berkeley: University of California, August, 1982.

Van de Graaff, John. "Great Britain." In *Academic Power: Patterns of Authority in Seven National Systems,* by John Van De Graaff, Burton R. Clark, Dorotea Furth, Dietrich Goldschmidt, and Donald Wheeler. New York: Praeger, 1978.

———. "Federal Republic of Germany." In *Academic Power: Patterns of Authority in Seven National Systems,* by John Van De Graaff, Burton R. Clark, Dorotea Furth, Dietrich Goldschmidt, and Donald Wheeler. New York: Praeger, 1978.

Van de Graaff, John, and Dorotea Furth. "France." In *Academic Power: Patterns of Authority in Seven National Systems* by John Van de Graaff, Burton R. Clark, Dorotea Furth, Dietrich Goldschmidt, and Donald Wheeler. New York: Praeger, 1978.

Van de Graaff, John, Burton R. Clark, Dorotea Furth, Dietrich Goldschmidt, and Donald Wheeler. *Academic Power: Patterns of Authority in Seven National Systems.* New York: Praeger, 1978.

Verger, Jacques. *Histoire des Universités Françaises.* Toulouse: Privat, 1985.

Verhoeven, Josef. "Belgium: Linguistic Communalism, Bureaucratisation and Democratisation." In *Universities, Politicians, and Bureaucrats,* ed. Hans Daalder and Edward Shils. Cambridge: Cambridge University Press, 1982.

Villanueva, Julio. "Spain: Restructuring, Reform and Research Policy." *European Journal of Education* 19, no. 2 (1984): 193–200.

Webler, Wolff-Dietrich. "The Student Movement in Germany and its Influence on Higher Education and Research." In *A Decade of Change*, ed. A. Armstrong. Guildford, England: Society for Research into Higher Education, 1979.

Weizsäcker, C. C. von. "Hochschulstruktur und Marktsystem." In *Der Doppelte Flaschenhals—Die Deutsche Hochschule Zwischen Numerus Clausus und Akademikerarbeitslosigkeit*, ed. U. Lohmar and G. E. Ortner. Hannover: Schroedel, 1975.

Williams, Gareth, Tessa Blackstone, and David Metcalf. *The Academic Labour Market*. Amsterdam, London, New York: Elsevier Scientific, 1974.

Zeldin, Theodore. "Higher Education in France, 1848–1940." *Journal of Contemporary History* 2, no. 13 (1967): 53–80.

6

The Disciplinary Shaping of the Profession

Tony Becher

The occupants of a space shuttle approaching earth will see, from a
few hundred miles, a uniform and undifferentiated sphere. As the
distance reduces, land masses can be distinguished from oceans,
cloudless from cloud-covered areas. Nearing touchdown, the visibility
of the whole planet gives place to a localized but much more detailed
view, which may well include coastlines and mountain ranges, forests
and lakes, and later, rivers, roads, railway tracks, houses, gardens,
trees, and traffic. After landing, the perspective is still more bounded
and more detailed—the kind of outlook we ordinarily see as we go
about our everyday business. At each successive stage, there is a
trade-off between comprehensiveness and specificity. To see the
whole is to see it in breadth, but without access to the particular; to
see the part is to see it in depth, but without the general overview.

So too it often is with social phenomena. There are those who seek
the global picture, choosing to explore a theme—it may be crime,
child-rearing, race relations, or one of a multitude of other facets of
human life—in a way that aims to capture its prominent features, its
general properties, and its salient regularities. There are those who
attend more closely to the fine detail, seeking to illuminate specific
processes and the network of causal connections that underpin them.
And there are those who opt for some intermediate position between
generality and particularity.

The study of the professions is no exception. An abundance of writing has been produced on professionalism as a whole. Although sociology of one persuasion or another accounts for most of the literature,[1] practitioners of other disciplines have made significant contributions. The emergence and growth of professionalism have been well documented by social historians;[2] there have also been occasional contributions from the perspective of psychology.[3]

Many such studies include some discussion of the academic profession not only as a relevant case but also as a source of preparatory training for a wide variety of other professional occupations. In this sense it could be termed—as indeed Harold Perkin has already termed it—a key profession.[4] It is scarcely surprising, then, that among the studies of particular professional groups, academics are popular subjects. If an issue remains for debate, it is whether university teachers can sensibly be regarded as members of a single profession or whether they are now so fragmented as to comprise a multiplicity of different professional groups. And here what is at stake may be more an issue of degree of specificity—of the choice of a frame of reference—than whether professions really have important features in common, or whether the academic profession can possibly be examined as a whole, or whether individual disciplines constitute the only legitimate form of occupational grouping.

The many studies that view academics as belonging to a single, homogenous profession[5] suggest that similarities outweigh differences. Writing from an anthropological standpoint, F. G. Bailey portrays a university as a "community culture" in which different tribes cohabit:

Each tribe has a name and a territory, settles its own affairs, goes to war with others, has a distinct language or at least a distinct dialect and a variety of symbolic ways of demonstrating its apartness from others. Nevertheless, the whole set of tribes possess a common culture: their ways of construing the world and the people who live in it are sufficiently similar for them to be able to understand, more or less, each other's culture and even, when necessary, to communicate with members of other tribes. Universities possess a single culture which directs interactions between the many distinct and often mutually hostile groups.[6]

But to other scholars the differences loom larger than the similarities. Donald Light is outspoken among the skeptics, declaring roundly that

the "academic profession" does not exist. In the world of scholarship, the activities . . . center on each discipline. Thus, theoretically at least, we have the academic professions, one for each discipline. Each discipline has its own history, its own intellectual style, a distinct sense of timing, different preferences for articles and books, and different career lines.[7]

He goes on to develop the point:

The academic man is a myth. Although we think of "the professor" as a distinct type in society . . . this image results from research which combines college teachers with research faculty, ignores the distinctly different experience of women in academic life, and overlooks important differences between disciplines.[8]

Biglan, in the more measured style of a psychologist concerned with qualitative matters, argues

the need to consider subject matter characteristics in studying academic organizations. They define limits on the extent to which studies in one area can be generalized to areas whose subject matter is different and indicate why studies of academic organizations should not lump together data that come from different areas.[9]

Although Biglan is ostensibly concerned, in this and in a closely related paper,[10] with contrasts between subject areas rather than with differences between groups of academics, he also says something about the characteristic attitudes, activities, and cognitive styles of practitioners in various disciplines. In general, the two themes seem so intertwined that it is not productive to try to separate them. What follows, then, will be based on evidence adduced both from the epistemological features of particular fields and from the cultural characteristics of the academics associated with those fields.[11]

The theme of the argument in this chapter is specific rather than universal. Its frame of reference is nearer to the ground than would be appropriate in a more holistic study of academics (the perspective of land masses and oceans), let alone an overview of professions as a whole (the perspective of an undifferentiated planet).[12] I take a vantage point similar to that of Light and Biglan, seeking to emphasize the significance, in understanding the academic profession, of differing intellectual tasks and the cultures associated with them. I do not, however, share Light's absolutist stance. There need be no inherent rivalry between the macro view and the micro view: astronomy does not have a monopoly on scientific truth, rendering the study of nuclear physics invalid. Alternative frames of reference may serve to illuminate different aspects of the same world.

CLUSTERS AND SEGMENTS

It is one thing to assert that the academic profession is better understood in its diversity than in its unity; it is another and more difficult
task to identify the key distinctions.

Some analysts find it useful to cluster cognate fields of knowledge
into groups which they then proceed to treat as homogeneous. Some
sociologists of science, for example, have coupled physics with chemistry and biology; others have linked it with engineering, medicine,
and one or more of the social sciences for good measure.[13] This need
to reduce the arena of discussion to a manageable size is understandable enough, but there is also a countervailing tendency to recognize
important distinctions within the framework of even a single discipline. In their influential study of branches of medicine, Bucher and
Strauss point out that specialties, which call the homogeneity of the
medical profession into question, are themselves often fragmented.[14]
To cite an example: "In psychiatry the conflict over the biological
versus the psychological basis of mental illness continues to produce
men who speak almost totally different languages."[15] They add that

within the profession . . . there are many identities, many values, and many
interests. These amount not merely to differentiation of simple variation.
They tend to become patterned and shared; coalitions develop and flourish—
and in opposition to some others. We shall call these groupings which emerge
within a profession "segments." (Specialities might be thought of as major
segments, except that a close look at a specialty betrays its claim to unity,
revealing that specialties, too, usually contain segments, and, if they ever
did have common definitions along all lines of professional identity, it was
probably at a very special, and early, period in their development.[16]

The same tendency toward segmentation may readily be established
in relation to academic disciplines.[17]

The classification systems are almost as numerous as the authors
who generate them. A study by Kolb in the tradition of social psychology was based on the contention that within the academic world,
"selection and socialization procedures combined to produce an increasingly impermeable and homogeneous disciplinary culture and
correspondingly specialized student orientations to learning."[18] Using
a Learning Style Inventory of his own construction, he divided students into concrete-abstract and active-reflective categories, obtaining
a reasonably clear-cut pattern of analysis:

In the abstract-reflective quadrant are clustered the *natural sciences and mathematics*, while the abstract-active quadrant includes the *science-based professions*,

most notably the engineering fields. The concrete-active quadrant encompasses what might be called the *social professions*, such as education, social work, and law. The concrete-reflective quadrant includes the *humanities and social sciences.*[19]

Kolb's account refers back to Biglan's earlier study, which adopted a more complex classification system based on faculty rather than student data.[20] Biglan asked 168 academics at the University of Illinois and 54 at a small western college to make "judgements about the similarities of the subject matter of different academic areas," and categorized the results in terms of hard versus soft, pure versus applied, and life system versus nonlife system.[21] The latter dimension, which serves to distinguish "biological and social areas from those that deal with inanimate objects,"[22] is played down by Kolb on the grounds that it accounted for less variance than the other two in Biglan's data. Intuitively, it seems to be less fundamental than the familiar pure-applied and hard-soft contrast.

Biglan's six groupings (later reified into "the Biglan model")[23] were taken up in several subsequent studies that matched his schema against salary patterns and the distribution of working time, sought its application to the process of faculty evaluation, checked its validity in relation to independently acquired data, and so on. Other classification systems are simpler, sometimes involving no more than a single linear scale. For example, in Ladd and Lipset's research on the political attitudes of academics, they discern a ranking from left wing to right wing, which would seem to hold generally constant over several separate themes.[24] The social scientists, true to stereotype, occupy the extreme left (with economists and political scientists as their most right-wing elements), adjoined by academics in the humanities and fine arts. Engineering and other applied scientists command the far right; physical and biological scientists take up the middle ground.

Another linear scale, closely related to the hard-soft spectrum, is used by Lodahl and Gordon in marking a number of distinctions between physics, chemistry, sociology, and political science.[25] They base their notions of high and low paradigm development on Kuhn's dicta that a paradigm "stands for the entire constellation of beliefs, values, techniques, and so on, shared by the members of a given [scientific] community," and that "a paradigm is what the members of a scientific community share, and conversely, a scientific community consists of men who share a paradigm."[26] The ranking of specified subject areas according to perceived levels of paradigmatic development proved to be remarkably consistent across the four disciplinary groups, numbering over 1000 academics in all.

Both Lodahl and Gordon and Biglan go beyond their initial exercises in classifying disciplines to comment on some differences in academic practice among those who occupy different areas of intellectual territory. Contrasts are drawn in terms of teaching activities, research patterns and output, relationships with graduate students, and the like. Biglan comments on "the way in which both the contents and the method in a field are linked to the cognitive processes of different areas."[27] Lodahl and Gordon, in similar terms, write of "the intimate relations between the structure of knowledge in different fields and the vastly different styles with which the university departments operate."[28] It is a nice irony that their findings were independently derived and published within a few months of each other; their conclusions were closely similar, but their modes of presentation noticeably different. Of a total of sixty-six citations between them, only four were common to both. Biglan's disciplinary affiliation is to psychology, Lodahl and Gordon's to sociology.

It may seem that a different choice has to be made in relation to all classification systems of this kind. Once attention is deflected from the academic profession as a whole to what Bucher and Strauss term its segments,[29] there is a temptation, because it makes for a simpler and more elegant analysis, to bracket apparently cognate disciplines together and draw out the significant contrasts between the groups. This procedure, however, serves to obscure some of the notable differences that underlie the similarities. Yet a move toward more detailed exploration at the subdisciplinary level threatens to destroy a coherent view.

As with the polarization earlier noted between academics as members of one profession or of many, the dilemma may prove to be a false one. Why disallow a move between one frame of reference and another, as long as the intellectual contexts and the transitions between them are clearly marked? Such a procedure would seem a logical outcome of the idea put forward by Bucher and Strauss, that professions ought to be seen as "loose amalgamations of segments pursuing different objectives in different manners and more or less delicately held together under a common name at a particular period in history," especially when (as they were earlier quoted as suggesting) the major segments, the specialties, may be seen to be further segmented in turn.[30]

In discussing evidence drawn from my own studies of disciplinary cultures and how such cultures help to shape the academic profession,

I propose to adopt a relativist stance. Where the argument seems to demand it, I shall aggregate a range of disciplines and regard them as a single if somewhat loosely knit entity. At other times the appropriate level of analysis may be the individual discipline; or the focus will shift to the subsidiary groupings within a discipline. These may on some occasions be regarded as entities in their own right, and on other occasions as components in a pattern running across subject boundaries to connect subspecialisms in apparently different intellectual settings.

For the present I propose to set aside any categorization of subdisciplinary groupings, as they are best discussed in their own particular contexts. I shall take the identification of individual disciplines for granted, even though the pattern is not entirely standard across academia. (There are, for example, significant differences between the organization of those universities with departments of botany and zoology and those with divisions of biological sciences.) However, it seems appropriate at this point to set out my proposed taxonomy in relation to mainstream academic disciplines.

The classification I have adopted is simpler than Biglan's eight-cell matrix (hard-soft, pure-applied, life systems–nonlife systems), but more complex than Lodahl and Gordon's linear scale from high to low paradigm development. It is very similar to Kolb's abstract-concrete, active-reflective framework, though I prefer Biglan's more familiar contrasts between hard and soft, pure and applied. Table 6.1 below anticipates some of the subsequent discussion in that it goes beyond a rough disciplinary grouping to outline the salient characteristics of the field of knowledge for each category. The next step will be to elaborate briefly on the notion of disciplinary cultures and to describe the empirical basis from which the categorization was derived.

DISCIPLINARY CULTURES AND KNOWLEDGE CATEGORIES

It is tempting, in any epistemological account of disciplines, to assume they represent a necessary and inevitable means of organizing knowledge. Yet, from a historical perspective, the introduction of specialized interests is contingent on a steady process of division of academic labor, in which the structure of university education was altered from being a means of acquainting students with the whole of human culture to being a federation of specialisms among which they were free to choose. Such subjects as philosophy, which once comprised "a rung in the ladder of an individual's intellectual and

TABLE 6.1

The Nature of Knowledge in Disciplinary Groupings

Disciplinary grouping	Nature of knowledge
Pure sciences (e.g., physics) "hard-pure"	Cumulative; atomistic (crystalline/tree-like); concerned with universals, quantities, simplification; resulting in discovery/explanation
Humanities (e.g., history) and pure social sciences (e.g., anthropology) "soft-pure"	Reiterative; holistic (organic/riverlike); concerned with particulars, qualities, complication; resulting in understanding/interpretation.
Technologies (e.g., mechanical engineering) "hard-applied"	Purposive; pragmatic (know-how via hard knowledge); concerned with mastery of physical environment; resulting in products/techniques
Applied social sciences (e.g., education) "soft-applied"	Functional; utilitarian (know-how via soft knowledge); concerned with enhancement of [semi-] professional practice; resulting in protocols/procedures

professional training," subsequently claimed for themselves "a special place in an impersonal map of learning." This shift in emphasis gave rise to a significant increase in intellectual productivity, at least in terms of research publications; it also succeeded in deepening the contrasts between those with specialized training and those without it. It became possible to refer not only to "the promotion and management of knowledge in the form of academic disciplines" but also to "a confiscation of epistemological authority from those outside the academy." The wider public, once the potential denizens of a commonwealth of knowledge, were haplessly cast into the role of spectators or outsiders.[31]

But if the nineteenth century still held out the promise of a common university culture, and with it perhaps a truly unified academic profession, the developments of the twentieth century progressively undermined that promise. Within the academic institution, the subject department has emerged as the basic element;[32] and correspondingly, within the academic world at large, it is the parent discipline that most strongly determines the characteristic features of its intellectual offspring. As Clark succinctly puts it:

The [academic] profession has long been a holding company of sorts, a secondary framework composed of persons who are objectively located in diverse fields, and who develop beliefs accordingly. . . . Around distinctive intellectual tasks, each discipline has a knowledge tradition—categories of thought—and related codes of conduct. . . . there is in each field a way of life into which new members are gradually inducted.[33]

With a view to understanding more clearly the epistemological and social characteristics of different disciplines, I embarked in 1980 on a study of six "mainstream" subject areas. In the pure sciences, I selected physics and biology (or, more precisely, botany and zoology); in the humanities and social sciences, history and sociology; in the professional domain, mechanical engineering and academic law. This selection was made before I had elaborated the categories set out in table 6.1 above, but as good luck would have it, there was a reasonable sectorial distribution: physics and biology in the hard-pure sector; history and sociology in the soft-pure sector; and engineering in the hard-applied sector. Whether law can be defined as a soft-applied subject depends largely on where its boundaries as a discipline are drawn.[34] Despite subsequent endeavors to widen the coverage, applied fields remain thinly represented.

For each of the six disciplines originally chosen I collected data based on unstructured interviews, the average length of which was one hour, with academic researchers and teachers in the relevant field. Because I wished to attempt a general portrayal of the culture of each discipline, it seemed sensible to select fairly typical and well-regarded university departments. In each case I conducted interviews in two or three departments in English universities and in the counterpart department at the University of California at Berkeley. A minimum of twenty and a maximum of twenty-four respondents were identified in each subject area, ranging from doctoral students to senior professors.[35] More recent inquiries into mathematics, chemistry, language and literature, and education have also been carried out on a similar basis, but they have involved smaller numbers and fewer departments. There have been over 150 respondents from the ten disciplines so far explored.

In the following sections some of the findings of this research will be used to illustrate the ways in which disciplines contribute to the shaping of the academic profession. First, however, I shall clarify some of the differences, already summarized in table 6.1, among the forms of knowledge characteristic of the four broad sectors—namely, hard-pure, soft-pure, hard-applied, and soft-applied.

One important distinction may be drawn in terms of whether knowledge is viewed as cumulative or whether it is reiterative and revisionist. In hard-pure subjects, such as physics, a clear meaning may be attached to the notion of a moving frontier of knowledge: each finding typically builds on previous ones in a linear progression. Characteristically, in this domain major problems can be subdivided into smaller segments and tackled piecemeal. The structure of inquiry is like a crystal, in that it grows by accretion and is neatly divisible; it is also like a tree, in that it continuously branches from its main stem.[36] Another characteristic of hard-pure disciplines is their concern with universality and often with quantifiability. The complexities of a problem are stripped away to expose the elegant regularities that underlie them. The outcome of a successful inquiry is a discovery, or at least an explanation, of the hitherto unknown.

In contrast, in soft-pure subjects, such as history, academic work often traverses ground already explored by others. Basic issues recur from one generation to the next: the same phenomena are examined by independent inquirers, each presenting individual findings. Here is how one historian puts it:

Perhaps that is essentially what the study of history is: the rereading of the past, so to speak, in the beginning because one wants to discover it for oneself and assimilate it, and later because what one looks for (hence sees) in familiar territory may be quite different from what one has discerned before or learned from others.[37]

The problems that form the starting points for most inquiries are multifaceted and not easily subdivisible. The mode of investigation is organic rather than crystalline. It grows in a complex way: like a river, it is fluid in substance and fickle in direction. Studies in this field are characteristically concerned with the particular instance, as against the general finding; the qualitative as against the quantitative. The concern is to comprehend complexity, not to simplify it. The typical end product is understanding, or at least interpretation, of what is already known.

Applied disciplines have a different set of characteristics. Their emphasis is as much on "knowing how" as on "knowing that"; work in these fields will always have some practical end in view. Hard-applied knowledge, as in engineering and the more science-based aspects of medicine, is not necessarily cumulative, though it may from time to time and area to area be heavily dependent on cumulative knowledge. Neither is it altogether quantitative, since application will always involve some element of qualitative judgment. Hard-applied subjects are concerned with ways of mastering the physical world. Their primary outcomes are products and techniques. They are typically judged by the effectiveness with which they work, that is, by purposive and pragmatic criteria.

By contrast, soft-applied knowledge is dependent on soft-pure knowledge in achieving the improvement of professional practice. But it uses soft-pure knowledge as a means of understanding and coming to terms with the complexity of human situations rather than as a way of explaining and mastering the material environment. Having a less evident sense of progression and being less stable than hard-applied knowledge, its basis is in the frequently reformulated interpretations of the humanities and the social sciences rather than in the steady growth of the natural sciences. Such subjects as education, social administration, and the more humanistic aspects of medicine have as their primary outcomes protocols and procedures; their effectiveness, as in hard-applied knowledge, is judged by functional and utilitarian criteria.

No sooner are such distinctions drawn than they have to be qualified. To carve up and label the whole realm of human knowledge in such simple terms is certainly to do violence to many important distinctions, to suppress crucial differences, and to ignore the richly subtle topography of the intellectual landscape. Any given discipline is itself fragmented along a variety of dimensions: to treat whole clusters as homogeneous is therefore to oversimplify to a dangerous degree. Nonetheless, if the dangers are recognized, such epistemological clustering can serve a useful purpose. It is introduced here to provide an explanatory framework for the basic, often quite straightforward differences in working practices between academics who respond to fundamentally different intellectual challenges.

An examination of the ways in which disciplines shape professional lives will also be divided—with similar dangers of distortion and oversimplification—into four main categories. The first will deal with initiation procedures; the second with patterns of social interaction; the third with specialization; and the last with mobility and change.

INITIATION

There is no precise point at which people begin to identify closely enough with a discipline to wish to become practitioners of it. Or at least, if some individuals can identify a clear moment of transition, the biographical locations of that moment will vary from one to another, ranging across the whole span from relatively early childhood to late maturity. Commonly, the characteristics of a given discipline begin to come quite sharply into focus at the undergraduate stage.

The intelligent student becomes more fully aware of the boundaries and content of the subject, and the perceptive student begins to recognize its specialized language, its permitted modes of argument, and its characteristic intellectual style.[38] Some who are not only intelligent and perceptive but also ambitious to achieve professional status may even begin to identify patterns of relationships within a field and pick up its folklore.

Nevertheless, in pure knowledge areas at least, it is not until a student is accepted into a department to undertake postgraduate work that the formal business of initiation begins. This acceptance will depend on a selection process in which quality of past performance and degree of present commitment are the most evident criteria. But while modes of recruitment are broadly similar across the hard-pure/soft-pure boundary, the implications of postgraduate study—the actual modes of initiation—vary in noticeable ways from one knowledge domain to another.

First, aspiring graduate students in hard-pure subjects may choose the department in which they wish to work; they may also be able to choose their research supervisor. Beyond this, they become, in a way, employees in an enterprise that requires their collaboration and their conformity. Like other members of the enterprise, they are expected to attend classes regularly and to keep reasonably habitual hours. Their research theme is defined for them by their research supervisor, who is likely to locate it within an area in which the supervisor and other researchers are engaged. Particularly in experimental subjects, the supervisors' involvements with students may be quite close: they may indeed see them for brief sessions every day. Doctoral students who succeed in producing interim results will normally be encouraged to publish them in joint authorship with the supervisor, and perhaps with one or more members of the research group who have had some share in the work.[39]

In soft-pure subjects the pattern is quite different. The graduate students are able to negotiate not only their departments and supervisors but also the themes of their research. Far from being regarded as employees, they are treated like self-employed persons or individuals of independent means. They are not required to observe any firm rules of attendance: the disposition of their time is a matter for them to control. Contact with their research supervisors is usually sporadic rather than regular—a question of mutual negotiation. If a student produces a paper for publication, it will appear unequivocally under his or her name.

Why do such differences arise? The obvious explanation lies in variations in knowledge contexts. If one is operating in a hard-pure field, where the problems are easily divisible, it makes good sense to adopt a cooperative approach, in which the members of a closely knit team tackle the distinct subproblems and then put them together to resolve the problem as a whole. And it is natural enough that any newcomer be assigned one of a set of outstanding tasks at an appropriate level of difficulty. Teamwork naturally implies conformity to group norms and a readiness to accept the sovereignty of the team leader. On the other hand, in a soft-pure subject, where knowledge is holistic and problems tend to be broadly defined and not readily amenable to subdivision, there is little incentive for collaborative work. Interpretation is essentially an individual activity: every scholar has to reappraise the evidence for himself. So it is not surprising that doctoral students are expected to work on a loose rein: there are no well-defined groups to which they can belong, and research supervisors take the role of critical commentators rather than that of directors of study.

Many applied areas exhibit a different picture. In engineering, for extrinsic, market-related reasons, very few students apply for doctoral programs immediately after qualification. The starting salaries offered in industry far exceed the most generous fellowships, and all except an eccentric few move immediately into the world of professional practice. Most recruits to the academic world are drawn from those who have been employed in industry and who have become disenchanted with it. Many but not all of them will study for a doctorate after their appointment to a university post.[40] Perhaps in part because current problems are more dispersed than they are in hard-pure domains, teamwork is less common and operates with relatively smaller groups. The same pattern is typical of academics in certain soft-applied areas, but for somewhat different reasons. In many people-oriented vocations, practical know-how tends to be valued more highly than theoretical knowledge, which is only loosely connected with the functional demands of the professional arena. Preference in recruitment is therefore commonly given to candidates who have had a certain amount of work experience. Again, higher degrees will often be gained after appointment to an academic post, though the proportion of doctorates in applied fields such as education (or, on indirect evidence, social administration) is noticeably lower than in hard-pure or soft-pure disciplines. There is no strong incentive to teamwork because most problems are not amenable to subdivision and are therefore addressed by individuals or occasionally by groups of two or three.

Not everyone who sets out to do so ends up in an academic post; an informal cooling-out process operates in every field, even though it is not identical across all knowledge domains. The process is at its most protracted in hard-pure subjects, such as physics and chemistry, where an individual is normally expected, because of the tight market conditions, to undertake at least one and possibly two postdoctoral research assignments, usually funded by a government agency or research foundation, before being judged ready for a permanent post. Each such assignment involves a three- to five-year attachment to a research team, in a more responsible role than that of a doctoral student, but still in a subservient relationship to the project director (who is almost invariably a tenured academic). Those aspirants who have failed to gain a regular appointment after three or more of such temporary research fellowships usually recognize that their chance is gone and move into industry or elsewhere; the few who refuse to take the hint usually end up as itinerant laborers, moving around to wherever the next job might be.

The possibility of extending the period of initiation beyond the point at which a doctorate is awarded clearly depends on the availability of research funds, which in turn depends on the field's attractiveness to grant-giving agencies. It is typically the hard-pure, high-cost areas of science that need the largest teams, promise the most spectacular results, and earn the largest share of outside financial support. Certainly, most soft-pure subjects, in which research is seldom dependent on expensive equipment and is conducted largely on an individual basis, do not have as evident a need for funding or as established a tradition of teamwork. Accordingly, they lack the scope that hard-pure subjects have for a lengthy holding period before the cooling out has to take place. In history, for example, those who attain doctorates can seldom afford to wait more than a few months for a vacancy. If they have not secured an academic post quite soon after completion, they have to set about finding a job elsewhere: research fellowships or other bridging posts are almost nonexistent.

The characteristic initiation process in both hard-applied and soft-applied areas is through professional experience; hence the award of a tenured academic post is more a matter of beckoning in the suitable candidates than of easing out the unsuitable ones.[41] But the substitution of practical know-how for theoretical inquiry is liable to exact its price later. Apart from the likely absence of a doctorate—a necessary passport to tenure in pure subject areas—the publication records of most applied academics, because they lag behind those of their pure counterparts by a critical five years or more, tend to look unimpressive in the promotion stakes.

A range of intrinsic and extrinsic factors, such as the nature of the subject or the state of the employment market, thus operate to bring about significant differences in the ways in which aspiring academics complete the process of initiation from the achievement of a first degree to a tenured appointment within the ranks of academe. Similar contrasts are reflected in the everyday patterns of activity of those who have successfully entered the profession, as we shall see in the following analysis.

SOCIAL INTERACTION

Those academics who aspire to be active in scholarship and research (the cosmopolitans) have a variety of contacts and commitments that are lacking in their colleagues who choose to concentrate instead on teaching and administration (the locals).[42] While the professional horizons of the locals tend to be bounded by their own institutions, the cosmopolitans belong to a wider community, the international network of like-minded people with whom they can share ideas and from whom they can seek intellectual support.

Though "invisible colleges"[43] exist in every field of inquiry, their characteristic operating modes differ from one knowledge domain to another. In hard-pure subject areas, where the topical issues are clearly identified and relatively few in number—where, as one physicist in my sample remarked, "There is a high people-to-problem ratio"—several geographically scattered teams may be working on closely related issues. The pace is rapid, and the demand for up-to-date reports on progress is strong. Accordingly, communication channels are geared for swift and frequent interchanges. Groups meet frequently in international conferences and colloquia; mutual visiting is commonplace; publication delays are overcome by the issue of preprints (photocopied typescripts of unpublished papers) and by the issuing of short published letters in periodicals designed to minimize waiting time to a few weeks. Personal contacts are maintained by the liberal use of international telephone services, on the grounds that postal links are too slow.

Academics in hard-applied areas adopt a somewhat different pattern. The problems here are more scattered, and there is less teamwork in research; consequently, the pace is more modest. Conferences are not as frequently attended; many of them attract a mixture of practitioners and academics. In engineering, membership on official committees is a valid alternative means of making useful contacts and knowing what is going on. Publication delays averaging six months to a year are expected and tolerated, because the speed with which results appear is not seen as crucial. Although there is a fair amount of mutual visiting, contact is generally maintained by correspondence.

The pace of interchange is more leisurely still in soft-pure areas. Because intellectual problems are primarily matters of personal concern, the public networks to which an individual scholar belongs are arenas for displaying social solidarity and exchanging general gossip rather than for the close sharing of ideas. Conference-going is occasional: one keeps in touch by reading what others publish. Delays in journal article publication may be more than a year; books may take twice as long to appear. A somewhat comparable pattern exists in soft-applied areas, where there is no strong requirement for rapid publication and conferences are relatively few and far between.

Lodahl and Gordon offer an indirectly related finding.[44] Quoting Zuckerman and Merton's study of average rejection rates by journals,[45] they note that "the humanities (pre-paradigm) have the highest rejection rates; the social and behavioural sciences are next high (low paradigm); while the physical, chemical and biological sciences (high paradigm) have low rejection rates." They conclude that "the most highly developed fields have the most efficient communication processes to speed development still further."

Leaving aside variations in publication patterns from one field to another, individual publication rates—the number of titles published annually by faculty members—also seem to reflect the characteristics of the associated knowledge domain. Several quantitative studies of research productivity have been made, but unfortunately few even differentiate between journal articles and books or between single as opposed to multiple authorship, let alone take into account the length of each contribution and the nature of its subject matter.[46] My data, though patchy and impressionistic, suggest a straightforward relationship between the typical scale of problems tackled and the resulting volume of publication. This information relates to quoted norms in elite research departments, however, not to averages derived systematically across the whole range of the disciplines in question.

Organic chemistry, a specialty in which problems are highly divisible, and in which the research teams may be sizable, probably takes pride of place. Papers reporting research results may number only three or four pages and may have three or four authors. It is scarcely surprising, then, that an applicant for a first appointment at the age of thirty might be expected to have about forty publications, or that a few researchers will publish over 500 papers in their careers. The contrast in style and professional way of life comes across clearly in the pattern among engineers, whose research problems may be comparatively complex. Their output may be no more than a couple of papers a year, but these would typically run from 3000 to 4000 words and have only single or dual authorship. In addition, many academics undertake industrial consultancies, for which they produce reports and develop patentable products, the latter counting toward promotion alongside published papers. Historians work on a still larger intellectual canvas. They may write one or two journal articles a year, averaging some twenty pages; but the expectation is that every few years they will also write a book around some major topic they have researched, particularly if they hope for professional advancement. Academic lawyers and educationists, like engineers, may establish professional connections that encourage them to produce expert opinions and consultancy reports. However, their pattern of journal publication is closer to that of historians, and they are also expected to produce the occasional book.

Biglan offers an analogous account:

Compared to scholars in soft or non-paradigmatic areas, those in hard or paradigmatic areas publish fewer monographs and more journal articles. In paradigmatic areas, it is not necessary to provide detailed descriptions of the content and method that underlie a piece of research; these are understood by anyone familiar with the paradigm. In this case, journal articles, with their restrictions on length, provide an appropriate means of communication. In the soft areas, where paradigms are not characteristic, the scholar must describe and justify the assumptions on which his work is based, delimit his method or approach to the problem, and establish criteria for evaluating his own response to the problem. Such an undertaking requires a monograph-length work.[47]

Other elements in the pattern of social interaction of academics in particular fields are reflections of the resources and responsibilities available within them.[48] Research with industrial applications, which may occur in hard-pure as well as hard-applied areas, tends to be associated with large-scale, high-cost apparatus, and with a related need for teamwork. The qualities of leadership, at a premium in such contexts, include tough-mindedness, organizing ability, and entrepreneurial flair. Once these qualities are promoted in an individual, he or she is more likely than colleagues who have led a relatively sheltered life (perhaps in a botany lab or a literature department) to go on to exercise them in a wider university context.[49]

A further set of distinctions exists in political status and prestige. The pecking order of academic disciplines is by no means constant across institutions or countries. Nonetheless, physics enjoys a strong political position not only within individual universities but also on a national and international scale. Collegial consensus is not difficult to achieve; in Lodahl and Gordon's terms, it is a "high-paradigm field."[50] Because a number of high cost areas are involved, it is in the collective interest that physicists speak with one voice about their needs, and exploit their high standing (both in the academy and in the world outside) to put sufficient pressure on government funding agencies to ensure that they are given adequate resources. The more they succeed in this enterprise, the more conspicuous the level of public investment in their research, the more their prestige is reinforced. This is an example at the macrolevel of the "Matthew effect," identified by Merton as operating at the microlevel.[51] Engineers, whose fields of research are less tightly knit, who are more inclined to squabble among themselves,[52] and those whose lack of academic purity is something of a liability, envy and perhaps resent the capacity physicists have to present a united front.

Education, among other soft-applied areas, because it draws in an eclectic way on the soft-pure knowledge of the humanities and pure social sciences, has an unstable intellectual base and is significantly less prestigious than any of the hard-applied disciplines, let alone the hard-pure ones. Its command of resources is weak, because educational research is often individualistic and inexpensive and also because it is relatively difficult, in a field divided by doctrinal arguments, to achieve consensus on the merit of grant proposals. History, with other subjects in the humanities, owes its relatively strong prestige within and outside the academic world to its established scholarly traditions; perhaps its prestige is also related to the accessibility of many of its products to informed members of the public.[53] Within the same soft-pure field, sociology is in a less happy position. A recent article in the British Sociological Association's newsletter attempts some explanation of the low esteem in which the discipline appears currently to be held:

> Sociologists are . . . a difficult lot to defend—their own worst enemies, with an alarming propensity to score 'own goals' . . . the well known spiral of self-labelling, stigmatization and amplification has caused sociologists to project a kind of self-fulfilling lack of confidence . . . there is no agreement as to whom we acknowledge as "leaders" . . . and certainly no deference of the kind that would give them the prestige and general recognition to speak out in defence of sociology, and be listened to.[54]

TABLE 6.2

KNOWLEDGE AND CULTURE, BY DISCIPLINARY GROUPING

Disciplinary grouping	Nature of knowledge	Nature of disciplinary culture
Pure sciences (e.g. physics) "hard-pure"	Cumulative; atomistic (crystalline/treelike); concerned with universals, quantities, simplification; resulting in discovery/explanation	Competitive, gregarious; politically well-organized; high publication rate; task-oriented
Humanities (e.g., history) and pure social sciences (e.g., anthropology) "soft-pure"	Reiterative; holistic (organic/riverlike); concerned with particulars, qualities, complication; resulting in understanding/ interpretation	Individualistic, pluralist; loosely structured; low publication rate; person-oriented
Technologies (e.g., mechanical engineering) "hard-applied"	Purposive; pragmatic (know-how via hard knowledge); concerned with mastery of physical environment; resulting in products/techniques	Entrepreneurial, cosmopolitan; dominated by professional values; patents substitutable for publications; role oriented
Applied social sciences (e.g., education) "soft-applied"	Functional; utilitarian (know-how via soft knowledge); concerned with enhancement of [semi-] professional practice; resulting in protocols/procedures	Outward-looking; uncertain in status; dominated by intellectual fashions; publication rates reduced by consultancies; power-oriented

The political standing of a discipline, as assessed in both internal and external terms, has particular significance in times of financial retrenchment, when the departments least able to defend themselves are often under the greatest threat.[55] Such collective vulnerability may drastically affect the professional lives of individual academics, even though safety devices exist (see chapter 8) in the form of faculty guilds and systemwide unionization.

So far, we have reviewed briefly the broad differences in forms of initiation and social interaction across the four basic knowledge domains displayed in table 6.1. These cultural characteristics of disciplinary groupings are summarized in table 6.2, which provides an extension of the earlier epistemological analysis.

The argument has been that noticeable distinctions in modes of academic life may be drawn in relation to the way initiates are received into the profession: the range, nature, and intensity of professional contacts; publication patterns; resources and responsibilities; political standing. Certainly, other contrasts may be drawn: for instance, how internal power and control are exercised, or the rationales for keeping up with and citing the literature. Taken together, these indicate the variety of connections between the intellectual tasks in a given domain of knowledge and the disciplinary cultures associated with that domain. The implication is that in order fully to understand the academic profession, one must consider at least the broad categories of inquiry in which members of that profession are engaged. Having done so, it becomes difficult to ignore the associated cultural differences that must weaken unqualified claims to unity.

SPECIALIZATION

The discussion to this point has had to sacrifice accuracy of detail to clarity of comprehension. The perspective from the metaphorical space shuttle has been of relatively large-scale topographical features—mountains, forests, and lakes—rather than of a close vision of cars, roads, houses, and fields from above the landing strip. Actually, no discipline entirely fits into any one of the four niches (hard-pure, soft-pure, hard-applied, soft-applied) around which the argument has hinged. Some appear to elude classification altogether. When subject fields are more closely scrutinized, it becomes evident that certain branches of physics, for instance, overlap into the hard-applied category; that conversely, the theoretical elements of mechanical engineering are best described as hard-pure; that there are some hard-pure aspects of disciplines—economics, for example—normally classed as soft-pure; and that there are some soft-pure edges of disciplines—the biological sciences, for instance—normally regarded as hard-pure. It is not easy to see where business studies falls within the hard-applied/soft-applied dichotomy, or where mathematics fits in at all. But despite these limitations, the division of knowledge into four (reasonably familiar) domains has, I would contend, a value in bringing out certain similarities within groups of disciplines and certain differences between them.

I propose now to take a closer vantage point, concentrating on specialized fields within individual disciplines, which constitute further sources of fragmentation of academia as a whole. Bucher and Strauss, writing about the medical profession, summarize the point neatly:

We should also recognize the great diversity of enterprise and endeavor that mark the profession; the cleavages that exist along with the division of labor; and the intellectual and specialist movements that occur within the broad rubric.[56]

Clark makes a similar comment, though richer in detail:

The major disciplines are extensively subdivided. For example, physics is broken down into such major subdisciplines as optics, mechanics, fluids, nuclear physics, and elementary particle physics—the latter dividing still further into cosmic ray physicists, who study natural particles, and high-energy physicists, who use accelerators. These major subfields, in turn, contain more specialities. . . . The division of labor accounts for large differences in originality and type and degree of competition.[57]

The range and variety of choice open to any individual, even after a main field of interest has been identified, is potentially very wide. Those areas where labor is most easily divisible are also those most prone to fragmentation. Lodahl and Gordon remark that "chemistry is clearly the most highly differentiated field [as against physics, sociology, and political science], and political science . . . is the least."[58] Nevertheless, most disciplines offer a diversity of intellectual and social styles. Perhaps this is in part what makes membership in the academic profession so personally satisfying.[59]

There certainly seems to be some matching between personality characteristics and fields of specialization. Gregarious individuals in predominantly solitary areas tend to be found in specialisms that put a premium on teamwork (among historical topics, they congregate in economic and demographic history); temperamental loners in predominantly gregarious areas are often identified with fields hospitable to individualistic inquiry (theoretical as against organic chemistry; meteorology as against particle physics). It is not clear from my research whether the predominant causal pattern is attributable to nurture or to nature: that is, whether academics' patterns of activity are molded by their specialisms, or whether they actively seek out those intellectual arenas within their discipline which best suit their temperaments. Perhaps, by analogy with current biological thinking, the answer may lie somewhere in between.

It is relatively easy, then, given the catholicity of specialisms available in most disciplines, for academics to establish themselves in a niche they find congenial. The initiation period helps to insure this. Doctoral students who find it difficult to come to terms with their research topic will often either change course at a relatively early stage or drop out altogether. Nevertheless, once an affiliation to a specialism is made, it tends to command strong personal loyalties. Both corporate activities (a sense of belonging) and personal commitment (an investment in ideas) may account, to some degree, for this attachment.

To affiliate with a particular specialism is to become, except in a few heavily populated areas, a member of a relatively small and close-knit community. An individual's intimate circle of reference, the people to whom one sends draft papers for comment, those to whom one readily turns for professional advice, and those with whom one keeps most closely in touch, will commonly number between six and twelve people,[60] though the wider reference group will often run into three figures (very seldom four). Some specialist groups, particularly in the humanities, social sciences, and people-oriented professions, are open to all comers, but others especially in the pure and applied sciences, have many characteristics of a clique. In the latter cases, one often must have published a substantial contribution to the relevant area of knowledge in an appropriate journal before gaining acceptance. Journals often represent and sometimes consciously symbolize the interests of a particular specialism. As Bucher and Strauss remark, "The journals a man reads . . . tend to reflect his methodological as well as his substantive interests."[61]

But an academic specialism is more than an affiliation representing particular sectional interests within a discipline. It is foremost an area of inquiry in which academics are prepared to invest substantial amounts of their time and effort. Although some specialist fields are fairly readily accessible to anyone with the necessary intelligence and material resources (books, equipment, and the like), others call for a quite prolonged period of induction. Thus medical sociology demands a lengthy and detailed familiarization with the complexities of the medical world; Latin American history requires mastery of at least two foreign languages; a full competence in most mathematical specialisms requires anything from one to three years' intensive study; in biology, those areas demanding a knowledge of electron microscopy and computing techniques take longer to enter than those requiring more straightforward skills. All such specialisms might reasonably be described as areas of comparatively high intellectual investment.

It is easy to predict—and the prediction is borne out by testimony—that those who become involved in a high investment area are reluctant to leave it until they feel they have adequately realized the dividends of that investment. Conversely, those who might wish to move into such an area are often dissuaded from doing so, particularly in mid- or late career, by the prospect of having to commit substantial intellectual capital to the entry process. Considerations of this kind help to maintain the boundaries of specialist fields and to promote a relatively stable pattern of activity within any given discipline. Nevertheless, there are equally powerful forces operating in a contrary direction.

CHANGE AND MOBILITY

The discussion so far has suggested that the characteristics of academic specialisms are reasonably constant and well defined. The picture that has emerged may seem somewhat akin to that of the academic culture of the Maoris in the midnineteenth century, when the priest of the school of learning at Wairarapa delivered this homily to his pupils:

There was no one universal system of teaching in the Whare Wananga (school of learning). Each tribe had its own priests, its own college, and its own methods. From tribe to tribe this was so; the teaching was led astray by the self-conceit of the priests which allowed of departure from their own doctrines to those of other schools of learning. My word to you is this: Hold steadfastly to our teaching; leave out of consideration that of other (tribes). Let their descendants adhere to their teaching, and you to yours, so that if you are wrong . . . it was we (your relatives) who declared it to you (and you are not responsible); and if you are right . . . it is we who gave you this treasured possession.[62]

A number of features of the contemporary academic world are inconsistent with this vision of a neatly contained and self-perpetuating pattern of intellectual activity. Some such features arise from the characteristics of the various knowledge domains themselves; others come from the effects on them of individual or collective decisions, though the two are not always easy to distinguish.

Unlike the boundaries of physics and economics, those of such subjects as history and botany are permeable to amateur practitioners with no formal qualifications. But some disciplines have boundaries that are permeable in a different sense: their pursuit allows for the incorporation of external values. Those chemists who wish to oppose chemical warfare, like those biologists who support conservation, can promote their views as private citizens, along with others; they may generally avoid making professional choices in conflict with such views; but they cannot explicitly incorporate them into the pursuit of their academic inquiries. In that sense such subjects are value-free. But in certain other disciplines, although individuals may make a conscious decision to suppress their own values, the possibility always remains to allow one's academic activities to be permeated by personal ideologies. To talk of a right-wing sociologist or educationist is to refer to the content of his or her work; to refer to a left-wing physicist or engineer is to characterize his or her nonacademic concerns.

The openness of a particular field to the incorporation of value issues will not necessarily affect its shape by polarizing it. History is as accessible as any subject to expressions of individual belief, but its practitioners generally manage to maintain a high degree of mutual tolerance. Nonetheless, in soft knowledge areas, the choice of topics for study, the ways in which they are studied, and thus the overall structure of the related disciplines are liable to be affected by changes in the wider climate of political opinion. In hard knowledge areas a different factor operates to much the same effect. Intellectual fashion in chemistry, for example, is powerfully influenced by the availability of funds: projects tend to cluster where the big money is. The trends are set in some areas by what large industrial sponsors currently happen to be developing, and in others by the preferences of government agencies and private foundations. Between them, these can bring about quite large-scale and long-term changes in the patterns of scientific and technological activity.

Sources of this type of change, which affect the nature and distribution of effort within a given field, are complemented by boundary changes resulting in a redrawing of disciplinary definitions. A recent example of the process is the disaffiliation of both statistics and computer studies from the framework of mathematics into separate departmental structures. A related but different process may occur when the boundaries of two disciplines overlap. In some cases, such overlaps seem relatively unproblematic, and there is thus no strong incentive to do anything about them. Researchers in certain areas of theoretical physics and pure mathematics, for example, are very close in their interests, though distinguishable enough in their styles of approach not to wish for a merger. In other instances the areas of common ground may give rise to a desire, if not for cooperation, then at least for boundary clarification: a case in point would be the overlap of political theory, a branch of political science, and political philosophy, a branch of philosophy.[63] But there are also times when a new discipline is born from the quest for a separate identity by those working in the shared territory between two established subject fields. To take a familiar illustration, biochemistry brings together the techniques of chemical analysis and the subject matter of cell biology.[64]

Shifts in the internal structures and the external boundaries of disciplines constitute a significant source of change in the world of learning. Their effect on the academic profession as a whole will be indirect, though their impact on individual member of it may be profound. Cumulatively, such local perturbations are frequent enough to create a sense of almost constant movement rather than permanence.

Viewing the careers of individual academics from a more detailed perspective, a somewhat comparable picture emerges. It was noted earlier that a cooling-out process occurs in separating prospective new members of the profession from the rest. At the other end of the professional career, in some disciplines at least, an inverse metaphor applies: those who are no longer able to keep up with the demands of the subject are subject to a process of burning out. There are a number of more or less honorable escape routes: to shift from active, empirical study to theorizing or synthesizing the findings of others; to concentrate largely on teaching; or to move into administration.

This particular form of intellectual emigration is not acknowledged at all as part of the career pattern in soft disciplines, where an increase in age betokens a parallel increase in experience and expertise. The burnout phenomenon is most commonly recognized in pure mathematics, where peak performance is often said to occur in the late twenties or thirties. The mathematicians in my sample (all over the age of thirty-five) were skeptical about this claim, but some acknowledged that the subject called for long periods of very close concentration when working through an argument and thus tended to favor those with high intellectual energy and a capacity for prolonged introspection. In physics and biology, some respondents offered a different explanation. In their view, the career menopause was closely connected with the life expectancy of one's research topic or experimental technique: "Your doctorate gives you momentum for ten or fifteen years—but by the time you are pushing forty, your training has already become out of date." That is the time to "pick up the pieces and update your technique, or change the emphasis of your research." Those who are unable or unwilling at this point to reinvest their intellectual capital are ipso facto opting out of an active research role.

Movement between specialisms is not by any means confined to those who want to avoid burning out. In some of the areas most subject to fashion, it can be a positive advantage to acquire the habit of, and the necessary skills for, mobility. Thus in the more highly competitive areas of physics, a grudging admiration is bestowed on "skimming the cream"—terms applied to those who are intellectually agile enough to concentrate on finding solutions to fundamental problems, but who then move on, leaving others to sort out the implications. Chemistry, a very different discipline in many respects, holds open the opposite temptation, of "turning the handle"—that is, of mechanically churning out a long succession of repetitive results. But once again, the pressure is toward tackling novel challenges rather than dwelling too long on familiar ones.

The patterns of migration among specialisms closely reflect the relative ease of transfer between the old and the new. We have observed that the barriers in mathematics between one specialism and another can be dauntingly high. Internal mobility is easier in the physical and biological sciences, particularly in the more theoretical areas. In history, law, and literature, it would appear easier still. One of the literature specialists in my sample had moved from a specialism in sixteenth-century poetry into a new expertise in the medieval English mystics; another migrated from seventeenth-century tragedy into modern drama.

Movement across boundaries between neighboring disciplines also takes place, though to a much more limited degree. The academics I interviewed included a biologist in a physics laboratory, a chemist in a zoology laboratory, an archaeologist in a history department, and a historian in an anthropology department. Another, quite common form of migration has already been remarked: namely, that from certain academic subjects, particularly in the hard-pure sciences, into industry; and from some professionally oriented subjects, such as engineering and law, into professional practice. In such applied subjects, too, there is a modest reverse flow of immigrants from the outside world into academia, most of them to take up junior appointments at the start of their academic careers.

We have noted the effects of some significant movements seen from the disciplinary standpoint: external values moving into particular disciplinary fields; change in the fashions set by funding bodies; and the creation of new subject areas. To obtain a more complete picture, these need to be taken in conjunction with movements seen from the standpoint of the individual academic: the phenomenon of midcareer burnout, the migration patterns between specialisms, the movement across disciplinary boundaries, the migration into and out of the system as a whole. The net effect is dramatically different from the image conveyed by the earlier discussion, encapsulated in the quotation about the academic culture of the Maoris with which this section began. It seems appropriate to provide an alternative portrayal of academia and its constituent parts, substituting a dynamic for a changeless image:

Perhaps . . . the nation is a complex of collective bodies, all in process of perpetual change and in a constantly varying relationship with one another. The static view of the nation as a precise entity that having once been forged is thereafter stable . . . is thus replaced by a Bergsonian model of continual interaction much closer to what actually went on.[65]

THE ONE AND THE MANY

An endless dispute in which philosophers of bygone days used to indulge concerned the question of the ontological priority of universals or particulars. There were those who argued, passionately and persuasively enough to convince even the most bigoted and myopic dissenter, that universals were the prime entities and particulars only the secondary, since particulars could be given no sense and accorded no significance unless they could be subsumed under an appropriate universal. But there were also those who, with equal degrees of passion and persuasion, pointed out that without particulars to instantiate and exemplify them, universals remained no more than empty abstractions: from this it could unquestionably be inferred that particulars were prime, and universals secondary. It was only in later, more sophisticated times that someone hit on the ingenious device of pointing out that each was essential to the other, and that it did not greatly matter what one said, provided that one clearly understood the nature of the relationship between the two. This intervention succeeded, if not in resolving the issue, at least in killing it stone dead.[66]

This chapter has contained within it the seeds of a closely related debate: Is there only one academic profession, or many? The universalists might contend that without the defining framework of higher education as a whole, there might be no meaningful role for the component elements, at whatever level of specificity (physics, early medieval history, the corrosion of nonferrous metals, the teaching of remedial mathematics in the middle years of schooling). The particularists might riposte that the academic profession is nothing more than a composite of its constituent specialisms, subspecialisms, subsubspecialisms (and so on, ad infinitum); hence that it is pointless to talk as if the whole were somehow one and indivisible, both independent of and greater than its parts. Would not the sophisticated answer be to point out the mutual interdependence of both positions, to acknowledge the importance of the relationships, and to conclude that it matters little what is then said?

The agnosticism is, I suggest, unnecessary. The commonalities between different elements of academic life are as plain to see as the divergences. Academics in a great variety of fields acknowledge the privileges of academic independence, admit an obsessional commitment to their work, express a high degree of job satisfaction, and share a common dislike of grading student essays and examination papers. They share many other, more far-reaching characteristics as well, which are described elsewhere in this book. In another context its editor has written, "Sweeping across all the fields and institutions, assumed by professors of biology, sociology, and classics alike, is the identity of 'academic man.' All such men and women, in the doctrines of the profession, are part of a single 'community of scholars,' sharing an interest that sets them apart from others."[67]

Paradoxically, the more it becomes possible to portray the components of the academic world as fragmented and particularized, and the more readily it can be shown that these components are in a constant state of change, the more one is inclined to apprehend that. world in its entirety. This chapter has attempted to show how the different disciplinary specialisms and subspecialisms contribute to the shaping of the profession, and to suggest that by understanding the parts and acknowledging their particularity one can better understand the whole. Surely it was in something of this spirit that one of the great federal nations adopted the familiar motto: e pluribus unum.

NOTES

I am grateful for constructive comments on earlier drafts, notably from Stephen Ball, Eric Hewton, Maurice Kogan, Jennifer Platt, Gary Rhoades, and Kenneth Ruscio. Ruscio's chapter in this volume is happily comparable in approach and complementary in subject matter: the two pieces might be read as extensions of each other's arguments.

1. A useful review of the field is contained in Atkinson, "Reproduction of the Professional Community."

2. One particularly interesting study, centered on the U.S., is Bledstein's *Culture of Professionalism;* another, covering a similar period in the U.K., though not exclusively concerned with professional issues, is Rothblatt's *Revolution of the Dons.*

3. They include Holland, *Psychology of Vocational Choice,* and Roe, *Psychology of Occupations.*

4. Perkin, *Key Profession:* an entertaining history of the Association of University Teachers, which also includes more general material on the changing fortunes of British academics.

5. Among the best-known and most widely quoted research in this genre is Halsey and Trow's *British Academics.*

6. Bailey, *Morality and Expediency*, p. 212.

7. Light, "Structure of the Academic Professions," p. 12.

8. Ibid., p. 14. The first three words in the quotation, perhaps intentionally, echo the title of a pioneering study by Wilson, *Academic Man*.

9. Biglan, "Relationships between Subject Matter Characteristics and the Structure and Output of University Departments," p. 213.

10. Biglan, "Characteristics of Subject Matter in Different Academic Areas."

11. Some of the relationships between the two are analyzed in Becher, "Cultural View."

12. It is not closely engaged with everyday realities (the perspective of the landing strip) as some ethnographic studies of academic life have been. To take one striking case, see Karin Knorr-Cetina's *Manufacture of Knowledge*.

13. Adherents of the Merton school illustrate the virtues and limitations of this approach: for a typical collection of writings, see Merton, *Sociology of Science*.

14. Bucher and Strauss, "Professions in Process."

15. Ibid., p. 328.

16. Ibid., p. 325.

17. Becher, "Towards a Definition of Disciplinary Cultures," especially pp. 115–117.

18. Kolb, "Learning Styles and Disciplinary Differences."

19. Ibid., p. 243.

20. Biglan, "Characteristics of Subject Matter in Different Academic Areas."

21. Ibid., p. 195.

22. Ibid., p. 202.

23. Follow-ups to Biglan's work are reviewed and summarized in Roskens, "Implications of Biglan Model Research for the Process of Faculty Advancement."

24. Ladd and Lipset, *Divided Academy*.

25. Lodahl and Gordon, "Structure of Scientific Fields and the Functioning of University Graduate Departments."

26. Kuhn, *Structure of Scientific Revolutions*, pp. 175, 176.

27. Biglan, "Characteristics of Subject Matter in Different Academic Areas," p. 202.

28. Lodahl and Gordon, "Structure of Scientific Fields and the Functioning of University Graduate Departments," p. 71.

29. Bucher and Strauss, "Professions in Process."

30. Ibid., p. 325.

31. I owe most of the ideas in this paragraph to Jonathan Rée, whose notes on the organization of knowledge and the history of academic disciplines so far remain unpublished.

32. See Becher and Kogan, *Process and Structure in Higher Education*, especially chap. 6.

33. Clark, *Higher Education System*, pp. 34, 76.

34. The ambiguity on this point underlines the rough-and-ready nature of

all attempts, my own included, to produce taxonomies of academic subjects. Although such exercise may be useful for particular purposes, there is a danger that they may be treated as if they were authoritative maps of knowledge, which they are invariably too simple to be.

35. The modus operandi of the inquiry is described in more detail in Becher, "Cultural View."

36. This is, of course, an account of what Kuhn and others have called "normal science": when conceptual upheavals occur in any given field, they may give rise to major discontinuities. See Kuhn, *Structure of Scientific Revolutions*.

37. Weber, *Peasants into Frenchmen*.

38. Such qualities are usually more evident at the undergraduate than the postgraduate stage, since the focus is on the basics of the subject rather than on its more subtle and complex elements.

39. An obvious exception is to be found in the less quantitative "whole organism" areas of biology, where the pattern is of individual and not collective research. Many respondents showed a positive disapproval of supervisors who habitually added their names to students' papers.

40. Scientific medicine deviates from this pattern because progression is often directly from medical school to project research. See the discussion in Bucher and Strauss, *Professions in Process*, p. 328, about specialties with minimal patient contact.

41. Insofar as law may be regarded as a soft-applied subject, it is atypical in this respect. In the U.K. (the pattern is not the same in the U.S.), many academic lawyers proceed straight from law school to a junior academic post, though some of them may go simultaneously into pupilage and subsequently engage in part-time practice. As in other soft-applied disciplines, however, only a small proportion of academic staff have doctoral degrees.

42. The distinction is enshrined in Gouldner's classic essay, "Locals and Cosmopolitans."

43. See Crane, *Invisible Colleges*, for a detailed discussion of the phenomenon in relation to scientific communities.

44. Lodahl and Gordon, "Structure of Scientific Fields and the Functioning of University Graduate Departments."

45. Zuckerman and Merton, "Patterns of Evaluation in Science."

46. One such study, Berelson's *Graduate Education in the United States*, reflects my findings, insofar as chemists head his league table and show only 17 percent of publications with single authorship, whereas historians are at the bottom of the table with 96 percent of publications having one author.

47. Biglan, "Relationships between Subject Matter Characteristics and the Structure and Output of University Departments," p. 211.

48. For an extended discussion of this issue, see Ziman, "What Are the Options?"

49. A number of chemists I interviewed pointed out, with proprietorial

pride, that chemistry as a discipline had considerably more than its proportional share of vice-chancellors in universities in Great Britain.

50. Lodahl and Gordon, "Structure of Scientific Fields and the Functioning of University Graduate Departments," p. 60.

51. Merton, *Sociology of Science*. The reference is to the well-known passage in St. Matthew's Gospel: "To those that have shall be given, and from those that have not shall be taken even that which they have."

52. A point confirmed by several of my respondents in mechanical engineering departments.

53. The continuing existence of an amateur tradition in certain disciplines—astronomy and branches of biology as well as history and archaeology—gives them a significant advantage both in public credibility and in the premium they place on clear, relatively jargon-free writing.

54. Porter, "Saint George or the Dragon?," p. 1.

55. An informative discussion of this point is to be found in Kogan and Kogan, *Attack on Higher Education*, especially pp. 66–70 and 95–96.

56. Bucher and Strauss, "Professions in Process," p. 326.

57. Clark, *Higher Education System*, pp. 35–36.

58. Lodahl and Gordon, "Structure of Scientific Fields and the Functioning of University Graduate Departments," p. 69.

59. Of the 150 or so academics I have interviewed to date, only a tiny minority have suggested that they are not doing the job they want above all others to do.

60. A figure of this order has, to my surprise, been commonly quoted in almost every field in each discipline I have so far studied, with the exception of the most fashionable and populous areas in physics and chemistry.

61. Bucher and Strauss, "Professions in Process," p. 327.

62. Smith, *Lore of the Whare Wananga*, quoted in Salmond, "Theoretical Landscapes," pp. 83–84.

63. See Barry, "Do Neighbours Make Good Fences?"

64. A highly theoretical but entertaining analysis of boundary changes of this kind may be found in Thompson, "Class, Caste, the Curriculum Cycle and the Cusp Catastrophe."

65. Weber, *Peasants into Frenchmen*, p. 103.

66. This is perhaps closer to a piece of fiction than it is to a contribution from the history of philosophy.

67. Clark, *Higher Education System*, p. 91.

BIBLIOGRAPHY

Atkinson, Paul. "The Reproduction of the Professional Community." In *The Sociology of the Profession*, ed. Robert Dingwall and Philip Lewis. London: Macmillan, 1983.

Bailey, F. G. *Morality and Expediency*. Oxford: Blackwell, 1977.

Barry, Brian. "Do Neighbours Make Good Fences?" *Political Theory* 9, no. 3, (1981): 293–301.

Becher, Tony. "Towards a Definition of Disciplinary Cultures." *Studies in Higher Education* 6, no. 2 (1981): 109–122.

————. "The Cultural View." In *Perspectives on Higher Education: Eight Disciplinary and Comparative Views*, ed. Burton R. Clark. Berkeley, Los Angeles, London: University of California Press, 1984.

Becher, Tony, and Maurice Kogan. *Process and Structure in Higher Education.* London: Heinemann, 1980.

Berelson, Bernard. *Graduate Education in the United States.* New York: McGraw-Hill, 1960.

Biglan, Anthony. "The Characteristics of Subject Matter in Different Academic Areas." *Journal of Applied Psychology* 57 (1973): 195–203.

————. "Relationships between Subject Matter Characteristics and the Structure and Output of University Departments." *Journal of Applied Psychology* 57 (1973): 204–213.

Bledstein, Burton J. *The Culture of Professionalism.* New York: Norton, 1976.

Bucher, Rue, and Anselm Strauss. "Professions in Process." *American Journal of Sociology* 66 (1961): 325–334.

Clark, Burton R. *The Higher Education System: Academic Organization in Cross-National Perspective.* Berkeley, Los Angeles, London: University of California Press, 1983.

Crane, Diana. *Invisible Colleges.* Chicago: University of Chicago Press, 1972.

Gouldner, Alvin W. "Locals and Cosmopolitans." *Administrative Science Quarterly* 1, no. 2 (1957): 281–306, 444–480.

Halsey, A. H., and Martin Trow, *The British Academics.* London: Faber, 1971.

Holland, J. *The Psychology of Vocational Choice.* Walton, Mass: Blaidsdell, 1966.

Hughes, Everett, C. *Men and Their Work.* Glencoe, Ill.: Free Press, 1958.

Knorr-Cetina, Karin D. *The Manufacture of Knowledge.* Oxford: Pergamon Press, 1981.

Kogan, Maurice, with David Kogan. *The Attack on Higher Education.* London: Kogan Page, 1983.

Kolb, David A. "Learning Styles and Disciplinary Differences." In *The Modern American College*, ed. Arthur W. Chickering. San Francisco: Jossey-Bass, 1981.

Kuhn, Thomas S. *The Structure of Scientific Revolutions.* 2d ed. Chicago: University of Chicago Press, 1970.

Ladd, Everett C., Jr., and Seymour M. Lipset. *The Divided Academy.* New York: McGraw-Hill, 1975.

Light, Donald, Jr. "The Structure of the Academic Professions." *Sociology of Education* 47 (1974): 2–28.

Lodahl, Janice Beyer, and Gerald Gordon. "The Structure of Scientific Fields and the Functioning of University Graduate Departments." *American Sociological Review* 37 (1972): 57–72.

Merton, Robert K. *The Sociology of Science*. Chicago: University of Chicago Press, 1973.

Perkin, Harold. *Key Profession*. London: Routledge, 1968.

Porter, Marilyn. "Saint George or the Dragon?" *Network* 29 (1984): 1–2.

Rée, Jonathan. Unpublished discussion papers. Mimeo.

Roe, Ann. *The Psychology of Occupations*. New York: John Wiley, 1956.

Roskens, Ronald W. "Implications of Biglan Model Research for the Process of Faculty Advancement." *Research in Higher Education* 18, no. 3 (1983): 285–297.

Rothblatt, Sheldon. *The Revolution of the Dons*. London: Faber, 1968.

Salmond, Anne. "Theoretical Landscapes: On Cross-cultural Conceptions of Knowledge." In *Semantic Anthropology*, ed. David Parkin. London: Academic Press, 1982.

Smith, S. P. *The Lore of the Whare Wananga*. Vols. 1 and 2. New Plymouth: Polynesian Society, 1913.

Thompson, Michael. "Class, Caste, the Curriculum Cycle and the Cusp Catastrophe." *Studies in Higher Education* 1, no. 1 (1976): 31–46.

Weber, Eugen. *Peasants into Frenchmen*. London: Chatto and Windus, 1977.

Wilson, Logan. *The Academic Man: Sociology of a Profession*. New York: Oxford University Press, 1942.

Ziman, John. "What are the Options? Social Determinants of Personal Research Plans." *Minerva* 19, no. 1 (1981): 1–42.

Zuckerman, Harriet, and Robert K. Merton. "Patterns of Evaluation in Science." *Minerva* 9, no. 1 (1971): 66–100.

7
Professional Schools in the American University

Sydney Ann Halpern

Although the term *academic profession* is often used to refer exclusively to faculty in the traditional disciplines of letters and science, professional school faculty are a dominant presence in American institutions of higher education. Their importance is reflected in both numbers and dollars. In American research universities, faculties of professional schools frequently constitute more than 60 percent of the total professoriat.[1] These schools command an impressive share of institutional resources. Among universities that offer medical training, medical school budgets alone comprise one-quarter of total university expenditures, and this excludes the very sizable budgets of university-owned teaching hospitals. It is not unusual for the combined budgets of a medical school and teaching hospital to exceed those of the remaining portions of their campus.[2] Professional schools and letters and science divisions are separate and parallel organizational units, with their own departments and administrative hierarchies. Schools for the major professions, (like medicine and law) exercise a substantial degree of autonomy in the management of internal affairs and have considerable impact on the university as a whole.

The large and influential professional school segments of the American professoriat occupy a special position in institutions of higher education. Janus-like they sit facing, on the one side, the university with its commitment to academic standards, and on the other, practicing professions with guild interests and commitments to client-oriented services. Sociologist Donald Light sees the American professional school as beset by structural ambiguity; it faces "cross-cutting pressures and expectations" due to its location "at the intersection of two social structures for which it has different meanings."[3] Professional colleges have disparate mandates, including the creation of knowledge and the transmission of distinctly vocational skills and attitudes. Such plurality of missions results in tensions within professional schools and between them and letters and science faculties.

This chapter examines the structural ambiguity of both American business and medical schools but focuses on academic medicine. Its principal emphasis is on temporal patterns: the changes over time in the balance of clinical and academic missions, and shifts in the relationship between professional schools and letters and science faculties and between the schools and letters and science disciplines. Business and medical schools display different patterns in the expression of professional and academic missions. The narrative explores structural origins of these differences. It draws upon both secondary literature and data gathered in the UCLA Academic Profession Study described in the introduction. As a participant in that study, I conducted one hundred and eight interviews at five American universities. Thirty-two of these interviews were with campus administrators and letters and science faculty. Seventy-six were with administrators and faculty of business and medical schools.

The chapter is organized into four sections. The first part identifies strains, characteristic of medical and business colleges, between clinical and academic missions. Medical schools at many organizational levels have high levels of tension between clinical and academic norms. Business schools typically have less internal conflict over divergent mandates, but they experience the pull of practical professionalism from without and are prone to crises of relevance. These differences arise in part from the structure of training programs. Medical education takes place largely in hospital wards; patient care is one of the routine tasks of medical faculty. But business students get practical experience outside the university; management faculty do not engage in practice as part of their academic duties. Attributes of the professions have an impact as well. Medicine has a socially sanctioned knowledge base and unorganized clients. Business administration has less prestigious intellectual foundations and extremely powerful clients.

The second section examines trends within professional schools during the early and midtwentieth century. I argue that business and medical schools moved toward greater conformity with university

research norms. The divergent mission of professional schools originated from the late nineteenth century when the American university
emerged in its modern form. Founders of the new institution had
strong commitments to both the production of knowledge and its
application to practical problems. They made professional training a
major function, creating separate organizational units for professional
and liberal arts training. Over time, medical and business schools
expanded their full-time faculty and placed greater importance upon
an individual's research productivity when making hiring and promotion decisions.

The third part discusses the reemergence of practical professionalism within business and medical schools during the 1970s and 1980s.
Management schools have endeavored to make training more consistent with practice and to forge stronger ties to the profession's
corporate clients. These efforts are a response to new contingencies
facing American business and are continuous with the perennial effort
of management schools to achieve relevance. Within medical schools,
clinical departments are under pressure to place greater emphasis on
patient care needs as a factor in promoting and hiring faculty. These
units have been making extensive use of nontenure-accruing appointments, creating a dual appointment structure: tenure-track lines for
research-oriented faculty and nontenure-accruing lines for service-
oriented faculty. These trends are related to the growing centrality of
teaching hospitals within the health care system and to the increasing
reliance of medical schools on patient care revenues.

The fourth section of the chapter explores more broadly the implications for the university of trends within professional schools. The
proliferation of nontenure-track appointments within medical schools
has been accompanied by conflict between medical and letters and
science faculty. This conflict centers on the viability of academic tenure
and the universal value of academic research norms. Finally, I examine
professional schools as work environments for faculty in academic
disciplines. Over the years increasing numbers of letters and science–
trained Ph.D.'s have found employment within professional schools.
I offer speculations about the implications of these trends for knowledge generated by disciplinary subfields.

VARIATIONS OF STRUCTURAL AMBIGUITY

Academic branches of professions differ in their positions in universities and in the nature and course of their academic-vocational
tensions. These differences arise both from characteristics of the

professional schools and from structural features of the professions themselves. Closer scrutiny of the two professions and their training institutions will make these points clearer.

The profession of medicine has a number of attributes that significantly influence the standing of its academic wing. Medicine has a dependent and unorganized clientele; it has also had, since the late nineteenth century, a powerful and politically effective guild organization and exceedingly legitimate intellectual foundations. These features enabled medicine to win an unprecedented degree of authority in society.[4] They also helped place its academic branches in a very strong position in the university. But perhaps the most influential factor that shapes the unfolding expression of academic and clinical missions in medical colleges is that vocational training actually takes place under the aegis of the university. University training programs in business, engineering, and law transmit the intellectual bases of professional practice. Entrants acquire practical skills after formal training in the early years of their careers. In medicine not only is clinical training a legal prerequisite for practice but much applied training takes place in institutions of higher education. Medical colleges, and other health training schools modeled after them, are the only professional schools in which students, trainees, and faculty routinely engage in hands-on professional practice.

The locus of this professional activity is the university teaching hospital. Of the 127 medical schools in the United States today, 65 own their own hospitals, and the majority of others control the management of one or more hospitals. Medical schools are divided into two types of academic units: basic science departments, such as anatomy, physiology, or biochemistry and clinical departments, such as internal medicine, surgery, or radiology. The former group is similar to departments in the letters and science division of their campuses; faculty conduct research, train graduate students in laboratory investigation, and provide classroom instruction to medical students in scientific fields relevant to the practice of medicine. The clinical departments, however, are as much a part of the hospital as a part of the medical school. Almost all teaching is done in the context of professional practice. Though research is conducted and is highly valued, a major function of each department is to manage and staff hospital service units. The clinical departments of American medical schools perform fundamentally different tasks than do the basic science and letters and science departments and have fundamentally different cultures.[5]

Just how these organizational arrangements arose is a very complex question. I will set aside the issue of origins for the moment and focus on the consequences of making professional practice a major function of academic departments. One outcome is that the academic and practicing branches of the profession are highly interdependent. The academic wing of medicine has a much greater impact on the organization and delivery of services outside the university than is the case in any other profession.[6] At the same time, medical schools are highly influenced by developments in the practicing profession and are vulnerable to the forces that affect the health care industry. The inclusion of professional practice in clinical departments also produces extremely sharp tensions between academic and vocational missions and values. These strains are probably sharper in medical colleges than in other professional schools.

Academic-vocational tensions occur in at least three different institutional arenas. In clinical departments of medical schools, faculty have substantial patient-care responsibilities in addition to the usual professorial duties of research, teaching, and administration. Many experience great difficulty in balancing clinical work with the research and publication requirements of promotion and academic tenure. The strain is particularly intense for faculty in subfields where research tends to be unrelated to patient-care activities. A second location of tension in medical schools is between clinical and basic science departments. These units vie over both the distribution of institutional resources and the appropriate priority of institutional missions. Their faculties may also be in conflict over what constitutes good research and what criteria ought to be used in tenure and promotion decisions.

A third arena of conflict occurs at the interface between medical and letters and science faculty. Major issues here include faculty appointment lines and tenure criteria. Medical school spokesmen argue that they must be able to keep faculty who are necessary for hospital functioning but are weak in research productivity or investigatory skills. Several physician informants who participated in the academic professions study cite the example of anesthesiologists who, according to their medical colleagues, are often deficient in scientific publications but indispensable to the patient-care obligations of the hospital. At each of the campuses visited in the study, some type of accommodation is made for service-oriented medical school faculty. At a few schools, tenure and promotion decision making is very decentralized; professional schools are, in essence, allowed to make their own personnel decisions. Tensions are greatest on campuses where a bona fide faculty review takes place above the level of professional-school deans. At one such school in our sample, special critieria are used in decisions regarding medical school appointees. At several institutions medical school departments are permitted to retain faculty rejected for tenure by switching them to nontenure-accruing faculty appointment lines. But these accommodations are uneasy ones, accompanied by dissatisfaction and perennial controversy.

The academic branch of management presents a different type of structural ambiguity. In business schools, attributes of the practicing profession are dominant in shaping the expression of vocational and academic missions. Business administrators must contend with corporate, not individual, clients. Unlike medicine, with a strong guild and dependent clients, the profession of management has almost no guild organization but has a very powerful clientele. Management practitioners gain status not through membership in the profession but through association with and mobility within large-scale corporations. Minimal use of licensure is one indication of weak guild organization; accounting is the only field in business in which certification is used. Aspiring managers do not need a license to obtain a job, nor do they need a professional degree to succeed at business. As one management professor put it, in business schools there is less consensus about what constitutes the knowledge base of professional practice and more variation among schools about what is actually taught than is the case with schools of medicine, engineering, or law. In business the link between university training and professional practice is tenuous.[7]

These characteristics shape the expression of academic and vocational missions within business schools in universities and colleges. In management schools tensions arise not from the presence of professional practice but from schools' efforts to satisfy competing sources of legitimacy. Status is derived from both academic respectability and the favorable opinion of business leaders. Like individual managers, business schools are affected by the power of the profession's corporate clients. Links with large-scale corporations are a source of prestige for management schools, as is the ability to place graduates in leading firms. The position of management schools in the university is enhanced by corporate gifts and collaborations. There are strong incentives for business school deans to court the favor and patronage of business and to gear academic programs to perceived corporate interests. At the same time, academic credentials are critical both for the business school's standing in the university and its reputation with business leaders. Historically the integration of training schools into the university was the basis of legitimacy for management as a profession. Academic reputation allows schools to attract the type of students that corporations feel make the best employees. But the route to academic respectability carries with it the danger that training will be perceived as irrelevant to management practice, a problem to which business schools are easily disposed. Strains associated with competing sources of legitimacy are particularly strong in management, because of the nature of its clientele and the equivocal link between knowledge and practice.

Disagreements surrounding executive training programs provide an example of academic-vocational tensions in management schools. Executive training is vocationally oriented short-term instruction for practicing managers. In the past several years, many business schools have initiated or expanded such programs, which are run independently of the regular academic curriculum. Executive training allows schools to strengthen links with the business community and—since it is extremely lucrative—provides schools and participating faculty with substantial additions to their income. But there is strong sentiment among the faculty of some schools that these programs conflict with academic functions, especially research activities.

Academic medicine confronts the demands of competing activities in the professional school; the academic wing of business strives to reconcile conflicting sources of legitimacy. The result for medical schools is acute and pervasive tension; for business schools it is a propensity for crises of relevance. The general point here is that characteristics of practicing professions, as well as features of the schools themselves, powerfully influence the dilemmas faced by professional schools and their faculties. Professions vary significantly in prestige and technologies and in the social location of service delivery, the nature of clientele, and degree of guild organization. All of these factors affect the academic branches and their evolving positions in the university.

ASSIMILATION OF UNIVERSITY NORMS

Professional training became a fundamental mission of American institutions of higher education during the late nineteenth and early twentieth centuries. During this period educational leaders initiated university training in new professional fields. They upgraded instruction in the older professions and brought existing professional schools more into the institutional fold. These developments were part of a series of radical changes that produced the American university in its modern form. The innovations contributing to this new species of organization are well documented. Colleges initiated masters' and doctoral programs as tiers above the preexisting baccalaureate programs, making graduate education a major educational function. Professional schools were part of the graduate tier, offering largely though not exclusively postbaccalaureate training. Administrators constituted discipline-based departments as the basic unit of academic organization. The leading schools embraced scientific norms and elevated research to a primary position among institutional goals.[8] Faculty roles were professionalized. A research-oriented science specialist supplanted the older, classically educated gentleman-scholar. Universities regularized academic careers through the introduction of sequenced and graded faculty positions. At the top schools, doctoral training became a requirement for faculty appointments and scholarly achievement requisite for academic advancement.[9]

The inclusion of professional training in the university was by no means inevitable. The American higher education system might have been more decentralized, with training in some or all vocational fields located in independent institutions or in schools with only loose university affiliations. There were in fact objections to some vocational programs; Veblen argued vociferously that training for business had no place in American universities.[10] In medicine also other patterns are conceivable: basic science and clinical training might have remained separate, with practical bedside instruction in teaching hospitals outside the university's purview.[11] But the architects of the American university were deeply committed both to scientific progress and to its application as professional expertise. The modern university emerged at a time when professions were becoming a dominant occupational type in American society. Leaders in education designed the university to transmit the skills and attitudes needed for success in an industralized and professionalized society.[12] They considered professional training a central function of higher education and constituted professional schools parallel to letters and science colleges, as major academic divisions. University presidents expected the faculty of these professional schools to engage in scientific research and other scholarly activities.

Professional schools, now part of the university, moved toward the assimilation of academic norms during the first half of the twentieth century. Progress was slow. The original faculties of professional schools were part-time teachers whose principal source of income was professional practice. Fully integrating scientific norms into professional schools required the creation of career tracks in research and teaching distinct from those in professional practice. Funds to establish full-time salaried professorships were limited. Furthermore, the introduction of regular academic posts in medicine caused controversy. The scientifically minded elite of the profession strongly supported full-time salaried appointments for medical faculty, but the practicing branch of medicine resisted.[13]

The basic science faculties of medical schools were functioning much like letters and science faculties as early as the late 1880s. But in clinical departments older traditions lingered. Medical practitioners used university appointments to attract upper-crust clientele to their private practices. Faculty posts were especially important to physicians who were establishing specialized practices. In the years before certifying boards and standardized residency training, physicians built reputations for specialized expertise through medical school and hospital appointments.[14] At the turn of the century, the professional elites that controlled American hospitals wielded substantial influence over the selection of clinical faculties in medical schools. Abraham Flexner complained bitterly about this in his writings on American medical training.[15] The scientific leadership of medicine mobilized to bring teaching hospitals under university management and wrest control of faculty appointments from the practicing profession. During the second decade of the century, medical schools negotiated contracts with hospitals; this gave academic units jurisdiction over hospital appointments.[16] But clinical departments were still staffed largely by part-time faculty, physicians who received small salaries for teaching and earned most of their income in private practice. Conformity to university norms required full-time appointments that allowed time for, and rewarded, research productivity.

The intitial funding for full-time clinical appointments in American medical schools was stimulated by the Flexner Report (itself a Carnegie Foundation effort) and was provided by private sources, most notably the Rockefeller Foundation.[17] Large increases in full-time posts came after World War II, supported by a massive influx of federal research funds. Between 1950 and 1980 the number of full-time faculty appointments in clinical departments rose from 2,300 to 37,700 while the total medical school posts (including clinical and basic science departments) increased from 3,900 to 50,500.[18] By the late fifties and sixties, clinical departments had made substantial movement toward assimilating university norms. At top schools academic standards were employed as the principal criterion in hiring and promotion decisions. American medical schools emerged as major centers for the conduct of biomedical research with scientific efforts occurring in both clinical and basic science departments. Huge increases in faculty posts were supported largely by soft money, rather than by institutional funds such as endowments or tuitions; this would eventually catch up with American medical schools, but not until after the boom period of the postwar era.

Adoption of academic norms occurred in business schools even later than in medicine. University training in management was itself introduced considerably after programs existed in medicine and law. The first collegiate business programs appeared in the late 1800s as offshoots of letters and science divisions, particularly in economics departments; these were undergraduate programs offering a variety of liberal arts training for the aspiring businessman. Between 1920 and 1940 more and more colleges and universities introduced business education, and enrollments expanded both in numbers and as a percentage of the undergraduate majors. Vocationally oriented graduate programs were also initiated during this period, becoming increasingly numerous after World War II. Still, business education remained largely an undergraduate field; of the 600 colleges and universities offering business training in the mid-1950s, only 125 conferred masters' degrees.[19] Graduate programs and faculties of that era had a strong trade school character. Among full-time business faculty at midcentury, only 40 percent held Ph.D.'s (of these doctoral degrees, 85 percent were in either economics or business).[20] Many schools relied heavily on part-time teachers and retired businessmen for academic staff.

The professionalizing of business faculties, begun in earnest during the late 1950s, was catalyzed by the efforts of the American Assembly of Collegiate Schools of Business (AACSB) and by the publication of two foundation studies, the Gordon and Howell report, sponsored by the Ford Foundation, and the Pierson report, supported by the Carnegie Foundation.[21] These studies criticized business schools for having a vocational orientation and low academic standards. Training programs were depicted as overly descriptive and insufficiently analytical; faculty were described as narrow in interests, intellectually obsolescent, and inadequate in research performance. Gordon and Howell advocated the building up of graduate over undergraduate programs. Both reports urged the upgrading of curriculum and academic staff, the latter through the hiring of full-time research-minded faculty from a range of academic disciplines. During the 1960s and 1970s, most of their recommendations were implemented. At leading schools scientific productivity became preeminent in decisions regarding hiring and promotion and, as in medicine, business faculties moved far in adopting university research norms.[22]

REEMERGENCE OF THE CLINICAL

In recent years there has been renewed talk of vocationalism in American universities. Enrollments in the traditional science and humanities disciplines have declined at both the undergraduate and graduate levels, with students migrating into fields having practical applicability and clear-cut career paths. Computer sciences, business, and other professional fields are among the popular areas of concentration.[23] Even within professional programs, student interests seem to have shifted. Medical educators complain that present-day trainees are less interested in research than were previous groups and that a higher proportion of graduates are entering careers in professional practice.[24] Shifts in student enrollments and interests are not the only suggestions of heightened vocationalism. Professional school faculty and administrators are sending new messages about the balance of academic and clinical missions.

Among business educators there have been rumblings during the past several years that professional training has lost relevance for management practice. Critics argue that degree recipients are sophisticated in the use of models and are adept at quantitative techniques but lack important management skills including the ability to set goals, make value judgments, identify problems, engage in entrepreneurial activity, and make decisions that involve complex trade-offs. Commentators blame business faculties who are described as lacking interest and experience in management practice and as being preoccupied with research in disciplines. In the words of one critic: "The research in business administration during the past twenty years would fail any reasonable test of applicability or relevance to consequential management problems. . . . The orientation of business faculty to the research concerns of their disciplines has gone so far as to give courses on management second class status."[25] At present there are two national panels in the United States looking into management training. One was initiated by business school deans and is being carried out through the AACSB. The other is sponsored by the Business Education Forum (an arm of the American Council on Education), which is composed of university presidents and corporate executive officers. Both panels are concerned with the adequacy of professional education for management practice. Within medical schools also, there are abundant signs that clinical concerns have gained renewed salience.

These developments suggest that the movement toward academic norms in business and medical schools may have peaked and that we may now be seeing a swing toward practical concerns, a reassertion of vocationalism. Does this mean that there have been, or will be, changes in the roles and commitments of business and medical school faculty? In management schools it is still too early to tell. Though there is considerable movement among business schools, it is not movement in a single direction. I argued earlier that the management profession derives status from both academic respectability and the favorable opinion of corporate leaders. These dual sources of legitimacy render business schools prone to crises of relevance. I believe that the current soul-searching going on among management educators is a response to development within business as an enterprise. There have been changes in the competitive position of American corporations in the world market as well as increased entrepreneurship in certain sectors of the American economy. Management schools seem to be in the process of adjusting to new realities facing American business. These adjustments are likely to be supported by university presidents, many of whom see stronger ties with industry as part of a solution to the fiscal problems of American higher education. It is no accident that one of the ongoing studies of management education is sponsored by a coalition of university and corporation presidents. But exactly where this process will lead with regard to academic life in business schools is not yet evident.

In medicine the trends are more long-standing and easier to interpret. Research remains a central mission of American medical colleges, but the impact of clinical practice is being felt more strongly and in ways that are new and sometimes subtle and unexpected. These developments are directly linked to the original inclusion of direct patient care within medical schools and to more recent financing arrangements. Clinical practice and funding patterns create imperatives for medical school faculties quite disparate from those arising from university research norms.

Some observations about university teaching hospitals and their importance in the American health care system shed light on the origins and course of these developments. Medical school hospitals are not simply teaching and research facilities: they are also very important service institutions. Beginning in the late nineteenth century, hospitals in general grew in size and scope and assumed a central position in medical delivery. Teaching hospitals grew also and, with the expansion of research activities among clinical faculties, became the locus for new developments in medical technology. Innovations originate in university faculties and from there spread to a wider range of treatment facilities. As hospitals became increasingly crucial to the delivery of medical services, teaching hospitals assumed a special and prominent position. By the 1960s university hospitals were functioning as tertiary-care centers, known for their ability to provide highly specialized, state-of-the-art treatment unavailable at most treatment facilities. Also, by that time, at least some academic physicians were complaining that the service functions of teaching hospitals had grown to be excessive and that too many demands were being made on medical school clinical faculties.[26]

During the 1960s and 1970s, growth of patient care activities among clinical faculties continued, a trend propelled largely by budgetary contingencies. American medical schools have relied heavily on financial support from outside the university, particularly on support from government agencies. Growth of medical faculties following World War II was funded largely by federal research dollars. In recent years the origins of external support have shifted; research grants leveled off in the 1970s while income from government insurance programs (Medicare and Medicaid) and from private insurance companies (e.g., Blue Cross and Blue Shield) increased substantially. The government also encouraged the expansion of certain patient-care programs directly; during the 1970s it created financial incentives for medical schools to establish primary-care training programs. These were intended to counterbalance the medical schools' strong emphasis on highly specialized training with education in general branches of medicine. Among the results were a proliferation of medical school ambulatory-care clinics and substantial growth in outpatient services. Meanwhile, the fiscal difficulties confronting American universities meant that institutional funds were dispensed with greater parsimony. For all these reasons, in the past two decades medical schools have become ever more dependent on patient-care revenues.

The principal source of this income is the professional billings of faculty in clinical departments of medical schools. At many schools physician billings are routed through fiscal and administrative units called Faculty Practice Plans (FPPs). These plans—really forms of group practice—were set up in the 1950s and 1960s when part-time teachers, then the bulk of medical school staff, were replaced by full-time faculty. In one type of plan, profits from faculty billings are pooled and then redistributed. Disbursement schemes vary widely; typically a percentage is directed into general medical school funds with the remainder going to clinical departments in proportion to the income each generates. Departments, in turn, use the largest portion of their share to pay faculty salaries. This type of FPP allows deans and department heads to monitor the patient-care activities of academic physicians and to control the rewards accompanying medical practice. Between 1965 and 1981 income derived from these activities rose from 5.6 to 30 percent of total medical school revenues.[27] During the same time span, FPP income rose from 3 percent to 17.5 percent of medical schools' total operating revenues.[28] Though the increases are impressive, even these figures do not indicate how essential patient care income has become to the functioning of clinical departments. Heads of departments of medicine interviewed during the UCLA Academic Profession Study indicate that FPP funds alone typically constitute a third or more of their department income.

Dependence on patient-care funds renders medical schools subject to the same forces that buffet the health industry in general, and at a time when the market for medical care is increasingly competitive. Federal policy during the late 1960s and early 1970s mandated the enlargement of medical school enrollments. In the view of many physicians, the result has been an oversupply of medical practitioners. Meanwhile, efforts by the federal government to control health-care costs have created widespread concern among hospitals about maintaining current revenue levels from patient-care activities. Medical school deans and department heads are more and more preoccupied with the balance sheet and are increasingly entrepreneurial in their strategies to maintain and enlarge patient-care revenues. Their tactics include initiating a variety of patient-care programs, including health maintenance organizations and preferred provider schemes, which may have little or no relationship to the research and teaching functions of the institution.

These trends have created powerful pressures within medical schools and have had profound consequences for academic physicians. In clinical departments, five developments are particularly striking. First, the working lives of clinical faculty have become exceedingly stressful. This is so in part because the financial problems facing medical schools have been transferred onto clinical departments and their academic staffs. In these departments, approximately two-thirds or more of faculty salaries are drawn from soft money, a combination of research funds and patient-care revenues. At many institutions, clinical faculty are under substantial pressure to generate their own income through either external grant support or clinical income. This creates severe strains for academic physicians, particularly those in the early stages of their careers. If a young faculty member does not succeed in acquiring research funding quickly, or if an older faculty member fails to maintain external funding, the department head may load on clinical duties that would make future research and grant activity close to impossible. Assistant professors with heavy patient-care duties are likely to have great difficulty publishing enough to obtain academic tenure. These types of pressures, and the routine strain of balancing research and clinical duties, produce pervasive anxieties among clinical faculties. A number of respondents in the study volunteered the opinion that life in clinical departments was more tension-ridden and less rewarding than it was in previous decades.

Second, new types of physicians are being added to the faculty of clinical departments, physicians whose greatest strengths are in patient care rather than in medical investigation. Some of the new academic personnel are hired to staff special patient-care programs like health maintenance organizations or ambulatory-care clinics. But many are integrated into established clinical departments and divisions. The head of cardiology at one elite medical school told me that competition with community cardiologists has become so fierce and the importance of clinical income so great that recently he was obliged to consider clinical skills rather than research as the preeminent criterion in hiring division faculty. He said that this had never occurred before in his division. The dean of another medical school, also an elite institution, reported that this trend was widespread. Medical schools sometimes have the option of hiring clinically oriented physicians for new faculty slots in, for example, temporary postdoctoral positions, or as hospital instead of medical school employees. But more often than not, they are brought in on some type of long-term academic appointment. These new recruits are similar in skills and orientation to the part-time teachers prevalent in clinical departments earlier in the century; the difference is that those in the recent group hold full-time faculty appointments.

Third, there has been a trend toward greater differentiation in the roles and activities of academic staff within clinical departments. Fewer faculty successfully combine professional practice and medical investigation; a greater portion can be identified as either primarily researchers or primarily patient-care providers. This trend has been discussed in a programmatic vein by Robert Petersdorf, a former medical school dean and frequent commentator in *The New England Journal of Medicine*. He argues that progressive role differentiation is necessary because medical research has become too complex to be pursued successfully on a part-time basis. Physicians who divide their time between patient care and research are no longer competitive in a biomedical research world populated with physicians and Ph.D.'s who are full-time investigators.[29] But there is another impetus as well. As patient-care activities have expanded and clinical income grows as a share of department revenues, at the top schools the value placed on research has not diminished. Increased role differentiation is the way competing pressures have been reconciled. Department heads at elite schools report that they routinely promote heavy patient-care loads for some of their physicians in order to create time and generate salary and laboratory support for their research-oriented faculty. As one might expect, there is a great deal of conflict within clinical departments over the distribution of FPP revenues. Not all faculty are happy about the use of clinical income to support research activities. One of the most universally voiced complaints among faculty with heavy patient-care obligations is that they receive too small a portion of the proceeds they generate.

Fourth, there has been a movement in medical schools toward the use of dual appointment systems. While regular tenure-track positions are still available to clinical departments, many schools have introduced nontenure-accruing lines or have used existing nontenure-track appointments more extensively. There is considerable variation in how nontenure-accruing posts are utilized. At some schools the positions are available to all university departments; in others they are restricted to the medical college. The titles of nontenure-track faculty vary across campuses. Some institutions have separate lines for different categories of irregular faculty—for example, clinical, research, and adjunct. Schools differ in the privileges and relative status accorded nontenure-track faculty. Incumbents may or may not be permitted to vote in faculty senates or be eligible for sabbatical and other benefits routinely available to regular academic staff. But there are several commonalities across schools in how clinical departments use nontenure-accruing appointments. The posts are held largely by practice-oriented physicians who carry substantial patient-care duties. Many in this group still hold tenure-track positions, but increasing numbers are being routed into alternative appointments. (Ph.D. researchers are also hired in nontenure-accruing posts in clinical departments.) Nontenure-accruing posts are not temporary positions. They are used to provide long-term (but not guaranteed) employment for physicians who are important to the teaching and service activities of medical schools, but who have not met (or are not expected to meet) the requirements of academic tenure. The appointments allow department heads to add faculty positions in their departments without making a permanent commitment of departmental resources. Data collected by the Association of American Medical Colleges (AAMC) indicate trends in the use of nontenure-track appointments. In 1975, 58 percent of American medical schools reported they had nontenure-accruing appointments with separate titles.[30] By 1983, 77 percent were using nontenure-track posts in clinical departments, 73 percent in basic science departments. During the latter year, 43 percent of American medical schools indicated that more than one-quarter of their faculties were in nontenure-track appointments.[31]

Fifth, academic tenure has become progressively less desirable for medical school faculty. This is in part because fewer faculty members are in tenure-accruing posts. But another important reason is that tenure guarantees little to academic physicians. As emphasized earlier, institutional funds provide only a fraction of faculty salaries in clinical departments; the largest share comes from research grants and patient-care revenues. These are generated by physicians themselves in the course of their professional activities. In response to an AAMC survey conducted in 1983, 40 percent of American medical schools indicated that tenure guaranteed a position but no income. In an additional 22 percent of schools, tenure assures only a portion of a faculty member's salary.[32] At one school visited during the course of the UCLA Academic Profession Study, special clauses that make future employment contingent on the continued availability of funding were included in the contracts of some tenure-track faculty.

Attitudes toward tenure among academic physicians are almost universally negative. In 1975, 70 percent of medical school deans reported they were against it in academic medicine,[33] and nearly all physicians interviewed in the study felt tenure was inappropriate to their professional school. Respondents argue that deadwood is exceptionally costly, given the prevailing salary scales in clinical departments. They maintain that tenure is irrelevant because physicians always have the option of leaving academia and going into professional practice. But there is an additional consideration underlying their hostility toward tenure: it creates invidious distinctions. Without firm income guarantees, the meaning of academic tenure in clinical departments is largely symbolic. The growing numbers of nontenure-accruing faculty feel like second-class citizens; this creates morale problems within clinical departments. Nontenure-track faculty with heavy patient-care obligations resent their low status, particularly in light of their importance to the economic viability of academic medicine. (At one medical school I visited, the administration handles these problems by concealing from its own faculty who is on a tenure track and who is not.) In recent years there have been recurrent debates about whether tenure in medical schools ought to be abolished.[34] But the reality is that, in academic medicine, the meaning of tenure has already substantially eroded.

THE PROFESSIONAL SCHOOL AND LETTERS AND SCIENCE FACULTIES

If the patterns described above have most direct impact on the work lives of academic physicians, letters and science faculties are affected as well. Recent trends have increased conflict between medical schools and liberal arts faculties, a major line of contention being appointment tracks for faculty with clinical leanings. Universities vary in the degree to which faculty senates are involved in decisions regarding appointment lines. Where the position of campuswide governance bodies is consequential, the introduction of nontenure-accruing clinical tracks has been controversial. Letters and science faculties view the creation of long-term but unguaranteed slots as a potential threat to academic tenure. They are concerned that proliferation of nontenure-track appointments will lower academic standards. There is discomfort about having, in the university's midst, large cadres of nontenure-track, vocationally oriented faculty with missions and commitments fundamentally different from those of regular academic staff. Letters and science faculty worry about the impact new appointees may have on important university decisions. Thus when nontenure-accruing lines have been approved by faculty senates, it has been with the inclusion of protective stipulations. At one campus I visited during the UCLA study, there is a ceiling on the percentage of medical school faculty permitted in nontenure-accruing posts. At others, nontenure-track faculty are excluded from faculty senates and denied benefits and privileges accorded to regular faculty. Conflicts surrounding these appointments are likely to sharpen in the foreseeable future. Medical schools would very much like to upgrade clinical tracks and remove the status differentials between them and regular faculty appointments. Many deans and department heads would be more than happy to abolish tenure for all medical school faculty. For their part, letters and science faculties would view such attempts as threats to their own job security and to university standards and values.

Developments in professional schools have had other effects on letters and science faculties which are more subtle and less readily apparent. I speak here of consequences for letters and science disciplines and for the work lives of discipline-based faculty. In the course of expanding research activities in the middle decades of the century, American professional schools absorbed a great many letters and sciences–trained Ph.D.'s into their faculties. Medical schools employed increasing numbers of biologists with Ph.D.'s in basic science departments. More recently they have added doctorates in the biological and social sciences to the faculty of clinical departments. Between 1965 and 1978 the portion of basic science faculty with Ph.D.'s (excluding those with both M.D.'s and Ph.D.'s) rose from 54 to 80 percent; the portion of faculty in clinical departments with Ph.D.'s rose from 10.5 to 14.2 percent.[35] (The latter figure underestimates the Ph.D. population in clinical departments; many hold academic but not faculty positions, and as a result go uncounted.) Comparable statistics do not exist for business schools; nevertheless, during the last two decades management schools generally have raised the proportion of Ph.D.'s in their departments and brought in doctoral recipients from a wider range of social and behavioral disciplines. Ph.D.'s are attracted to professional schools by the substantially higher salaries than those in letters and science departments and by opportunities to do applied work and consulting. With the recent constriction of job openings in letters and science disciplines, professional schools have offered some individuals their only possibility of academic employment. The influx of Ph.D's has raised research standards in professional schools and has provided new job opportunities for doctoral recipients. At the same time it has created groups of letters and science–trained academics with very different work environments and career contingencies than faculty in the same discipline in letters and science departments.

The pressures and problems faced by Ph.D.'s in professional schools vary markedly by discipline and institutional location. Biologists in medical school basic science departments are in a relatively enviable position, particularly those at top medical schools. They report that their research environments are good and that they typically earn higher salaries and carry lighter teaching loads than biologists in letters and science departments on the same campuses. Some respondents feel that medical school departments have more difficulty attracting the high-quality graduate students necessary for the functioning of laboratories than do biology departments. Another perceived drawback of employment in a basic science department of a medical school is that funding for faculty salaries, even tenured posts, rests partly on soft money. (Biology departments in letters and science divisions have avoided the practice of relying on extramural funds to pay faculty salaries.) Like the physician faculty of medical schools, biologists very often must generate some portion of their own income. This intensifies already severe pressures to secure research grants. The chairman of biochemistry at one top medical school quipped that "a faculty position here is equivalent to a hunting license." At nonelite schools, biological scientists face more substantial difficulties. Clinical departments frequently dominate institutional policymaking, and support for basic research is likely to be minimal. At one school I visited, the medical college required that all indirect costs and overhead associated with research grants be covered by external funding; this limited the range of funding agencies from which biologists could seek support and thus hampered research efforts.

Biologists in clinical departments experience even more severe problems. They are very likely to be in nontenure-accruing posts supported entirely on soft money. Many work in laboratories directed by physicians and have little autonomy in conducting or initiating research; they serve, as one respondent put it, as supertechnicians. Those permitted to serve as principal investigators and to obtain their own grant support are often prevented, by lack of professorial status, from having graduate students and setting up their own research groups. Because teaching opportunities for Ph.D.'s in clinical departments are scarce, these individuals encounter difficulties shifting into tenure-track positions and qualifying for academic tenure later in their careers. Even those in relatively good positions are likely to feel like second-class citizens, peripheral to the major activities of clinical departments. A participant in the study declared that the physician chairman of his clinical department showed him off to visitors with, " 'I'd like you to meet our Ph.D. immunologist.' Like, I'd like you to see my pet cocker spaniel." Finally, Ph.D.'s in clinical departments tend to be isolated from others in their discipline and experience difficulty maintaining their professional identities.[36]

The experience of medical social scientists also varies substantially by professional school. Letters and science–trained social scientists find management schools to be reasonably benign academic environments; they hold regular academic appointments, and their status is good relative to business administration doctorates. But in medical schools, social scientists encounter a familiar litany of problems: low status, nontenure-accruing posts, soft salary support. Many are on a grant-support treadmill, under pressure to conduct easily fundable, policy-relevant, quick turnaround research. The pressures of this type of work world push social scientists far from their original disciplinary moorings.

The influx of doctorates into professional schools not only creates new work contingencies for letters and science–trained faculty; it may also be affecting the type of knowledge American universities produce. Ph.D.'s in professional schools typically conduct research in subfields also pursued in letters and science departments; they often attend the same conferences and belong to the same disciplinary associations. Long-term patterns in Ph.D. employment have pushed some fields away from discipline-grounded and toward problem-oriented research. An example of this phenomenon is found in medical sociology, which emerged as a discrete area of research in the 1950s; a separate section for this subfield was created within the American Sociological Association (ASA) in 1962. During the first two decades of its development, researchers focused on issues central to the discipline of sociology. They examined the functions of medicine in society, the roles played by physicians and patients, the dynamics of professional socialization, the organization of medical professions and of medical institutions. During the 1970s and 1980s research took a decidedly practical turn, addressing questions consistent with the perspective of medical care providers. When and why do people engage in health-enhancing behavior? What social factors contribute to the etiology of disease? Under what conditions do people seek care and comply with physicians' orders? While discipline-grounded work still goes on, the bulk of recent research in medical sociology uses social science techniques to address questions of an applied nature. No one factor alone accounts for disciplinary drift of this sort; trends in the funding of social research are undoubtedly partly responsible. I maintain that employment patterns are an important factor as well. Though jobs for sociologists in health training programs were relatively scarce in the 1950s and 1960s, more positions have opened in academic health centers during the last fifteen years. Scrutiny of the current membership list of the ASA's medical sociology section reveals that, among those who list work addresses, more than 40 percent are employed in schools of medicine, nursing, or public health. Sociologists in these professional schools are influenced by the vocational bias of their settings and are highly vulnerable to the impact of funding contingencies on the content of social science research.

I believe that trends of this sort may be widespread among letters and science subfields. Unfortunately, data necessary to make a very strong case to this effect are simply not available. AAMC statistics indicate that Ph.D.'s constitute a growing percentage of the medical school faculty. But at present no hard data exists on whether larger proportions of Ph.D. recipients in given disciplines—for example, biochemistry—have entered medical school than letters and science departments. Nor is there aggregate data on the relative rates of growth of professional school and letters and science faculties. Much to my surprise, individual schools participating in the academic profession study could not provide information on growth patterns for their professional school and letters and science faculties. Our research universities simply do not know how the composition of their professoriats is evolving. Respondents in the study offered some impressions. Biological scientists (from both letters and science departments and medical schools) thought it likely that higher portions of biology Ph.D.'s were accepting medical school posts. They reported a related trend: basic science departments have initiated their own Ph.D. programs with the help of National Institutes of Health (NIH) grants, and increasing numbers of biology Ph.D.'s are being trained in medical schools. These doctoral recipients take jobs in medical schools or industry, rarely entering letters and science departments.

There is also some evidence that professional school employment is influencing the content of research conducted in disciplinary fields. Among interviewed biologists, about half felt that basic science departments, as work environments, were sufficiently different from letters and science departments to affect the character of research products. They reported that the former departments encourage investigation of disease-relevant phenomena, and the latter work on basic biological processes. Virtually all felt that Ph.D.'s in clinical departments were under strong pressure to conduct applied research. Respondents from the business schools also provide impressions of the impact of employment locale on research content. Several reported that after a number of years of teaching in a business school, faculty frequently shift their research agendas away from public nonprofit organizations toward private profit-making corporations. If Ph.D. employment trends are influencing letters and science fields, the impact would be felt not in disciplines at large but in their discrete subfields. Research areas close to the knowledge base of professional practice would be particularly subject to such influence.

Finally, the topic of future prospects of scientific research in American medical schools deserves some comment. To date, basic science departments have remained relatively insulated from pressures facing the clinical wing of academic medicine. But medical educators express concern that this situation may not continue. Basic science departments are made vulnerable by their reliance on external research grants and on money originating from faculty practice. The latter support is received directly from deans' funds and indirectly through cost sharing on research grants. In the next decade economic problems facing medical schools are expected to intensify. Medical school deans are extremely worried about the potential impact of market competition and changes in Medicare and Medicaid reimbursement practices. If the financial plight of medical schools significantly worsens, basic science departments may be faced with declining institutional support and increasing pressures from the clinical wing of academic medicine. The dean of one elite medical school offered his perceptions: "Medical schools are becoming more like big corporations. That's what they are. We have the health care business, the industry right in the middle of the university. . . . The kinds of controls that a dean can exert are largely economic and managerial rather than moral or related to a vision of academic life. . . . [In the future] it will be much more difficult to see the academic health center as a place for the creation of knowledge for its own sake."

NOTES

1. Data provided by the National Center for Education Statistics on the disciplinary areas of four-year college and university professors suggests that 60 percent is a good estimate for the portion of the faculty in professional and vocational fields. In each of five universities examined in the UCLA Academic Profession Study, professional and vocational faculty made up 60 percent or more of the entire professoriat.

2. Wilson, Knapp, and Jones, "Growing Managerial Imperative of the Academic Medical Center," p. 101; information from staff members at the Association of American Medical Colleges.

3. Light, "Development of Professional Schools in America," pp. 345–346. Light's concept borrows from Robert Merton's notion of sociological ambivalence. See Merton, "Sociological Ambivalence," pp. 3–31.

4. Starr, Social Transformation of American Medicine.

5. I am indebted to Donald Light for emphasizing this point. See also Bucher, "Social Process and Power in a Medical School."

6. Jencks and Riesman, Academic Revolution, p. 218; also Lewis and Sheps, Sick Citadel.

7. Collins argues that employers value business degrees not because they are thought to ensure technical skills but because they indicate appropriate motivation and attitudes. See "Functional and Conflict Theories of Educational Stratification," pp. 1011–1012. On the nonscientific nature of business education, see Veblen, Higher Learning in America, p. 205.

8. Veysey, Emergence of the American University; Jencks and Riesman, Academic Revolution, pp. 12–20.

9. Parsons, "Professions," p. 542; Berelson, Graduate Education in the United States, p. 13.

10. Veblen, Higher Learning in America, pp. 203–210.

11. Even some present-day medical educators advocate the separation of basic science and clinical training. See, for example, Ebert, "Can the Education of the Physician Be Made More Rational?"

12. Wiebe, Search for Order; Bledstein, Culture of Professionalism.

13. Ludmerer, *Learning to Heal*, pp. 207–218.

14. Halpern, *The Emergent Profession*.

15. Flexner, *Medical Education in the United States and Canada;* Flexner, *Medical Education*.

16. Ludmerer, *Learning to Heal*, pp. 219–233.

17. Brown, *Rockefeller Medicine Man*.

18. Association of American Medical Colleges, "Full Time Medical School Faculty," p. 1; *Journal of the American Medical Association*, "81st Annual Report on Medical Education," p. 2913.

19. Gordon and Howell, *Higher Education for Business*, p. 247.

20. Ibid., p. 343.

21. Ibid.; Pierson, *Education of American Businessmen*.

22. On the history of business education, see Gordon and Howell, *Higher Education for Business;* Pierson, *Education of American Businessmen;* Kephart, McNulty, and McGrath, *Liberal Education and Business;* Cheit, *Useful Arts and the Liberal Tradition*, pp. 83–107.

23. National Center for Education Statistics, *Condition of Education*, p. 123. On long-term trends toward professional and preprofessional curriculums, see McGrath and Russell, *Are Liberal Arts Colleges Becoming Professional Schools?* pp. 9–12.

24. Wyngaarden, "Clinical Investigator as an Endangered Species," pp. 417–424; Siperstein, "Training of Internal Medicine Faculty—1980," pp. 5–9.

25. Behrman and Levin, "Are Business Schools Doing Their Jobs?" p. 141. Other critiques include Grayson, "Business of Business Schools"; Hacker, "Shame of Professional Schools."

26. Seldin, "Some Reflections on the Role of Basic Research and Service in Clinical Departments," p. 979.

27. Relman, "Who Will Pay for Medical Education in our Teaching Hospitals?" p. 21.

28. Figures provided by the Association of American Medical Colleges.

29. Petersdorf, "Is the Establishment Defensible?" p. 1056.

30. Spellman and Meiklejohn, "Faculty Tenure in American Medical Schools," p. 625.

31. Association of American Medical Colleges, *Faculty Appointment Policies and Practices*, p. 15.

32. Association of American Medical Colleges, "*Faculty Appointment Policies and Practices*," p. 8.

33. Spellman and Meiklejohn, "Faculty Tenure in American Medical Schools," p. 624.

34. Petersdorf, "Case Against Tenure in Medical Schools"; Spitzberg, "Academic Freedom and Tenure, Governance, and the Quality of Medical Education"; Smythe, Jones, and Wilson, "Tenure in Medical Schools in the 1980s."

35. Association of American Medical Colleges, "Full Time Faculty in 78

Medical Schools," p. 1; Fishman and Jolly, "Ph.D.'s in Clinical Departments," p. 19.

36. Gillis, "Role of the Basic Scientist in an Academic Clinical Setting," p. 2357.

BIBLIOGRAPHY

Association of American Medical Colleges. "Full Time Medical School Faculty." *Datagrams* 7 (1966): 1–2.

————. "Full Time Faculty in 78 U.S. Medical Schools." *Datagrams* 9 (1967): 1–2.

————. *Faculty Appointment Polices and Practices.* Vol. 1. Chicago, 1983.

Berelson, Bernard. *Graduate Education in the United States.* New York: McGraw-Hill, 1960.

Behrman, Jack N., and Richard Levin. "Are Business Schools Doing Their Job?" *Harvard Business Review* (January–February 1984): 140–147.

Bledstein, Burton J. *The Culture of Professionalism.* New York: Norton, 1976.

Brown, E. Richard. *Rockefeller Medicine Man.* Berkeley, Los Angeles, London: University of California Press, 1979.

Bucher, Rue. "Social Process and Power in a Medical School." In *Power in Organizations,* ed. Mayer Zald, 3–48. Nashville, Tenn.: Vanderbilt University Press, 1970.

Cheit, Earl F. *The Useful Arts and the Liberal Tradition.* New York: McGraw-Hill, 1975.

Collins, Randall. "Functional and Conflict Theories of Educational Stratification." *American Sociological Review* 36 (1971): 1002–1019.

Ebert, Robert H. "Can the Education of the Physician Be Made More Rational?" *New England Journal of Medicine* 305 (1981): 1343–1346.

Fishman, Alfred P., and Paul Jolly. "Ph.D.'s in Clinical Departments." *The Psychologist* 24 (1981): 17–21.

Flexner, Abraham. *Medical Education in the U.S. and Canada.* New York: Carnegie Foundation for the Advancement of Teaching, 1910.

————. *Medical Education: A Comparative Study.* New York: Macmillan, 1925.

Gillis, C. N. "The Role of the Basic Scientist in an Academic Clinical Setting." *Federation Proceedings* 2 (1979): 2355–2358.

Gordon, Robert A., and James E. Howell. *Higher Education for Business.* New York: Columbia University Press, 1959.

Grayson, C. Jackson. "The Business of Business Schools." *The Wharton Magazine* (Spring 1977): 46–81.

Hacker, Andrew. "The Shame of Professional Schools." *Harpers* 263 (1981): 22–28.

Halpern, Sydney A. *The Emergent Profession: A Social History of American Pediatrics.* Berkeley, Los Angeles, London: University of California Press. Forthcoming.

Jencks, Christopher, and David Riesman. *The Academic Revolution.* New York: Doubleday, 1968.

Journal of the American Medical Association. "81st Annual Report on Medical Education in the U.S., 1980–1981" 246 (1981): 2913–2986.

Kephart, William M., James E. McNulty, and Earl J. McGrath. *Liberal Education and Business.* New York: Teachers College, Columbia University, 1963.

Lewis, Irving J., and Cecil G. Sheps. *The Sick Citadel.* Cambridge, Mass.: Oelgeschlager, Gunn and Hain, 1983.

Light, Donald W. "The Development of Professional Schools in America." In *The Transformation of Higher Learning 1860–1930,* ed. Konrad H. Jarausch. Chicago: University of Chicago Press, 1983.

Ludmerer, Kenneth M. *Learning To Heal: The Development of American Medical Education.* New York: Basic Books, 1985.

McGrath, Earl J., and Charles H. Russell. *Are Liberal Arts Colleges Becoming Professional Schools?* New York: Teachers College Press, 1958.

Merton, Robert K. "Sociological Ambivalence." In *Sociological Ambivalence and Other Essays,* ed. Robert K. Merton, 3–31. New York: Free Press, 1976.

National Center for Education Statistics. *The Condition of Education* (1983): 123.

Parsons, Talcott. "Professions." In *International Encyclopedia of the Social Sciences,* ed. David L. Sills. 12: 536–547. New York: Macmillan and Free Press, 1968.

Petersdorf, Robert G. "Is the Establishment Defensible?" *The New England Journal of Medicine* 309 (1983): 1053–1057.

————. "The Case Against Tenure in Medical Schools." *Journal of the American Medical Association* 251 (1984): 920–924.

Pierson, Frank C. *The Education of American Businessmen.* New York: McGraw-Hill, 1959.

Relman, Arnold S. "Who Will Pay for Medical Education in Our Teaching Hospitals?" *Science* 226 (1984): 20–23.

Seldin, Donald W. "Some Reflections on the Role of Basic Research and Service in Clinical Departments." *Journal of Clinical Investigation* 45 (1966): 976–979.

Siperstein, Marvin D. "The Training of Internal Medicine Faculty—1980." *Transactions of the Association of American Physicians* 93 (1980): 1–13.

Smythe, Cheves McC., Amber B. Jones, and Marjorie P. Wilson. "Tenure in Medical Schools in the 1980s." *Journal of Medical Education* 57 (1982): 349–360.

Spellman, Mitchell W., and Gordon Meiklejohn. "Faculty Tenure in American Medical Schools." *Journal of Medical Education* 52 (1977): 623–632.

Spitzberg, Irving J. "Academic Freedom and Tenure, Governance, and the Quality of Medical Education." Unpublished paper.

Starr, Paul. *The Social Transformation of American Medicine.* New York: Basic Books, 1983.

Veblen, Thorstein. *The Higher Learning in America.* New York: Heubsch, 1918.

Veysey, Laurence R. *The Emergence of the American University.* Chicago: University of Chicago Press, 1965.

Wiebe, Robert H. *The Search for Order.* New York: Hill and Wang, 1967.

Wilson, Marjorie P., Richard M. Knapp, and Amber B. Jones. "The Growing
    Managerial Imperative of the Academic Medical Center." In *Health Man-
    agement for Tomorrow,* ed. Samuel Levey and Thomas McCarthy. Philadel-
    phia: Lippincott, 1980.
Wyngaarden, James B. "The Clinical Investigator as an Endangered Species."
    Bulletin of the New York Academy of Medicine 57 (1981): 415–426.

8
Many Sectors, Many Professions

Kenneth P. Ruscio

The roles of academics—their tasks and attitudes and behaviors, their sense of professionalism and sense of being part of a larger academic community—are functions of the institutions to which they are attached. But the institution is not the sole determinant; the discipline also exerts a powerful influence. Both discipline and institution thus link the individual to the profession. Contrary to some descriptions, the two do not compete until one subdues the other, transforming the professor into either a "local" or a "cosmopolitan." Instead a subtle, intricate interaction with many nuances occurs as we move through the various disciplines and across the many institutions, each with its own culture. Biologists speak of a genotype and a phenotype. The genotype represents the fundamental instructions to the organism and its potential for survival and growth; the phenotype represents the actual manifestation of that potential in a particular physical setting. In the nature-nurture debate a middle position is increasingly agreed upon: each organism has a blueprint, the expression of which depends on the environment, with some traits and characteristics remaining forever latent and others fully revealing themselves. From this perspective we view the American academic profession as a creature of its organizational setting. What distinguishes the American professoriat and makes it so complicated and intriguing is not its genotype (the academic profession everywhere organizes itself around areas of knowledge or disciplines) but its phenotype: American higher education is characterized by an array of extremely diverse institutional settings.

If academics in the United States have come to accept institutional diversity and the consequent division of labor as admirable accommodations to the widely scattered and often conflicting demands placed on the system of higher education, they at times seem unwilling to accept, or are uncomfortable with, the academic profession as a mirror for that diversity. Acknowledging that the academician at a modest unknown college and his purported counterpart at an elite research university perform differently, have different incentives, and receive awards based on different criteria rubs against the belief that all academics are united by a common bond of lofty values, sometimes called a scientific ethos. Perhaps some of the discomfort derives from the "united we stand, divided we fall" notion, which implies that a plurality of interests is vulnerable to greater control from nonprofessional, nonacademic powers outside the academy. A countervailing aphorism then might be "know thyself." To overlook the diversity within the profession is to induce a false sense of solidarity. This chapter describes the heterogeneity within the profession in arrangements of work, patterns of institutional governance, and the values and beliefs of academics. The discussion is guided by the following premises:

1. Institutional structure shapes the professorial role. Structures of postsecondary educational institutions reflect their missions. Because missions vary considerably, structures and professorial roles will similarly differ. Consequently, a political scientist who belongs to a department with only one other colleague and who devotes 20 percent of his time to research probably conducts a very different type of investigation than a political scientist in a much larger department who also spends 20 percent of his time in research.

2. Institutional differences operate more covertly than disciplinary differences. Diverse disciplinary cultures are a readily acknowledged condition of the profession and receive tacit acceptance through the formal structures of departments (this is not to say that we understand the implications of the disciplinary differences). Institutional differences, however, remain in the shadows. A discipline is the first mark of identity a professor receives; institutional affiliation comes after the training, after the socialization. It is often depicted as a necessary evil to be tolerated in the performance of a professor's real duties. A discipline provides the opportunity; an institution imposes the obligation. And, except in rare cases of highly distinctive colleges, the in-

stitutional ethos lacks the clarity and sharpness of the disciplinary one. Yet institutional affiliation is indispensable to a professor's identity.

3. The preceding two propositions imply a greater division of labor within the professoriat. It also suggests the rise of separate professions, taking *profession* to mean different work styles, reference groups, objectives, organization of authority, and attitudes.

4. The turbulence of the higher education system in the United States causes some institutions, over time, to accumulate various missions that layer themselves like geological rock strata one upon the other, resulting in peculiar combinations. This in turn leads to idiosyncratic combinations of academics.

Though institutional boundaries conveniently demarcate clusters of academics, the situation is actually more complicated. There is diversity within diversity as different types of professionals exist side by side in the same setting.

The observations presented here are largely the products of intensive interviews, lasting between one and two hours, with nearly 150 members of the American professoriat; they are the outcomes of research done as part of the UCLA Academic Profession Study. The sample was chosen to range across different kinds of universities and colleges as well as across disciplines: the interviews were conducted in sixteen institutions representing six institutional types, from leading research universities to community colleges, and in six subject fields—physics, biology, political science, English, medicine, and business. The preceding two chapters in this volume focused on disciplinary differences. Here my attention is given to institutional settings and their effects.

I set out by establishing and portraying the rich institutional diversity of American higher education. Three areas of analysis follow: the implications of this diversity for an academic's work, his participation in institutional governance, and his values and attitudes. These components were not chosen randomly. They provide important bases for cross-national comparisons among systems of higher education.[1]

DIVERSITY

Diversity is the central feature of American higher education, but differences in the professoriat in different institutions have never attracted much attention. When Logan Wilson wrote *The Academic Man* in 1942, he confined his research to such leading universities as Harvard, Chicago, Columbia, and "others that rank high in the universe of learning." These places were surely more pleasant and easier to visit than an isolated liberal arts or a rural land-grant college, but even then were unlike other institutions in the country. Understandably, Wilson's academic man was a scholar frustrated by the burdens of administration and teaching.[2]

Despite a few such important statements as Lazarfeld and Thielens's *The Academic Mind*, research on the profession faltered; it wasn't until the 1960s that the topic was resurrected—and then in a dramatic fashion. Reporting on the "academic revolution," Jencks and Riesman found that the academic profession had taken over higher education. "The shape of American higher education," they wrote, "is largely a response to the assumptions and demands of the academic profession."[3] To demonstrate their thesis, they studied colleges with highly distinctive missions, such as historically black, church-related, and single-sex institutions. Finding consistencies throughout the colleges more significant than differences, they predicted that "the model for the future is the 'university-college,' and the result is likely to be a continuing trend toward meritocracy."[4]

Responding in part to Jencks and Riesman, Ladd and Lipset asserted, a few years later, that the picture was considerably altered. In their study *The Divided Academy*, they found a variety of political attitudes and opinions among what was purportedly a relatively homogeneous group of professors. Curiously, they attributed the differences primarily to individual disciplinary backgrounds, and it wasn't until they discussed unionization and collective bargaining that institutional differences seemed to have become a central concern. An intriguing paradox surfaced: the most politically conservative professors were among those more frequently found at nonelite colleges and the more liberally inclined were those at the elite universities; the sentiment for faculty unionization was much stronger among the most conservative. The authors attributed this in part to the very different views of the profession, and thus cast some doubt on the idea of a consistent, agreed-upon definition of an "academic."[5]

A different kind of book came along more recently (1983); its subtitle, *The Management Revolution*, suggests that its thesis runs counter to the theories of Jencks and Riesman. George Keller attacks the notion that the academic profession is a self-regulating group of scholars who run their institutions: "The basic myth is that each college is close to an Athenian democracy of professorial scholars who know each other and share a bundle of values and aspirations which they practice in their institutional lives."[6] Faculty ought to recognize that their professional identities are also intertwined with membership in an organization. Sounding the call for an academic counterrevolution, Keller proclaimed, "Retrenchment, constricting finances, new competition, marketing, and rapid changes in the academic and demographic areas all spell the end of the traditional, unobtrusive style of organizational leadership on campuses."[7]

The interaction between the professor and the institution is thus an issue of some significance and timeliness. The first task, then, is to describe the institutional setting, especially its diversity, and offer an explanation of why differences among colleges are increasing.

In 1982, 12.3 million students, 86 percent of whom were undergraduates, attended 2,661 postsecondary institutions. Doctoral-granting universities accounted for 6.2 percent of the total institutional population, comprehensive colleges (diverse postgraduate programs, but no significant doctoral production) 15.3 percent, general baccalaureate-awarding colleges 27.4 percent, and two-year institutions 45.6 percent. Enrollments differ widely among institutions, with some colleges accepting about one hundred students and some universities having close to 50,000. Faculty size also varies considerably. Although nearly half of the institutions are community colleges, they enlist less than a quarter (22 percent) of the full-time institutional faculty while universities, fewer in number, employ nearly 32 percent. Four-year colleges make up the difference (46 percent).[8] The diversity becomes even more apparent when the significant influence of part-time faculty is taken into account. No reliable figures exist on that group; one frequently cited estimate claims that nearly one-third of the total number of 667,000 faculty are part-time.[9] Moreover, the use of part-timers varies throughout the system: community colleges rely disproportionately on these individuals, a strategy that permits them to respond to the often volatile demands on their curricula.

But the raw statistics cannot possibly convey the extreme qualitative differences existing throughout the system and within the sectors. As higher education moved from an elite system to one that offered virtually unlimited access to graduates of secondary schools, the institutions began to distinguish themselves from one another, to carve out portions of a diverse market, and to adapt to the numerous demands placed on them by diverse constituencies. There was a division of labor. No single institution or single sector could possibly simultanously accommodate demands for excellence and access; thus colleges and universities, sometimes deliberately and sometimes compelled by external forces, acquired functions and developed roles different from their postsecondary cousins—circumstances that enabled the system to responsively enlarge its place in society.

Clearly, institutional missions, whether of research universities or community colleges, elite or nonelite liberal arts colleges, state universities or comprehensive colleges, are undergoing reassessment and introspection. Consider, for example, the state colleges. Pulled by the research glamour of the leading universities, pushed by the preferences of budget-controlling legislatures to contribute to the economic growth of the state, and confused by the pragmatic demands of the students who enroll in such large numbers, the "college of the forgotten American" is allowing its "once sharp mission" to fade into an "undistinguished comprehensiveness." As put by George Weathersby, "Many state colleges have decided that a clear mission is less desirable than a large institution that is diffuse in purpose. Such vagueness of purpose has in turn led to confusion in the minds of students, employers, potential donors, and legislators about the identity, purpose and priorities of these institutions."[10] Attempts to define the role are usually processes of elimination cast in negative terms: state colleges are not research universities or liberal arts colleges, nor are they supposed to preempt the technical and vocational training of the community colleges. But an overview of a state college would show some research, some conventional liberal arts instruction, and some vocational services, in varying degrees, depending on the specific institution.

Research universities also have their concerns. "The leading American universities have never had any clear objectives; the university is confused as to its social role and political obligations, is divided internally, and is the object of political dispute."[11] But what appears to be confusion may be an ingenious adaptation to conflicting demands. Clark Kerr argues that in the multiversity, the organizational complexity of the modern research university is actually a means of coping with an array of research, teaching, and service missions.[12] Whatever the interpretation, research universities have at least a set of objectives, which may be contradictory; the trick is to minimize the situations where many contradictory objectives collide.

Community colleges are perhaps organizationally the most confusing, since enormous variation exists within that sector. In some regions, especially the Northeast, community colleges traditionally educate students along conventional lines, intending to transfer them to other colleges for completion of the baccalaureate. In other locations this transfer function is shared with and frequently surpassed by an occupational one. The colleges also differ by size, which is perhaps the primary predictor of other differences. Though the diversity within this sector cannot be fully addressed here, one characteristic ought to be noted. Students, even within the same college and the same classroom, may range from high school seniors to retired workers seeking continuing education to college graduates retraining for a new career. This last category—the "reverse transfer"—is becoming an increasingly widespread phenomenon. In short, the demands on the community college are multiple; a common thread, however, would surely center around the overwhelmingly complex instructional burden.

If diversity is predictable in the community college sector, a relatively new group of colleges that arose during a short period of time, it is not predictable in the liberal arts sector, which has existed throughout the history of higher education in the United States. Liberal arts colleges have maintained a relatively consistent commitment to the ideal of providing general knowledge and the development of intellectual capacities. Once the distinction between nonelite and elite is acknowledged, some uniformity across the colleges appears. Unlike community colleges, liberal arts colleges are almost entirely private and are uniformly small. Students are usually from the traditional eighteen- to twenty-two-year-old age group, although several nonelite colleges facing severe declines in the numbers of these students are designing alternative programs to attract the nontraditional student. Even in this seemingly homogeneous world, mission is under stress. Lord Ashby has noted that "the prime purpose of the liberal arts bachelor course in a four-year college is not clear any longer, and in many colleges the concentration on preparing students to enter professional schools makes it difficult for those colleges to develop an independent and indigenous curriculum."[13] Barzun noted that liberal arts colleges are being threatened from two directions: from below, high schools and community colleges invade the first two years of the curriculum; from above, graduate and professional schools infiltrate the last two years.[14] The result is that some colleges trade up and others trade down, a practice that may result in severe tensions between liberal arts and occupational subjects.[15] Some colleges now claim the "applied" liberal arts as their forte, a semantic creation that allows them to maintain credibility with their old constituencies while seducing new ones.

The point is not that the missions of the sectors are confused or ambiguous. Rather they are different and set apart from other institutions, having been designed to accommodate a particular segment of the higher education market. This may be explained in part by an almost unalterable law of organizational behavior: as demands increase and constituencies diversify, there must be a structural response by the system, usually in the form of increased differentiation.

In higher education a more subtle explanation also bears heavily on a discussion of the professoriat. In general, American higher education is highly interactive with its constituencies. Walter Metzger has pointed out that colleges and universities today are "delocalized." Though an institution used to operate with little direct interference from society and made decisions relatively unimpeded by outside forces, we may now observe "the flow of decisional power from authorities on the campus to those resident outside. Richer, larger, more complex than before, the typical modern institution is less self-directive than before."[16] While delocalization may be a pervasive trend throughout higher education, and important too for a discussion of the professoriat, it assumes different patterns in different institutions and sectors: there are in fact distinctly "local" patterns of delocalization. The influence of the federal government on a university that receives a substantial amount of research support from it will be, for example, significantly different than the impact of the local or state government on a community college. Conversely, the impact of the surrounding town will be far different for a community college than for a research university and will differ in still other ways for a state college.

For higher education systems, "fragmentation is the dominant force. It is in the nature of academic systems to be increasingly pluralistic in the production of patterns of thought and in the precise definitions of proper behavior."[17] The impact of this fragmentation on the academic profession and the resulting differences among the academic professoriat are very likely not simply small adjustments of a pervasive ethos to minor local variations; instead, they are significant phenomena that severely question the existence of a unified, integrated community of scholars.

WORK

The transmission and creation of knowledge require a mixture of tasks that joined together reflect individual preferences, disciplinary backgrounds, and institutional imperatives. The academic world has a relatively high tolerance for idiosyncrasy in work habits; styles vary considerably within departments and institutions. They also vary across sectors, where random differences appear to arrange them-

TABLE 8.1

RESEARCH ACTIVITY OF FACULTY BY TYPE AND QUALITY OF INSTITUTION
(percentage of faculty)

	Type of Institution							
	Universities			*Four-year colleges*			*Community*	*All*
Research activity	*High*	*Medium*	*Low*	*High*	*Medium*	*Low*	*colleges*	*institutions*
Inactive, not currently publishing	9	14	21	23	37	48	70	33
Active, no recent publications	12	15	23	23	26	24	16	20
Few current publications	51	52	46	45	34	26	12	37
Many current publications	28	20	11	9	3	3	2	11

SOURCE: Trow and Fulton, "Research Activity in American Higher Education," 1975.

selves into discernible patterns. Three propositions about the sectorial activities of academics are here suggested.

First, some research is performed in all sectors. True, not all academics engage in research, nor do they practice it in equal amounts in all sectors. According to Fulton and Trow's analysis of the 1969 Carnegie Commission survey data,[18] and as shown in table 8.1, research (defined as publication) hangs by a slim thread in community colleges, but nearly 80 percent of those employed in high-quality research universities claim it as an activity they perform. Between these two extremes, research activity and institutional quality decrease in tandem, with a sharp break occurring between universities of medium and low quality and another between four-year colleges of high and medium quality. There are thus four general categories: high- and medium-quality universities, lower-level universities and elite four-year colleges, other four-year colleges, and community colleges.

Defining research in terms of publication has its problems, although it is hard to think of a more appropriate surrogate measure. Even so, other evidence tends to corroborate that academics in different sectors devote a significant amount of time to noninstructional activities. In 1981 the National Science Foundation reported the results of an intensive survey of science, social science, and engineering faculty.[19] With the sample divided into two broad institutional categories— universities (doctorate-granting) and four-year colleges (non-doctorate-granting)—the survey requested the faculty to keep a weekly log of how they spent their time. Tables 8.2 and 8.3 display some interesting and predictable patterns. University faculty devote significantly more time to research and less time to instructional activities. They also spend slightly more time on general administrative tasks and on efforts that produce income beyond the faculty salary.

Across the disciplines, different patterns, even within the same sector, are evident. In universities, for example, political scientists spend considerably more time on instructional activities in, and especially out of, the classroom and considerably less time on research than do their colleagues in the biological sciences. Some of the data also support Fulton and Trow's hypothesis that research activity in a research setting translates into institutional power: individuals in disciplines with higher rates of research spend more time on administrative tasks. The exceptions are in engineering and economics, two disciplines in which a more than average amount of time is spent on consulting. In those subject areas that tend to be highly interactive with their constituencies, consulting opportunities may be a function of previous success in research, and consulting may supplant some portion of research time.

All disciplines make relatively heavy demands for teaching in four-year colleges, but the heaviest are in the natural, not the social, sciences, a reversal of the pattern found in universities. This is very likely a result of the laboratory time required. Also, to judge from this data, the most active researchers in non-doctorate-granting colleges are in the social sciences. Fulton and Trow found few differences in publication rates among the disciplines in these institutions; this raises questions about the ways in which research is construed across the disciplines and, as we shall see below, across the institutions.[20]

A second proposition strongly supported in the literature is that, despite the presence of research in all sectors, teaching is the dominant preferred activity. Again, the results of the Carnegie survey are instructive. In answer to the question, "Do your interests lie primarily in teaching or research?," only 4 percent indicated a strong attraction for research while another 20 percent leaned toward it. A heavy interest in teaching was reported by 43 percent, while 34 percent were inclined toward it. Table 8.4 shows that, predictably, these interests vary by sector. Like the distribution of research activity, research preference falls into the same four categories: high- and medium-quality universities, low-quality universities and elite four-year colleges, other four-year colleges, and community colleges.

Such findings permit Everett Ladd to state, "There is, on the surface, a fairly good fit between what faculty want to do—as teachers and researchers—and what they are required to do."[21] Interviews with

TABLE 8.2

HOURS PER WEEK DEVOTED TO PROFESSIONAL ACTIVITIES IN DOCTORATE-GRANTING INSTITUTIONS

Type of activity	All fields	Engineering	Life sciences	Biological sciences	Physical sciences	Social sciences	Economics	Political science
				Disciplines and Professional Fields				
Total instructional	14.9	15.5	13.4	13.5	13.8	18.2	17.2	23.1
Classroom	4.3	4.6	4.1	4.2	3.2	4.9	5.1	5.6
Other	10.5	10.8	9.2	9.3	10.6	13.3	12.1	17.4
Total research	15.6	14.7	18.8	20.0	20.5	10.5	14.1	7.8
Total public services, administration, & miscellaneous professional	9.5	10.0	11.0	10.2	8.0	8.4	8.8	6.1
Public service	1.6	1.7	2.2	1.3	.6	1.6	2.2	1.3
Administration	5.3	6.1	5.4	5.5	5.3	4.8	5.1	3.3
Miscellaneous professional	2.6	2.1	3.4	3.4	2.2	2.0	1.6	1.4
Total outside income-producing activities	4.2	5.8	3.6	3.7	3.9	4.8	2.8	3.8
Consulting	1.2	3.3	.8	.8	1.1	.9	1.3	.6
Publication	2.4	1.7	2.1	2.3	2.5	3.6	1.1	2.9
Other	.6	.8	.7	.6	.3	.3	.4	.3
Continuing & educational professional enrichment	4.1	3.0	3.9	4.2	3.4	6.1	4.7	6.0
All activities	48.2	49.1	50.6	51.7	49.6	48.1	47.6	46.8

SOURCE: NSF, "Activities of Science and Engineering Faculty," 1981.

TABLE 8.3

Hours per Week Devoted to Professional Activities in Non-Doctorate-Granting Institutions

Type of activity	All fields	Disciplines and Professional Fields						
		Engineering	Life sciences	Biological sciences	Physical sciences	Social sciences	Economics	Political science
Total instructional	21.6	23.2	21.0	21.1	23.9	19.4	17.6	14.9
Classroom	8.4	9.8	8.2	8.4	10.0	7.4	7.9	6.6
Other	13.2	13.3	12.8	12.7	13.9	12.0	9.6	8.3
Total research	5.0	3.2	6.5	6.7	3.8	5.9	7.7	7.0
Total public services, administration, & miscellaneous professional	7.4	6.0	8.5	8.5	6.8	6.5	8.9	6.9
Public service	2.1	1.2	4.3	4.4	1.4	1.6	2.1	1.4
Administration	4.3	3.6	3.6	3.5	4.4	3.8	5.9	4.0
Miscellaneous professional	1.0	1.2	.6	.6	.9	1.1	.9	1.5
Total outside income-producing activities	3.1	10.3	1.7	1.2	2.7	2.1	2.2	3.4
Consulting	1.2	4.8	.3	.3	.5	.5	1.5	.1
Publication	1.3	4.4	.6	.6	1.6	1.4	.1	2.7
Other	.7	1.2	.9	.3	.6	.2	.5	.6
Continuing & educational professional enrichment	5.5	3.2	5.5	5.6	4.9	6.7	6.0	5.8
All activities	42.7	43.6	43.2	43.2	42.1	40.6	42.3	37.9

Source: NSF, "Activities of Science and Engineering Faculty," 1981.

TABLE 8.4

PRIMARY PROFESSIONAL INTERESTS OF FACULTY MEMBERS BY
INSTITUTIONAL TYPE
(percentage of faculty)

	Type of Institution							
	Universities			*Four-year colleges*			*Community*	*All*
Primary interest	High	Medium	Low	High	Medium	Low	*colleges*	*institutions*
Very heavily in research	9	7	4	4	1	1	1	4
Both research and teaching but leaning toward research	41	33	24	22	11	9	4	20
Both research and teaching but leaning toward teaching	35	37	39	39	37	34	18	34
Very heavily in teaching	15	23	23	35	51	56	77	43

SOURCE: Trow and Fulton, "Research Activity in American Higher Education," 1975.

faculty tend to support that interpretation. At one elite liberal arts college, an assistant professor in physics reports that he spends about 80 percent of his work time (sixty to seventy hours per week) on teaching.

Teaching is an extremely high priority for me. I am in these kinds of institutions because I like to teach, and it is very important to me. It is very challenging, it is very satisfying. Research is also challenging, satisfying, and rewarding but I find teaching a little more so. Therefore, my priorities will always be on that side, not to the extent of excluding research, just to the extent of it not being more important and not taking a greater percentage of my time.

There may, of course, be resistance to oppressive teaching loads regardless of the sector: a preference for teaching relative to research is not the same as a request for more courses to teach. When asked how they would prefer to spend their time—not how they actually spend it—most academics mention a desire for more research time. If this is interpreted more broadly as discretionary time that would allow the academic to "keep up in the field" (in teaching settings) or to be relieved of administrative chores (in all settings), such requests are not inconsistent with the earlier findings of a teaching temperament throughout academia. One English professor who teaches eight different courses a year lamented the time spent in teaching. "As a faculty we have been trying to negotiate any kind of lightening of the teaching load. I find, increasingly, that by the time I have done the work that I have to for school—preparation, and the like—there is no time left for anything else. . . . Even to read a whole novel seems like a complete frivolity." When asked if he would like to do research with any extra time, he said he "would probably do just enough to get tenure."

If the favored normative stance of academics is teaching, then the third proposition about the work styles of academics is somewhat paradoxical: "Faculty believe that the most meritorious behavior of academic man is the performance of significant research."[22] This stands as one of the most curious characteristics of American higher education. Wilson found in 1942 that "professional recognition is achieved through activities engaging a minor portion of the average man's energies."[23] Some twenty years later, Caplow and McGee also noted the anomaly: "Perhaps the leading problem for the individual faculty member," they wrote, "is the incongruity between his job assignment and the work which determines his success or failure in the discipline."[24] Certainly part of the reason for this is a "Gresham's law" of academic evaluation: the hard, tangible results of research productivity drive out the soft, intangible contributions of teaching or service to the institution. And academic status or national recognition still depends on criteria that can be easily compared across institutions; the relatively ambiguous criterion of instructional quality stands in poor contrast to reputation in the discipline.

These three propositions together present a confusing state. Patterns of work across institutions differ significantly, yet there is only one model for the profession.[25] Depending on the setting, this one model has several different versions. Each sector seems to worship the god of research, but organized religion reflects the local culture. Some are more religious than others, and some allow religion to play a different role in their lives.

Clearly, disciplinary labor is divided. The activities of the professor and the rationale for those activities reflect the mission of the college; because the structures of the institutions vary so much, they also influence the way certain tasks are performed. Taking the clearest example—the liberal arts college—discussions with faculty members in the sciences, social sciences, and the humanities reveal a cynical attitude toward the leaders in the discipline. "Trivial," "insignificant," and "narrow" are used to describe most of the research found in the leading journals. Such failings are blamed, by liberal arts college members, on the counterproductive publish-or-perish syndrome. As one less critical biology professor termed it, those in the research universities excel in "vertical" research; by contrast, those in the high-quality liberal arts college excel in "horizontal" research that transcends the disciplines and provides innovative ways of looking at the current state of knowledge.

There are good reasons a faculty member at a liberal arts college would take this stance. He or she teaches undergraduates, most of whom have only a rudimentary knowledge of the discipline, and whose interest will likely extend no farther than the next semester. Also, the faculty member belongs to a department consisting of only a few colleagues chosen to cover the entire discipline. Rarely do two members of the same subfield have the opportunity to work together. The teaching load is heavy, the coverage of topics broad, the audience are generalists, and colleagues specialize in different fields.

Nevertheless, an obstacle in one setting may turn out to be an opportunity in another. The chances of socializing and collaborating with faculty members in other disciplines appear to be greater in liberal arts colleges. A biologist was planning a course with members of the drama department on how scientists are viewed in films, while a political scientist and a literature professor jointly taught a course on politics and the novel, a subject about which they had also written. The breadth required to teach a variety of courses forces the teacher to make connections across subfields, a luxury not afforded those who must specialize.

Within institutions and departments there is a research context shaped by interrelated structural variables. These include department size, generality of courses (for example, ratio of graduate to undergraduate courses taught by an individual), teaching load, coverage of subfields, and interaction with other departments. We can hypothesize that the nature of research is determined in part by the organizational setting.

Other major influences shaping the nature of research are its rationale or purpose and the institutional attitudes toward it. At a liberal arts college one department responded to faculty dissatisfaction with teaching obligations by instituting a policy whereby faculty were expected to spend one day a week "investing in future students," a euphemism for research. Teaching remains the core activity around which other activities revolve. In this case faculty would spend roughly 20 percent of their time keeping up in the field, conducting research, and writing—activities taking them away from current students but enabling them to better serve future students. A molecular biologist at a leading research university, in contrast, spoke of his

love of teaching because he was training future researchers in biochemistry. His commitment to teaching sounded as passionate as any
voiced at a liberal arts college but for a very different reason: a much
different activity reinforced a commitment to advancement of the
discipline which was clearly his primary motivation.

Along with these diverse rationales for research come different
definitions for it. At a leading research university, the demands for
excellence in scholarship are apt to be precise and well understood.
On the other hand, scholarship at a liberal arts college may be more
broadly defined. One respondent spoke of tenure awarded on the
basis of a "gestalt." Here, in evaluating a professor's record, the department and the administration look for contributions demonstrating
professional vitality, their precise nature varying from case to case.
In another liberal arts college, a rating of excellence in scholarship is
awarded if the individual has met the following conditions: (1) pursued a systematic research and study program leading toward further
publication or the presentation of a new course; (2) authored a high-
quality book or an equivalent set of articles and/or monographs; or
instead of this (3) devised a set of procedures or a syllabus that may
be expected to substantially change the teaching of the discipline in
first-rate colleges and universities.[26]

The contrast between research at a liberal arts college and at a
research university illustrates a trend that is likely to exacerbate this
disciplinary division of labor. Repeatedly, we heard that disciplines
themselves are increasingly fragmented because of the specialization
required to make a contribution. Historically, biology has been a federated discipline comprised of numerous subfields. In the United
States there are now over 100 professional associations in this field,
two of which periodically attempt, always unsuccessfully, to unite
some of the others. Physics is a more integrated field. Still, most of
the scientific conferences tend to consist of irregular meetings of specialists focusing on a particular problem. In this way the invisible
college is institutionalized, placing further barriers between leading
researchers and those doing horizontal research. The American Political Science Association reported a 25 percent decrease in membership over the last ten years; it blames this decline on increasing specialization and proliferation of splinter organizations.[27] As disciplines
become more fragmented and the need to specialize becomes greater,
academics in institutions that emphasize undergraduate teaching and
introductory courses will find themselves either having less affinity
with the academic research community or experiencing a sharper and
less complementary distinction between research and teaching. In-

creasing differentiation among institutions interacts with increasing fragmentation of the disciplines.

Liberal arts colleges and research universities provide excellent illustrations of the differences in work patterns, but structures and missions of colleges in other sectors also place their distinctive imprint on the work of academics. Instructors at a community college identified themselves as educators, not as members of a discipline (e.g., political scientists, biologists, physicists, and the like). According to the president of the college, "The discipline is the means for the community college teacher—not the end. We simply view the discipline as the means, the tool. . . . I am reaching students, but my means happens to be English composition, or American history, or economics." In this college there were no departments, only divisions; the teaching load for each instructor was five courses a semester. One instructor with a doctorate in American diplomatic history taught courses in political science, American history, American government, and European history. Given these structural constraints, it is not surprising that instructors devote nearly all of their time to teaching and working with students.

Yet another pattern may emerge at a state or comprehensive college. These institutions vary from state to state and region to region. But in some colleges where the teaching load is heavy and where research is encouraged but only minimally supported, academics can fashion innovative professional careers outside the college and outside the conventional boundaries of the discipline. An example is the English professor who appears regularly on local television and who edits a quasi-serious, widely read newsletter lampooning the educational system. Another is a political scientist located near Washington and New York who writes commentaries for newspapers and consults frequently with international organizations. A business professor consults nearly three days a week with a real estate firm. A political scientist becomes heavily involved in environmental causes, assuming a variety of leadership roles in associations committed to the cause. Though all were reluctant to call these activities research, they did consider them an important part of their professional lives. Academics in other sectors occasionally assume these roles, but the incidence of this pattern in state and comprehensive colleges seems to surpass the practice elsewhere, suggesting that the broad missions of these institutions and the affinity these institutions have for these local constituencies are reflected in extremely catholic views of the profession among its faculty.

Work patterns differ among the professoriat, but there are other ways of viewing fragmentation. How faculty govern themselves, for example, varies by institution. It is to these differences we now turn.

AUTHORITY

Education, as a process, does not easily fit within organizational constraints. Organizations, by definition, impose routines, eliminate personal vagaries, and have a predisposition toward an efficiency not always hospitable to the creativity and individualism required in the pursuit of knowledge. Nevertheless, the activities of higher education do indeed occur in organizations and must therefore continually balance administrative and educative imperatives. Of course not every decision has both an administrative and an educational dimension, nor do the two necessarily clash, the one prevailing over the other. On the contrary, any decision results from the blend. Kim Cameron explained, in a slightly different context, that higher education institutions are "Janusian." Like the two-faced Roman god Janus, they must always look in two directions simultaneously and must act on apparently contradictory demands.[28] But as we look across the sectors of higher education and peer more closely at specific institutions, we find some settings characterized by a management temperament and others by an academic temperament. This distinction is akin to the difference between collegial and bureaucratic forms of governance, but "temperament" better conveys the idea that authority arrangements, aside from having a formal structure, also depend on the attitudes and perceptions of the participants.

The present situation in higher education is extremely complex. There are distinctly local forms of governance fashioned by the history of the institution, the organizational structure, the leadership style of past and present administrators, and the overall mission of the college. As these independent variables change, each form of governance changes—and so does the temperament. A managerial spirit arises in settings where the faculty, their representatives, and the administration debate issues similar to those in a conventional employer-employee relationship. There are managers and employees. There are discussions about work loads, assigned office hours, and salaries. Organizational expectations for individuals become formalized and quantified. By contrast, an academic temperament reflects a more guildlike approach: decentralized decisions; reliance on the professional's expertise; and tolerance for redundancy and ambiguity in decision making.

An institution does not have one temperament to the exclusion of the other; more often one type sets the tone for some decisions, whereas the other provides a particular ambience for different ones. But the distinction has some validity on its face. As higher education institutions require more and more management, the role of the faculty in governance evolves and adjusts to local conditions. The patterns become distinctly different, and the severity of the tension between a managerial and an academic perspective is one general indicator of the differences. To explain this a more systematic approach is required, beginning with the construction of a simple model.

The faculty role in governance is shaped by organizational design. A model of the design is a heuristic device that does not capture reality; it serves as a standard. After the organization's deviation from the standard is determined, comparisons may be made among institutions and across sectors.

The basic components are the organizational units. They form a chain beginning with individual faculty members and move in sequence to the department, the school or division, the college, the system, and the governmental bodies. Each link in the chain constitutes an authority relationship, and each relationship has different characteristics. The connection between the individual and his department, for example, though formal and rule-bound in some respects, may also be very informal, marked by exchanges in the corridor, advice from senior to junior members, or lunches at the faculty center. In contrast, the connection between the institution and the system assumes the intricate configuration of an organization in relation to its environment.

But the authority arrangements in higher education are not a simple hierarchy. Among many other permutations there is a network of relations between the individual and the college, the department and the legal bodies, so that complexity can best be conveyed by arranging the components—there are five in this very simple case—horizontally and vertically in a matrix. The resulting five-by-five matrix forms twenty-five cells, each having its own distinctive relationships. An individual's role in governance becomes a function of interaction with the department, the college, the system, and the legal bodies.

The matrix becomes a web and complexity becomes even more apparent when mechanisms for collective faculty action enter the picture. Faculty senates, collective bargaining agents, and ubiquitous committees weave in and out of the matrix, raising the number of interactions geometrically and rendering governance structures even more complex. At one small liberal arts college the list of committees and subcommittees assigned to handle certain issues could not be described in less than four pages. Also, a faculty senate ratified such decisions as course changes, but not others, budget and tenure, for instance. The college was not part of a large public system nor did it have many divisions, such as graduate or professional schools, but it was a complex structure. To discover the precise location of a decision was difficult; to trace the informal influences or formal constraints on the decision was especially so.

Referring to this simple model, the following examples illustrate how faculty members fit into very different authority structures. The diversity is apparent. What is less apparent are the generalizable explanations for the disparities. Clearly, authority arrangements are moving from simple to complex, from informal to formal, from normative to instrumental, from soft to hard, from unspoken to spoken. In large public systems "the drift of authority for a quarter century has been steadily upward, toward a growing web of multicampus administrations, coordinating boards of higher education, state legislative committees and executive offices, regional associations and a large number of agencies of the federal government."[29] Along with this upward flow, there is a steady downward movement of constraints that circumscribe decisions. Though the nominal decision may remain in the hands of a department or a faculty senate, other units of authority may significantly limit the options. The first example illustrates this quite well, as it also illustrates the tension between the managerial and academic temperaments.

At a small community college where faculty morale seems fairly high, an instructor explained his ability to influence decisions by saying "the administration gives us a lot of power." When asked if this formulation ought to be reversed if it were said that the power was already in the hands of the faculty to give, he replied that in any organization the responsibility for the consequences of a decision must be clearly assigned and therefore could not be apportioned among a collective body. The president of the college echoed this philosophy:

The faculty does not run the college, not at all. First of all, we are a very tight state system. I believe that, ultimately, the president, within the bounds of the (State) Board guidelines, must make the final decision. The faculty member has a right to participate in the decision-making process. The point is not who makes the decisions, but the process you use in arriving at the decision.

At a liberal arts college with a strong academic reputation, the academic dean wields an enormous amount of power and influence. The faculty understands that he will closely review hiring, tenure, and promotion decisions. He will also involve himself in the particulars of curriculum revision and other academic matters. His influence results in part from the complexities of a committee structure so intricate that decisions become lost in its machinations. Ironically, the system was the creation of a president who hoped to revitalize faculty participation in the college in the aftermath of his predecessor's benevolent dictatorship. But the cumbersomeness of the structure and the inability of the committees to coordinate themselves left the decisions, by default, to the president and the dean.

Nevertheless, the faculty is not disenchanted; their culture does not place a high value on participation in committee work or administrative tasks, but there is a perceived compatibility between their values and those of the administration. Mulkay and Williams conducted a study of a physics department run autocratically by a powerful chairman, whose members were quite content to be left out of decision making because everyone agreed on the goals.[30] Though running a department differs in scale and complexity from running a college, even at a small liberal arts college the principle is the same: where there is a consensus on norms and expectations among the faculty, and where the administration is perceived to be a trustee of those norms and expectations, faculty will exercise their authority collegially. One assistant professor, when asked what she valued most about the institution, said, "the lack of red tape."

The level of bureaucratization, that is, the degree of differentiation and organizational complexity, is not a reliable predictor of whether faculty feel they run their institution. At a major university, the organization chart of which would rival that of any multinational corporation, the faculty report that they make all decisions on "issues that are important to the faculty," In contrast, a faculty member at a medium quality liberal arts college interpreted his situation this way: "I think the faculty feels a certain sense of powerlessness. The administration . . . is not even geographically in the same place we are. It is somewhere else on campus doing God knows what, has ultimate authority over our lives, does all of this like the Wizard of Oz, and is kind of faceless." At an urban comprehensive college, more complex than the liberal arts college but still simpler than the research university, a professor described the mechanism of hiring new faculty as "the whispering in the ear method; we all go whisper in [the chairman's ear]"; tenure criteria are "who you know and who likes you." When asked who has the power at the institutional level, she replied, "Who knows? I don't know what goes on up there." A better predictor of the ability of faculty to control their professional lives seems to be a "cultural" factor: administrators and faculty stand in an almost inevitable tension with each other, but the tension is minimized to the extent that the outlooks of the faculty and the administration are, or are perceived to be, similar.

An example of how the different cells of the model interact and how some units of authority constrain the individual faculty member is found in the research university. If there is an axiom to be gleaned from the literature on faculty authority, it is that direct connections between a faculty member and an external funding agency have the potential to redistribute influence within the university.[31] Specifically, influence shifts from the faculty as a whole to those individuals who have enhanced their position by attracting financial support.[32] This situation first appeared in the 1960s in response to the rapid growth of federal research support, and some secondary effects can now be seen. One leading political scientist at a major research university lamented the lack of institutional support for research and claimed that faculty positions became merely "hunting licenses," to obtain external support. A biologist at another research university frankly conceded that the ability to obtain grants was an important element in hiring, promotion, and tenure decisions. Most significant grants (at least those from the federal government) were awarded only after extensive peer review. They could therefore serve as a surrogate measure of the individual's standing in the field. This is a subtle form of delocalization, as internal criteria for decision making mingle with external criteria—that is, standards applied by those outside the institution and, strictly speaking, outside the discipline. But this phenomenon is a sectorial one confined to research universities: approximately 85 percent of federal research funds are awarded to 100 institutions, and federal funds account for nearly all external funding of academic research.[33]

Another trend that parallels the movement from internal to external criteria is the shifting from normative forms of control to instrumental ones. Faculty autonomy is increasingly bound by formal constraints often imposed from outside the university. When a University of California scientist agrees to perform research sponsored by a private company, he must disclose his financial holdings in that company to the California Fair Political Practices Committee, a group whose primary mission is to police the ethical conduct of elected and appointed public officials. Like a politician, the faculty member may violate the public trust by using his position for private benefit, but the vehicle for regulation is not one devised by the institution or the profession. Instead a group that stands apart from the academy monitors the scientist's choice of research topic; in so doing, it reorders (although minimally in this case) the relationship between the university and the faculty member.[34]

Faculty subcultures have institutional as well as disciplinary foundations. To speak of "the faculty interest" is to ignore the coalitional politics that may develop over any particular issue. Divisions between full-time and part-time faculty exist, although generally part-time faculty have only a token role, if any, in university governance. Another division, sometimes more prominent, is between junior and senior faculty. In recent years this has become more acute because expectations for tenure have risen as a function of the low demand and high supply of prospective academics. Under some circumstances junior faculty perceive themselves as being held to standards not met by their senior colleagues; this injects further strain into the already tense process of awarding tenure.

More complicated are the divisions that may arise over collective bargaining. In colleges where collective bargaining has been in place for many years, relations between management and labor can be combative but stable; collective bargaining quickly becomes a fact of life. But the primary forum for articulating faculty interests tends to shift to the contract negotiation. Although campuses with collective bargaining retain their faculty senates, and although by agreement academic matters are left to those bodies and employment conditions are left to the contract bargaining, there can be turf battles over numerous issues that are not neatly divisible. On one campus, after negotiating a contract with a recently elected bargaining agent, the administration (which historically had a testy relationship with the faculty) insisted that "consulting with the faculty" according to the terms of the contract meant consulting with the academic senate. The senate, however, remained in the control of a rival union that had lost the election for a bargaining agent. Thus the representation of faculty can become an extremely complicated process. By its very nature, collective bargaining forces the identification and articulation of the faculty interest, but a diverse group of individuals may have a diverse set of interests. Coalitions within the faculty on most campuses belie the myth of a common interest.

The variety of authority arrangements illustrated by these examples are outgrowths of several factors, including the history of the institution, the disposition of the administration, and the structure of authority on a campus. Added to this de facto diversity, mainly created by local circumstances, there are now rudiments of a de jure differentiation brought on by some recent complications over the legal status of unionization and collective bargaining in American higher education.

Traditionally, the notion of faculty authority implied the formation of a guild through which the direction of the institution was influenced. To those outside the academy this was somewhat confusing because many different forms of this authority existed in practice. At no time was this perplexity more apparent than in 1980 when the United States Supreme Court was faced with the task of deciding whether faculty members at Yeshiva University were managerial employees and therefore ineligible, under the provisions of federal law, to form a union for the purpose of engaging in collective bargaining.[35] The court agonized over its decision: the opinions of the judges revealed a determined effort to interpret the atypical arrangements found in academia. But as the five-four vote indicated, the result was a deeply divided and confused court. Writing for the majority, which decided that the faculty were not eligible to join a union, Justice Lewis Powell concluded:

The faculty of Yeshiva University exercises authority which in any other context would unquestionably be managerial. Their authority in academic matters is absolute. . . . To the extent the industrial analogy applies, the faculty determines within each school the product to be produced, the terms upon which it will be offered, and the customers who will be served.

This provoked a rather sharp dissent from Justice William Brennan.

The court's perception of the Yeshiva faculty's status is distorted by the rose-colored lens through which it views the governance structure of the modern day university. The court's conclusion that the faculty's professional interests are indistinguishable from those of the administration is bottomed on an idealized model of collegial decision making that is a vestige of the great medieval university. But the university of today bears little resemblance to the "community of scholars" of yesteryear. . . . The task of operating the university enterprise has been transferred from the faculty to an autonomous administration.[36]

Allowing that the Yeshiva decision illustrates that the concept of faculty authority may confuse a detached observer, it is important because it creates a de jure distinction among types of instutitions, a distinction reinforced by the administrative rulings of the National Labor Relations Board (NLRB) and by federal and state legislation. In the United States the authority to unionize and bargain collectively forms a quiltlike pattern. Public universities and colleges receive their authority to unionize or bargain from state governments. Private institutions fall under federal labor law. The Yeshiva decision and subsequent rulings by the NLRB which are limited to private institutions have thus had a chilling effect on unionization in that sector. In 1981 there were ninety-two private institutions with bargaining agents; in 1983 there were seventy-four, arresting and reversing what had been a consistent growth.[37] Because some groups of colleges are predominantly private and others predominantly public (e.g., community colleges) these de jure constraints are likely to lead to greater diversity in patterns of faculty authority.

To make a final statement on authority, I develop a proposition derived from my model and suggested by the examples. The location of the formal decision—who awards tenure, who approves curriculum changes, and who sets work rules—varies by institution and is of obvious importance in any discussion of authority. But it is only part of the picture, the other factor being constraints on the decision. I propose that a critical difference between a management temperament and an academic temperament is that in the former the constraints are imposed from on high by individuals whose range of vision spans departments and disciplines, but is limited to the particular institution. In an institution with a more academic temperament, the tone is set from below, and although still subject to legal and institutional constraints in the exercise of power, faculty may make all decisions important to them. This helps to explain why, in some institutions, faculty are pleased to be given power by the administration, while in others, such as in the liberal arts college with the powerful dean, faculty see themselves as the originator of the power delegation. This invisible control over the institution is a critical consideration in a discussion of faculty authority, and it varies in institutions throughout the system.

VALUES AND BELIEFS

As systems of higher education divide into the separate worlds of different work settings and local patterns of governance, do the beliefs, attitudes, and ideologies of the academic profession also become fragmented? Or do they serve as the profession's only remaining bond? Edward Shils finds that there is a common academic ethic.

The fundamental obligations of university teachers for teaching, research and academic citizenship are the same for all academics. All these activities are necessary for the university to perform its indispensable tasks for modern activities and modern intellectual culture and it falls to the individual academic to contribute to the best of his capacity to the performance of those tasks.

Not all academics are equally endowed or equally inclined, for whatever reason, to the activities needed to meet these obligations. . . . Nevertheless to abstain from any of these totally and to show no respect for them is contrary to the obligations of an academic career.[38]

Is an academic in one setting kin to his or her counterpart in another, or do local circumstances encourage indigenous ideologies? These issues challenge the profession more acutely than do questions about a division of labor or different approaches to institutional governance; for the most fundamental, most basic definitional component of any profession is a consistent set of values that integrates a community of individuals and distinguishes it from other professional and occupational groups. If this ideology becomes fragmented, pluralistic, less unifying, the distinctiveness of the profession diminishes; professionalism itself diminishes.

The most sensitive topic is also the most difficult to analyze. Certainly it is not amenable to precise answers or, for that matter, precise questions: asking academics what they value and then tabulating the results is not the same as asking them what they do and tabulating those responses. Discussions of academic ideology are themselves tinted with ideology, and participants rarely hesitate to offer interpretations. Because of the inherently subjective nature of the topic, we are all experts.

In the following section we attempt to disentangle complications and avoid temptations of prescription and advocacy. Here we are guided by Clark's assertion, "It is still the case that academic ideologies may be seen as a form of emotional bonding and even of moral capital for all the levels of organization in higher education—a relatively strong form compared to that found in most non-academic organizations. But the relatively intangible bonds of symbol, emotion, and morality are evermore pluralistic."[39]

One device for eliciting statements from academics about what they consider important and what they think the profession considers important is to ask them to construct a model of an outstanding academic. Across different sectors of higher education the answers were similar in some ways, different in others. The differences, whether of degree or kind, are seen in the statements from individuals in various sectors of higher education which follow. They reveal concerns ranging from the humane to the scholarly and illustrate the kinds of circumstances where values come into play. All are responses to questions asking for a description of an outstanding academic.

I will define that in relation to the community college, with the understanding that if I were to define it in relation to a research institution it would be a different definition. . . . A good teacher—a person who enjoyed teaching and one who would understand the discipline . . . would continue to read professional journals within his discipline, but he would also read the literature relating to the community college as a whole; in other words, understanding our philosophy and our mission, our students, and so on. He would be one who would serve on the important committees and occasionally chair those committees. . . . He should get along well with colleagues and his students, understand the discipline, enjoy teaching, and be able to view what he is doing in a larger context. (A community college president)

I knew a grand old man—courtly in an almost old-fashioned way. In class he was meandering and rambling, but he was a wonder and a very charming man. A lot of students liked to do their dissertations with him because of his personality . . . [he had] a humanity and ability to relate in an unpretentious way to the students. (English professor, nonelite liberal arts college)

Basically I have been impressed with [someone who] can say what he wants to say in a way that makes sense to me . . . an innovative thinker and a good communicator . . . a well-rounded perspective . . . I find multidisciplinary scholarship very exciting. (Physics professor, elite liberal arts college)

Truthfulness . . . in contributing to and increasing our field of knowledge you want to bring in the purest material possible . . . personal integrity as far as representation of yourself, and what you do and do not know. Something else that is important to me, and I don't know if it is important for an academic, is simply compassion. (Biology professor, state college)

I said to someone who I respect very much, "It must be great to do research and find yourself very prominent as a result." He said he never did research for that purpose. "I was always out there to learn something," he told me, "that is what drives me." He is such a sincere person that it really hit home. The second attribute is thoroughness, making sure something is right and complete before you send it out. So I guess I would say that it is the lust for knowledge and the willingness to work on something until it is really meaningful as a research piece. (Business professor, research university)

What makes any analysis of values so murky is the platitudinous terminology. No one at a community college would deny that thoroughness is admirable, nor would most people at a research university scoff at the idea of compassion, but while the responses may seem inoffensive to academics they nevertheless also reveal some differences in emphasis. The question did not ask for a description of an outstanding academic in the specific sector in which the individual is located; it asked for one of an outstanding academic. The models do, however, suggest variations reflecting the culture of different sectors and a range of priorities and concerns.

Similarities and recurring themes were also evident. Many academics mentioned lust for knowledge; an inquisitive mind; a cognitive ability to focus on a particular question while understanding the broader context, introducing perspectives from outside the discipline; and, somewhat surprising in its frequency, a concern for the human side of the profession, including an ability to work with people and communicate with them. For example, a young molecular biologist at a leading research university, who is already establishing a national reputation and has a substantial federal research grant that insures him the resources to develop his reputation, described his outstanding academic this way: "Certainly a creative scientist and an interactive person, someone who is able to interact with many kinds of people in terms of training them and being a good teacher. . . . I have been trained for seven or eight years as a researcher, and I get to a university and become a psychologist, administrator, and writer, none of which I am trained for. The people who can handle it are great but rare." While his comment gainsays the stereotype of the research professor obsessed with publication, isolated in his lab, and communicating only through journals and an occasional conference, a professor at a nonelite liberal arts college belies that sector's stereotype—an individual cast as "Mr. Chips"—who is concerned only with the moral and personal growth of his student. For him an outstanding academic is someone "who has continued making contributions in his field of expertise by scholarly endeavors"; he ought to "have the ability to convey his enthusiasm for the subject to those he comes in contact with, his students." From two very different settings come similar responses, suggesting at least some agreement with Shils's premise that the "distinctive task of the academic profession is the discovery and the transmission of truth."[40]

How then to interpret the differences and similarities? Are the differences unimportant nuances and the similarities substantial, or is it the other way around? Let me offer at least one possible interpretation.

The importance of socialization should not be minimized. When asked why they entered the academic profession, nearly all respondents described the decision as one they fell into without carefully considering the career implications. Lured primarily by interest in a particular subject and inspired perhaps by a teacher of that subject, they sought an opportunity to continue learning about that field. The discipline was clearly the motivation in almost all cases; once in the rarified atmosphere of graduate school, the individual, looking for a further opportunity to continue studying the subject, saw the academic profession as the most inviting. It insured freedom.

The intensity of the socialization process is severe. Work concerns (often domestic concerns, too, as divorce rates among graduate students attest) are subordinated to scholarly endeavors. Teaching, if the opportunity presents itself, becomes a means to the end of writing a dissertation without starving. There is little incentive for a teaching assistant to spend time with students, but a wealth of it to become deeply involved in the subject matter; at no point in an individual's career will he have a broader understanding of his discipline than on the day of his qualifying exams.

The process of socialization into a scholarly career consists of imparting and then balancing two separate cognitive dispositions. The first is a creative, liberating, cerebral approach to problems that encourages the scholar to entertain a range of ideas, consider novel interpretations, and challenge accepted wisdom. The second is a healthy bias against certitude, which constrains the promulgation of unsubstantiated findings and binds the exuberance of the novice researcher. Together these liberating and constraining outlooks impart an ideology. Lomnitz and Fortes's study of the socialization of scientists describes this ideology as

being of paramount importance . . . because it represents a world view, a code of conduct and a character of behavior on the social, cognitive, and emotional levels. It must be internalized by the individual in order to identify with his scattered community. This affords a mutual acknowledgment and a feeling of identity and belonging. . . . It is the acquisition of an individual's traits, his ideological commitments, and the recognition by the scientific community which makes him a scientist.[41]

For academics newly inducted into the scholarly world, no similar process exists for socialization into the specific colleges or universities where they are to be employed. The former students leave graduate school with virgin ideologies and find them frequently violated by the organization. Academics are often surprised by their organizational obligations, committee work, teaching loads, and advising duties. Departmental or college feuds, despite their curious and unfortunate pervasiveness, are always impossible for the academic to explain and are always seen as intruding on his ability to do what he is supposed to do. Said one professor, "I came to my college presuming a rational model, but I learned quickly about bureaucratic politics."

Socialization into the organization comes after an intense introduction into the world of scholarship. The sequence causes the academic to see the second process as inhibiting what he was trained to do in the first. While scholarly socialization is an ordeal willingly entered into, organizational socialization is reluctantly tolerated. At

least some of the infused ideology, but usually not all of it, can with-
stand the organizational influence, which partly explains the similar
descriptions of outstanding academics.

A few statistics lend further support to this. Assume that institutions with the strongest commitment to the scholarly ideology are
leading research universities, those operationally defined in the Carnegie categories as Research Universities I and II. Of the 100 most
fertile institutional producers of Ph.D.'s in the sciences, social sciences, and engineering between 1960 and 1981, 77 came from these
two categories. During that period, they produced 78.9 percent of the
total number of Ph.D.'s. Research I Universities (45 of the top 100
producers) alone produced 58 percent.[42] Therefore, to the extent that
various sectors rely upon the doctorate, substantial numbers of academics were first introduced to the profession through the intense
scholarly track. With credentials in hand, typically, they were then
placed in organizations, each with different commitments, to undergo
a quite different introduction to the profession.

An obvious caveat is the absence of significant numbers of doctorates in some institutions, especially community colleges. Table 8.5
shows a sectorial distribution of doctorate-holding faculty, by percentage.[43] The humanities faculty are not necessarily representative
of other disciplines, but the broad trend of lesser reliance on the
doctorate in the community college is undoubtedly the same in other
fields. Do doctorates in the community college have different outlooks
than their nondoctorate colleagues? Very little research is available
on this topic (it would be a good test of a socialization hypothesis).
One recent study showed similarities, but it dealt mainly with instructional goals and techniques, not with broader views about the
profession.[44] Another study, now somewhat dated, showed that
Ph.D.'s in the community colleges were more ambivalent about the
goals of the community college than those without the doctorate.[45]
One of our respondents, an instructor in English at a community
college, articulated the nature of this division. "The Ph.D. in this
place separates people from other people. Now, I have no particular
respect for a system that sets up arbitrary boundaries in the way of
obtaining a Ph.D. At the same time, those who have gotten through
it have some interest and respect for literature and maybe even a
passion for writing. . . . The M.A. mentality is to get through and
get a job; their real lives are perhaps lived elsewhere than on the
page." While the evidence is mixed, the weight is on the side of the
Ph.D. carrying some influence that endures despite the organizational
setting.

TABLE 8.5

HUMANITIES AND ENGLISH FACULTY BY INSTITUTIONAL TYPE AND HIGHEST DEGREE ATTAINED
(percentage of faculty)

	Humanities				English			
	Doctorate	Master	Other		Doctorate	Master	Other	
Universities								
Private	90.4	8.4	1.3	(n = 4,612)	87.2	11.6	1.1	(n = 1,654)
Public	85.7	12.3	1.9	(n = 11,992)	77.5	19.9	2.6	(n = 5,147)
Four-year colleges								
Private	70.7	28.4	0.9	(n = 13,229)	63.5	35.8	0.7	(n = 5,487)
Public	72.6	25.3	2.1	(n = 14,689)	64.9	32.6	2.8	(n = 6,767)
Community colleges								
Private	18.6	74.3	7.2	(n = 1,383)	18.2	70.4	11.4	(n = 869)
Public	20.0	74.5	5.6	(n = 12,682)	16.4	77.8	5.8	(n = 8,153)
All institutions	63.6	33.8	2.6	(n = 58,587)	52.7	44.0	3.4	(n = 28,076)

SOURCE: Atelsek and Gomberg, "Selected Characteristics of Full-Time Humanities Faculty, Fall 1979," 1981.

The similarities across the sectors—the language used to describe an outstanding academic, the respect for research, and the like—may be partly explained by an intense and sequential socialization. Some residual symbolic bonding remains from an academic's training: a belief in the value of transmitting knowledge, familiarity with the subject matter, and being able to work with people.

Academics are able to articulate a general model, but they may not agree on its specific applications, or they may not adopt it as their own personal ideal. Some professors who described an outstanding academic in very conventional terms and who conceded that such an individual could never exist in their institutions are not necessarily eager to leave their positions for "better" ones. If indeed they do wish to leave, they occasionally resemble the political scientist at a state college who spoke with fervor about his extra-academic involvement in political and community activities and how the flexibility of his present position allowed him to do that. Having made that statement, he continued: "I still wistfully dream on occasion about holding a position at a major institution. I think I would welcome the pressure to write articles and publish if I had the ability to do it. But I won't do it. It's too late now. I'm old and set."

Strains on the common ideology will persist and increase as the similarities among the different sectors decrease. To be sure, the Ph.D., except in the community colleges (but even there, in some cases), remains valued, and in the current academic labor market, most institutions will have little difficulty in requiring recruits to have it. As nearly all institutions pay some lip service to the objective of discovering as well as transmitting knowledge (the community college is again the exception), the research norm will not vanish, although the increasingly broad definitions of research will lead to a differentiated research community. Those factors notwithstanding, the trend toward a greater fragmentation and a more pluralistic definition of the profession will accelerate. Socialization imparts norms, but mutual interaction reinforces them. If academics continue to define their values to make them consistent with their institutional settings, if they tend to define professional concerns locally, and if research and professional associations continue to exhibit distinctly local patterns, we can expect the centrifugal forces to challenge and to weaken further the already tenuous normative core of the profession.

CONCLUSION

The academic profession exhibits important behavioral and ideological differences across institutional sectors: distinct cultures linked to the missions of various colleges and universities are emerging, and different research contexts are influencing the nature and quantity of research. A "fault line," postulated by Fulton and Trow, separates teaching styles and classroom objectives of academics from one sector to another: where the teaching load is heavy, the courses general, and the audiences diverse, instructors find pedagogical rewards different from those that come from training future leaders in the disciplines in graduate schools. Fragmentation is a fundamental feature of the academic profession.

We begin to understand the significance of this institutional fragmentation by contrasting it with another apparent source of fragmentation: the disciplines. Tony Becher tells us (chapter 5) that disciplines have very different cultures. It is difficult to imagine the physicist understanding the intellectual sparks that ignite the inquisitive fires of a political scientist; for that matter, the theoretical physicist is often perplexed by his experimental brethren. Disciplines and subdisciplines vary by styles of presentation, preferred modes of investigation, and by the "permeability of their boundaries," the degree to which they draw upon other fields and respond to nonscientific constituencies.[46]

But for all these differences, the disciplines share a common ethos, a compensatory integrating mechanism. Clark wrote that the norms of science are the norms of the (academic) profession;[47] is it not also true that the norms of science are the norms of the disciplines? However broadly "knowledge" is defined, disciplines impart a respect for it. They also establish such procedural expectations as the sharing of information among researchers, the importance of disinterestedly reviewing evidence, and the privilege—indeed the responsibility—of exercising self-regulation, as "only the holy can know what is holy." Insofar as the disciplines fragment the profession, then, a paradox arises. Ben-David, in his discussion of science as a profession, explains that as fields of study develop and become more sophisticated, they also become more distinct from other fields and more protective of their body of knowledge. They also become more committed to a professional temperament, in which the separation of disciplines is countered by an increasingly stronger commitment to a scientific professional ethos.

If we look at the profession across institutions the situation is different; it is difficult to find any mechanism, normative or instrumental, to compensate for the fragmentation. Academics in different sectors are developing distinct interests. This may be so because the constituencies of higher education vary by institutional setting. Diverse student populations, state governments, the federal government, and business present demands that vary by sector, resulting in a variety of organizational cultures that require academics to respond differently. In settings where collective bargaining was habitual our respondents regretted the introduction of a union. But they considered it unavoidable in light of their collective powerlessness relative to their institution, the system, or the public authorities—a condition that might be absent elsewhere. The community for a community college instructor is not like the community for someone in a research university. Graduate students at a research university have different expectations than undergraduates have at a smaller, teaching-oriented college. The relationship of the academic profession to society becomes defined in terms of the sector, particularly the sector's constituencies.

Higher education in the United States is clearly evolving toward sharper distinctions among institutions. Inevitably, for the professoriat, a more diverse set of interests is being built around the local conditions for each institution. It would not be amiss to speculate that separate professions or separate cadres of academics, each with its interests endemic to its own institutional setting, may sprout, root, and endure.

NOTES

The author wishes to acknowledge with appreciation the assistance of his former colleagues at the UCLA Comparative Higher Education Research Group, especially to Burton R. Clark and Gary Rhoades for their advice, and to Marie Freeman and Mitchell Bard for their research assistance.

1. Clark, *Higher Education System.*
2. Wilson, *Academic Man.*
3. Jencks and Riesman, *Academic Revolution*, p. 480.
4. Ibid., p. 27.
5. Ladd and Lipset, *Divided Academy*, especially chaps. 4 and 10.
6. Keller, *Academic Strategy*, p. 30.
7. Ibid., p. 39.
8. National Center for Education Statistics, *Condition of Education 1983*, pp. 94, 95.
9. Ibid.
10. Weathersby, "State Colleges in Transition," p. 26.
11. Norman Birnbaum cited in Froomkin, "Research Universities," p. 34.
12. Kerr, *Uses of the University.*
13. Pfinster, "Role of the Liberal Arts College," p. 165.
14. Ibid., p. 163.
15. Ibid., p. 166.

16. Metzger, "Academic Freedom in Delocalized Academic Institutions," p. 15.

17. Clark, *Higher Education System*, p. 106.

18. Fulton and Trow, "Research Activity in American Higher Education."

19. National Science Foundation, *Activities of Science and Engineering Faculty in Universities and Four-Year Colleges.*

20. Fulton and Trow, "Research Activity," p. 54.

21. Ladd, "Work Experience of American College Professors," p. 4.

22. Ibid., p. 5.

23. Wilson, *Academic Man*, p. 194.

24. Caplow and McGee, *Academic Marketplace*, p. 189.

25. Light, "Introduction: The Structure of the Academic Professions," p. 16.

26. Michalak and Friedrich, "Research Productivity and Teaching Effectiveness at a Small Liberal Arts College," p. 585.

27. American Political Science Association, "Learned Societies," p. 2.

28. Cameron, "Organizational Adaptation and Higher Education," p. 136.

29. Clark, *Higher Education System*, p. 130.

30. Mulkay and Williams, "A Sociological Study of a Physics Department," pp. 68–82.

31. Clark, "Faculty Organization and Authority," p. 49.

32. Kerr, *Uses of the University*, pp. 52–55.

33. National Science Foundation, *Federal Support to Universities, Colleges, and Selected Nonprofit Institutions, Fiscal Year 1980.*

34. Sanger, "University of California Puts Limits on Private Research Pacts," *New York Times* (21 August 1983), p. 22.

35. U.S. Supreme Court, *NLRB v. Yeshiva*, p. 686.

36. Ibid., p. 702.

37. Douglas (with De Bona), *Directory of Faculty Contracts and Bargaining Agents*, p. VIII.

38. Shils, *Academic Ethics*, p. 104.

39. Clark, "Academic Culture," p. 25.

40. Shils, *Academic Ethic*, p. 3.

41. Lomnitz and Fortes, "Socialization of Scientists," p. 27.

42. National Science Foundation, *Science and Engineering Doctorates: 1960–1981*, pp. 85–86.

43. Atelsek and Gomberg, "Selected Characteristics of Full-Time Humanities Faculty, Fall 1979," p. 23.

44. Green, "Does the Doctorate Make a Difference?"

45. Bloom, Gillie, and Leslie, *Goals and Ambivalence.*

46. Becher, "The Cultural View."

47. Clark, *Higher Education System*, p. 93.

BIBLIOGRAPHY

American Political Science Association. "Learned Societies: Self-Study and Institutional Planning." A research proposal to the National Endowment for the Humanities, Washington, D.C., 1984.

Atelsek, Frank J., and Irene L. Gomberg. "Selected Characteristics of Full-Time Humanities Faculty, Fall 1979." Washington, D.C.: American Council on Education, August, 1981.

Becher, Tony. "The Cultural View." In Perspectives on Higher Education: Eight Disciplinary and Comparative Views, ed. Burton R. Clark, 165–198. Berkeley, Los Angeles, London: University of California Press, 1984.

Bloom, Karen L., Angelo C. Gillie, and Larry L. Leslie. Goals and Ambivalence: Faculty Values and the Community College Philosophy. Center for the Study of Higher Education, The Pennsylvania State University, Report no. 13. University Park, Pa., November 1971.

Cameron, Kim S. "Organizational Adaptation and Higher Education." Journal of Higher Education 55, no. 2 (1984): 122–144.

Caplow, Theodore, and Reese J. McGee. The Academic Marketplace. Garden City, N.Y.: Doubleday, 1965.

Clark, Burton R. "Faculty Culture." In The Study of Campus Cultures, ed. Terry F. Lunsford. Boulder, Col.: Western Interstate Commission for Higher Education, 1963.

––––––. "Faculty Organization and Authority." In Academic Governance, ed. J. Victor Baldridge, 236–250. Berkeley, Calif.: McCutchan, 1971.

––––––. "Academic Culture." Higher Education Research Group Working Paper, YHERG-42. New Haven: Yale University, 1980.

––––––. The Higher Education System: Academic Organization in Cross-National Perspective. Berkeley, Los Angeles, London: University of California Press, 1983.

Douglas, Joel N. (with Lorraine DeBona). Directory of Faculty Contacts and Bargaining Agents in Institutions of Higher Education. National Center for the Study of Collective Bargaining in Higher Education and the Professions, vol. 10. New York: Baruch College of the City University of New York, January, 1984.

Froomkin, Joseph. "The Research Universities." In The Crisis in Higher Education, ed. Joseph Froomkin. Academy of Political Science, Proceedings 35, no. 2 (1983): 23–34.

Fulton, Oliver, and Martin Trow. "Research Activity in American Higher Education." In Teachers and Students, ed. Martin Trow. New York: McGraw-Hill, 1975.

Green, Kenneth C. "Does the Doctorate Make a Difference? In The Humanities and Sciences in Two-Year Colleges, ed. Florence B. Brawer, 102–112. Los Angeles: Eric Clearinghouse for Junior Colleges, 1980.

Jencks, Christopher, and David Riesman. The Academic Revolution. Garden City, N.Y.: Doubleday, 1969.

Keller, George. *Academic Strategy: The Management Revolution.* Baltimore: The Johns Hopkins University Press, 1983.

Kerr, Clark. *The Uses of the University.* Cambridge, Mass.: Harvard University Press, 1982.

Ladd, Everett Carll, Jr., and Seymour Martin Lipset. *The Divided Academy.* New York: Norton, 1975.

————. "The Work Experience of American College Professors: Some Data and an Argument." *Current Issues in Higher Education 1979,* 3–12. Washington, D.C.: American Association for Higher Education, 1979.

Lazarsfeld, Paul F., and Wagner Thielens, Jr. *The Academic Mind: Professors and Politics.* Glencoe, Ill.: Free Press, 1958.

Lee, Barbara, and James P. Begin. "Criteria for Evaluating the Managerial Status of College Faculty: Applications of Yeshiva University by the NLRB." *Journal of College and University Law* 10, no. 4 (1984): 515–537.

Light, Donald. "Introduction: The Structure of the Academic Professions." *Sociology of Education* 47, no. 1 (1974): 2–29.

Light, D. W., Jr., L. R. Mardsen, and T. C. Corl. *The Impact of the Academic Revolution on Faculty Careers.* Washington, D.C.: American Association for Higher Education, 1973.

Lomnitz, Larissa, and Jacqueline Fortes. "Socialization of Scientists: The Internationalization of a Myth." Unpublished paper.

Metzger, Walter P. "Academic Freedom in Delocalized Academic Institutions." In *Dimensions of Academic Freedom,* ed. Walter Metzger, 1–33. Urbana: University of Illinois Press, 1969.

Michalak, Stanley, Jr., and Robert J. Friedrich. "Research Productivity and Teaching Effectiveness at a Small Liberal Arts College." *Journal of Higher Education* 52, pt. 6 (1981): 578–597.

Mulkay, M. J., and Anthony T. Williams. "A Sociological Study of a Physics Department." *British Journal of Sociology* 22, pt. 1 (1971): 68–82.

National Center for Education Statistics. *The Condition of Education 1983.* Washington, D.C., 1984.

National Science Foundation, *Science and Engineering Doctorates: 1960–1981.* Washington, D.C., 1983.

————. *Activities of Science and Engineering Faculty in Universities and Four-Year Colleges.* Washington, D.C., 1981.

————. *Federal Support to Universities, Colleges, and Selected Nonprofit Institutions, Fiscal Year 1980.* Washington, D.C., 1982.

Pfinster, Allan O. "The Role of the Liberal Arts College: A Historical Overview of the Debates." *Journal of Higher Education* 55, no. 2 (1984): 145–170.

Shils, Edward. *The Academic Ethic.* Chicago: University of Chicago Press, 1983.

Stadtman, Verne A. *Academic Adaptations.* San Francisco: Jossey-Bass, 1980.

U.S. Supreme Court, *NLRB v. Yeshiva.* In *U.S. Reports* 44: 672–702. Washington, D.C.: Government Printing Office, 1980.

Weathersby, George B. "State Colleges in Transition." In *The Crisis in Higher Education*, ed. Joseph Froomkin. The Academy of Political Science, *Proceedings* 35, no. 2 (1983): 23–33.

Wenzlau, Thomas E. "The Outlook for Liberal-Arts Colleges." In *The Crisis in Higher Education*, ed. Joseph Froomkin. Academy of Political Science, *Proceedings*. 35, no. 2 (1983): 1–13.

Wilson, Logan. *The Academic Man.* London: Oxford University Press, 1942.

PART III
CONCLUSIONS

9
Conclusions

Burton R. Clark

Ranging across national, disciplinary, and institutional contexts, the foregoing eight chapters have shed considerable light on the academic profession. Among nations we find profound differences in the convictions and conduct of academicians but also subtle similarities. Across disciplines we observed subcultures that are a world apart but also values that unite. Across enterprises we encounter subworlds that offer diverse conditions of work, opposite forms of authority, and dissimilar convictions but still share an occupational identity. The many settings that make this occupation a patchwork are tied by lines of affiliation that partly knit together the profession's unraveling pattern. In this most varied profession the tension between the many and the one is deeply rooted in reality. Indeed, antithetical identities and commitments abound: the academic profession is haunted by the play of contrary forces.

Consider the following contradictions. For over a century the academic profession in most of the major international centers of learning has been driven by a research imperative that rewards for individuality in thought and conduct. There is a bias for anomic behavior, an inclination for groups to be ripped asunder. Yet the profession is mainly and increasingly composed of individuals who are caught up in large local and national administrative frameworks, often intensely bureaucratic ones, which systematize their duties and privileges and convert them into employees. In turn, these workers manage to convince outsiders as well as themselves that, unequivocally, they are not mere employees but instead are, and should be seen as, privileged members of a virtually independent professional community. As if it were a birthright, they struggle for self-government, invoking powerful doctrines—academic freedom, community of scholars, freedom of research—which serve both as guild ideologies and as the justification of unusual personal liberties. The contradictions could hardly be sharper: a strong stress on individuality occurs within guildlike and communitylike social units that are in turn encapsulated or closely supported by large bureaucracies and the modern state. A strange profession indeed, with uniquely intricate features that seem more significant than the usual characteristics attributed to all the other leading professions.

Much of the discussion in this volume has been directed by an interest in the strain between fragmentation and integration. How to divide work and authority and still have the parts interrelated is the central problem of formal organizations and professions. My first purpose here is to consider the findings of the earlier chapters on how academics and their work are conditioned by national settings, how they are differentiated by institutional sectors, and how they are affected by the increasingly powerful thrust of the disciplines. With these major axes of differentiation in place, I then face the question of the nature of academic authority: is it still largely collegial, even guildlike, or is it now cast in bureaucratic molds and in inherently political forms of group representation? Is self-government the heart of profession, and if so, what are the conditions and forms that sustain it?

Next, I take up the larger issues of the internal integration of the profession and its integration with society. Internal integration is partly structural: disciplines and institutions connect as well as divide academics; modern formal systems add new linkages. Integration is also normative, sometimes powerfully so, when academics uphold a moral vision, share an identity infused with sentiment, and thereby create intangible bonds of morality and emotion. In such matters the current state of knowledge is deficient, but some reflections are warranted. The integration of the profession with society is even less charted, but the ultimate questions about any profession must be posed. How does the modern academic profession relate to other sectors of society? Who is served, in what fashion, and how effectively? "Service to society" may be the final justification, but the services of the academic profession now vary enormously in kind. I offer a first approximation on how they may be untangled and clarified.

The volume closes on the theme of the one and the many, the issue with which we began this collective pursuit of the profession. The strain between differentiation and integration, which is at the center of the problem of social order in complex societies, is strongly recapitulated in this profession of professions, this conglomerate of diverging groups. The task for the future is to become better informed about the contrary forces that underlie this strain, penetrating more of the ambiguity that leaves outsiders bewildered by the ways of this uncommon occupation and its members bemused about its identity.

NATIONAL CONTEXTS

We have seen that the academic profession is quite differently organized in each of the international centers of learning discussed in the first four chapters. The profession in Britain is relatively unitary, even in the face of some hostile divisions, with a professional self-consciousness not matched in France. The French do not even conceive of an academic profession on a plane with the learned professions of law and medicine; instead, they define academics as civil servants within the framework of public employment, assembled as bureaucratic strata that are considerably isolated from one another. In Germany the old-style dominance of chaired professors has been countered during the last two decades by increased state and bureaucratic control from above and by formalized participation of junior faculty, students, and even nonprofessional staff from below, producing a politicization qualitatively different from the structure of academic authority found in the United Kingdom and more so in the United States. The American profession in turn ranges widely; it encompassed those at small religious colleges, for example, and a third of its ranks are inhabited by those at two-year community colleges, a domain that professors in research universities are bound to perceive as peripheral to their own world, because it shares more characteristics with secondary-school teaching than with life in the graduate schools. In America the qualitative difference is the massive extension of the original profession into institutional sectors that fragment it severely, especially at the level of open access.

What is it about national contexts that helps to determine these differences? The strongest influence is government. It is the main sponsor and supporter, the allocator of resources, superior virtually everywhere to the church and the private groups that were often central in the past. In the European tradition and throughout the areas of the world affected by that heritage, government has also been the job market, the primary locus of employment for graduates, from top government circles to schoolteaching. Beyond government itself, higher education is shaped by popular beliefs, labor force demands, and a host of influences from many other sectors of society, all of which at first glance are difficult to grasp systematically. But such influences are somewhat systematized for us in that so many of them are mobilized and articulated through the actions of government. Public officials mediate, interpret, and rearrange many of the external understandings and demands: one example is the so-called labor-force demands that become manpower projections estimated by officials and then applied by them to higher education as plans for access, curriculum, and certification.

The influences of government on the academic profession are many, ranging from niggling details of categorical budgeting to wholesale suppression of academic freedom. But the most common long-run forces seem to lie in the capacity of government, as founder and sponsor, to determine the size and complexity of the system, thereby shaping the institutional and disciplinary foundations on which the professoriat is built. Governments have an influential if not a controlling voice in determining whether access to higher education is elite, mass, or universal; whether graduates proceed only to government and the learned professions or to private employment as well; whether research is placed within the universities or located in a separate set of academies and institutes. As a government acts to limit or expand size, so is the academic profession influenced: to be a numerically small profession or a large one; to be a privileged occupation primarily serving a privileged clientele or a more common occupation serving nearly everyone. Thus governments not only provide the bulk of yearly resources that directly affect size but also have a central role in defining student and employer clienteles.

Regarding complexity in the form of institutional sectors, it was government that opted for a binary policy in Great Britain. It assembled institutions on each side of a dividing line and then arranged two sets of allocating and coordinating devices—the University Grants Committee (UGC) on the one side, with its own history and culture, and the newer Council for National Academic Awards (CNAA) and the National Advisory Board (NAB) on the other, with a separate set of possibilities and constraints. And it is governments and their immediate academic advisors which promulgate master plans in American state systems, establishing thereby in some cases a multisector division of institutions and the professoriat, and attempting in other instances to establish a unitary framework that permits institutions and professors to pretend they are all equal. On the European continent the hands of government on the steering wheels of systems have long been strong, particularly in the French nationalized style in which decisions made by Napoleon over a century and a half ago still echo down the corridors of the state–higher education relationship. The historical imprint of national context in France is such that central officials must constantly and consciously attempt to steer the system as a whole, even when painfully aware that each central pronouncement will excite a powerful countervailing reaction from the field.

In no small way do governments influence the type and amount of disciplinary specialization found within the academic profession. The disciplines are less controllable than institutions, since most of them have lines of affiliation that pierce national boundaries. But governments still have a substantial role in admitting subjects to higher education and in liberating the inner imperatives of the many disciplines and professional areas of study. The permanent civil servants of the British government as well as the oligarchs of the UGC have been inhospitable to applied science and technology; they have supported relevant programs and staffs late in history and cut them first when push came to shove. Nationalized procedures for approving courses and assigning staff, as in France and Italy, institutionalize the power of old fields over new ones, as members of traditional fields sitting on central governmental councils veto changes sought by newer fields that seem suspect educationally or that threaten to dilute one's own powers and resources. In contrast, the American system— formally a nonsystem—stands close to the opposite pole. More than elsewhere among the advanced societies, the leading representatives of disciplines maneuver in a marketlike setting, as institutions compete for their services and their prestige. No single government is in control of the more dynamic fields, such as physics, mathematics, biology, computer science, engineering, law, medicine, and business administration, as long as campuses in Texas seek to draw talent away from campuses in California, and campuses in both states attempt to raid universities in Michigan, Ohio, and Wisconsin. As long as a small private university like Princeton fights back by investing tens of millions of dollars in the biological sciences and sets out to hire, at whatever cost, the best professors that can be found, control of the profession will remain dispersed. This type of competitive dynamism shapes the American academic profession, accentuating the rewards of individual achievement at the top of one discipline after another at the expense of group cooperation, institutional loyalty, and commitment to undergraduate teaching. The ever-present possibility that key academics will take their talent and reputation elsewhere is an important source of professional clout in leading universities, the very settings in which the best graduate students are socialized into the meanings and ways of the profession. The characteristic American academic features of rugged individualism and high mobility have their sources first in a radical decentralization of overall authority, both governmental and private.

Thus national context also becomes defined as interior fixations of the system of higher education and of the academic profession itself. Many individual institutions take on a character rich in meaning, full of tradition and habit: they become ends in themselves. In turn, the ongoing profession works to define and control its supporting system. The profession undergoes its own changes, which then shape changes in the system at large, right down to the fundamental matter of whether the system will grow by reaching out to new subjects and services and more people. The American case is particularly revealing. As Walter Metzger revealed in chapter 4, much of the diversification of American higher education, particularly in the nineteenth and early twentieth centuries, was a product of "substantive growth," an absorption of new subject matters by the system through processes of parturition, affiliation, dignification, and dispersion. Diversification, he claims, defined the system. Changes in the professoriat drove this diversification from within and made academics receptive to knowledge in sundry forms. The faculty gradually became more secularized, and hence less bounded by religious doctrines that would constrict academic thought. They increasingly reached toward research, were tempted by its personal rewards as well as its social promises, and institutionalized it as the central activity in the more advanced universities. In the years between 1870 and 1900, they organized th eir specialties in two forms that were to strongly support science an rapid generation of new knowledge: locally, the department, a more flexible and readily expandable unit than the chair-institute combination found in continental Europe; and nationally, the association, an inclusive meeting ground for like-minded specialists that simultaneously lubricates communication, defines innovative work, and allocates jobs.

More important, American academics gleefully put their shoulders to the wheel of institutional competition, playing the game for great personal profit as well as for scientific and scholarly advance. Those of gathering reputation became the critical resource for university presidents, trustees, and supporters in public and private office. The academic transformation of locals into cosmopolitans became an essential part of the machinery of competition. Compared to Europe, state controls remained minimal: no royal commissions, let alone regulatory ministries, stood in the way of a free-for-all determination of constancy and change. Institutional controls could readily be pushed back: if important professors were not given voices where they were, they could easily leave to find the freedom promised them elsewhere. Openness then became characteristic of the system, an openness that allowed and encouraged the processes that effected so much substantive growth. The profession and the system that supported it took their modern shape before the great "reactive growth" of the more recent decades.

Professions are active players. They steadily seek the roads to dominance. To push back constraints and to enhance discretion, they constantly test their environments, particularly the tolerances of donors and clients and the relative power of nearby occupations. There is always an interaction in which those who have the most to gain or lose, the practicing professionals, seek to shape the larger frameworks to serve their own ideals and their own material interests. The academic profession is no different on this score, except that it is so radically fractured by discipline, and often by institutional sector, that its ideals and interests become extensively differentiated. In short, in each national context, as a product of past efforts as well as historical conditions, the academic profession will have characteristic ways of defending itself and affecting the rest of society.

THE LAYERING OF THE PROFESSION

As systems of higher education become more complex, the academic profession inescapably becomes more differentiated. What was a university profession becomes a postsecondary profession. In one country after another, academics locate in institutions quite different from the traditional university, even in ones designed to counter university practices. There may even be special sectors, as in the classic case of the *grandes écoles* in France, that evolve into a position superior to that of the universities. In every country where they develop, the differentiated sectors position themselves in a prestige hierarchy.[1] The academic profession is thereby systematically layered.

Such layering has three primary dimensions, the first of which is the sheer extent of differentiation, the number of recognized major divisions. Italy has had one sector—a unified national system of public universities.[2] Britain in recent decades has been strongly binary—university and nonuniversity, the "independent sector" and "the public sector." France has a tripartite division: the grandes écoles, the universities, and a powerful separately funded set of research units. The United States has a sixfold breakdown at minimum—public and private universities, public and private four- and five-year colleges, public and private two-year colleges—and a ten- to twentyfold one when analysts more closely approximate the realities of differences among 3,000 institutions.[3] In all cases the sectors differentiate the work and careers of academics. They also differentiate academic authority in different proportions of collegial and bureaucratic, oligarchic and managerial. They may or may not strongly differentiate academic beliefs, a matter to which I shall return.

A second dimension of the layering of the profession by sectors is the firmness and clarity of the divisions. The dividing lines may be hard and clear with categorical divisions, or soft and ambiguous with fuzzy separations. State action tends to produce the first, market interaction the second. The formal bracketing of institutions in a national system works to produce categorical divisions, since the central government must decide on an overall framework, apportion institutional titles, and define budget allocations. It needs clear categories, large and small, to help it decide which institutions ought to do what. It seeks to control institutional aggrandizement. France is one clear case of such categorical division, with the separation of academic workers in three virtually watertight compartments ratified by explicit and detailed separate civil service definitions for grandes écoles instructors, university personnel, and full-time researchers in the third stream. Britain has moved rapidly toward the categorical approach. The binary policy set down in the mid-1960s clearly divides English academic life into distinct parts, each topped (in the early 1980s) by a specific coordinating body that constantly struggles to clarify its mission and jurisdiction.

In contrast, a nonunified, more marketlike system produces ambiguous divisions as well as multiple ones. There is not sufficient formal control to lay down an embracing scheme and to keep institutions from wandering somewhat as they pursue individual ambitions. Again, the United States is the classic case: public and private sectors blend into one another; teachers' colleges shade into comprehensive colleges that offer graduate work. These colleges in turn overlap with "service universities" that do little research and produce only a few Ph.D's. Ambiguity surrounds the boundaries of the many layers. Only the two-year colleges establish a clearly separate category, because the collegiate work of their faculties is limited to the first two years. Even here radical decentralization of control has allowed community colleges to roam around in the higher education domain, where they absorb much of the country's adult education clientele in a catch-as-catch-can fashion, including persons who already have a B.A., M.A., or Ph.D.

A third dimension of layering is the degree of homogeneity within declared or observed strata. Governments may lay down clear categories, but they have enormous difficulty in making institutions into carbon copies of one another within those boxes. Thus in France it turns out that the grandes écoles sector, normally described as monolithic, is actually composed of quite different places, individualistic in nature and under private as well as public sponsorship. In Britain the university and nonuniversity sectors are each internally complex, with differences that cause observers to remark that certain polytechnics ought to be classified as universities and certain universities as polytechnics. In each case some of the internal diversity had developed in the past and had existed before the government ascribed major demarcations. But institutional diversity in higher education is a restless thing: it is steadily produced in the normal course of affairs as institutions work out individual niches in the ecology of the whole, each ultimately having a unique configuration of ambition, organizational capability, and environmental constraint.

In the United States, nearly all the major layers of academic life are internally heterogeneous as well as blurred at the boundaries. Among private universities, for example, some are secular and others are religious, some are privileged bastions of research and high scholarship—veritable think tanks—and others offer academics the chance to labor at low pay while teaching many courses in the salt mines of undergraduate vocational curricula in a downtown center serving students who read at a precollege level. In turn, the hundreds of private liberal arts colleges range all over the map in quality of staff, student selectivity, purity of program, and secular commitment. Even among public institutions often formally treated as if they were alike, much college-by-college differentiation individualizes the conditions under which academics work; the overall beliefs from which they take meaning; and the patterns of control that apportion authority within their ranks and between them, the administrators, and trustees. Among the nineteen campuses of the California State University System (the state college part of the California planned tripartite structure), the large, urban, relatively prestigious campuses in San Diego and San Francisco are very different locales for academic life than the small, more isolated, less prestigious centers in Bakersfield and Humboldt.

Over the long run the increasing complexity of knowledge drives institutional differentiation, which in turn powerfully divides the academic profession. The profession is inescapably layered, turned into a hierarchy of subprofessions organized by institutional sectors that vary in status. The odds on achieving a parity of esteem between noted professors in leading universities and part-time teachers in two-year programs seem no higher than the odds on developing a classless society. Differentiation overwhelms; and prestige is a valuable commodity in the higher education system and its mainline profession.

This is not to say that this trend is unopposed. There are always important social, administrative, and academic interests that want it otherwise. Social groups strongly committed to egalitarian ideals are deeply offended by the invidious distinctions found in a layered profession: they seek to effect, generally through left-of-center governments (as in Sweden), singular frameworks that embrace all academic units under the umbrella of "university." Administrations committed to bureaucratic ideals of fairness find layering troublesome to administer and defend: they move toward an institutional form of comparable worth. The "have-not" academics located in the lower reaches of the prestige hierarchy have a self-interest in parity: they press government for official redress. Thus various groups within and without seek a planned dedifferentiation.

Furthermore, unplanned delayering takes place through academic drift. "Lower" institutions attempt to converge on "higher" ones as they are driven by the ambitions of professors and administrators to make a better world for themselves. They want a converging profession, with more institutional look-alikes and greater similarity in work and rewards. Especially in countries where central governments are little inclined or poorly positioned to plan convergence, drift is the main counterforce to layering. But all such forces, planned and unplanned, swim upstream against the strong flow of differentiation. One may use common labels and all-embracing formal frameworks, but the differentiation of subjects, services, and clienteles does not thereby cease. And differentiation means that dissimilar components possessing different social and personal value will, in the nature of things, be ranked.

Among the features of institutional layering that affect the unity of the profession none loom larger than the permeability of sector boundaries; it is not the number of sectors that is decisive, but whether the sectors are sharply separated or blur into one another. A two-sector system that operates as two distinct compartments divides the profession into halves that cannot trade with each other. A ten-sector system in which sectors overlap, boundaries are blurred, and intersector mobility of staff is possible places the internal differentiation of the profession on a gradient. Some trade flourishes: students acquire credit in one type of institution which is good currency in another; faculty members may move from a college to a university or vice versa, or, barring such personal mobility, they may at least have a sense that they are somewhat interchangeable in training, talent, and value with colleagues in other places. Permeability is a foundation on which a number of integrating mechanisms, discussed later, may be strengthened. It is formal categorical layering that most splits the profession or estate into separate worlds.

THE DISCIPLINARY BASES OF THE PROFESSION

Everywhere higher education is organized primarily by discipline. This specialized form of organization knits together historians and historians, psychologists and psychologists, chemists and chemists, thereby cutting across institutions and institutional sectors, fragmenting them internally.[4] The discipline (and the professional area of study) is a domain of knowledge with a life and a dynamic of its own. Norton Long, in a classic essay published over thirty years ago, cogently pointed out that such scientific disciplines as physics and chemistry are "going concerns with problems and procedures that have taken form through generations of effort and have emerged into highly conscious goal-oriented activities."[5] These going concerns are not organized to carry out the will of nominal superiors in organized hierarchies; instead they develop their own incentives and their own forms of cooperation around a subject matter and its problems. Disciplines have conscious goals. In fact it is their intentions and strivings and not those stated as the broad aims of higher education which determine the real goals of the many departments, schools, and sub-colleges that make up the operating levels of universities and colleges. The operating units are as much if not more the arms of the disciplines as they are the arms of the institutions, especially when research is emphasized over teaching and specialized training is more important than liberal education.

It is no wonder, then, that universities and colleges are a bottom-heavy form of organization. Each internal disciplinary unit has self-evident primacy in a front-line task, each possesses the authority of its own field, and each takes its behavioral cues from peers, departmental and individual, located elsewhere in the country and the world. It is not astonishing that the academic profession as a whole is primarily fragmented rather than integrated by professionalism, because professional attachment forms first around the discipline. The academic profession is qualitatively different from all other professions in the extent of this fragmentation. It is inherently a secondary organization of persons located in numerous diverse fields that operate as primary centers of membership, identity, and loyalty.

In chapter 6, Tony Becher took us down many of the byways of these "going concerns," each of which may be properly thought of—in British-American terminology—as a profession in itself. In this essay and in previous work,[6] Becher has emphasized and clarified how the very knowledge base of a discipline shapes thought and behavior within it: physics leads to a culture different from that of political science, with Einstein, Heisenberg, and Oppenheimer as heroic figures in the one and Machiavelli, de Tocqueville, and Dahl as defining (if not heroic) figures in the other. The disciplines develop different ways of training and initiating new members, and they influence how members specialize, interact with one another, and move among positions within the field.

The main disciplinary fault line perhaps lies between members in professional schools and those in letters and science departments. Medicine and its branches in dentistry and nursing is the extreme case of the professional school setting that is infused more with the orientations and practices of an outside profession than with those of the faculty in the "basic disciplines." In chapter 7, Sydney Halpern instructed us in the vast proliferation of tasks occurring in the American campus domains of modern medicine. Here, faculty roles differ by categories of full-time and part-time, clinical and academic, tenured and nontenured, in a way qualitatively different from the relatively singular track of status and rank that letters and science departments seek to uphold.

But our conception of disciplines-within-the-profession cannot stop with a one-way account of the disciplinary imperative shaping the profession, because the disciplines are shaped in turn by the manner in which the profession develops in national contexts. A crucial instance is found in the differences between chair and department organization explored by Guy Neave and Gary Rhoades in chapter 5. The traditional clustering of junior and support personnel around the single senior chairholder in traditional Continental systems balkanized many disciplines. "Invisible-college" linkages, which extend across the universities of a nation as like-minded researchers and scholars write, phone, meet, and otherwise communicate with one another, are broken and are restricted to local clusters when the institute directed by a senior professor publishes a nonrefereed journal, sponsors the work of its own members to the virtual exclusion of others, and renders the careers of young scholars dependent on the goodwill and patronage of the padrone and his circle. Such blockages within disciplines break cardinal rules of the scientific ethos when they restrict the wide distribution of ideas and the results of research, weaken the corrective capacity of critical review, and make a career placement more dependent on sycophancy than scholarly achievement.

In contrast, department organization tends to break up such individual-centered fiefdoms, distributing power locally among a number of full professors all equal in formal power, and in lesser amounts to associate and assistant professors on a gradient of rank and responsibility. Local members are then free to participate in the larger circles of the discipline: the rawest of recruits are found at the front of the room at national and international meetings of associations and societies, presenting the results of their own research and learning how to communicate and compete in the larger arenas. Sponsorship still counts, and institutional location measurably adds or detracts. But compared to chair sponsorship and its tendency toward inbreeding, under organization by department individuals are more on their own. And in the competitive race for status in which American university departments engage, the recruitment and retention of talent becomes pressing. Inbreeding is suspect, a weakness to be guarded against, since the odds are normally high that the best person is not one's own.

In short, fragmentation of the academic profession by discipline is as fundamental and consequential as fragmentation by type of institution. The disciplines are powerful points of commitment and identity in those systems where organizational forms encourage individual scholars to be cosmopolitans. However, the disciplines are themselves fractured where the institutional foundations encourage academics to be locals. The disciplinary imperative may well be *the* driving force in modern higher education. But it is powerfully shaped in turn by the imperatives of institutional sectors and the large structures of incentive and reward that characterize the national settings.

THE QUESTION OF AUTHORITY

In higher education professional authority is distributed in disciplinary, institutional, and governmental frameworks.[7] Within each modern national system, the academic profession develops its own grass-roots organization in the disciplinary foundations and then uses those forms as the principal base for extending influence in the institutional and national arrangements. For the profession, the road to power is essentially from the bottom up. And that road is paved with blocks of knowledge. If knowledge is power anywhere, it is so in the academic world.

The characteristic forms of professorial influence are personal rulership and collegial control. Systems of higher education are saturated with the personalized rule of superiors over subordinates. Individual professors supervise and otherwise command the work of students and often the labors of junior teachers, researchers, and support staff, with the judgments of superiors circumscribed neither by bureaucratic rules nor by collegial norms that would foreclose individual discretion. The personal rule of professors has historical roots in the dominance of the master in early academic guilds; it is functionally founded on sheer expertise: "She's the only one around here who knows anything about that subject." It allows the personal leeway that seemingly promotes creative thought and critical detachment; it receives strong ideological backing in the central academic doctrines of freedom of teaching and research. Highly personalized control is even promoted by national bureaucratic structures in which professors acquire niches in the civil service and accumulate projected rights and privileges. In many daily interactions and ongoing relationships, individually they may do as they please, whether choosing research topics or grading the work of students or providing institutional and community services. There may be a myriad of rules in nationalized systems which multiply each year, but enactment is one thing and enforcement another. Whenever bureaucracies encapsulate the academic profession, investigative procedures are notably weak.

Collegial rulership is also pervasive. Collective control by a body of peers is a classic form of traditional authority, one that has worn well in academic systems. Widespread in the academic world from the twelfth century to the present, it is congenial to the expression of expert judgment and has exceedingly strong ideological support in the blended doctrines of academic and scientific freedom. Collegiality is the form of authority about which the profession expresses the greatest pride. It has democratic, antibureaucratic overtones, as decisions are to be made not by a boss but by a group of peers; equality is operationalized in one-person-one-vote procedures.

The characteristic academic compound of the personal and the collegial amounts to guild authority. The individual master has a personal domain within which he or she controls or heavily influences subordinates—in the classroom, the laboratory, the tutorial session, the supervision of the dissertation. The masters then come together periodically as a body of nominal equals to exercise joint control over a larger territory of work—a specialization within a department, a department, a school, a faculty, or the entire university. The controlling stratum in a guild is composed of persons who are simultaneously autocrats and colleagues; they are bosses with individual rights of command as well as good democrats who submit to the rule of a limited populace. The combination has worn well. It may tilt toward the personal, and edge into the dangers of particularistic judgment patronage. Or it may tilt toward the collegial, then to face the weaknesses of logrolling and suppression of individuality. But whatever the balance, this guildlike compound commonly dominates the authority substructure of institutions and national systems, even those that are heavily weighted with top-down bureaucratic and political constraints.

From their operative bases in departments, chairs, and institutes, academics stretch their authority in two directions. The first thrust is upward in the structure of institutional, regional, and national administration. At the institutional level, the academics' favorite collective bodies—senates, faculties, and the like—contend with campus bureaucrats, trustees, and other lay persons who have been granted some voice. Faculties then work out shared authority with these groups, or they slip into an adversarial posture based on interest groups. At the system levels, they gain privileged access to central councils and offices, even becoming the most important members of bodies that allocate financial resources and decide on personnel appointments. They institutionalize peer review within one central body after another, most notably in science councils. They advise officials throughout government. In the transactions of higher education, they often become the most important constituency for bureaucratic and political officials. By means of election, appointment, and informal exchange, academics transfer their discipline-rooted local power into some significant degree of systemwide academic oligarchy. National systems may be, and have been, legitimately ruled by professors.

The second direction in which academics extend their forms of governance is in regional, national, and international disciplinary organizations, which mostly take the forms of associations and societies. Stepping out of their local shops, the masters, journeymen, and apprentices form large interrelated guilds, usually now called professional associations—for example, Western Sociological Association, American Sociological Association, International Sociological Association—to help extend control over membership and practices. Within these associations they develop special sections that recapitulate the practicing specialties of the disciplines. Further, they link their associations in larger clusters—a national academy of science, a social science research council, a council of learned societies. Such associational structures may be and often are powerful centers of authority and influence, reflecting sharply the disciplinary thrusts of academic effort.

In the extreme case of the United States, where great disciplinary specialization has built on the strong American tradition of voluntary association, the forming and strengthening of one's own national association is a key part of the legitimation of a field of study. Hence one finds hundreds of such specialized associations that supplement the all-encompassing associations in such mainline disciplines as physics, economics, and English: the Society for Italian Historical Studies, the American Folklore Society, the Psychometric Society, and the American Association of Teacher Education in Agriculture. These American associations are a powerful class of organizations that are entirely separate from such institutional ones as the Association of American Universities and the Association of American Colleges. The latter, also numerous, are clubs for presidents and other administrators. The papers presented at meetings of these two major classes of academic organizations could hardly be more dissimilar, with the one focused on the separate subjects of the many disciplines and specialties—"Toward a Reconsideration of Marx, Weber, and Durkheim"—and the other on institutional concerns and administrative problems—"Some Thoughts on a New Program of Student Personnel Services."

Professorial authority thus comes well equipped, with a supporting base in local personal and collegial forms and with two main branches upward from that base, one to influence and possibly control the coordinating machinery of institutions and systems, the other to organize academics in national and international disciplinary frames that operate separately from the institutional structures.

But much has happened in the twentieth century, particularly since World War II, to oppose professorial authority and to change its nature. Higher education may or may not be "the axial institution of modern society,"[8] but it is now too valuable and too expensive for governments to ignore. In an extended historical perspective like the one presented by Harold Perkin (chapter 1), the modern period can be characterized as one in which "the traditional autonomy of the university, which has served it well since the twelfth century, is increasingly at the mercy of the bureaucratic corporate state," a state that is in turn closely linked to "the huge impersonal bureaucracies of private and public industry and the 'corporations' of employers' associations, trade unions, and the professions." Higher education itself tends to become a corporate bureaucracy; it is encased in a series of nested administrative units and is often structured internally around numerous strata of personnel which organize around their own particular interests and which lobby the government accordingly. Bureaucratic coordination has its own means of increased influence: it expands jurisdictions, adds layers, enlarges the administrative work force, makes administration more specialized, expands the rule book. Political coordination has also gained almost universally in recent decades. As higher education assumed a higher priority in government budgets, politicians found there were votes and responsibilities to be reaped, and outside interest groups sought greater influence. The counterforces to academic self-rule have clearly become more conspicuous, working mainly through the offices of the modern administrative state.

In certain settings academic self-rule has, critically, divided along a new dimension. Erhard Friedberg and Christine Musselin in their chapter on France, Wolfgang Mommsen in his discussion of recent changes in West Germany, and Guy Neave and Gary Rhoades in chapter 5 all indicated that "the academic estate" in the systems of Continental Europe has developed a basic fissure along lines of rank: junior faculty divides from senior faculty to an extent qualitatively different from the academic structure found in Britain and America. The schism in Europe is linked to the chair-faculty structure typical until the 1960s. Senior figures were sharply set off and especially as patrons had extensive power over junior staffs. Expansion overloaded this relationship: junior faculty numbers became much larger, absolutely, and relatively to the number of professors. Patronage became less dependable, advancement more doubtful, and feelings of exploitation and powerlessness were exacerbated. Finding courage as well as power in their swollen numbers, the younger faculty then organized themselves as a stratum, turning to trade union activity or to associations of their own which pressured and worked through governmental bodies to redistribute power in universities. "Participation" and "democratization" became the watchwords, and from operating units to central councils, the junior faculty acquired new rights. Their efforts were initiatives from within that helped to replace the chair-faculty structure with new units of organization. In the process a fragmentation of the academic estate by rank became formalized

388 *Burton R. Clark*

in laws that spelled out respective rights, and in union and associational bodies that represented academic interests.

Looking more broadly across national systems, sheer size clearly strains traditional informal give-and-take, the collegiality idealized in bygone days. Academic senates move toward representative government in place of direct democracy: a few are elected to go to meetings, representing disciplines and professional fields of study. Academic unions spread and take on more adversarial postures. The ways in which the profession organizes itself move from the informal toward the formal, from the soft to the hard. Though authority is always political, we can say that authority in the modern academic profession has become more political. It is more sharply so, with the profession and its many parts more intensely involved in conflict over who does what to whom.

But beneath all the strengthening of the hands of bureaucrats, politicians, and corporate groups, and beneath the segmenting and hardening of academic interests, the sense of professional expertise grows ever more important as a cornerstone of autonomous academic authority, for individuals and for groups large and small. When asked who is qualified to judge him, the academic will surely answer that not administrators, not trustees, not members of the general public, not even all the members of his discipline or professional area of study can do so. He will accept only those few who are schooled and proven in his specialty. Tony Becher pointed out in chapter 6 that the more academic people specialize, the greater is their sense of separateness. Their bundles of knowledge are the basis for their power. And that foundation of authority, grounded in disciplines and in institutional locations, continues to expand. The silent drift of authority to expertise helps explain why, in the face of so many bureaucratic and political interventions, academics go on running faculties, departments, and institutes, maintaining a primacy of influence in those matters about which they care most.

THE INTEGRATION OF THE PROFESSION

Professions, like organizations, are integrated along the two dimensions of social structure and normative order.[9] Either dimension may be weak or strong and the two lines may or may not correlate closely. The academic profession is a fascinating case of structural and normative integration, one that requires some stretching of a sociological imagination. Throughout this volume we have emphasized fragmentation, the play of institutional and disciplinary differences that set academic people apart from one another. The forces of frag-mentation run strong: specialization will not cease, institutional dif-ferentiation goes on. We know that with each passing decade the academic division of labour will become finer and more extensive. What then still binds, if anything, in this profession of professions? Where do we look if we wish to search for the forces of integration?

THE STRUCTURE OF INTEGRATION

Within disciplines roles emerge that serve to link specialists. A study of the specialties found in high-energy physics in Britain offered the principle, "When roles became segmented one role will emerge whose function it is to bind the separate components into a cohesive group."[10] Some specialists specialize as generalists. In a host of fields, methodologists and theorists serve as such specialists, working with methods or ideas that reach across subfields. Among disciplines, in turn, interpersonal linkages form around problems not special to a particular discipline, as in Latin American studies, education, health, or environmental pollution. Here the interdisciplinary groups serve to lure specialists out of their tunnels, at least some of the time, to mix with others on general topics. Professional schools increasingly are hotbeds of such crosshatching of specialty and broad subject.

At the level of institutions, senior professors take up all-campus tasks. Professorial oligarchy may be strongly integrative: leaders of an academic senate move toward integrating frames of reference as they struggle with such campuswide issues as the criteria for pro-motion to tenure. Central administrators often become key sources of integration. The campus head—president, vice-chancellor, rector— may symbolize the whole. The administrators who specialize, such as a vice-president for finance or a dean of student affairs, generally bridge across the many divisions of academic specialization. In short, the bureaucracy integrates. And so on, up the line, through the sys-tem-building arrangements in multicampus universities, the admin-istrative and professional linkages that form in major institutional sectors, the regional networks, and the national system. Formal link-ages are apparent almost everywhere. And relatively invisible infor-mal and quasi-formal ties that form webs of relationship around the formal lines are, in most settings, likely to play an even greater role.

Central to our understanding of the possible integration of the academic profession in its increasingly varied settings in different countries is a recognition of how membership in small units may be a link to membership in large ones. Here our story of disciplinary and institutional fragmentation may be turned on its head. If individuals can be simultaneously citizens of California and the United States, or of Berlin and the Federal Republic of Germany, or identified with Tuscany and also Italy as a whole, academics can be simultaneously members of a discipline and members of the academic profession as a whole, members of both a particular institution and a national system. Using a pluralist explanation of integration, the discipline and the institution may be seen as units that mediate between the individual and the profession at large. The refrain would be: "I am an academic biologist, therefore I am a member of the academic profession," as biology so obviously belongs to the academic family. And: "I am a Stanford professor, therefore I am an academic," as Stanford so obviously belongs to the academic world. We can adopt an essentially federalist perspective on a profession composed of autonomous segments: in belonging to the smaller state, one is made part of the larger nation. Thus a professor of biology at Stanford is linked to the American professoriat at some minimal but still significant level, so long as his discipline and his institution fall within the socially defined boundaries of the higher education sector of society. And each affiliation separates academics from nonacademics to some degree. In short, there is a natural federalism in the composition of the profession in which dualities of membership, power, and status may link as well as divide.

THE NORMATIVE ORDER

Kenneth Ruscio stressed in chapter 8 that, unlike institutional differences, disciplinary differences are confronted by compensatory integrating mechanisms that are normative. The norms of science have spread as a professional ethos, penetrating one discipline after another. This spread is the hidden agenda of the infusion of science into higher education. Academics in the various disciplines understand that they are committed to the advancement of knowledge. They all respect research. They develop shared procedural expectations: that information should be shared, that evidence should be reviewed impartially, that academics are responsible for some self-regulation. Academics think of plagiarism and the falsification of research results as the worst occupational crimes, compared to which running away with a colleague's spouse or money pales into insignificance. Stealing ideas and falsifying research are severely judged because they violate basic academic codes of intellectual honesty and the pursuit of truth. There seem to be some norms widely held within national systems, and even across them, which may serve to link institutional sectors as well as to embrace disciplines in a single normative order.

There may be large elements of professional consensus, broader still than scientific values, which are best sensed in a general anthropological perspective. Ronald Dore has argued persuasively that in Japan, the United States, and in most other countries academics commonly believe that brighter is better and that higher social placement based on quality is legitimate.[11] There is a primary belief in the intrinsic value of academic quality and the related awarding of prestige to individuals and institutions. With all its inequalities, a prestige hierarchy is thereby valued. In Dore's terms, there is a "consensual hierarchy." And inside this consensus, such disparate items as school marks, salary levels, and campus prestige march together. And once these hierarchies are institutionalized in national systems, such values are held particularly strongly by elites who are in a position to dominate. This type of value consensus is also a primary source of academic drift: academics push their own institutions toward the posture of those that are in a more favored position. Call it hope or color it envy, the ambition that causes institutions to converge indicates a consensus about quality and what is most worth doing.

Perhaps even more basic are the academic interpretations of the concepts of community, freedom, and individualism. The guild has long spoken of itself—locally, nationally, and even internationally— as a "community of scholars." And still today in universities with tens of thousands of anonymous students, several thousands of professors who are strangers to one another, and many thousands of support staff, we find professors and administrators voicing the same doctrine at lunch in the faculty club, at meetings of the academic senate, at all the occasions when wounds need to be bound, and for all time at inaugurations and commencements. Consciously manipulated or honestly stated, the idea of communality clearly serves to integrate. It goes with the flowing robes, the colorful banners flapping in the breeze, the spires of academic architecture, and the flagstones of college landscaping. The academic profession remains uncommonly able to turn "corporate bureaucracies" into "communities," able to extract rich meaning and emotion from the shining ideals of educating the young, advancing the frontiers of knowledge, and otherwise serving society—all requiring, according to academics, the loving hands of a community of craftsmen rather than the ministrations of a body of corporation employees. Doctrines of community, blessed with loving overtones of togetherness, still serve.

Even more salient is the academic interpretation of freedom, one that at first glance seems to lead to radical individualism. Academics enshrine the idea of freedom in one or more of three forms: freedom of research, freedom of teaching, and freedom of learning. They thereby strongly value a reasoned individualism. As put by Emile Durkheim, the ideal of individualism "has as its primary dogma the autonomy of reason and as its primary rite the doctrine of free inquiry."[12] Individualism may become a shared value, one that academics sense they share and one that inculcates respect for the choices and actions of others. For instance, academics readily understand that individual divergence may be good for collectives:

Where most other social institutions require their members to adopt convergent values and practices, universities—and, to a growing extent, polytechnics and colleges—put a premium on creative divergence. Individual distinction, competitively assessed, in research or consultancy or scholarship, is held to strengthen the reputation of the basic unit which has housed and sponsored the work, and more remotely that of the institution which has provided resources for it.[13]

Serving as a flexible normative frame, individualism has an elective affinity for the always varied nature of academic work.

THE INTEGRATION OF PROFESSION AND SOCIETY

In the relationship of the academic profession to the general society, one dimension ranges from elite bonds to mass linkages. Close to the first pole is the pattern in Europe in which the profession links directly to the senior civil service, to advanced levels of schoolteaching, and to a few leading outside professions, preeminently law and medicine. In that classic European relationship, the profession taught a few students a few subjects to certify them for a few occupations. Research, if carried out, was to be pure, detached from the immediate preoccupations of the world. Elite occupations, high-status students, and respected subjects interacted in a virtuous circle of status enhancement. The profession became part of a larger exclusive network. It profited from social exclusion and earned credit for isolating itself from business and commerce, as well as from the overwhelming majority of the population. It sharply limited its student clientele and its coverage of subjects and services and was able to avoid activities considered vulgar. The tasks of stocking government with top-grade officials and preparing able individuals to staff the best secondary schools were central. Tack on preparation for the learned professions and of course for the academic world itself, and not many "relations to society" were left to worry about.

Close to the other pole of mass linkages is the pattern prevailing in the United States, where the profession early became absorbed in trying to do everything for everybody. Employment in government was never the first resort for graduates: it was far more prestigious to become a captain of industry or commerce. And the outside professions could be less learned: for example, forestry, social work, librarianship, and nursing, as well as law and medicine. Great masses of young people—15 percent of the age group by 1940—were admitted to undergraduate programs to improve their minds and characters by means of the ever-elusive "liberal education," as well as to acquire job skills by means of a host of vocational-technical-technological programs. They were then sent forth with a bachelor's degree in hand to find whatever jobs they could, even to tend homes and raise children. Compared to European counterparts, the American academic profession has been unparticular about what it does. Its internal diffusion has been part of a broad, ambiguous connection to society and its needs. In a classic pattern toward which many other countries are now moving, a broad coverage of clientele and fields of study has gone hand in hand with a broad array of services and linkages to many parts of society. In the European pattern, as Guy Neave and Gary Rhoades emphasized in chapter 5, everyday life and academic life were separated by a wide breach. In the American pattern that breach became minimal.

In a democratic age it is written in stone that the elite pattern brings with it the great danger of limited popular support. This is the outcome that has now become such a threat to the British academic profession, where the barriers to mass access remain so rugged and the outputs to industry relatively meager. In contrast, the mass pattern, at once diffuse and disorderly, "buys" popular support.

Running parallel to the dimension of elite-to-mass linkage is one of closeness to government. The European academic pattern of distance from society correlates with closeness to government; the American pattern in contrast incorporates closeness to the general economy and to a plethora of societal institutions and groups but displays relatively considerable distance from government. One of the most revealing points for Americans working cross-nationally is the European academy-government proximity, where, simply, the academic estate is so intimately a part of the state as to be embedded in its civil service. Not only does government monopolize the financing of the estate, but it does so in the most intimate way possible: through direct salary subsidy allocated according to civil-service rank and privilege, with all the bureaucratic classifying and rule-making that is a normal part of modern governmental procedure. In the words of Neave and Rhoades, academics are then a "national profession,"an estate situated within the state. This fundamental structural underpinning means that, willy-nilly, the internal affairs of the estate are then automatically translated into relations with the state.

The now classic case is the uprising of the academic subclass, the junior faculty, in Europe in the 1960s and 1970s. To effect their interests, as pointed out earlier, they hardened their interest-group representation and took their case directly to government, using trade unions and other outside groups to pressure government officials. Confirmation or rejection of academic interests then became an intensely political matter. Left-of-center governments tended to support the junior faculty, students, and others who were the party of change in the distribution of power within the estate; right-of-center governments favored the senior professors, even to the point of mounting counterreformations. The point is clear: when the academic estate is intimately a part of government, it is vulnerable to changes in the dominant political ideologies of government.

In the United States, in contrast, as fully described by Walter Metzger in chapter 4, the profession is housed in private as well as in public institutions. Membership in the private places is the antithesis of civil service: each institution behaves like a private corporation or a voluntary association—"a tub on its own bottom"—hiring, promoting, and firing on its own. In public institutions there is an awareness of being on the public payroll but little sense that one has joined the organized ranks of state public employees, and of course no sense of embeddedness in any national corps. Overhead administrative services are located primarily in campus administrative offices or in academic systemwide administrative locations in the states, rather than in state offices. Many state university systems have considerable constitutional autonomy (for instance, the University of California) which helps to push the profession away from the embrace of government. Trustees often become a buffer, representing the institution to the state rather than the other way around.

The private housing of the profession that is significant in Japan as well as in the United States is more widespread elsewhere in the world than is usually seen.[14] And what we may expect to increasingly see in more countries and in more sectors within them is a pattern of mixed public and private support in the financing of the profession, with a greater number of lines of support in each: basic institutional funding from two or more levels of government; multiple public channels for the support of research; governmental student aid, arranged in various packages; private contributions to endowment; private annual support; parental payments for tuition. The public-private distinction in the financial base is being replaced in many countries by a distinction between single and multiple sources. The effects of the latter are crucial to the autonomy of the modern profession. A single source is able to make broad moves, leaving the academy and the professoriat vulnerable to massive intervention. Multiple sources spread dependency, building a certain redundancy into the capacity of the system and its main profession to survive and prosper. Multiple dependencies are a source of institutional and professional autonomy.

Autonomy within the modern pattern of mass integration may be a more than adequate substitute for the autonomy of the old arrangement in which, in various countries, the academic profession was isolated from mass pressures. The autonomy offered by multiple dependencies is untidy. But this disarray seems to be near the core of any explanation of how, for example, the American professoriat can be so dependent on the goodwill of so many different groups in society and at the same time be so highly autonomous in its most prestigious institutional sectors and disciplines. Complex financing makes for ruggedness in comprehensive academic institutions and a comprehensive academic profession.

THE DIVERSIFICATION OF CLIENTELE SERVICES

As sectors and disciplines proliferate, so do academic services. Different sectors admit different arrays of students and send graduates to different job markets. Disciplines and professional studies are notoriously different in their services to applicants and graduates. Some admit only a few on highly selective grounds and later certify them for well-paying prestigious occupations, while others admit virtually all applicants with little regard to achievement or aptitude and then graduate survivors who must maneuver in an open job market. Any intelligent account of how the academic profession serves society by means of its service to individual clients has to recognize the differentiation and diversity intrinsic to the profession. The transition from higher education to work becomes more segmented, as internal diversity connects to an ever-finer division of labor in the general society.

And so for the services bound up in relationships with major donors, public and private. Government receives various types of profes-

sional cadres from the academy to serve its many diverse bureaus—
from road-building engineers to policy analysts, from foresters to
doctors—in an endlessly widening array. The corporate executive
depends on a lawyer on one side, an economist on the other, and an
accountant in front, as obligatory fountainheads of professional advice, all to be gotten from different parts of the academy and all to
be trained in diverse divisions of the firm. Rich firms can pay for the
very best and hence recruit from the top sectors of universities and
colleges. Enterprises with modest resources work further down the
line, taking graduates of less prestigious institutions, right down to
the night-school lawyer and the graduate of a barely accredited business administration program. Segmentation is the basic trend in the
service relationship between those who do the academic training and
the major institutional donors who finance their work.

But the academic profession does much more than merely service
individual, governmental, and corporate clients directly. Its more ultimate commitments are rooted in its role as a central location for the
handling of knowledge. There is the cultural heritage to be preserved,
ample reason in itself in well-organized institutions to place the university library at the center of the campus and to be proud of having
millions of books, most of which are seldom if ever used. There is
the commitment to the creation of new knowledge, embedded in the
research imperative. There is the task of shaping the minds of future
generations, sometimes even their characters, which is institutionalized in the most common duty of the profession, that of teaching.
A broad involvement in the care and feeding of knowledge means a
fiduciary relation to society's culture in general. These broad societal
services are the bases for the loftiest ideals and pretenses of the profession, the ones on which claims of professional altruism can best be
founded. Always ambiguous and always edging into myth and cant,
the services to knowledge, culture, and future generations are part
and parcel of what the profession is about. They are also the outcomes
of academic effort that are most remote to the touch of efficiency
criteria and accountability demands. Hence they are the strongest
bases for claims of trust: if you cannot direct their work, you have to
trust them to get it right.

THE ONE AND THE MANY

What was always so is now much more so: the academic profession
is many professions, a loosely coupled array of varied interests. The
nineteenth- and twentieth-century expansion of higher education has

multiplied the settings that are the foundations of academic work, belief, and authority. Student clientele has shifted from elite to mass; subjects have proliferated in a broadening stream of knowledge; outputs of graduates and services are unremittingly numerous and varied. Moving further into complexity, the profession comes to resemble a caucus of subprofessions, and that array, we have seen, will be arranged differently in different countries by the interaction of the national, institutional, and disciplinary settings on which we have concentrated. National contexts shape the institutional and disciplinary ones, as in the nineteenth-century Bonapartist definition of a single national university for all of France. Disciplinary thrusts condition all national and institutional settings, as in the sweep to power first of physics and then of biology in all advanced systems in the twentieth century. And institutional arrangements shape national and disciplinary ones, as when competitive sectors of universities, colleges, and short-cycle units diverge and converge in a market dynamic. What we see is a proliferation that can no longer, if it ever properly could, be characterized in a global type. The profession is the many and not the one.

Still, we sense strands that help to hold this profession of professions together, within a country and even internationally. There are the memberships we have identified that link academics in segments by discipline and by institution, with those segments in turn tied into the academic system. There are the shared understandings we have fleetingly highlighted: the commitment to subject, the awareness that specialization pays, the mandate of the pursuit of truth, and the converging understanding that academics ought to differ in thought and behavior. What remains particularly problematic is the strength of such bonds, often intangible and remote, against the forces of fragmentation. Since the reach of this profession is so great, we have mainly emphasized its division into autonomous segments. We have been taken with "the many." But in the many there remain some signs of the one. The profession remains a puzzle, a subject clearly in need of a variety of perspectives that may stimulate the imagination and point further analysis in quite different directions.

This modern "key profession" is a product of eight centuries of higher education in the Western world. Inescapably, it will continue to have a central role in society, even as it becomes more difficult to grasp. If social analysis pursues worthy problems, then it will invest more fully in the effort to grasp the constancy and the change in the lives of academics and to base views of their work and their services on fact rather than fiction. To date, such inquiry has occurred only

398 Burton R. Clark

in fits and starts, with long pauses in between. Perhaps the collective effort mounted in this volume will direct reflection and research toward the day when we systematically will know much more about the one and the many, and the interaction between the two, in a profession that is an art as much as a science, a place where dreamers dream alongside tinkerers who tinker, all in the name of the highest values of society.

NOTES

1. On institutional sectors and hierarchies in higher education, see Clark, *Higher Education System*, pp. 53–69, 254–262; and Trow, "Analysis of Status," chap. 5.
2. See Clark, *Academic Power in Italy*.
3. See the Carnegie classifications of the 1970s, as reported in Carnegie Council on Policy Studies in Higher Education, *Classification of Institutions of Higher Education*.
4. On the cross-cutting of disciplines and enterprises in a grand matrix of academic organization, see Clark, *Higher Education System*, pp. 28–34; and Clark, "Organizational Conception," chap. 4.
5. Norton Long, *Polity*, p. 83.
6. See particularly Becher, "Cultural View," chap. 6.
7. The following section draws heavily upon Clark, *Higher Education System*, pp. 110–123.
8. See Harold Perkin's discussion in chap. 1, which refers to earlier work by Daniel Bell.
9. The following section draws upon Clark, *Higher Education System*, pp. 102–106.
10. Gaston, *Originality and Competition in Science*, p. 172.
11. Prepared comments at the Bellagio Conference, July 30–August 3, 1984, for which the papers of this volume were originally prepared.
12. Durkheim, "Individualism and the Intellectuals," chap. 4, quotation from p. 49.
13. Becher and Kogan, *Process and Structure in Higher Education*, p. 110.
14. See Geiger, *Private Sectors in Higher Education;* and Levy, *Higher Education and the State in Latin America*.

BIBLIOGRAPHY

Becher, Tony. "The Cultural View." In *Perspectives on Higher Education: Eight Disciplinary and Comparative Views*, ed. Burton R. Clark, 165–198. Berkeley, Los Angeles, London: University of California Press, 1984.
Becher, Tony, and Maurice Kogan. *Process and Structure in Higher Education*. London: Heinemann, 1980.

Carnegie Council on Policy Studies in Higher Education. *A Classification of Institutions of Higher Education.* Berkeley, Calif., 1973. Rev. ed., 1976.

Clark, Burton R. *Academic Power in Italy: Bureaucracy and Oligarchy In a National University System.* Chicago: University of Chicago Press, 1977.

———. *The Higher Education System.* Berkeley, Los Angeles, London: University of California Press, 1983.

———. "The Organizational Conception." In *Perspectives on Higher Education: Eight Disciplinary and Comparative Views,* ed. Burton R. Clark, 107–131. Berkeley, Los Angeles, London: University of California Press, 1984.

Durkheim, Emile. "Individualism and the Intellectuals." In *Emile Durkheim on Morality and Society,* ed. Robert N. Bellah. Chicago: University of Chicago Press, 1973.

Gaston, Jerry. *Originality and Competition in Science: A Study of the British High Energy Physics Community.* Chicago: University of Chicago Press, 1973.

Geiger, Roger L. *Private Sectors in Higher Education: Structure, Function, and Change in Eight Countries.* Ann Arbor: University of Michigan Press, 1986.

Levy, Daniel C. *Higher Education and the State in Latin America: Private Challenges to Public Dominance.* Chicago: University of Chicago Press, 1986.

Long, Norton. *The Polity.* Chicago: Rand McNally, 1962.

Trow, Martin A. "The Analysis of Status." In *Perspectives on Higher Education: Eight Disciplinary and Comparative Views,* ed. Burton R. Clark, 132–164. Berkeley, Los Angeles, London: University of California Press, 1984.

Conference Participants

Professor Tony Becher, Chairman
Education Area
University of Sussex
Sussex, England

Dr. Eskil Björklund
Research Program Administrator
National Board of Universities and Colleges
Stockholm, Sweden

Dr. Erik Bolle, Vice Rector
Twente University
Enschede, The Netherlands

Dr. Ernest Boyer, President
Carnegie Foundation for the Advancement of Teaching
Princeton, New Jersey

Dr. Barbara Burn, Director
International Programs
University of Massachusetts
Amherst, Massachusetts

Dr. Ladislav Cerych, Director
European Institute of Education and Social Policy
Université de Paris IX
Paris, France

Professor Burton R. Clark, Chairman
Comparative Higher Education Research Group

Graduate School of Education
University of California
Los Angeles, California

Professor Arthur Cohen
Graduate School of Education
University of California
Los Angeles, California

Professor Ronald Dore
Technical Change Centre
London, England

Dr. Erhard Friedberg, Associate Director
Centre de Sociologie des Organisations
Paris, France

Dr. Dorotea Furth, Program Officer
Organisation for Economic Co-operation and Development
Paris, France

Professor Sydney Ann Halpern
Department of Sociology
University of Illinois
Chicago, Illinois

Professor A. H. Halsey, Director
Department of Social and Administrative Studies
University of Oxford
Oxford, England

Professor Maurice Kogan, Head
Department of Government
Brunel University
Uxbridge, England

Professor Daniel C. Levy
Department of Educational Administration and Policy Studies
State University of New York
Albany, New York

Professor Alberto Martinelli
Department of Political Science
University of Milan
Milan, Italy

Professor Walter P. Metzger
Department of History
Columbia University
New York, New York

Professor Wolfgang J. Mommsen
Historisches Seminar
Universität Düsseldorf
Düsseldorf, Federal Republic of Germany

Professor Guy Neave
Institute of Education
University of London
London, England

Professor Harold J. Perkin
Department of History
Northwestern University
Chicago, Illinois

Professor Gary Rhoades
Center for the Study of Higher Education
University of Arizona
Tucson, Arizona

Professor Sheldon Rothblatt, Chairman
Department of History
University of California
Berkeley, California

Professor Olof Ruin, Chairman
Department of Political Science
University of Stockholm
Stockholm, Sweden

Professor Kenneth P. Ruscio
Department of Social Sciences and Policy Studies
Worcester Polytechnic Institute
Worcester, Massachusetts

Professor Rosemary Stevens
Department of History and Sociology of Science
University of Pennsylvania
Philadelphia, Pennsylvania

Professor Ulrich Teichler, Director
Wissenschaftliches Zentrum für Berufs- und Hochschulforschung
Gesamthochschule Kassel
Kassel, Federal Republic of Germany

Index